FATHERHOOD:
Research, Interventions
and Policies

FATHERHOOD: Research, Interventions and Policies has been co-published simultaneously as *Marriage & Family Review,* Volume 29, Numbers 2/3 and 4 2000.

The *Marriage & Family Review* Monographic "Separates"

Below is a list of "separates," which in serials librarianship means a special issue simultaneously published as a special journal issue or double-issue *and* as a "separate" hardbound monograph. (This is a format which we also call a "DocuSerial.")

"Separates" are published because specialized libraries or professionals may wish to purchase a specific thematic issue by itself in a format which can be separately cataloged and shelved, as opposed to purchasing the journal on an on-going basis. Faculty members may also more easily consider a "separate" for classroom adoption.

"Separates" are carefully classified separately with the major book jobbers so that the journal tie-in can be noted on new book order slips to avoid duplicate purchasing.

You may wish to visit Haworth's website at . . .

http://www.haworthpressinc.com

. . . to search our online catalog for complete tables of contents of these separates and related publications.

You may also call 1-800-HAWORTH (outside US/Canada: 607-722-5857), or Fax 1-800-895-0582 (outside US/Canada: 607-771-0012), or e-mail at:

getinfo@haworthpressinc.com

FATHERHOOD: Research, Interventions and Policies, edited by H. Elizabeth Peters, PhD, Gary W. Peterson, PhD, Suzanne K. Steinmetz, PhD, and Randal D. Day, PhD (Vol. 29, No. 2/3/4, 2000). *Brings together the latest facts to help researchers explore the father-child relationship and determine what factors lead fathers to be more or less involved in the lives of their children, including human social behavior, not living with a child, being denied visiting privileges, and social norms regarding gender differences versus work responsibilities.*

Concepts and Definitions of Family for the 21st Century, edited by Barbara H. Settles, PhD, Suzanne K. Steinmetz, PhD, MSW, Gary W. Peterson, PhD, and Marvin B. Sussman, PhD (Vol. 28, No. 3/4, 1999). *Views family from a U. S. perspective and from many different cultures and societies. The controversial question "What is family?" is thoroughly examined as it has become an increasingly important social policy concern in recent years as the traditional family has changed.*

The Role of the Hospitality Industry in the Lives of Individuals and Families, edited by Pamela R. Cummings, PhD, Francis A. Kwansa, PhD, and Marvin B. Sussman, PhD (Vol. 28, No. 1/2, 1998). *"A must for human resource directors and hospitality educators." (Dr. Lynn Huffman, Director, Restaurant, Hotel, and Institutional Management, Texas Tech University, Lubbock, Texas)*

Stepfamilies: History, Research, and Policy, edited by Irene Levin, PhD, and Marvin B. Sussman, PhD (Vol. 26, No. 1/2/3/4, 1997). *"A wide range of individually valuable and stimulating chapters that form a wonderfully rich menu from which readers of many different kinds will find exciting and satisfying selections." (Jon Bernardes, PhD, Principal Lecturer in Sociology, University of Wolverhampton, Castle View Dudley, United Kingdom)*

Families and Adoption, edited by Harriet E. Gross, PhD, and Marvin B. Sussman, PhD (Vol. 25, No. 1/2/3/4, 1997). *"Written in a lucid and easy-to-read style, this volume will make an invaluable contribution to the adoption literature." (Paul Sachdev, PhD, Professor, School of Social Work, Memorial University of Newfoundland, St. John's, Newfoundland, Canada)*

The Methods and Methodologies of Qualitative Family Research, edited by Jane F. Gilgun, PhD, LICSW, and Marvin B. Sussman, PhD (Vol 24, No. 1/2/3/4, 1997). *"An authoritative look at the usefulness of qualitative research methods to the family scholar." (Family Relations)*

Intercultural Variation in Family Research and Theory: Implications for Cross-National Studies, Volumes I and II, edited by Marvin B. Sussman, PhD, and Roma S. Hanks, PhD (Vol. 22, No. 1/2/3/4, and Vol. 23, No. 1/2/3/4, 1997). *Documents the development of family research in theory in societies around the world, and inspires continued cross-national collaboration on current research topics.*

Families and Law, edited by Lisa J. McIntyre, PhD, and Marvin B. Sussman, PhD (Vol. 21, No. 3/4, 1995). *With this new volume, family practitioners and scholars can begin to increase the family's position in relation to the law and legal system.*

Exemplary Social Intervention Programs for Members and Their Families, edited by David Guttmann, DSW, and Marvin B. Sussman, PhD (Vol. 21, No. 1/2, 1995). *An eye-opening look at organizations and individuals who have created model family programs that bring desired results.*

Single Parent Families: Diversity, Myths and Realities, edited by Shirley M. H. Hanson, RN, PhD, Marsha L. Heims, RN, EdD, Doris J. Julian, RN, EdD, and Marvin B. Sussman, PhD (Vol. 20, No. 12/3/4, 1994). *"Remarkable! . . . A significant work and is important reading for multidisciplinary family professionals including sociologists, educators, health care professionals, and policymakers." (Maureen Leahey, RN, PhD, Director, Outpatient Mental Health Program, Director, Family Therapy Training Program, Calgary District Hospital Group)*

Families on the Move: Immigration, Migration, and Mobility, edited by Barbara H. Settles, PhD, Daniel E. Hanks III, MS, and Marvin B. Sussman, PhD (Vol 19, No 1/2/3/4, 1993). *Examine the current research on family mobility, migration and immigration and discover new directions for understanding the relationship between mobility and family life.*

American Families and the Future: Analyses of Possible Destinies, edited by Barbara H. Settles, PhD, Roma S. Hanks, PhD, and Marvin B. Sussman, PhD (Vol. 18, No. 3/4, 1993). *This book discusses a variety of issues that face and will continue to face families in coming years and describes various strategies families can use in their decisionmaking processes.*

Publishing in Journals on the Family: Essays on Publishing, edited by Roma S. Hanks, PhD, Linda Matocha, PhD, RN, and Marvin B. Sussman, PhD (Vol. 18, No. 1/2, 1993). *This helpful book contains varied perspectives from scholars at different career stages and from editors of major publication outlets, providing readers with important information necessary to help them systemically plan a productive scholarly career.*

Publishing in Journals on the Family: A Survey and Guide for Scholars, Practitioners, and Students, edited by Roma S. Hanks, PhD, Linda Matocha, PhD, RN, and Marvin B. Sussman, PhD (Vol. 17, No. 3/4, 1992). *"Comprehensive. . . . Includes listings for some 200 social science journals whose editors have expressed an interest in publishing empirical research and theoretical articles about the family." (Reference & Research Book News)*

Wider Families: New Traditional Family Forms, edited by Teresa D. Marciano, PhD, and Marvin B. Sussman, PhD (Vol. 17, No. 1/2, 1992). *"An insightful and informative compilation of essays on the subject of wider families." (Journal of Marriage and the Family)*

Families: Intergenerational and Generational Connections, edited by Susan K. Pfeifer, PhD, and Marvin B. Sussman, PhD (Vol. 16, No. 1/2/3/4, 1991). *"The contributors challenge and move dramatically from outdated myths and stereotypes concerning who and what is family, what its members do, and how they continue its traditions to contemporary views of families and their relationships." (Contemporary Psychology)*

Corporations, Businesses, and Families, edited by Roma S. Hanks, PhD, and Marvin B. Sussman, PhD (Vol. 15, No. 3/4, 1991). *"Examines the changing relationship between family systems and work organizations." (Economic Books)*

Families in Community Settings: Interdisciplinary Perspectives, edited by Donald G. Unger, PhD, and Marvin B. Sussman, PhD (Vol. 15, No. 1/2, 1990). *"An excellent introduction in which to frame and understand the central issues." (Abraham Wandersman, PhD, Professor, Department of Psychology, University of South Carolina)*

Homosexuality and Family Relations, edited by Frederick W. Bozett, RN, DNS, and Marvin B. Sussman, PhD (Vol. 14, No. 3/4, 1990). *"Offers a smorgasbord of familial topics. . . . Provides references for those seeking more information." (Lesbian News)*

Cross-Cultural Perspectives on Families, Work, and Change, edited by Katja Boh, PhD, Giovanni Sgritta, PhD, and Marvin B. Sussman, PhD (Vol. 14, No. 1/2, 1990). *"On the cutting edge of this new perspective that sees a modern society as a set of influences that affect human beings and not just a collection of individual orphans." (John Mogey, DSc, Adjunct Professor of Sociology, Arizona State University)*

Museum Visits and Activities for Family Life Enrichment, edited by Barbara H. Butler, PhD, and Marvin B. Sussman, PhD (Vol. 13, No. 3/4, 1989). *"Very interesting reading . . . a fine synthesis of current thinking concerning families in museums." (Jane R. Glaser, Special Assistant, Office of the Assistant Secretary for Museums, Smithsonian Institution, Washington, DC)*

AIDS and Families, edited by Eleanor D. Macklin, PhD (Vol. 13, No. 1/2, 1989). *"A highly recommended book. Will provide family professionals, policymakers, and researchers with a foundation for further exploration on the largely unresearched topic of AIDS and the family." (Family Relations)*

Transitions to Parenthood, edited by Rob Palkovitz, PhD, and Marvin B. Sussman, PhD (Vol. 12, No. 3/4, 1989). *In this insightful volume, experts discuss the issues, changes, and problems involved in becoming a parent.*

Deviance and the Family, edited by Frank E. Hagan, PhD, and Marvin B. Sussman, PhD (Vol. 12, No. 1/2, 1988). *Leading experts in the fields of criminal justice, sociology, and family services explain the causes of deviance as well as the role of the family.*

Alternative Health Maintenance and Healing Systems for Families, edited by Doris Y. Wilkinson, PhD, and Marvin B. Sussman, PhD (Vol. 11, No. 3/4, 1988). *This important book offers timely discussions of current approaches and treatments in modern medicine that have had great impact upon the family health care.*

'Til Death Do Us Part: How Couples Stay Together, edited by Jeanette C. Lauer and Robert C. Lauer (Supp. #1, 1987). *"A landmark study that will serve as a classic for the emerging ethic of commitment to marriage, family, and community." (Gregory W. Brock, PhD, Professor of Family Science and Marriage and Family Therapy, University of Wisconsin)*

Childhood Disability and Family Systems, edited by Michael Ferrari, PhD, and Marvin B. Sussman, PhD (Vol. 11, No. 1/2, 1987). *A motivating book for professionals working with disabled children and their families that offers new and enlightening perspectives.*

Family Medicine: The Maturing of a Discipline, edited by William J. Doherty, PhD, Charles E. Christianson, MD, ScM, and Marvin B. Sussman, PhD (Vol. 10, No. 3/4, 1987). *"Well-written essays and a superb introduction concerning various aspects of the field of family medicine (or as it is sometimes called, family practice)." (The American Journal of Family Therapy)*

Families and the Prospect of Nuclear Attack/Holocaust, edited by Teresa D. Marciano, PhD, and Marvin B. Sussman, PhD (Vol. 10, No. 2, 1986). *Experts address the issues and effects of the continuing threat of nuclear holocaust on the behavior of families.*

The Charybdis Complex: Redemption of Rejected Marriage and Family Journal Articles, edited by Marvin B. Sussman, PhD (Vol. 10, No. 1, 1986). *An examination of the "publish-or-perish" syndrome of academic publishing, with a frank look at peer review.*

Men's Changing Roles in the Family, edited by Robert A. Lewis, PhD, and Marvin B. Sussman, PhD (Vol. 9, No. 3/4, 1986). *"Brings together a wealth of findings on men's family role enactment . . . provides a well-integrated, carefully documented summary of the literature on men's roles in the family that should be useful to both family scholars (in their own work and the classroom) and practitioners." (Contemporary Sociology)*

Families and the Energy Transition, edited by John Byrne, David A. Schulz, and Marvin B. Sussman, PhD (Vol. 9, No. 1/2, 1985). *An important appraisal of the future of energy consumption by families the the family's adaptions to decreasing energy availability.*

Pets and the Family, edited by Marvin B. Sussman, PhD (Vol. 8, No. 3/4, 1985). *"Informative and thorough coverage of what is currently known about the animal/human bond." (Canada's Mental Health)*

Personal Computers and the Family, edited by Marvin B. Sussman, PhD (Vol 8, No. 1/2, 1985). *A pioneering volume that explores the impact of the personal computer on the modern family.*

Women and the Family: Two Decades of Change, edited by Beth B. Hess, PhD, and Marvin B. Sussman, PhD (Vol. 7, No. 3/4, 1984). *"A scholarly, thorough, readable, informative, well-integrated, current overview of social science research on women and the family." (Journal of Gerontology)*

Obesity and the Family, edited by David J. Kallen, PhD, and Marvin B. Sussman, PhD (Vol. 7, No. 1/2, 1984). *"Should be required reading for all persons touched by the problem of obesity–the teachers, the practitioners of every discipline, and the obese themselves." (Journal of Nutrition Education)*

Human Sexuality and the Family, edited by James W. Maddock, PhD, Gerhard Neubeck, EdD, and Marvin B. Sussman, PhD (Vol. 6, No. 3/4, 1984). *"Twelve chapters that not only add some new ideas about the place of sexuality in the family but also go beyond this to show how widely sexuality influences human behavior and thought . . . excellent." (Siecus Report)*

Social Stress and the Family: Advances and Developments in Family Stress Theory and Research, edited by Hamilton I. McCubbin, Marvin B. Sussman, PhD, and Joan M. Patterson (Vol. 6, No. 1/2, 1983). *An informative anthology of recent theory and research developments pertinent to family stress.*

The Ties That Bind: Men's and Women's Social Networks, edited by Laura Lein, PhD, and Marvin B. Sussman, PhD (Vol. 5, No. 4, 1983). *An examination of the networks for men and women in a variety of social contexts.*

Family Systems and Inheritance Patterns, edited by Judith N. Cates and Marvin B. Sussman, PhD (Vol. 5, No. 3, 1983). *Specialists in economics, law, psychology, and sociology provide a comprehensive examination of the disposition of property following a death.*

Alternatives to Traditional Family Living, edited by Harriet Gross, PhD, and Marvin B. Sussman, PhD (Vol. 5, No. 2, 1982). *"Professionals interested in the lifestyles described will find well-written essays on these topics." (The Amercian Journal of Family Therapy)*

Intermarriage in the United States, edited by Gary A. Crester, PhD, and Joseph J. Leon, PhD (Vol. 5, No. 1, 1982). *"A very good compendium of knowledge and of theoretical and technical issues in the study of intermarriage." (Journal of Comparative Family Studies)*

Cults and the Family, edited by Florence Kaslow, PhD, and Marvin B. Sussman, PhD (Vol. 4, No. 3/4, 1982). *"Enlightens not only the professional but the lay reader as well. It provides support and understanding for families . . . gives insight and . . . enables parents, friends, and loved ones to better understand what happens when one joins a cult." (The Family Psychologist)*

Family Medicine: A New Approach to Health Care, edited by Betty Cogswell and Marvin B. Sussman (Vol. 4, No. 1/2, 1982). *The history, rationale, and the continuing developments in this medical specialty all in one readable volume.*

Marriage and the Family: Current Critical Issues, edited by Marvin B. Sussman (Vol. 1, No. 1, 1979). *Covers pluralistic family forms, family violence, never married persons, dual career families, the "roleless" role (widowhood), and non-marital, heterosexual cohabitation.*

FATHERHOOD: Research, Interventions and Policies

H. Elizabeth Peters
Gary W. Peterson
Suzanne K. Steinmetz
Randal D. Day
Editors

FATHERHOOD: Research, Interventions and Policies has been co-published simultaneously as *Marriage & Family Review,* Volume 29, Numbers 2/3 and 4 2000.

The Haworth Press, Inc.
New York • London • Oxford

FATHERHOOD: Research, Interventions and Policies has been co-published simultaneously as *Marriage & Family Review,* Volume 29, Numbers 2/3 and 4 2000.

Cover design by Thomas J. Mayshock Jr.

Library of Congress Cataloging-in-Publication Data

Fatherhood : research, interventions and policies / H. Elizabeth Peters, Gary W. Peterson, Suzanne K. Steinmetz, Randal D. Day, editors.
      p. cm.
    Includes bibliographical references and index.
    ISBN 0-7890-1015-1 (alk. paper)–ISBN 0-7890-1016-X (alk. paper)
      1. Fatherhood. 2. Fathers. I. Peters, Elizabeth, 1955- II. Day, Randal D., 1948-
HQ756 .F3817 2000
306.874'2–dc21
                                        00-025431

INDEXING & ABSTRACTING

Contributions to this publication are selectively indexed or abstracted in print, electronic, online, or CD-ROM version(s) of the reference tools and information services listed below. This list is current as of the copyright date of this publication. See the end of this section for additional notes.

- *Abstracts in Social Gerontology: Current Literature on Aging*
- *Abstracts of Research in Pastoral Care & Counseling*
- *Academic Abstracts/CD-ROM*
- *Academic Search: database of 2,000 selected academic serials, updated monthly*
- *AGRICOLA Database*
- *Applied Social Sciences Index & Abstracts (ASSIA) (Online: ASSI via Data-Star) (CDRom: ASSIA Plus)*
- *AURSI African Urban & Regional Science Index*
- *BUBL Information Service, an Internet-based Information Service for the UK higher education community <URL: http//bubl.ac.uk/>*
- *CNPIEC Reference Guide: Chinese National Directory of Foreign Periodicals*
- *Contemporary Women's Issues*
- *Current Contents: Clinical Medicine/Life Sciences (CC:CM/LS) (weekly Table of Contents Service), and Social Science Citation Index. Articles also searchable through Social SciSearch, ISI's online database and in ISI's Research Alert current awareness service*
- *Expanded Academic Index*
- *Family Studies Database (online and CD/ROM)*
- *Family Violence & Sexual Assault Bulletin*
- *FINDEX, free Internet directory of over 150,000 publications from around the world (www.publist.com)*
- *GenderWatch*
- *Guide to Social Science and Religion*
- *IBZ International Bibliography of Periodical Literature*
- *Index to Periodical Articles Related to Law*

(continued)

- *MasterFILE: updated database from EBSCO Publishing*
- *PASCAL, c/o Institute de L'Information Scientifique et Technique*
- *Periodical Abstracts, Research I (general & basic reference indexing & abstracting data-base from University Microfilms International (UMI))*
- *Periodical Abstracts, Research II (broad coverage indexing & abstracting data-base from University Microfilms International (UMI))*
- *Population Index*
- *Psychological Abstracts (PsycINFO)*
- *Sage Family Studies Abstracts (SFSA)*
- *Social Services Abstracts*
- *Social Science Source: coverage of 400 journals in the social sciences area, updated monthly, EBSCO Publishing*
- *Social Sciences Index (from Volume 1 & continuing)*
- *Social Work Abstracts*
- *Sociological Abstracts (SA)*
- *Special Educational Needs Abstracts*
- *Studies on Women Abstracts*
- *Violence and Abuse Abstracts: A Review of Current Literature on Interpersonal Violence (VAA)*

Special Bibliographic Notes related to special journal issues (separates) and indexing/abstracting:

- indexing/abstracting services in this list will also cover material in any "separate" that is co-published simultaneously with Haworth's special thematic journal issue or DocuSerial. Indexing/abstracting usually covers material at the article/chapter level.
- monographic co-editions are intended for either non-subscribers or libraries which intend to purchase a second copy for their circulating collections.
- monographic co-editions are reported to all jobbers/wholesalers/approval plans. The source journal is listed as the "series" to assist the prevention of duplicate purchasing in the same manner utilized for books-in-series.
- to facilitate user/access services all indexing/abstracting services are encouraged to utilize the co-indexing entry note indicated at the bottom of the first page of each article/chapter/contribution.
- this is intended to assist a library user of any reference tool (whether print, electronic, online, or CD-ROM) to locate the monographic version if the library has purchased this version but not a subscription to the source journal.
- individual articles/chapters in any Haworth publication are also available through the Haworth Document Delivery Service (HDDS).

ABOUT THE EDITORS

H. Elizabeth Peters, PhD, is Associate Professor in the Department of Policy Analysis and Management at Cornell University, and a senior partner in the Family and Child Well-being Network sponsored by the National Institute of Child Health and Human Development. Dr. Peters' research focuses on economics and family policy issues related to divorce, child support, nonmarital childbearing, child care, and welfare reform. Her publications have appeared in such journals as the *American Economic Review*, the *Review of Economics and Statistics*, the *Journal of Human Resources*, *Demography* and *Family Issues*.

Gary W. Peterson, PhD, is Chair and Professor, Department of Human Development, Washington State University, Pullman, Washington. He is former Professor and Chair of the Department of Sociology at Arizona State University. He is also former Chair of the Department of Family Resources and Human Development at Arizona State University. Dr. Peterson's general area of research and scholarly expertise is adolescent development within the context of family and parent-child relationships. Currently, he is analyzing the impact of ethnic and cultural issues in samples of adolescents from the Peoples' Republic of China, Russia, India, Mexico, Chile, and the U.S. Previous research using samples from the U.S. examined health issues in Mexican-American populations of adolescents and young adults as well as influences on the life plans of low-income, rural youth from Appalachian areas of the United States. Peterson's research papers have appeared in such publications as *Journal of Marriage and the Family, Family Relations, Journal of Adolescent Research, Youth and Society, Family Science Review, Family Process,* and *Family Issues.* He was co-editor of *Handbook of Marriage and the Family* (2nd ed.) and *Adolescents in Families.* Major review articles on parent-child and parent-adolescent relationships have appeared in several books including *Advances in Adolescent Development, Handbook for Family Diversity, Handbook of Marriage and the Family* (1st and 2nd editions), and *Families Across Time: A Life Course Perspective.* Dr. Peterson has been a guest editor for special issues of several research journals and has been a member of the Board of Directors for the National Council on Family Relations.

Suzanne K. Steinmetz, PhD, MSW, DAPA, is Professor and former Chair of Sociology at Indiana University-Purdue University at Indianapolis (IUPUI). She is certified as a civil and family mediator and mediates neighborhood disputes for Indianapolis Superior Courts. Dr. Steinmetz does pro bono therapy with a focus on individuals with a diagnosis of Dissociative Identity Disorder. Credited as being one of the founders of the field of family violence, she was the first scholar to bring the problem of battered husbands and elder abuse into the public arena as a result of her congressional testimony in 1978. She served on the Board of Directors of the Society for the Study for Social Problems and was President of both the University of Delaware's and Indiana University's chapters of Sigma Xi, the National Science Society. Steinmetz has authored two research monographs, *Duty Bound: Elder Abuse and Family Care,* and *Cycle of Violence: Assertive, Aggressive and Abusive Family Interaction*; co-authored *Behind Closed Doors: Violence in American Families* and *Marriage and Family Reality: Historical and Contemporary Analysis*; and edited *Family and Support Systems Across the Life Span* and *Violence in the Family.* She also co-edited *Handbook of Marriage and the Family* (1st and 2nd editions) and *Sourcebook of Family Theory and Methods: A Contextual Approach*, two major reference books in the discipline. Steinmetz has also authored over 70 additional publications, and produced a curriculum for reducing conflict and violence in the school (K-9), two videos on elder abuse, and a computerized decision-making game for adolescents.

Randal D. Day, PhD, is Professor of Marriage, Family and Human Development at Brigham Young University. He has written several articles on father involvement and family processes, and is co-author of an introductory text entitled *Family Science.*

FATHERHOOD:
Research, Interventions and Policies

CONTENTS

Editors' Introduction

H. Elizabeth Peters
Randal D. Day

A lively and often heated public debate on the value of two-parent families–and more specifically on the value of the father in a family–has been underway in the United States for much of the 1990s. Despite this strong and persistent interest in fathers and concern about their absence in children's lives, we are far from understanding the complex ways in which fathers make contributions to their families and children.

It is often assumed that the father's primary role is economic, but few researchers have attempted to ascertain what the bulk of fathers accomplish in families, how they approach this role, or how it is different from what the mother does. For example, how does the economic contribution of fathers affect families both directly and indirectly through a broad band of other resources? What are the substantial contributions they make as nurturers, caretakers, and role models? How are these roles altered when children live in female headed households due to divorce or nonmarital childbearing, or when children live only with their fathers, as is the case in a small but growing number of families? What factors lead fathers to be more or less involved with their children?

To examine these issues, the NICHD Family and Child Well-Being Network commissioned papers by leading scholars from anthropology, demography, economics, family science, psychology, and sociology to address two related questions: (a) What is the impact of father involvement on child outcomes? and (b) What factors predict increased involvement of fathers? Many of the papers also addressed the implications of father involvement for family policy issues including family leave, child care, and child support. These papers were presented at the Conference on Father Involvement that was held on October 10-11, 1996 on the NIH campus. The conference at-

[Haworth co-indexing entry note]: "Editors' Introduction." Peters, H. Elizabeth, and Randal D. Day. Co-published simultaneously in *Marriage & Family Review* (The Haworth Press, Inc.) Vol. 29, No. 2/3, 2000, pp. 1-9; and: *FATHERHOOD: Research, Interventions and Policies* (ed: H. Elizabeth Peters et al.) The Haworth Press, Inc., 2000, pp. 1-9. Single or multiple copies of this article are available for a fee from The Haworth Document Delivery Service [1-800-342-9678, 9:00 a.m. - 5:00 p.m. (EST). E-mail address: getinfo@haworthpressinc.com].

tracted considerable attention in the research and policy communities. The audience consisted of more than 150 participants from government, academia, policy research and consulting firms, and family and child advocacy organizations. This volume on "Father Involvement" is the collection and synthesis of many of the papers presented at the conference.

A common theme among the papers in this volume is diversity. The Lamb paper discusses how the fathers' roles and social norms about fatherhood have changed over time. Hewlett emphasizes the differences in fathers' roles across different cultures, using as examples several African cultures studied by anthropologists. Many of the papers also discuss the diversity in fathers' behaviors across different SES, race, and ethnic groups in the U.S. Moreover, differences in father involvement can be caused by social and structural barriers such as (a) the logistical difficulties in maintaining involvement when a father does not live with his child or when the mother denies him access, (b) public policies such as child custody laws which, historically, did not encourage joint or father custody, and (c) social norms regarding gender differences in family versus work responsibilities. In addition, several of the papers highlight the diversity in the effects of father involvement on children's outcomes–especially differences for sons versus daughters. Finally, the papers show how different methodologies and measures–both quantitative and qualitative–can be used to inform our understanding of father involvement and its consequences.

The collection of papers included in the volume is unique in a number of ways. First, much of the existing work on fathers has been done by psychologists, sociologists and family scientists and tends to focus on white intact middle-class families. In contrast, the contributors to this volume represent a broader range of disciplines including anthropology, demography, economics, as well as family science, psychology, and sociology. Second, many of the studies of father involvement in this volume use large nationally representative data sets that allow the analysis and comparison of a variety of family contexts and backgrounds including differences by race and ethnicity and across two-parent versus non-resident father families.

The papers in this volume are organized into several broad groupings. The first set of papers summarizes the recent history of work on fatherhood and provides several "thought pieces" written by scholars from different disciplinary perspectives on what is important about fathers and how different methodologies and perspectives can contribute to the social and policy debate about fathers' roles. The remaining papers in the volume present new empirical findings about father involvement in three different family types: (a) fathers in intact families, (b) single-father families, and fathers raising non-marital children, (c) non-resident fathers who are divorced or separated from their children's mother. This section also provides information on intervention programs and policy implications of fatherhood and father involvement.

HISTORY OF FATHERHOOD RESEARCH AND PERSPECTIVES ON FATHER INVOLVEMENT

The first paper in this section, by James Garbarino, asks us to consider the "soul" of fatherhood. In this discourse, he proposes several lenses through which one can look past the obvious roles of fathers and see into the meaning that fatherhood has for our culture. He suggests that we are reinventing social fatherhood and redefining what it means to protect and how the very language of who we are as parents is shifting.

The next two papers in this volume are written by two of the early pioneers in father research, Michael Lamb and Ross Parke. In "The History of Research on Father Involvement," Lamb provides an overview of how the social construct of fatherhood and research on fatherhood have changed over time. Many of the themes outlined in his paper are echoed in the other papers in this volume. He identifies four types of father roles that have received differing emphasis over different time periods: (a) the moral teacher or guide, most important before the Industrial Revolution; (b) the breadwinner, which was dominant from the Industrial Revolution to the Great Depression, (c) the sex-role model which attained prominence during the 1930s and 1940s; and (d) the new nurturant father which became popular beginning in the 1970s. This typology has influenced much of the research on fatherhood and is also evident in many of the papers in this volume. In addition, Lamb discusses the different methodologies that have been used to examine father involvement ranging from the qualitative information provided by letters and popular literature to quantitative data from time-use studies. He argues that a mix of quantitative and qualitative data would provide a richer picture of the diversity of father involvement.

In the paper "Father Involvement: A Developmental Psychological Perspective," Parke emphasizes the need for a developmental and life course perspective. He argues that our research on fathers should be sensitive to (a) the child's life course (i.e., differences in the predictors and consequences of father involvement by the child's age), (b) the father's life course (the effects of the timing of his entry into parenthood), (c) the family's life course (the timing of transitional events for families such as residential mobility, divorce or separation), and the life course within the context of historical time. He also advocates for observational methods as being essential to capture the complexities of the life course perspective. Parke reinforces the importance of diversity and cautions against stereotyping. For example, he points out that the research on white fathers (primarily from middle-class intact families) generally portrays these fathers in a positive light; whereas the research on African American fathers (usually from lower income families with nonresidential fathers) tends to show these fathers in a negative light. He urges researchers to expand their studies to middle-class African American fathers, lower class white fathers, and fathers from other ethnic groups such as Latinos, Asian-Americans, and Native Americans.

Barry Hewlett writes from the perspective of an anthropologist. In the paper "Culture, History, and Sex: Anthropological Contributions to Conceptualizing Father Involvement," Hewlett uses ethnographic data to describe the fathering practices of several African cultures and points out how foreign these practices sound to us from the perspective of 20th century western culture. While emphasizing that the nature of father involvement differs greatly across different cultures, he also discusses how cross-cultural studies can be used to understand common patterns across cultures. Anthropological research shows that father involvement is related to intra- and intercultural factors such as the closeness of the husband and wife relationship, equality of males and females in providing for the material well-being of the family, a lack of regular warfare, and a diminished importance of material wealth.

The final paper in this section, by Marsiglio and Cohan, "Contextualizing Father Involvement and Paternal Influence: Sociological and Qualitative Themes," presents an in-depth examination of father involvement from a traditional sociological perspective. Their analysis emphasizes the interplay between social structures and processes while keeping an eye on the on social psychological issues. In particular, they examine the social, organizational, and cultural contexts for fathering, fathers' social capital contributions, the construction and maintenance of father identities, and fathering as a co-constructed accomplishment. A key to this analysis is an understanding of how men perceive themselves as fathers as that perception is shaped by race, gender, and economic considerations, a father's relationships with his child's mother and others in the community.

FATHERS IN INTACT FAMILIES

Research on father involvement in these types of families has typically been done by psychologists and has often included only small middle-class White families in the analysis. Moreover, the research has been focused primarily on understanding family processes rather than directly informing policy or evaluating a specific policy program. In contrast, the two papers on fathers in intact families in this volume use large nationally representative data sets. In addition, the results from the Averett, Gennetian, and Peters paper provide evidence on how work place polices can impact father involvement.

In "Putting Fathers Back in the Picture: Parental Activities and Children's Adult Outcomes," Yeung, Duncan, and Hill use data from the Panel Study of Income Dynamics (PSID) to examine the unique contribution of fathers' activities and characteristics on their children's adult outcomes (e.g., education, wage rates, and nonmarital childbearing). Their results show that fathers' abilities and activities such as church attendance add substantial predictive power to models based on maternal characteristics. One of their most intriguing findings relates to how fathers' risk-taking behavior (e.g., wearing seatbelts, having car insurance, and having savings) may provide a role model for sons and, in turn, affect sons' risk taking behavior and adult outcomes. Although their data do not include information about the quality of the interactions or the nature of the relationships between fathers and their children, this paper illustrates how a simple accounting of fathers' activities can be used to provide a richer picture of what fathers do and how fathers affect their children's outcomes.

Using data from the National Longitudinal Survey of Youth, 79 (NLSY79), the paper by Averett, Gennetian and Peters, "Patterns and Determinants of Paternal Child Care During a Child's First Three Years of Life" focuses on one specific activity of fathers: child care by fathers while mothers are at work. Not only is father care important to facilitate labor force participation by mothers, it is also an important and understudied type of father involvement. Their paper shows that two types of factors are important in predicting whether a father will provide this type of care: (a) preferences about child care that are associated with cultural differences and attitudes about gender roles and (b) the availability of fathers that is associated with parents' work schedules. Their findings suggest that policies supporting flexible work schedules could facilitate this type of father involvement.

SINGLE FATHERS AND FATHERS
WITH NONMARITAL CHILDREN

Today more than one out of every three children is born to unmarried parents. These children are generally at higher risk of negative outcomes. They are more likely to live in families with low income and in families that receive public assistance. For these reasons families with nonmarital children have been the focus of recent policy debates and legislation. Two of the stated goals of the 1996 welfare reform legislation were to reduce nonmarital childbearing and to make nonresident fathers take greater responsibility for the support of their children. For a number of reasons, the barriers to father involvement with nonmarital children are likely to be greater than for fathers of children born in marriage. Not only do many of these fathers live apart from their children, but they are also required to go through a formal paternity establishment process to be able to legally acknowledge their relationship with the child. Several papers in this volume address the special circumstances of nonmarital fathering. One of the papers looks exclusively at nonmarital fathers; three papers address father involvement using samples that are primarily fathers of nonmarital children or single fathers.

In "Father Involvement with Their Nonmarital Children," Lerman and Sorensen use data from the NLSY79 to look at the dynamics of fathers' involvement over time and the relationship between involvement and earnings. Their paper documents several important facts that are often overlooked in discussions of nonmarital fathers. First, they show that from a father's perspective, involvement with a nonmarital child is much higher than commonly perceived. More than half of these fathers were actually living with one or more of their nonmarital children, either as a single father or through cohabitation or later marriage with the mother. An additional 20% reported visiting a nonmarital child at least once a week. They also show that changes in involvement can go up or down over time. For example, visitation sometimes becomes cohabitation or marriage with the mother; cohabitation may turn into frequent or less frequent visitation. The paper also reports racial and ethnic differences in the patterns of father involvement. Initially, Hispanics are more likely to be living with a nonmarital child through cohabitation with the mother, but the level of their involvement decreases over time. African American fathers, on the other hand, have lower initial levels of involvement (they are most likely to visit weekly, and least likely to live with the child), but their level of involvement does not drop substantially over time. Finally, Lerman and Sorensen investigate the relationship between labor market potential and father involvement. Does involvement with nonmarital children motivate fathers to work more hours or find a better job? Or does success in the job market enable fathers to maintain their involvement? Using the time sequencing of events to try to sort out the direction of causation, they find that an increase in father's involvement in an earlier time period is associated with later increases in hours of work and earnings.

Greene and Moore in their paper, "Nonresident Father Involvement and Child Well-Being Among Young Children in Families on Welfare," analyze the patterns and consequences of nonresident father involvement in a sample of (mostly never married) African American mothers and children on welfare. They include measures of father involvement that previously have been ignored in the literature, specifically, informal support from fathers such as providing money, groceries, clothes, or other items outside the formal child support system. Although only 17% of the nonresidental fathers provided formal child support, 42% gave some kind of informal support and two-thirds visited at least once in the past year. They find that many of the determinants of informal support and visitation are similar; however, formal child support appears to be determined by a different set of factors. One interesting finding in their multivariate analysis is that support from the father's family increases the likelihood of all three types of involvement: visitation, formal child support, and informal support. (A different kind of three-generation relationship is explored in more detail in the Furstenberg and Weiss paper.) Finally, Greene and Moore report that contributions provided informally are positively associated with several developmental outcomes for children and with the child's home environment. A concern that is mentioned in several of the papers in this volume is the disincentive to pay formal child support that is inherent in the welfare system. One implication of the Greene and Moore paper is that as long as fathers are supporting their children informally, nonpayment of formal child support may not have large negative consequences for children. However, under the 1996 welfare reform legislation, mothers are sanctioned for not cooperating with the formal child support system. Some policy analysts fear that enforcing a formal child support obligation may have the unintended consequences of making some low income fathers who previously provided some informal support, disappear from their children's lives instead.

In their paper "Intergenerational Transmission of Fathering Roles in At Risk Families," Furstenberg and Weiss present a very different kind of analysis from the two papers just discussed. Their paper looks at intergenerational linkages between a male's experiences with his own father and his probability of becoming a responsible father himself. They define responsible fatherhood as either living with their child or waiting to have a child until later in life. Their results show that early fatherhood is more likely to occur if men did not grow up living with their fathers. This association was not explained either by the closeness of the relationship with their father or by differences in economic resources. They note that, unlike other research, their finding about the importance of fathers in affecting responsible parenting is limited to males. The theme of gender differences in the effect of father involvement was also seen in the Yeung et al. paper discussed above.

The final paper in this section, "The Single-Father Family: Demographic, Economic, and Public Transfer Use Characteristics," by Brett Brown, documents the increase in the number of children living in single-father families and distinguishes between single fathers who are cohabiting (and thus by official Census definitions, are single) versus those who are not cohabiting. He finds that a substantial number of never-married fathers assume primary parental responsibility for their children. Most single fathers are heads of their own households; however, some single fathers live with their parents. This shared living arrangement may be economically beneficial and may assist fathers with child care and supervision. Compared to married fathers, single fathers are more likely to receive public assistance; in contrast, they are much less likely to receive public assistance than are single-mother families. The substantial changes in public assistance resulting from the 1996 welfare reform legislation are likely to have only a small impact on the financial well-being of single-father families, because the types of assistance they are most likely to receive–Food Stamps and, especially, the Earned Income Tax Credit–were not substantially reduced by welfare reform.

MARITAL DISRUPTION AND PARENT-CHILD RELATIONSHIPS: INTERVENTIONS AND POLICIES ON FATHERHOOD

The last section contains empirical papers which focus on the effect of the parental relationship on the quality of the parent-child relationship. One paper presents interventions; a final paper presents some policy implications on a variety of aspects of fatherhood.

The two empirical papers, however, come from very different perspectives and are trying to answer different questions. Orbuch, Thornton, and Cancio in their paper, "The Impact of Marital Quality, Divorce, and Remarriage on the Relationships Between Parents and their Children," ask how the relationship between the adult child and his or her parents is affected by the parents' marital quality or by whether the parents divorced. They find that the answer to their question differs substantially for sons versus daughters. Parental divorce without remarriage negatively influences mothers' relationships with sons, but improves their relationships with daughters. Divorce and remarriage, however, decreases the quality of the mother-child relationship. The quality of father-child relationships is also negatively affected by divorce for both sons and daughters, although the effect is stronger for daughters. They argue that this finding may be due to a greater sharing of interests and activities between fathers and sons.

The Braver and Griffin paper, "Engaging Fathers in the Post-Divorce Family," explains the lack of father involvement with children after divorce as due to "gatekeeping" behavior of mothers rather than to a lack of desire on the part of fathers to maintain their involvement. They suggest that the relationship between the parents can affect the limits that mothers impose on a father's involvement. When the parental relationship is not hostile, a mother is more likely to encourage or facilitate a father's involvement with his children. Their results also show that fathers often feel disenfranchised by the legal system; they are required to support their children financially, but do not have the rights to be involved in their children's lives. These findings about the importance of the parents' relationship have direct implications for policy and program interventions. The paper describes a program called DADS FOR LIFE, an intervention that they have developed to help fathers learn to interact with their ex-wives in a way that reduces hostilities. They find that this intervention has had positive effects on fathers' ability to maintain a quality relationship with their children after divorce.

The final paper in this section (and volume) focuses on the intersection between research and policy. The paper describes the "Fatherhood Initiative," a set of activities sponsored by the Federal government that focused on improving data and research about fathers. This paper also summarizes what we know about the effects on father involvement of policies such as welfare reform, child support, work place policies, responsible fatherhood programs, and other fatherhood interventions. It provides examples of new programs and initiatives on father involvement and suggests directions for future research on fathers that can inform the policy process.

I. THE HISTORY OF FATHERHOOD RESEARCH AND PERSPECTIVES ON FATHER INVOLVEMENT

The Soul of Fatherhood

James Garbarino

SUMMARY. This paper proposes several lenses through which one can look past the obvious roles of fathers and see into the meaning that fatherhood has for our culture. The paper suggests that we are reinventing social fatherhood and redefining what it means to protect. It also describes how the very language of who we are as parents is shifting. *[Article copies available for a fee from The Haworth Document Delivery Service: 1-800-342-9678. E-mail address: getinfo@haworthpressinc.com <Website: http://www.haworthpressinc.com>]*

KEYWORDS. Fatherhood, culture

James Garbarino is Director, Family Life Development Center, and Professor, Human Development and Family Studies, Cornell University.

Based upon a presentation to the NICHD Conference on Father Involvement, Bethesda, Maryland, October 10, 1996. The author expresses appreciation for the contributions of Claire Bedard to this paper.

[Haworth co-indexing entry note]: "The Soul of Fatherhood." Garbarino, James. Co-published simultaneously in *Marriage & Family Review* (The Haworth Press, Inc.) Vol. 29, No. 2/3, 2000, pp. 11-21; and: *FATHERHOOD: Research, Interventions and Policies* (ed: H. Elizabeth Peters et al.) The Haworth Press, Inc., 2000, pp. 11-21. Single or multiple copies of this article are available for a fee from The Haworth Document Delivery Service [1-800-342-9678, 9:00 a.m. - 5:00 p.m. (EST). E-mail address: getinfo@haworthpressinc.com].

In this paper I am concerned with three forms of discourse, or the interchange about ideas about reality, as they bear on the task of understanding fatherhood. Each form or "level" of discourse has its own methodological approaches; each its central issues. Each form of discourse can enrich our understanding of current fatherhood issues in human development, public policy and personal life. These three forms of discourse about fatherhood are social science, human studies, and soul searching.

Social science. The first form of discourse, social science, is the conventional domain of sociologists, anthropologists, and psychologists who seek to demonstrate the objective empirical realities of fatherhood. They seek to understand empirical patterns, statistical relationships, and predictive and verifiable hypotheses concerning the objective features of fatherhood. The central questions might include: When and how do men become fathers? What do they do as fathers? What effects do these behaviors have on mothers and children? This is the predominant discourse in academic pursuit and policy making.

Human studies. Set within this social map of fatherhood is the experience of men as fathers, which leads us to the study of subjectivity, a concept central to what Dilthey, Weber and Cohler refer to as "human studies" (Cohler, 1998: 555). As Dilthey explains, "the study of life history is intrinsically the study of meanings that persons impute to their lives and communicate to others" (Cohler, 1988: 555). When we study the means by which people make sense of their lives, roles, and experiences, we must allow room for a perspective which moves beyond the constraints of objectivity and verification. We must allow for subjective information to become a valid vehicle for understanding fatherhood. Dilthey warns us that the complexity of constructions of the life experience "transcend(ed) reductionist scientistic objectivity" (Rickman, 1979). Human studies is the documentation of identity: it is studying my life story and your life story.

Soul searching. The third form of discourse is soul searching, in which the goal is to make and sustain contact with human spiritual realities (Hillman, 1996). This approach starts from the reality of human beings as spiritual beings having a physical experience. Does anything in human experience really mean anything beyond the contextual construction made by individuals, groups, and cultures? Is there anything more than psychology, sociology, and anthropology? Without soul searching, the answer is "no." Only soul searching can expand these stories by integrating them into the eternal realities of spirituality. Only by incorporating all three forms of discourse can we adequately approach and understand current issues in fatherhood.

In what follows, I illustrate the idea of soul searching through a brief look at four enduring issues relevant to today's public and private discussions of fatherhood: the social invention and reinvention of fatherhood, the language of fatherhood in the stories we tell of our fathers, the role of fathers in dangerous environments, and the role of androgyny in fatherhood.

ENDURING ISSUES IN FATHERHOOD

The Social Invention and Reinvention of Fatherhood

Margaret Mead once wrote that "motherhood is a biological necessity, but fatherhood is a social invention." Although parenthood for women is clear; it is tied to their essential biological role in the process of bringing children into the world, the role of the father is intrinsically ambiguous and relies upon cultural prescription. Once a child is conceived, it is a biological given that it dominate a woman's life for the better part of a year; the child's continued existence depends upon the nourishment and care it receives from its mother, in her arms and at her breast. A script exists for women to follow, should they choose to do so, a script of unconditional nurture, commitment, and love. Even in our fractured modern society, a woman who gives birth knows that she is the mother of "her" child.

The big issue today is not the existence of motherhood, but how to reconcile it with other interests, roles, and demands. How is a woman to incorporate it into a life plan that includes work outside the home (in the cash economy) and a generally greater sense of options and opportunities independent of her role as mother. On the other hand, fatherhood has been quite different. Fathers play their role in the moment of conception, to be sure. Biologically, it is only a brief, albeit dramatic, contribution of genetic material to get the process of child development started (much like the deistic view of God and the universe, in which God wound things up and let them go). Sociobiologists argue that what "makes sense" evolutionarily for men is to maximize their opportunities for paternity since their investment (and the costs to them) of each child is small relative to that of women.

Unlike motherhood, paternity is always in doubt, and belief in one's paternity is always an act of faith based in a particular relationship and person. It is also faith in the strength and validity of a set of social conventions designed to structure the roles of men and women. Thus, fatherhood is essentially a social invention with diverse forms. Social science documents that some cultures have all but done away with fatherhood as a social role linked to biological relationship. Others have found ways to bind men to their children closely and intimately and some of those ways are illuminated in this volume.

Individual men wrestle with their own paternity. The stories of their lives are full of their efforts to make sense of fatherhood–being the son of a father, or being a father. Absent fathers seem to generate some of the most intense

narrative efforts. In most cases, including Judeo-Christian culture, a definition of what a father is and what he is to do is tied up in myths. In contrast to
the mother who came before Solomon, ready to give up her claim to her child
(her rights) so that the child may live, there is Abraham, who is ready and
willing to sacrifice his son out of loyalty to his god. Modern interpreters of
myth, such as Hillman (1996: 80-81), provide in the following, a result of
soul searching for fatherhood:

> His job is elsewhere . . . because his fundamental value to the family is
> maintaining the connection to the elsewhere . . . Fathers have been far
> away for centuries: on military campaigns, as sailors on distant seas for
> years at a time; as cattle drivers, travelers, trappers, prospectors, mes-
> sengers, prisoners, jobbers, peddlers, slavers, pirates, missionaries, mi-
> grant workers. The work week was once seventy-two hours. The
> construct "fatherhood" shows widely different faces in different coun-
> tries, classes, occupations, and historical times. Only today is absence
> so shaming, and declared a criminal, even criminal-producing behavior.

How could Hillman speak this way of father absence? He can do so
because he seeks to relate the social science and human studies of fatherhood
to the fruits of soul searching. He recognizes that "father" is a social category and a character in a personal narrative. He further recognizes that there is a
point to the story, the individual's "daimon" or spirit, the spiritual purpose of
the individual person who is a parent. Looked at in this light, the issue is not
the physical presence or absence of the man, but how well he lives his
spiritual calling so that his life story can inspire his child who will then make
sense of the father's life.

I had demonstrated elsewhere (Garbarino, 1992) in longitudinal research
covering a 50-year span, that kids value fathers who spend time with them.
Access to one's father and a sense of his personal investment in you has been
a dominant issue in the relationships of children to their fathers, at least in this
century. Thus, in 1924, 63% of the teens in one city reported that the most
desirable attribute of a father is that he spends time with his children. By
1977, the figure had risen to 68%. This reflects the fact that children, who
know that fathers have other callings, appreciate fathers who take the time to
be with them. Children may not differentiate on qualitative grounds among
these callings–e.g., being a drunk vs. being a civic leader. They focus on
whether or not the father is loyal to the child. Research also confirms that
what matters most to kids about their non-custodial fathers is whether they
remember birthdays, call on special occasions, or remember the details of the
child's hobbies, athletics, and artistic endeavors. What seems to matter is that
fathers place children in a special place in their minds and hearts–a highly

symbolic dimension to father-child relationships–indicating that the father is connected psychologically, if not present physically.

What about mothers? In 1924, most kids took for granted that their mothers were available to them–perhaps they even took them for granted. Some 38% of the kids said that the most important thing about a mother is that she spends time with her kids. By 1977, the figure had risen sharply to 62%. Thus, in this realm at least, women have achieved equality with men. But what does that equality mean? From soul searching we can conclude that it means that some women have found ways to live out their call more fully, and so their children can respect them better. Of course, for others, the time away from children has little payoff because it is not spent listening to the call but only making ends meet.

Some researchers report a continuing decline in the amount of active time spent with children by their parents (Garbarino, 1995). This decrease is linked to a disturbing rise in depression and social maladjustment among children, and a sense of being estranged and useless. The stress so many children feel today, the unsettling sense of being "on approval" and "on your own" is related to the speeding up of daily life around them, the exit of adults from their lives, and the demands for ever earlier maturity and independence. A *New Yorker* cartoon from a while back shows a father instructing his child in the modern way, "Well son, you're six years old now, so I'm turning your development over to you."

Soul searching always resonates with the ecological proposition that context matters, and with the human studies proposition that a good story shapes the impact of any psychological or sociological fact. The presence or absence of fathers is no simple phenomenon. It requires a full scale investigation that recognizes the multiple significance of fathers–as mapped by social science, as chronicled by human studies, and as illuminated by soul searching.

The Language of Fatherhood

What is the subjective core of many social science issues related to fatherhood? Surrounding the social science of paternal involvement, step-fathering, child support by non-custodial fathers, and other contemporary issues is the fact that the subjective experience of fatherhood is tied to the power that lies in the emotional intensity and psychological ramifications of making love with a child's mother.

Being "sexually active" with a child's mother is at the core of it because it affects a step-father's feelings (for whom the child represents that inescapable fact that the child's mother used to have sex with another man); a divorced father's feelings (for whom the central fact is that his child's mother may be having sex with someone else); and a child's feelings (for the child must cope with the fact that his mother may be sleeping with someone who is not his father and that his father may be sleeping with someone who is not his mother). Each narrator tells a story of fatherhood that is steeped in the emotionally laden language of subjective experience, even as it may be grossly fit into objective categories for statistical analysis.

How often do we tell our own stories to illuminate the social science of fatherhood? As I reflect upon my own narrative account, I recognize that some of my thoughts and feelings about fatherhood grow out of my own stories of myself as a son and as a father. My own father died in 1989, too soon and with shocking unexpectedness. He was a good father and his story taught me many important lessons–some negative, some positive. He was a man who had grown up in the tough world of the immigrant slums of New York City. He had been a tough kid and was a soldier in World War II. He suffered from all the liabilities that implies: quick to take offense, committed to the need to "defend yourself" with your fists if necessary, and believing in the masculine values. But he also carried with him some important virtues that I seek to sustain: a sense of humor, love of family, and a sense of responsibility. In his later years he mellowed a great deal. Thus, I remember him as a gentle whale in a world of sharks and barracudas.

People took advantage of him in business and financial matters, and at his funeral two of his ex-partners came guiltily to the service, perhaps in the hope of expiating their sins against him. But he had the wisdom to recognize that even while he envied their worldly success, he had something much more important: the love and regard of his children. Nothing pleased him more than to sit down to dinner surrounded by his children and their families. A smile would light up his face, and it told the whole story of what he cared about and whom he cared for. "This is what's important," he would say, "the whole family together." We teased him about it (of course), but we appreciated it and learned from it.

My dad was a talented musician. When he died, musicians from all over called or visited to express their appreciation for him as an accordion player and as a friend. One said, "He knew all the tunes." I was reminded of the times when as a young child I accompanied him to the open Musicians Union meetings in New York where his colleagues would often take me aside and tell me what a good man he was, "and don't you forget it kid!" Affirmation and challenge!

He wasn't an easy person by any means, but he was kind-hearted. He listened to radio talk shows and talked back to them. In his last years he and his musician cronies would meet weekly for lunch to remember the good old days and set the world straight. I'd be falsely sentimentalizing our relationship, our story, to say I agreed with him about the practical matters of day-to-day life or social policy or any of that. I didn't. In these areas he was a bit of a crank.

My story is told from the perspective of the emotional fact that I loved him for loving me, for the time he spent with me as a boy when he taught me to play baseball, for the stories of the old days he told, for his genuine pleasure in my successes and accomplishments, for accepting my wife into the family, for treating my children to ice cream cones at the beach, for his sense of responsibility for our family–even when he himself felt unappreciated and not cared for, as he often did over the years. In his last years he became my sister's best friend and my brother's close friend. This is *my* fatherhood story. What's *yours*?

Fathers and Security in a Dangerous World

We can learn about the changing nature of the role of the father with regard to security by understanding the story of Dantrell Davis, a little boy who lived in Chicago until the fall of 1992. Each morning his mother walked him to school. His teachers were waiting on the steps of the school, and there were cops on the corner. And yet, as he walked the 75 feet between his mother and the school he was shot in the back of the head and killed. His death sends an important message to other children: adults can't protect you; you are on your own. This is what I call "Dantrell's Secret" (Garbarino, 1995). Dantrell's Secret teaches children that you may be left alone in the face of threat. One of the truisms of research on children growing up in war zones around the world is that the first line of defense against fear and trauma is parental protection.

Children enter into a social contract with adults. The terms of this contract are roughly these: I will obey and trust you, and in return you will protect and care for me. Dantrell's Secret voids this contract. Once I visited with a little boy living in a refugee camp who had learned Dantrell's Secret months earlier. Soldiers had come into the camp looking for someone. With the boy's mother standing next to him, a soldier grabbed the boy and put a knife to his throat. "Tell me where Omar is," he said to the mother, "or I'll cut your boy's throat." That this could happen to him while his mother stood powerless was the most traumatic element of the experience.

Beyond such dramatic incidents are situations in which it is the corrosive effects of parental depression, especially maternal depression, that are the source of the problem. When I visited a Cambodian displaced persons camp in Thailand a few years ago, I was struck by how hideous it was for mothers. Men played a marginal role, often disappearing for long periods to return to Cambodia to fight in the civil war. The future was uncertain–no one knew when, if ever, families would return to their homeland. There was a high level of domestic violence in the camp, and weapons abounded. The moderating influence of the outside world departed at 5:00 p.m. every day when the international workers left and the camps were under the control of gangs.

Not surprisingly, this environment produced high levels of maternal de-

pression. A recent survey had reported that 50% of the mothers were seriously depressed. Perhaps the only question was, why wasn't it 100%! Unfortunately, children of depressed mothers tend to receive inadequate adult
supervision, and therefore are more likely to be injured in accidents. And so it
was, according to a pediatrician who worked in the camp, that the children
were always getting run over, drowning in the irrigation ditches, burning
themselves up or getting hurt playing with weapons they found. And, these
same depressed mothers were psychologically unavailable to help children
deal with the stresses and potentially traumatic events they encountered.

I thought of these Cambodian mothers again when a week later I had
occasion to visit a public housing project in Chicago. The parallels were
striking. Here too men were in marginal roles, always disappearing to escape
the police, the welfare authorities, or some conflict with a rival group or
individual in the neighborhood. The future was uncertain, there was a high
level of domestic violence, and weapons were abundant–and used. Gangs
were in control after 5:00 when the social workers and teachers representing
the outside world went home. So it came as no surprise when a research
group in New Orleans (Osofsky et al., 1993) conducted a mental health
survey in a similar public housing project, that 50% of the mothers were
seriously depressed. They also found that 40% of the mother-child attachment relationships in the first year of life were disrupted ("disorganized" to
use the investigators' term).

Such an environment is precisely suited to increase the traumatic nature of
violent experiences. Without parents being actively in charge children learn
Dantrell's Secret and have it reinforced daily. To cope with this knowledge
that they have to fend for themselves in a dangerous environment, they cope
as best as they can, including banding together in gangs for protection. A boy
in Michigan once told me, "If I join a gang, I'm 50% safe. If I don't join a
gang, I'm 0% safe." Adults just don't figure into the equation.

This is a special challenge for fathers because the mythic father is the
child's protector *in the world.* Children look to fathers to project the kind of
involved strength that sustains a feeling of security among children and
adolescents in the community beyond the family. This mythic recognition is
the wisdom that lies behind programs such as "Mad Dads," begun in Omaha,
Nebraska, which encourages adult men to venture out onto the streets of the
city at night, wearing green jackets, in a team to represent strong fatherhood
to youth who have learned Dantrell's Secret. In so doing, it sends the message
that "grown men, the fathers of the community, are in charge–not 15-year-
olds with guns."

This message has special appeal to me because of the visits I have made to
children in war zones and situations of community conflict over the last five
years (Garbarino, Kostelny and Dubrow, 1991; Garbarino, Dubrow, Kostelny

and Pardo, 1992). Fathers are *both* the focal point for security and strength and the origins of the masculine voice that underlies aggression. Children are being sacrificed daily to the male impulse that presents a deadly mix of power, self-defined rights, and aggression that generates and sustains war and other forms of community violence. To be sure, women–mothers–sometimes play a role in sustaining these conflicts by valuing the little soldier in their sons, and by teaching "at the breast" some of the stereotypes that sustain racism and exclusive ideologies and identities. But by and large, it is the masculine voice of the fathers that makes war in the name of love–love of country, love of political party, love of being right, love of power. Until we reinvent fatherhood to retain the father as mythic protector while changing his voice from *Warrior* to *Peacemaker*, men will continue to be the principal origin of the problem of violence. For most fathers to speak with this voice will mean a move towards androgyny.

Hybrid Vigor: The Imperative for Androgyny

When her son was killed in Northern Ireland, a woman who worked with a peace group (Women Together) said: "I am a totally non-violent person. Phillip's death will make me more determined to work for peace. This will make me more capable of feeling the burden others are feeling." How can men speak more fully with the human voice of *Peace* while retaining their special strength? We need to invent a new kind of father. We need to encourage a new kind of man. In *My Fair Lady*, Professor Higgins asks, "Why can't a woman be more like a man?" It's time to ask the opposite question–a rewriting of the parenting script to emphasize nurturing and the investment of self in children's lives. We need to ask, "Why can't a man be more like a woman?"

This is necessary to give back the balance in the lives of children that they need to become the kind of people the world needs. In coming generations the self-esteem and empathy that comes from such a balance will be essential to master the intricate challenges of living cooperatively and non-violently. With its emphasis on domination, power assertion, and emotional distance, traditional masculinity is the problem. Carol Gilligan and others suggest that while men tend to represent powerful activity such as assertion and aggression, women, in contrast, tend to portray acts of *nurturing* as acts of strength. For most men, it is taking what you deserve that indicates personal power; for most women it is giving what is needed.

Women tend to see aggression as a problem born of fractured relationships. The appropriate response then is to try to mend and strengthen those relationships. This places an enormous burden on the shoulders of women, who must provide a disproportionate share of the caring and healing required to sustain the world. Jesus may have died for our sins, but Mary lived through them. And where was Joseph anyway when it came time to take care?

Women have asked for a re-negotiation of the demands that this ethic of caring implies. For men to be prepared to become the kind of fathers we need them to be, they must first and foremost be invested in their children early, so that they may build the kind of skills and feelings that sustain closeness later on. As we well know, some men *are* making this change; there is a whole crop of "new" fathers out there. By and large they are finding that early investment in child care is a distinctly humanizing experience (just as many women are finding that participating in the public world beyond the home has its special rewards). Both genders can listen better to their spiritual core, their daimon, in such an androgynous world.

One way to help men become the kind of people they need to be, prepared to be the kind of fathers we need, is to involve them more fully in the day-to-day realities of child care, particularly infant care. And along the way, diaper-changing men will be doing the good work of reinventing fatherhood in a way that makes good sense for society and the children who must grow up in it. It takes practice, of course. It takes learning how to do "nothing" with interest and humor on a little person's timetable. Nothing teaches humility and patience like caring for a young child–if you let it happen. And it can promote the kind of "mindfulness" (to use a Buddhist term) that nurtures the soul.

To achieve this goal of androgyny we must harness what biologists call "hybrid vigor," the special energy that comes from combining two different strains of the same species. In this case, it is the combining of the masculine and feminine personas within one person. The deepest myths speak to this. Plato speculated that originally human beings contained both the feminine and the masculine, and as a result were self-sufficient. It was the reaction of the Gods to the divine aspirations of these complete beings that led to their being split in half, left to wander the Earth in search of their complementary other (what we now call their "soul mate").

CONCLUSION

Social science, human studies and soul searching coordinate to provide a vision for human development. Social science documents the dimensions of father involvement, the ways in which boys without fathers are prone to insecurity and compensatory aggression and the androgyny as a basis for resilience. Human studies explores the narrative accounts of individual men making sense of their complete selves as they mature, and shows us how both the masculine and feminine voices contribute to a full narrative accounting. Soul searching focuses on the mythic identities and roles of fathers, the larger meaning of "father absence," and the vital importance of achieving a connection with the spiritual domain through loving the soulmate. A complete analysis of fatherhood rests upon a complete human discourse, one that integrates social science, human studies, and soul searching.

REFERENCES

Cohen, L. & Manion, L. (1994). *Research Methods in Education*. London: Routledge.

Cohler, B.J. (1982). Personal Narrative and Life Course. *Life Span Development and Behavior, 4*, 205-241.

Cohler, B.J. (1988). The Human Studies and the Life History: The Social Service Review Lecture. *The Social Service Review, 62*, 555-574.

Garbarino, J., Kostelny, K., & Dubrow, N. (1991). *No place to be a child: Growing up in a war zone*. Lexington, MA: Lexington Books.

Garbarino, J., Dubrow, N., Kostelny, K., & Pardo, C. (1992). *Children in Danger: Coping with the consequences of community violence*. San Francisco: Jossey-Bass.

Garbarino, J. (1992). *Children & Families in the Social Environment (2nd Ed)*. New York: Aldine.

Garbarino, J. (1995). *Raising Children in a Socially Toxic Environment*. San Francisco: Jossey-Bass.

Gilligan, J. (1996). *Violence: Our Deadly Epidemic & Its Causes*. New York: Putnam.

Hillman, J. (1996). *The Soul's Code: In Search of Character and Calling*. New York: Random House.

Osofsky, et. al. (1993). Chronic Community Violence: What is happening to our children? *Psychiatry, 56*, 36-45.

Rickman, L. (1979) *Wilhelm Dilthey: Pioneer of Human Studies*, Berkeley & Los Angeles: University of California Press.

van den Berghe, P. (1979). *Human Family Systems: An Evolutionary View*. New York: Elsevier.

The History of Research on Father Involvement: An Overview

Michael E. Lamb

SUMMARY. Both our understanding and operationalization of father-hood and father involvement have changed over time. Fatherhood has always been a multifaceted concept, although over time the dominant or defining motif has shifted in turn from moral guidance to breadwinning to sex-role modeling, marital support, and finally nurturance. As a result of these changing concepts, the extent of father involvement has been viewed and indexed in different ways at different times. In the late 1960s and early 1970s, at a time when societal concerns about the effects of fatherlessness were coming to the fore, social scientists also became much more interested in quantification of concepts such as father involvement, motivated in part by the emergence and popularity of time-use methodologies. This prompted a shift from a focus on qualitative dimensions (such as masculinity and dominance) to quanti-fiable dimensions (the amount of time spent by fathers with their chil-dren). This led to a restricted focus on paternal nurturance with little if any attention paid to the other functions or aspects of fatherhood. The narrowly focused view of fatherhood that resulted, ignored subcultural

---

Michael E. Lamb is affiliated with the National Institute of Child Health and Human Development.

Address correspondence to: Michael E. Lamb, Section on Social and Emotional Development, National Institute of Child Health and Human Development, 9190 Rockville Pike, Bethesda, MD 20814.

An earlier version of this paper was presented to a conference on Father Involve-ment held at the National Institutes of Health's Natcher Conference Center, Bethes-da, Maryland, in October 1996.

[Haworth co-indexing entry note]: "The History of Research on Father Involvement: An Overview." Lamb, Michael E. Co-published simultaneously in *Marriage & Family Review* (The Haworth Press, Inc.) Vol. 29, No. 2/3, 2000, pp. 23-42; and: *FATHERHOOD: Research, Interventions and Policies* (ed: H. Elizabeth Peters et al.) The Haworth Press, Inc., 2000, pp. 23-42. Single or multiple copies of this article are available for a fee from The Haworth Document Delivery Service [1-800-342-9678, 9:00 a.m. - 5:00 p.m. (EST). E-mail address: getinfo@haworthpressinc.com].

23

variation in the definition and understanding of fatherhood. Social scientists are only now beginning to seek a broader and more inclusive understanding of fatherhood–efforts that should permit more insightful research on the effects of variations in performance of the relevant roles. *[Article copies available for a fee from The Haworth Document Delivery Service: 1-800-342-9678. E-mail address: getinfo@haworthpressinc.com <Website: http:// www.haworthpressinc.com>]*

KEYWORDS. Father involvement, fatherhood, history

Fatherhood has been of interest to at least some social scientists and authorities on mental health since the turn of the century and has been the focus of considerable research, theory, and speculation over the last three decades. As a result, a large body of literature has accumulated, and substantial advances have been made in efforts to understand father-child relationships, paternal influences on child development, and the particular impact of father involvement on children and families (see Lamb, 1997b, for a detailed review). Over the course of the twentieth century, however, the ways in which fatherhood has been operationalized or implicitly defined have changed in important ways. As we attempt to appraise the current status of knowledge and to articulate fruitful avenues for research in the future, it is perhaps helpful to review the evolution of ideas concerning the central issues in this area. One goal of this paper is to describe the changing and rather narrow conceptions of fatherhood and paternal involvement that have dominated the research and theoretical literatures, particularly in the last two decades with a focus limited to the social aspects of fatherhood. The more biological aspects of fatherhood such as sexuality, fertility, and procreation, which have had little effect to date on the literature concerned with the social aspects of fatherhood, are not addressed in this paper.

The history of fatherhood and father involvement are discussed in this paper, with special focus on how our understanding and operationalization of these crucial concepts have changed over time. Fatherhood has always been a multifaceted concept, although over time the dominant or defining motif has shifted in succession from an emphasis on moral guidance, to a focus on breadwinning, then to sex-role modeling, marital support, and finally, nurturance. Corresponding with the changing conceptualization of the essence of fatherhood, paternal involvement has been viewed and indexed in different ways at different times. This makes cross-time comparisons of the extent of paternal involvement both difficult to conduct and difficult to interpret. Moreover, these difficulties became magnified because social scientists' conceptions of parental involvement were emerging simultaneously with, and were heavily influenced by, the growing popularity of time use methodologies. This prompted a shift from a focus on qualitative dimensions of fatherhood (including such traits as masculinity and dominance) to quantifiable dimensions (such as the amount of time spent by fathers with their children).

At the same time, feminist critiques of both contemporary social mores and traditional parental roles were gaining popularity. Such ideological redefinition of ideal parental roles prompted a restricted focus on paternal nurturance and involvement in day-to-day child care, with little, if any, attention paid to the other functions or aspects of fatherhood. Social scientists ignored not only the other features of fatherhood, but also subcultural variations in the definition and conceptualization of fatherhood. Consequently, we are only now beginning to seek a broader and more inclusive understanding of fatherhood. These efforts should permit more insightful research on the motivations and behavior of contemporary fathers, as well as on the effects of variations in paternal behavior on child development. Because my focus is so broad, I do not attempt to review or cite the primary literature; instead I refer to major reviews where readers can find further and more detailed discussion of the issues addressed here.

A BRIEF HISTORY OF FATHERHOOD

Within the sprawling literature on the social (as opposed to the biological or procreative) aspect of fatherhood, one can discern at least three broad and widely recognized dimensions of fatherhood. First of all, current concerns about fatherlessness and "deadbeat dads" highlight the implicit equation of responsible fatherhood with successful provisioning or bread-winning. Second, some scholars (especially developmental psychologists) have focused on the direct interactions between fathers and children in the provision of care, discipline, coaching, education, companionship, play, and supervision. A third set of writings have focused on the relationships between fathers and mothers–a primary determinant of the family climate which, in turn, affects child development and adjustment in profound ways. These three aspects of fatherhood are all of central importance. However, both researchers and theorists have tended to restrict their focus to individual components of fatherhood, ignoring or paying minimal attention to the interactions among multiple roles and the ways in which a broader and more inclusive conception of fatherhood might both enrich and change our analysis and understanding. This narrow or restrictive conception of fatherhood, rather than a more inclusive and complex portrait, reflects, in part, the changing ways in which fatherhood has been viewed within the broader society which social scientists shape and by which they are simultaneously shaped.

The available data are obviously limited, but social historians argue that much can be learned by examining letters (even though admittedly few of our forebears wrote letters, and even fewer thought to preserve them for posterity) and the literature or popular writing during particular eras in the past. The sequence of changes in popular concerns identified by scholars such as La Rossa (1988) and others who have analyzed such historical materials (LaRossa, Gordon, Wilson, Bairan, & Jaret, 1991; Mintz, 1998; Pleck & Pleck, 1997; Rotundo, 1993; Demos, 1982; 1986), are of interest not only because they help articulate our past, but also because they may help us understand the contemporary concern with and confusion about fatherhood. According to Pleck (1984), one can actually discern four phases or periods over the last two centuries of American social history. In each of these, a different dominant motif became prominent in writing to or about fathers, making other aspects of the complex, multifaceted role seem much less important by comparison.

The Moral Teacher or Guide

The earliest phase was one that extended from Puritan times through the Colonial period into early Republican times. During this lengthy period, the father's role was predominately defined by responsibility for moral oversight and moral teaching. By popular consensus, fathers were deemed primarily responsible for ensuring that their children grew up with an appropriate sense of values, acquired primarily from the study of religious materials like the Bible. To the extent that a broader role was defined, fathers assumed responsibility for the education of children–not necessarily because education and literacy were valued in their own right (although they might have been so evaluated by some), but because children had to be literate to read the Scriptures. Helping children become literate served to advance the father's role as moral guardian by ensuring that children were academically equipped to adopt and maintain Christian ways. In their more detailed and thorough reviews, both Demos (1982) and Pleck (1984) pointed out that, during this era, good fathers were defined as men who provided a model of good Christian living and whose children were well versed in the Scriptures.

The Breadwinner

Around the time of centralized industrialization, however, a shift occurred in the dominant conceptualization of the father's role (Pleck, 1984). Instead of being defined in terms of moral teaching, fathers came to be defined largely by their responsibility for breadwinning. This almost uni-dimensional conceptualization of the father endured from the mid-nineteenth century through the Great Depression (Pleck, 1984). An analysis of the then-popular literature and of letters written between fathers and children during that period confirms the dominant conception of fathers as breadwinners. This is not to say that other aspects of the father's role, such as the presumed responsibility for moral guardianship, had disappeared. Nor does this focus imply that, before industrialization, breadwinning had been insignificant. However, prior to industrialization, mothers and fathers had clearly shared the responsibility of provisioning. After industrializaton, the reduction in the importance of subsistence agriculture and home industry forced a separation between in- and out-of-home work. With industrialization, breadwinning became the most important and defining characteristic of fatherhood–*the* criterion by which "good fathers" were appraised.

The Sex-Role Model

Perhaps as a result of the disruption and dislocation brought about in rapid succession by the Great Depression, the New Deal, and the Second World War, the 1940s brought to prominence a new conceptualization of fatherhood, manifested primarily in a literature focused on the inadequacy of many fathers. Although breadwinning and moral guardianship remained important, focus shifted in the 1930s and early 1940s to the father's function as a sex-role model, especially for his sons (Pleck, 1981). Many books and articles in the professional and popular literature focused on the need for strong sex-role models, with many professionals concluding that fathers were clearly not doing a good job in this regard (e.g., Levy, 1943; Strecker, 1946; Wylie, 1942). Their alleged or apparent inadequacies were underscored in dramatic works such as *Rebel Without a Cause*, and were ridiculed in such comedies and cartoons as *Blondie* and *All in the Family* (Ehrenreich & English, 1979).

The New Nurturant Father

Around the mid-1970s a fourth stage emerged. For the first time, many writers and commentators emphasized that fathers could and should be nurturant parents who were actively involved in the day-to-day care of their children. Active parenting was defined as the central component of fatherhood and was implicitly (sometimes even explicitly) portrayed as the yardstick by which "good fathers" might be assessed. This redefinition of successful fatherhood was popularized in fictional works such as *Kramer vs. Kramer* and *The World According to Garp*, but professional interest in "the new fatherhood" soon followed. As Griswold (1995) noted, fathers had been exhorted to be more involved in the care of their children since early in the century, but the 1970s marked a change in the relative and defining importance of such behavior.

CHANGING FATHERHOOD:
THE SOCIAL SCIENTISTS' PERSPECTIVE

The systematic or scientific study of fatherhood and father-child relationships has, of course, a much shorter history than that explored by family historians. Many historians of science identify the turn of the century as the approximate time that the social sciences, including psychology and sociology, became differentiated from philosophy, biology, and medicine. It was not long after this transition that social scientists began to consider the social roles of fathers; as products and producers of their times. Moreover, the implicit and explicit conceptions enunciated by various social scientists, not surprisingly, reflected those of the wider society in which they lived.

Given the preoccupations and conceptions of turn-of-the-century society, it is not surprising that Sigmund Freud's archetypal father was characterized by classic masculine characteristics (e.g., Freud, 1909; 1924). He was to be psychologically strong, dominant within the family, assertive, decisive, and successful as a provider. Within psychoanalytic theory, the father functioned primarily in the context of a motivational system in which boys sought to identify with their fathers. Building on this notion, psychologists devoted considerable efforts in the years between 1920 and 1940 to research loosely focused on identification. In practice, the dominant concern during this era was with the extent to which children behaved, acted, or saw themselves as being similar to their fathers (Lynn, 1969; Mussen, 1967). Consequently, the modal study was one in which some aspect of the father's masculinity, in particular, or personality, more generally, was correlated with some aspect (usually the same aspect) of the son's personality in an effort to evaluate the degree to which identification had been effective. The focus was thus on qualitative characteristics such as masculinity, dominance, assertiveness, and the like.

The Second World War, which scarred the middle decades of the twentieth century, fostered two remarkably significant concerns within psychology that had tremendous implications for contemporaneous and future research on fatherhood. One was the literature on maternal deprivation, which comprised a number of reports, mostly by psychiatrists, purporting to demonstrate that children raised in orphanages or hospital settings were seriously affected by these early rearing circumstances. In his masterful integration of this literature, John Bowlby (1951), a British psychiatrist, eloquently argued that the absence of motherly love, as represented by access to the continuous care and affection of a single individual in the early months of life, effectively doomed children to serious psycho-social disadvantage.

A parallel body of literature focused on father absence. The results of many studies and the contents of many commentaries suggested that children, especially boys, were irrevocably harmed when they grew up in families without fathers, either because their fathers had been killed or were deployed away from home for long stretches of time (e.g., Sears, 1951). Ironically, both the maternal deprivation and father absence literatures over-simplified the relationships between traumatic events and the alleged outcomes or effects, and each ignored the many other potential risk factors that might better explain the apparent effects. Superb critiques of both the father absence and maternal deprivation literatures, laying bare many of their methodological inadequacies and fallacies, were published in the early 1970s (Herzog & Sudia, 1973; Rutter, 1972) but did not noticeably diminish the impact of the work itself. The maternal deprivation literature directly shaped the emergent attachment theory (Bowlby, 1958, 1969) which is easily the most important theoretical advance in the study of socialization since the emergence of psychoanalysis. Attachment theory led to a single-minded focus on mothers, and seriously undervalued the potential for influence by others (including fathers, siblings, and peers). In reaction to it researchers undertook a number of studies in the 1970s designed to evaluate Bowlby's "monotropic" hypothesis (see Lamb, 1981a; 1997a, for reviews). In the meantime, the father absence literature, with its single- and simple-minded focus on whether or not fathers were present, had a somewhat similar heuristic effect. Specifically, this literature encouraged researchers to explore the impact of variations in the extent of father presence instead of simply viewing fatherhood as a dichotomous (present *vs.* absent) construct. The emergent concern with the extent of paternal presence helped promote a very quantitative concern with variations in the amounts of time that fathers spent with their children.

Two other factors also fostered this quantitative approach. Perhaps most important was the feminist movement which led many social scientists to question some of the fundamental implicit assumptions of previous psychological research (Pleck, 1981). For example, noting that masculine fathers were believed to promote filial masculinity, many social scientists were forced to ask whether it was, in fact, desirable for boys to be more masculine and girls more feminine and whether the greater aggressiveness of boys was something to be praised or bemoaned. Perhaps in order to avoid taking stands on such value-laden issues, many psychologists apparently found it comforting to focus instead on objective dimensions (such as the extent of paternal involvement) rather than on the qualitative dimensions (such as masculinity, aggressiveness, dominance, and passivity) that had captured the attention of social scientists in preceding decades.

The popularity of quantitative measures of paternal involvement was also fostered by the reemergence of interest in time-use methodologies. These methodologies had been utilized by social scientists and home economists in the 1920s, but they fell from favor in the succeeding decades (Caplow &

Chadwick, 1979). The 1970s saw a reemergence of interest in time-use studies and this further fed the new concern with evaluating the amount of time that fathers spend with their children (e.g., Robinson, 1977).

Thus, for a variety of reasons, when psychologists turned their attention to father involvement in the late 1970s, they evinced a very narrow interest in the amount of time that fathers spent with their children. Their perspective was narrow first because the focus was limited to amount of time involved without recognizing differences in the quality of interaction. A second limiting factor was the focus on the components of fatherhood that involved direct interaction, while ignoring the other ways in which fathers could make important contributions to their children's welfare and development such as supporting their families financially or by providing emotional support for the children's mothers. At minimum, however, these scientists felt they would be able to accumulate some good "hard" data on at least one aspect of fatherhood. Unfortunately, as I indicate in the next section, the first generation of researchers who attempted to determine how much time the average father spent interacting with his children found it much more difficult than expected to obtain answers to this question (Lamb, Pleck, Charnov, & Levine, 1985; 1987; Pleck, 1983; 1997).

HOW HAVE RESEARCHERS COMPARED LEVELS OF PATERNAL INVOLVEMENT?

Many of the studies designed to determine both how much time fathers spent with their children and what sorts of activities occupied that time have involved small and often unrepresentative samples–a perennial problem in developmental research. Fortunately, however, this area of research can also boast several studies involving nationally representative samples of individuals (both mothers and fathers) who have been asked what fathers do and how much they do, although the gaps in our knowledge remain legion.

Given the availability of these data, it would seem easy to determine how much time the average father spends with his children. A preliminary evaluation of the evidence available in the mid-to-late 1970s, however, yielded estimates that ranged from as little as 37 seconds per day (Rebelsky & Hanks, 1971) to as much as 8 hours per day (DeFrain, 1975). Such dramatic and irreconcilable differences fostered intensive and systematic efforts to understand both why the data were so unreliable and how more reliable estimates could be obtained.

Engagement, Accessibility, and Responsibility

One problem is that the implicit definitions of parental involvement often vary from study to study, with different activities being included in the operational definitions of paternal involvement, making comparisons difficult at best. To make sense of the data, therefore, my colleagues and I (Lamb, Pleck, Charnov, & Levine, 1985; 1987) first found it necessary to group the studies with regard to similarities in the implicit definitions of paternal involvement employed. For purposes of analysis, one can distinguish three components of parental involvement.

Engagement. The first and most restrictive type of paternal involvement involves time spent in actual one-on-one interaction with the child (whether feeding her, helping him with homework, or playing catch in the garden). Such involvement, which we labeled engagement or interaction, does not include time spent in child-related housework or time spent sitting in one room while the child plays in the next room.

Accessibility. We included these times in a second category comprising activities characterized by less intense degrees of interaction. These activities imply parental accessibility to the child, rather than direct interaction. Cooking in the kitchen while the child plays in the next room, or even cooking in the kitchen while the child plays at the parent's feet, are examples of accessibility.

Responsibility. The final type of involvement is the hardest to define, but is perhaps the most important of all inasmuch as it reflects the extent to which the parent takes ultimate responsibility for the child's welfare and care. Responsibility involves knowing when the child needs to go to the pediatrician, making the appointment, and making sure that the child meets this appointment. Responsibility involves making child-care and baby-sitting arrangements, ensuring that the child has clothes to wear, and making arrangements for care and nurturance when the child is sick. It involves more than "helping out" or "baby-sitting." Much of the time involved in being a responsible parent is not spent in direct interaction with the child, and thus survey researchers can easily overlook this type of involvement. It is also hard to quantify the personal commitments involved, particularly because the anxiety, worry, and contingency planning that characterize parental responsibility often occur when the parent is ostensibly doing something else.

Comparison of findings. Once we had differentiated among the different components of parental involvement, my colleagues and I observed greater consistency from study to study; but a considerable degree of inconsistency remained. In part, this is because the distinctions among the three types of involvement were applied retrospectively to the results of independent investigations conducted years earlier, and thus differences across studies in specific definitions of engagement, accessibility, and responsibility remained. For example, "watching TV together" might be considered a form of engagement in one study, but a component of accessibility in others.

To integrate and compare the findings of different studies more meaningfully, Lamb et al. (1987) observed, each researcher's idiosyncratic definition of involvement had to be respected, with relative rather than absolute measures of paternal involvement used to compare results. Instead of comparing those figures purporting to measure the amount of time that fathers spend "interacting with" their children, therefore, proportional figures must first be computed (i.e., compared with the amount of time that mothers devote to interaction, how much time do fathers devote to it?). When these proportional figures are then compared, the picture becomes much clearer. Surprisingly similar results are obtained in the various studies, despite major differences in the methods used to assess time use (diary versus estimate), the size and regional representation of the samples employed, and the date when the studies were conducted.

Extent of Paternal Involvement

Consider, first, figures concerning the involvement of fathers in two-parent families in which mothers are not employed (Lamb et al., 1987; Pleck, 1983; 1997). In such families, the data reviewed by Lamb and his colleagues suggested that the average father spends about 20% to 25% as much time as the mother does in direct interaction or engagement with his children, and about a third as much time being accessible to his children. The largest discrepancy between paternal and maternal involvement was in the area of responsibility. Many studies indicated that fathers assumed essentially no responsibility (as previously defined) for their children's care or rearing.

In two-parent families with employed mothers, the levels of paternal compared with maternal engagement and accessibility are both substantially higher than in families with non-employed mothers (Lamb et al., 1987; Pleck, 1983; 1997). Lamb and colleagues reported figures for direct interaction and accessibility averaging 33% and 65% respectively, whereas Pleck's (1997) later review reported that the averages had increased to 44% and 66%, respectively, by the early 1990s. As far as responsibility is concerned, however, there was initially no evidence that maternal employment had a major effect on the level of paternal involvement. Even when both mother and father are employed 30 or more hours per week, the amount of responsibility assumed by fathers appeared as little as when mothers were not employed. As noted below, however, the situation appears to have changed by the 1990s.

In light of the controversies that have arisen on this score (Hoffman, 1977; Gottfried, Gottfried, & Bathurst, 1988; Pleck, 1983; 1985), it is worth noting that, on average, fathers do not appear to spend more time interacting with their children when mothers are employed. Instead, the proportions just cited appear to increase because mothers are doing less. Thus, fathers are proportionately more involved when mothers are employed, even though the depth of their involvement, in absolute terms, remains essentially unchanged.

The existing studies focused on time use, on the other hand, pay scant attention to the quality of maternal and paternal behavior. It is quite possible that maternal employment has led to changes in the types of activities in which fathers engage and (as noted below) to increases in the extent of paternal responsibility.

Child and family characteristics have much less affect on paternal involvement than one might expect (Pleck, 1983). Both parents spend more time with their children when the children are younger–a trend that, although understandable, contradicts the popular assumption that fathers become more involved as their children get older. Although fathers may know more about, feel more comfortable and competent with, and appear more interested in older than younger children, they apparently do not spend more time with them. In part, this may be because older children no longer want to interact with parents as much, preferring instead to interact with peers or siblings.

Popular presumptions are correct, however, so far as the effects of the child's gender are concerned (Lamb, 1981b; 1997c). Fathers are indeed more interested in and more involved with their sons than their daughters, tending to spend more time with boys than with girls, regardless of the children's ages (Pleck, 1997). However, beyond these variations associated with age and gender, there are no consistent regional, ethnic, or religious variations in the amount of time that parents–mothers or fathers–spend with their children (Pleck, 1983).

Changes Over Time

The term "new fatherhood" implies that fathers in the 1980s began to perform differently than fathers in earlier times. Unfortunately, few data are available concerning changes over time in levels of paternal involvement. Some relevant data were reported by Juster (1985), who compared figures from a 1975 national survey with figures obtained in a follow-up survey undertaken six years later. In 1981, the average father spent much more time (26% more) in the most intensive type of child care (direct interaction) than in 1975. The percentage increase for mothers was substantially smaller (7%), at least in part because the changes for mothers took place relative to higher baseline levels. In any event, the discrepancy between the levels of maternal and paternal involvement remained large: Mothers in 1981 still engaged in substantially more interaction with their children than did fathers, despite the larger increase in paternal involvement. In both 1976 and 1981, paternal involvement was about one-third that of mothers, rising from 29% in 1976 to 34% in 1981.

In his most comprehensive review, Pleck (1997) examined and compared the data on father involvement obtained from studies conducted between the mid-1970s and early 1980s and those conducted in the later 1980s and early

1990s. Pleck concluded that the average levels of father involvement, whether viewed in absolute or relative terms, had indeed increased. The average father spent approximately one-third as much time as the average mother in direct interaction in the late 1970s, whereas that figure had increased to approximately 43% by the early '90s. Likewise, whereas the average father was accessible to his children about half as much time as the average mother in the earlier surveys, this figure has increased to almost two-thirds as much time by the early 1990s. Time-use data, however, do not yield good estimates of responsibility.

Although these statistics all suggest continuing increases in the average level of paternal involvement over time, it is important to avoid over-interpretation of the findings. First, these studies have focused primarily on the amount of time that fathers spend with their children rather than on the content and quality of the interaction. Second, they focus primarily on the children in two-parent families who obviously represent only a portion–a declining portion–of the total number of children in the country. Indeed, as the more recent wave of studies on father involvement has become prominent, another group of social scientists have been drawing attention to a parallel social trend. Reference is made to the dramatic increase in the number of children growing up in fatherless families–fatherless either because the children were born out-of-wedlock to single women, or because the families were disrupted by divorce or separation (Popenoe, 1997). These statistics demonstrate that more than half of the children in the country spend at least a portion of their childhood in such families, with the proportion continuing to increase each year (U.S. Bureau of Census, 1992). The existence of such large numbers of children having little or no contact with their biological fathers underscores the fallacy of focusing exclusively on average levels of paternal involvement.

BEHAVIORAL AND MOTIVATIONAL DIFFERENCES BETWEEN MOTHERS AND FATHERS

Other researchers have criticized the time-use studies on the grounds that they examine how much time parents spend with their children, while ignoring possible variations in the content of their interactions. Both observational and survey data have in fact long suggested that mothers and fathers engage in rather different types of interaction with their children (Lamb, 1981a; 1981b; 1997a). Mothers' interactions with their children are dominated by caretaking, whereas fathers are behaviorally defined as playmates. Mothers actually play with their children much more than fathers, but as a proportion of the total amount of child-parent interaction, play is a much more prominent component of father-child interaction. In contrast, caretaking is a more salient component of mother-child interaction. A related point is that these differences are evident from early infancy and persist at least into childhood.

Although mothers are associated with caretaking and fathers with play, we cannot assume that fathers are less capable of child care. A number of researchers have attempted to investigate the relative competencies of mothers and fathers with respect to caretaking and parenting functions, and the results of these studies are fairly clear (Lamb, 1981a; 1997a; Lamb & Goldberg, 1982). First, they show that, during the newborn period, there are no differences in competence between mothers and fathers–both parents can do equally well (or equally poorly). Contrary to the notion of a maternal instinct, parenting skills are usually acquired "on the job" by both mothers and fathers. However, mothers are "on the job" more than fathers, and not surprisingly, mothers become more sensitive to their children, more in tune with them, and more aware of each child's characteristics and needs. By virtue of their lack of experience, fathers become correspondingly less sensitive and come to feel less confidence in their parenting abilities. Fathers thus continue to defer to and cede responsibility to mothers, whereas mothers increasingly assume responsibility. In this way, the imbalanced distribution of parental responsibility discussed earlier is consolidated. The crucial question thus becomes: What explains the different motivations or commitments of mothers and fathers?

Motivation

Obviously, different conceptions or definitions of fatherhood are associated with different sets of motivations. Whether or not biological drives or tendencies impel men in general, conceptions of fatherhood, as well as the extent to which individual fathers are motivated to behave accordingly, appear to be determined by the men's socio-cultural background, their current social circumstances, and their earlier experiences, particularly the behavior of their own parents. Therefore, instead of trying to rank motivations in order of importance or associate them with particular functions, it may be more productive to enumerate the most important motivational or explanatory categories that have been hypothesized. We must acknowledge, however, that empirical research in this area is, at best, scanty.

Sociobiologists emphasize that both men and women strive to maximize the representation of their genes in future generations (Trivers, 1972). Several implications flow from their observation that males (unlike females) can be biologically involved in many pregnancies simultaneously and do not need to make major physiological contributions to the physical survival of their offspring after insemination. The "down side," according to these same theorists, is that men can never really be sure of paternity, and thus always face the risk of investing resources in someone else's children (genes). Several predictions flow from these simple (if controversial) observations:

1. Men invest less in individual offspring because the costs of not investing are so much lower and the risks of mis-investment are so much higher than they are for women.
2. Men support their partners and offspring economically and socially (rather than physiologically).
3. Biologically determined differences in male and female investment may continue after delivery.
4. Like mothers, fathers invest time in the care and rearing of their children in order to bring children to reproductive maturity. Unlike mothers, their behavior does not appear to be hormonally facilitated.
5. The more men invest in partners and their children, the more they want to be sure of paternity; the extent to which they provide economic and socio-emotional support may affect the extent to which their partners' later children have the same fathers.
6. The fewer the children, the greater the motivation to invest time and resources in the success of each.

The clarity of some of these predictions is offset by the fact that the motivations are unconscious and must therefore be studied. Subsequent investigations must proceed, therefore, not by probing attitudes and values in interviews, but by studying the effects, often at the level of population groups rather than individuals. Fortunately, the desire to be a father is not driven solely (or even consciously) by the desire to propagate one's genes, and sociobiological explanations in terms of ultimate causes involve a different level of analysis than psychological and sociological explanations.

Being a father denotes maturity and confers status in many societies and subcultures, while participation in shaping the growth and development of another person brings fulfillment to many men and women. Such participation is hard to quantify empirically, but time-use measures come closest, especially when they illuminate both *what* and *how much* fathers do for or with their children. No large-scale studies measure *how well* fathers perform these roles or tasks–rather, that is the focus of smaller scale studies that are informed by direct observation.

Likewise, social status attaches to those whose partners and children are well-provisioned and successful (for example, as denoted by school performance, sports achievement, college admissions, and career attainment). Attitude surveys may indicate the relative, if not absolute importance of these motivations, as well as differing perceptions of the ways in which these desired outcomes can best be hastened (by coaching, supervision, warmth, play, physical provisioning, etc.). The type and extent of individual involvement in fathering may also be affected by recollections of the fathering experienced by men as children. Some men, particularly those who embrace hands-on involvement and avoid being defined solely as breadwinners, are motivated to emulate the behavior of their fathers. In contrast other men who behave in this way are apparently driven by a desire to be better fathers than were their own fathers. Finally, although spending time with children may or may not be an important aspect of fatherhood to the individuals concerned, the time diary studies have shown that the amount of time fathers spend with, and the amount of responsibility fathers assume for their children is associated with several factors. Specifically, we refer to socioeconomic class membership (lower class fathers tend to spend more time with their children), child's age (fathers spend more time with younger than with older children), child's gender (fathers spend more time with boys than with girls), and maternal employment status (fathers assume more responsibility when their partners are employed).

COMPONENTS OF FATHER INVOLVEMENT

Clearly, the single-minded focus on quantitative and unidimensional conceptions of fatherhood and paternal involvement that dominated scholarship in the 1970s and 1980s has, in the last several years, yielded to broader and more inclusive definitions of fatherhood. All four of the images or functions discerned by family historians discussed above remain important today, although the extent of their importance varies across cultural, ethnic, religious, and social class groupings. In any pluralistic society, various conceptions of the father's role coexist, so that while journalists and filmmakers in the United States have been lauding active and nurturant fatherhood for the last 10 years, many citizens continue to hold very different conceptions of fathering. In addition, one must recognize that fathers fill many roles, and the relative importance of each varies from one cultural context to another. Thus, active fathering must be viewed in the context of the multiple activities that fathers undertake for and with their children (for example, breadwinning, sex-role modeling, moral guidance, emotional support of mothers).

Perhaps the most striking features of father involvement, as it is now conceptualized, are the diverse array of functions viewed as aspects of father involvement and the vast individual and subcultural variability in the definition of and investment in these functions. Because the core features of mothering (nurturance and protection) are more universally recognized, much greater consensus exists about "good mothers" than about "good fathers." Committed fathers may perform in vastly different ways, and the same performances may be viewed as successful or unsuccessful depending on the implicit definitions held by those making the evaluations. These facts obviously complicate efforts to explore and articulate the motivations surrounding father involvement.

Economic provisioning, or breadwinning, is one feature of fatherhood that is probably viewed as central by most, if not all, of the defining stakeholders. A second feature is the psychosocial and emotional support of female partners (the mothers of the men's children) with special emphasis on the current partners. Third is the provision of nurturance and care to young children, an area in which widespread disagreement exists about the importance of this function. Although evaluated positively, however, the importance of nurturance and care may vary, depending on the age and gender of the children. While (or perhaps because) this function approximates "mothering" in many respects, it is almost universally viewed today as secondary–less important than mothering by mothers and less important than the other functions of fatherhood. Fourth, the role of moral and ethical guidance is viewed as a core feature of fatherhood within most religious traditions, even though, in reality, most such guidance or socialization within the family is performed by mothers. Moreover, when fathers are involved in socialization of this sort, they often function as enforcers, sternly administering sentences issued by mothers.

Although all of these (and perhaps other) aspects or features of fatherhood would be acknowledged by the majority of fathers and evaluators in most subcultural groups, their relative importance varies among individuals and socio-cultural groups. Consequently, it is not very informative to ask individuals about the importance of fatherhood without first ascertaining what fatherhood means to them. Because few researchers have done this, the motivational bases of fatherhood remain poorly understood. In fact, when studies have been conducted, it is not always clear that the researchers' conception of fatherhood has matched the respondents'. In order to assess the fulfillment of each aspect or dimension of fatherhood, one must use different metrics. Furthermore, fathers' performance of these dimensions is clearly easier to measure in some areas (e.g., economic provisioning) than in others (e.g., moral guidance). Outside the narrow research contexts, the easiest data to gather involve economic provisioning and time use, although the available statistics fail to clearly tap either paternal motivations or involvement.

MODES OF PATERNAL INFLUENCE

When we recognize the diverse roles that fathers are expected to play in different families and communities, it becomes apparent that we must recognize the variety of ways in which fathers can influence their children's development. Clearly, breadwinning remains a key component of the father's role in most segments of society today. Even in the vast majority of families in which there are two wage-earners, the father is still seen as the primary breadwinner, if only because of continuing disparities between the salaries of male and female workers. Economic support of the family constitutes an indirect but important way in which fathers contribute to the rearing and emotional health of their children.

A second important but indirect source of influence stems from the father's role as a source of emotional support to the other people, principally the mother, involved in the direct care of children (Parke, Power, & Gottman, 1979). The father's functioning as a source of emotional support for the mother and others in the family tends to enhance the quality of the mother-child relationship, and thus facilitates positive adjustment by the children. By contrast, when fathers are unsupportive or when there is conflict between the parents, children often suffer (Cummings & O'Reilly, 1997). Fathers can also affect the quality of family dynamics by being involved in child-related housework, thus easing the mother's workload (Pleck, 1983; 1984; 1985). Paternal involvement in housework may also provide a good model for children.

Fathers also influence their children by interacting with the children directly in the course of caretaking, teaching, play, and one-on-one interaction with particular children (Lamb, 1981b; 1995). Although fathers obviously can and do affect their children's development in many ways beyond direct interaction, most of the research on paternal influences is concerned with these direct influence patterns (Lamb, 1995; 1997b).

CONCLUSION

We have learned a great deal about fatherhood and father involvement over the last several decades, yet, it is clear that we have obtained a much more narrow understanding of the phenomena than we might have wished. In the next several years, it will be most important for researchers and theorists to pursue a more complete understanding of fatherhood and father involvement. Attention should be paid, not only to direct interaction between fathers and children, but also to fathers' other roles and responsibilities. Of particular importance are the breadwinning function and their influences on child development as mediated by the quality of their relationships with the children's mothers. We know little about the ways in which these different aspects of the paternal role are mediated, or the relative importance attributed to these different roles across subgroups within the society. Presumably, the impact on children will vary depending not only on ways that fathers fulfill their various functions, but also on the extent to which their behavior corresponds with paternal roles that are expected by relevant family members and others in the immediate community.

REFERENCES

Bowlby, J. (1951). *Maternal care and mental health.* Geneva: World Health Organization.

Bowlby, J. (1958). The nature of the child's tie to his mother. *International Journal of Psychoanalysis, 39,* 350-375.

Bowlby, J. (1969). *Attachment and loss. Vol. 1. Attachment.* New York: Basic Books.

Caplow, T. & Chadwick, P. (1979). Inequality and lifestyles in Middletown, 1920-1978. *Social Science Quarterly, 60,* 367-385.

Cummings, E. M. & O'Reilly, A. W. (1997). Fathers in family context: Effects of marital quality on child adjustment. In. M. E. Lamb (Ed.), *The role of the father in child development* (Third edition, pp. 49-65). New York: Wiley.

DeFrain, J. (1979). Androgynous parents tell who they are and what they need. *Family Coordinator, 28,* 237-243.

Demos, J. (1982). The changing faces of fatherhood. In S. H. Cath, A. R. Gurwitt, & J. M. Ross (Eds.), *Father and child: Developmental and clinical perspectives* (pp. 425-445). Boston, MA: Little Brown.

Demos, J. (1986). *Past, present, and personal: The family and the life course in the nineteenth century.* New York: Oxford University Press.

Enrenreich, B. & English, D. (1979). *For her own good.* New York: Anchor Books.

Freud, S. (1909/1963). Analysis of a phobia in a five-year-old boy. In: *The sexual enlightenment of children.* New York: Collier.

Freud, S. (1924). The passing of the Oedipus complex. In *Collected Papers,* Vol. 2. London: Hogarth.

Gottfried, A. E., Gottfried, A. G., & Bathurst, K. (1988). Maternal employment, family environment, and children's development: Infancy through the school years. In. A. E. Gottfried & A. W. Gottfried (Eds.), *Maternal employment and children's development: Longitudinal research* (pp. 11-58). New York: Plenum.

Griswold, R. L. (1995). *Fatherhood in America: A history.* New York: Basic Books.

Herzog, E., & Sudia, C. (1973). *Children in fatherless families.* In B. M. Caldwell & H. N. Ricciuti (Eds.), *Review of child development research* (Vol. 3, pp. 141-232). Chicago: University of Chicago Press.

Hoffman, L. W. (1977). Changes in family roles, socialization, and sex differences. *American Psychologist, 32,* 644-657.

Juster, F. T. (1985). A note on recent changes in time use. In. F. T. Juster & F. Stafford (Eds.), *Time, goods, and well-being* (pp. 313-332). Ann Arbor, MI: Institute for Social Research.

Lamb, M. E. (1981a). The development of father-infant relationships. In M. E. Lamb (Ed.), *The role of the father in child development* (Revised edition, pp. 459-488). New York: Wiley.

Lamb, M. E. (1981b). Fathers and child development: An integrative overview. In M. E. Lamb (Ed.), *The role of the father in child development* (Revised edition; pp. 1-70). New York: Wiley.

Lamb, M. E. (1995). Paternal influences on child development. In M. C. P. van Dongen, G. A. B. Frinking, & M. J. G. Jacobs (Eds.), *Changing fatherhood: An interdisciplinary perspective* (pp. 145-157). Amsterdam, The Netherlands: Thesis Publishers.

Lamb, M. E. (1997a). The development of father-infant relationships. In M. E. Lamb (Ed.), *The role of the father in child development* (Third edition; pp. 104-120; 332-342). New York: Wiley.

Lamb, M. E. (Ed.) (1997b). *The role of the father in child development* (Third edition). New York: Wiley, 1997.

Lamb, M. E. (1997c). The role of the father in child development: An introductory overview and guide. In M. E. Lamb (Ed.), *The role of the father in child development* (Third edition; pp. 1-18; 309-313). New York: Wiley.

Lamb, M. E., & Goldberg, W. A. (1982). The father-child relationship: A synthesis of biological, evolutionary and social perspectives. In L. W. Hoffman, R. Gandelman, & H. R. Schiffman (Eds.), *Parenting: Its causes and consequences* (pp. 55-73). Hillsdale, N.J.: Lawrence Erlbaum Associates.

Lamb, M. E., Pleck, J. H., Charnov, E. L., & Levine, J. A. (1985). Paternal behavior in humans. *American Zoologist, 25*, 883-894.

Lamb, M. E., Pleck, J. H., Charnov, E. L., & Levine, J. A. (1987). A biosocial perspective on paternal behavior and involvement. In J. B. Lancaster, J. Altmann, A. S. Rossi, & L.R. Sherrod (Eds.), *Parenting across the lifespan: Biosocial dimensions* (pp. 111-142). Hawthorne, NY: Aldine.

LaRossa, R. (1988). Fatherhood and social change. *Family Relations, 36*, 451-458.

LaRossa, R., Gordon, B. A., Wilson, R. J., Bairan, A., & Jaret, C. (1991). The fluctuating image of the 20th century American father. *Journal of Marriage and the Family, 53*, 987-997.

Levy, D. (1943). *Maternal overprotection.* New York: Columbia University Press.

Lynn, D. B. (1969). *Parental and sex-role identification.* Berkeley, CA: McCutchan Publishing.

Mintz, S. (1998). From patriarchy to androgyny and other myths: Placing men's family roles in historical perspective. In A. Booth and N. Crouter (Eds.), *Men in families: When do they get involved? What difference does it make?* (pp. 3-30). Mahwah, NJ: Erlbaum.

Mussen, P. H. (1967). Early socialization: Learning and identification. In T. M. Newcomb (Ed.), *New directions in psychology* (Vol. III, pp. 51-110). New York: Holt, Rinehart & Winston.

Parke, R. D., Power, T. G., & Gottman, J. M. (1979). Conceptualizing and quantifying influence patterns in the family triad. In M. E. Lamb, S. J. Suomi, & G. R. Stephenson (Eds.), *Social interaction analysis: Methodological issues* (pp. 231-252). Madison, WI: University of Wisconsin Press.

Pleck, E. H., & Pleck, J. H. (1997). Fatherhood ideals in the United States: Historical dimensions. In M. E. Lamb (Ed.), *The role of the father in child development* (Third edition; pp. 33-48). New York: Wiley.

Pleck, J. H. (1981). *The myth of masculinity.* Cambridge, MA: MIT Press.

Pleck, J. H. (1983). Husbands' paid work and family roles: Current research issues. In H. Lopata & J. Pleck (Eds.), *Research in the interweave of social roles.* Vol. 3. *Families and jobs* (pp. 231-333). Greenwich, CT: JAI Press.

Pleck, J. H. (1984). *Changing fatherhood.* Unpublished manuscript, Wellesley, MA: Wellesley College Center for Research on Women.

Pleck, J. H. (1985). *Working wives, working husbands.* Beverly Hills, CA: Sage.

Pleck, J. H. (1997). Paternal involvement: Levels, sources, and consequences. In M. E. Lamb (Ed.), *The role of the father in child development* (Third edition; pp. 66-103). New York: Wiley.

Popenoe, D. (1997). *Life without father.* New York: Free Press.

Rebelsky, F. G., & Hanks, C. (1971). Fathers' verbal interaction with infants in the first three months of life. *Child Development, 42*, 63-68.

Robinson, J. (1977). *How Americans use time: A social psychological analysis.* New York: Praeger.

Rotundo, A. (1993). *American manhood: Transformations in masculinity from the revolution to the modern era.* New York: Basic Books.

Rutter, M. (1972). *Maternal deprivation reassessed.* Harmondsworth, England: Penguin.

Sears, P. S. (1951). Doll play aggression in normal young children: Influence of sex, age, sibling status, father's absence. *Psychological Monographs, 65*, No. 6.

Strecker, E. (1946). *Their mothers' sons: The psychiatrist examines an American problem.* Philadelphia: Lippincott.

Trivers, R. L. (1972). Parental investment and sexual selection. In. B. G. Campbell (Ed.), *Sexual selection and the descent of man: 1871-1971* (pp. 136-179). Chicago: Aldine.

U. S. Bureau of the Census (1992). Studies in marriage and the family: Married couple families with children. *Current Population Reports* (series P-23, No. 162). Washington, DC: U.S. Government Printing Office.

Wylie, P. (1942). *A generation of vipers.* New York: Rinehart.

Father Involvement:
A Developmental Psychological Perspective

Ross D. Parke

SUMMARY. This paper assumes a developmental focus to provide a psychological perspective of father involvement. A key element of this objective is to recognize how difficult it is to define the complexities of father involvement. Components of father involvement include such relationship components as direct interaction, availability, and the managerial function, all of which are conceptually distinct. Other issues worthy of careful consideration are the context of father involvement, processes used to index involvement, and dimensions of involvement. In addition to examining father involvement from a developmental perspective, future research needs to study father involvement within a greater variety of ethnic-minority groups so that both cross-group and within-group variability can be appreciated. Finally, a more complete understanding of father involvement will require the use of multiple research methods involving both experimental and nonexperimental approaches. *[Article copies available for a fee from The Haworth Document Delivery Service: 1-800-342-9678. E-mail address: getinfo@haworthpressinc.com <Website: http://www.haworthpressinc.com>]*

KEYWORDS. Father involvement, developmental, parenting, definitions

The aim of this paper is to provide a psychological perspective on father involvement. Some of the issues that are addressed represent a psychological perspective, but increasingly the disciplinary boundaries between psychology

Ross D. Parke is affiliated with the Department of Psychology and Center for Family Studies, University of California, Riverside.

[Haworth co-indexing entry note]: "Father Involvement: A Developmental Psychological Perspective." Parke, Ross D. Co-published simultaneously in *Marriage & Family Review* (The Haworth Press, Inc.) Vol. 29, No. 2/3, 2000, pp. 43-58; and: *FATHERHOOD: Research, Interventions and Policies* (ed: H. Elizabeth Peters et al.) The Haworth Press, Inc., 2000, pp. 43-58. Single or multiple copies of this article are available for a fee from The Haworth Document Delivery Service [1-800-342-9678, 9:00 a.m. - 5:00 p.m. (EST). E-mail address: getinfo@haworthpressinc.com].

and related disciplines such as sociology, demography, and anthropology are becoming blurry. Perhaps we are beginning to recognize that fathers and families are too important and too complex to be left to the scrutiny of a single discipline–even psychology. Instead a multi-disciplinary perspective, in the final analysis, is likely to be more useful.

TOWARD A DEFINITION OF INVOLVEMENT

One of the continuing difficulties in this area is the definition of father involvement. Much of the confusion in the literature stems from different definitions of this central term and from different strategies for assessment of involvement. Psychologists, in particular, have recognized the need to move beyond crude distinctions between father presence versus father absence as an approximation of involvement. Although the structural level of analysis is often useful (e.g., McLanahan & Sandefur, 1994), it leaves unaddressed the variations in father involvement in father-present homes. Perhaps the most important contribution of psychology to this issue is its efforts to distinguish among different forms of involvement in father-present families or in the types of involvement when non-custodial fathers do have contact with their children.

Not all forms of father involvement are conceptually equivalent. Several researchers have distinguished various types of father involvement (Barnett & Baruch, 1987; Lamb, Pleck, & Levine, 1985; Radin, 1993). The most influential scheme was offered by Lamb and his colleagues (Lamb, 1987; Lamb, Pleck, & Levine, 1985) who suggested three components: interaction, availability, and responsibility:

> Interaction refers to the father's direct contact with his child through care giving and shared activities. Availability is a related concept concerning the father's potential availability for interaction, by virtue of being present or accessible to the child whether or not direct interaction is occurring. Responsibility refers to the role the father takes in ascertaining that the child is taken care of and arranging for resources to be available for the child. (Lamb, Pleck, Charnov, & Levine., 1987:125)

As several authors (e.g., McBride, 1989; Palkovitz, 1997; Parke, 1995) have noted, most of the literature has focused on direct interaction or engagement between the father and his offspring, while the other aspects have received less systematic attention. To a large degree this emphasis reflects the common assumption that parental influence takes place directly through face-to-face interaction or indirectly through the impact of the interaction on another family member. Only recently have researchers and theorists begun to recognize the managerial function of parents (i.e., Lamb's "responsibility" notion) and to appreciate the impact of variations in how this managerial function influences child development (Hartup, 1979; Parke, 1978; Parke, Burks, Carson, Neville, & Boyum, 1994). By managerial, we refer to the ways in which parents organize and arrange the child's home environment and set limits on the range of the home settings to which the child has access and the opportunities for social contact with playmates and socializing agents outside the family. The managerial role may be just as important as the parent's role as stimulator, because the amount of time that children spend interacting with the inanimate environment far exceeds their social interaction time (White, Kaban, Shapiro, & Attonucci, 1976).

Mothers and fathers differ in their degree of responsibility for management of family tasks. From infancy through middle childhood, mothers are more likely to assume the managerial role than fathers. In infancy, this means setting boundaries for play (Power & Parke, 1982), taking the child to the doctor, or arranging daycare. Mothers are higher in all of these domains than fathers. In middle childhood, Russell and Russell (1987) found that mothers continue to assume more managerial responsibility (e.g., directing the child to have a bath, to eat a meal, or to put away toys).

Nor is the managerial role restricted to family activities but includes initiating and arranging children's access to peers and playmates (Bhavnageri & Parke, 1991; Ladd, Profilet, & Hart, 1992; Parke & Bhavnagri, 1989). In addition, parents function as supervisors or overseers of children's interactions with age mates, especially with younger children. While laboratory studies show that both mothers and fathers are equally capable of this type of supervisory behavior (Bhavnagri, & Parke, 1985; 1991), in home contexts fathers are less likely than mothers to perform this supervisory role (Bhavnagri & Parke, 1991; Ladd et al., 1992).

Even in the 1990s and in the case of families where husbands and wives share roles, fathers are less likely to engage in management of the household and childcare. As Coltrane (1996:175) notes:

> In most families, husbands notice less about what needs to be done, wait to be asked to do various chores and require explicit directions if they are to complete the tasks successfully . . . most couples continue to characterize husbands contributions to housework or child care as "helping" their wives.

Several further distinctions have been offered (Beitel & Parke, 1998; Palkovitz, 1997; Radin, 1993). Specifically, it is important to distinguish between the levels of involvement, the contexts of involvement, the types of processes identified to index involvement, and the dimensions along which involvement can vary.

Context of Involvement

Several authors have distinguished between the contexts of involvement, such as play, leisure, and affiliative activities with the child, direct (e.g., feeding, diapering, bathing) and indirect (packing diaper bag, washing clothes, selecting clothes for an outing) care and teaching or achievement-oriented activities (homework, teaching alphabet or numbers). (See Beitel & Parke, 1998; Palkovitz, 1997; Pleck, 1997; Radin, 1993 for further elaboration of these distinctions.) Palkovitz (1997) has recently provided an extensive 15-category list of ways in which fathers are involved, but unfortunately his categories confound contexts of involvement (e.g., teaching) with levels or components of involvement (e.g., availability). However, his refinement and especially his myriad examples ought to promote more detailed and complete assessments of father involvement in the future. The importance of this distinction between components and contexts is that there are different determinants of father involvement in different contexts or activities (Beitel & Parke, 1998; Grossman, Pollack & Golding, 1998; Levy-Schiff & Israelashvili, 1988).

Processes Used to Index Involvement

Although behavioral measures (e.g., talking, touching, feeding, etc.) which are easily observed and quantified are the most commonly used indices of involvement (Palkovitz, 1997; McBride, 1989), affective and cognitive processes can also reflect involvement (Palkovitz, 1997). Affective dimensions such as type and amount of positive and negative emotions have received attention (Boyum & Parke, 1995; Carson & Parke, 1996; Isley, O'Neil & Parke, 1996), but generally within the context of ongoing interaction between fathers and children. Less is known about fathers' emotional ruminations about their children's activities, accomplishments, or failures, either when they are present or during their absence (e.g., worries, guilt, shame, joy, pride); many of these felt emotions may not be overtly expressed and therefore are inaccessible to direct observation. Less attention has been devoted to the cognitive aspects of father involvement. As Palkovitz (1997:208) argues, "our conceptualizations of involvement need to be more inclusive of thought processes and other cognitive components." Just as in the case of affective involvement, cognitive involvement can be manifest both overtly (e.g., joint planning and decision making between father and child (Gauvain, 1999); or covertly (e.g., anticipating a child's future funds for college, planning an activity for his child, thinking about the child's social, emotional, or academic needs). Even such fundamental notions as "the psychological presence of the child in the parents' cognitions" is another dimension that needs to be represented in our conceptualizations of involvement (Palkovitz, 1997:209-210).

Dimensions of Involvement

It is useful to distinguish various dimensions that can be used to characterize the quantity and quality of involvement (Palkovitz, 1997; Pleck, 1997; Radin, 1993). These include dimensions that characterize an individual father's involvement, such as the degree, salience, observability, and directness (Palkovitz, 1997), while other dimensions require an assessment of the father's contributions in relation to other family members (Radin, 1993), such as the relative vs. absolute levels of involvement. As Pleck (1981; 1997) has shown, relative and absolute indices of involvement are independent and may affect both children's behavior and adults' views of role distribution in different ways.

Finally, the quality/quantity distinction, a long-established one, remains of central importance. In spite of the current rhetoric concerning the importance of father presence as a solution to a myriad of social problems, developmental psychologists have repeatedly demonstrated that in intact father-present families, the quality of father-child involvement is more clearly linked to children's development outcomes than quantity of involvement per se (Parke, 1996). In fact, if the quality is inferior or harmful (e.g., in case of an abusive father) more father involvement can be linked to poorer developmental outcomes for the child (Parke, 1996; Palkovitz, 1997). More involvement is sometimes better if the quality of involvement is high, but more involvement is clearly not always linked with better outcomes.

A Developmental Perspective on Father Involvement Is Necessary

The placement of fathers in a developmental perspective is critical for understanding fathers' role in families. A developmental view can assume a variety of forms. First, the traditional issue that concerns developmental psychologists, namely, the changing nature of the father-child relationship as a function of the age of the child needs to be considered (Parke, 1995; 1996). Closely related to this issue is the impact of the father-child relationship on the child's social, emotional, physical, and cognitive development. Surprisingly, in the late 1990s we still have only a sketchy picture of these issues (Lamb, 1997). Most of our descriptive studies of father-offspring interaction have focused on infancy. There is some recent interest in father-adolescent relationships, but this work is only beginning to emerge (Larson & Richards, 1994). We are particularly uninformed about any changes in the father-child relationship in the early school years or in middle childhood (Collins &

Russell, 1991; Russell & Russell, 1987). Nor do we know much about the impact of fathers on children's development in these latter age periods.

There is an urgent need to move beyond either simple descriptions of father-offspring interaction or noting simple links between father-child interaction and child outcomes. Studies that detail the processes or mechanisms through which fathers achieve their effects are sorely needed. Are the effects achieved directly through interaction with their children or indirectly through changes in maternal attitudes and behaviors? What emotional and cognitive processes are implicated in mediating between father behavior and child outcomes? We have, to date, a relatively shallow process-based account of how fathers, in fact, affect their children's development (see Parke, 1996 for a summary).

Another meaning of development flows from a life-course view of fathering (Elder, 1998; Parke, 1996). In contrast to the usual view that all fathers are alike regardless of their age at the time of entry into parenthood, the life course view alerts us to the importance of the timing of fatherhood. The location of the father in terms of his age, life style, occupation, and education are important determinants of his involvement. Older and younger fathers may differ in a myriad of ways, including energy and health, educational, occupational roles and their readiness to assume fathering roles (Parke, 1995; 1996; Tinsley & Parke, 1988). Recent evidence suggests that older and on-time fathers have different patterns of interaction with their children. MacDonald and Parke (1986), in a survey of 300 fathers, found that age of fathers is negatively related to frequency of physical play.

Recent observational studies of father-child interaction confirm these early self-report investigations. Volling and Belsky (1991) who studied fathers interacting with their infants at three and nine months found that older fathers were more responsive, stimulating, and affectionate at both three and nine months. In another observational study, Neville and Parke (1997) examined the play patterns of early- and late-timed fathers interacting with their preschool-age children. Early and delayed fathers' play styles differed; the early fathers relied on physical arousal to engage their children, whereas the delayed fathers relied on more cognitive mechanisms to remain engaged.

Timing effects are important not just for fathers, but for grandfathers as well. It is not just the age, per se, that is important, but the timing of entry into familial roles may be a determinant of interactional style as well. In their study of grandfathers interacting with their seven-month-old infants, Tinsley and Parke (1988) found that grandfather age related to the level of stimulating play. Grandfathers were divided into three categories: younger (36-49 years), middle (50-56), and older (57-68). Grandfathers in the middle age group were rated significantly higher on competence (e.g., confident, smooth, accepting), affect (e.g., warm, interested, affectionate, attentive), and play style (e.g., playful, responsive, stimulatory). From a life-span developmental perspective, the middle group of grandfathers could be viewed as being optimally ready for grandparenthood, both physically and psychologically. Unlike the oldest group of grandfathers, they were less likely to be chronically tired or to have been ill with age-linked diseases. And, unlike the youngest grandfathers, they have completed the career-building position of their lives and were prepared to devote more of their time to family-related endeavors. Moreover, the age of the middle group of grandfathers fits the normative age at which grandparenthood is most often achieved; thus, for these men, the role of grandfather was more age-appropriate than it was for the youngest and oldest groups of grandfathers.

"Father time," or the point at which the individual becomes a father, is not the only important timing issue. Fathers are embedded in dyadic relationships with children as well as with wives or partners, and these dyadic units may each follow separate developmental trajectories that can produce a diverse set of effects on how fathers enact their parenting role (Parke, 1988; Parke & Tinsley, 1984). For example, the mother-father relationship may follow a different pathway than the father-child relationship; the father's relationship with two siblings may differ which, in turn, could alter both sets of relationships, especially if there is conflict engendered by the discrepancies between the trajectories followed by the different relationships. Recent research on siblings' perceptions of differential treatment by parents underscores the importance of examining the sets of relationships that fathers develop with different family members (Dunn & Plomin, 1991).

The family as a unit and its developmental course, in turn, can profoundly influence fathers' involvement. "Family time," or the timing of transitional events for the family as a unit, is important for understanding fathers. Family time includes such events as residential mobility or divorce, separation. As argued elsewhere (Parke, 1988), these different units of analysis–individual, dyadic, and familial–do not operate independently, but rather mutually influence each other. To fully appreciate fathering involvement, multiple sets of developmental trajectories need to be considered.

Finally, a life-course view alerts us to the importance of the historical context in which the father is operating (Coltrane & Parke, 1999; Parke & Stearns, 1993; Parke & Tinsley, 1984; Stearns, 1991). While there is considerable historical continuity, there have also been important shifts in the secular sphere that have profoundly altered men's fathering roles, for example, the Great Depression (Elder, 1974) and the Midwest Farm Crisis (Conger & Elder, 1994). The life-course view alerts us to these historical shifts. Again, the interplay among father time, family time, and historical time is often complex and often does not harmonize.

It is clear that the understanding of the determinants of father involvement requires a multi-level, multi-factor framework. As presented recently, Parke (1996) has offered such a framework which emphasizes four levels of determinants–individual, familial, extrafamilial, and cultural–each of which has multiple components (see Table 1).

The main feature is the systemic nature of these different levels of analysis, with changes in any level influencing the operation of the other aspects of the model. Some factors such as our culture's attitude concerning roles for males and females and the differential socialization of boys and girls may be

TABLE 1. Determinants of Father Involvement: A Systems View

Individual Influences

1. Attitudes, beliefs and motivation of father
2. Relationship with family of origin
3. Timing of entry into parental role
4. Child gender

Family (Dyadic and Triadic)

1. Mother-child relationships; Father-child relationships
2. Husband-wife relationship
3. Father-mother-child relationship

Extra-Familial Influences

Informal Support Systems

1. Relationships with relatives
2. Relationships with neighbors
3. Relationships with friends

Institutional or Formal Influences

1. Work-family relationships
2. Hospital and health care delivery systems

Cultural Influences

1. Childhood cultures of boys and girls
2. Attitudes concerning father/mother gender roles
3. Ethnicity-related family values and beliefs

Source: Parke, 1996, p. 77.

most helpful in accounting for overall levels of involvement in caregiving between mothers and fathers as a group or as a member of a particular gender category (Parke & Brott, 1999). Other factors are most useful in understanding differences among individual fathers. For example, the amount of support a father receives from his spouse or the amount of gatekeeping that a spouse engages in may facilitate or suppress the degree of father involvement (Allen & Hawkins, 1999; Beitel & Parke, 1998). For a review of these determinants of father involvement, see Doherty, Kouneski and Erickson (1998), Levine and Pettinsky (1997), Parke (1996), and Parke and Brott (1999).

BEYOND STEREOTYPES OF MINORITY FATHERS

One of the greatest challenges for the field is to move beyond current stereotypes about fathers of different ethnic backgrounds. Recently, two relatively distinct fathering literatures have emerged in the social sciences. First, a substantial body of literature exists on paternal issues within intact families where the focus is on fathers who are white and middle class (Lamb, 1997). In addition, a second literature exists on young fathers or fathers of adolescent women, many of whom are African American, poor, and unmarried (Lerman & Ooms, 1993). Separate literatures of this kind have led to the propagation of stereotypes that cast white fathers in a positive light, while suggesting that African American fathers are likely to father children by young adolescent women and then neglect both their partners and their children. Moreover, only limited effort has been made to integrate these two literatures (for a recent exception, see Gadsden, 1999). Are similar processes operating in determining father involvement in these two sets of fathers? Or, are there enough distinctive contextual and developmental differences to justify treating these two groups as distinctive with their own unique determinants?

An obvious need exists to study middle-class African-American fathers, as McAdoo (1993) urged, and to assess lower class Caucasian young fathers, as Mott (1994) has done. There are some interesting results that have emerged. For example, the distribution of father involvement in African-American families is similar to Caucasian families. In both cases fathers are secondary caregivers and more often playmates (see Hossain & Roopnarine, 1994). On the other hand, studies of African-American fathers reveal that fathers do not interact more with boys than girls, a finding consistent with less gender role distinction in African-American families (Gibbs, 1989).

Another urgent need exists to expand the cast of fathers from other ethnic groups to include Latino, Asian-American, and Native American fathers (see Ishii-Kuntz, 1995; Mirande, 1991; Williams, Radin, & Coggins, 1993). Moreover, it is critical to recognize the within group variability among these different ethnic groups. Cubans, Puerto Ricans, and Mexican-Americans each represent distinctive cultural traditions that, in turn, may shape father relationships with other family members including wives and children as well as relationships with extended family (Parke & Buriel, 1998). Acculturation, ethnic identity and generational status will play critical roles in shaping fathering patterns. We are just beginning to sketch the levels and determinants of involvement in fathers of different ethnic backgrounds. As we move into the 21st century and as we become an increasingly multi-cultural society, we need to meet this challenge.

Multiple Methods Are Necessary for Understanding Fathers

Increasingly, psychologists and other social scientists are using a number of methodological approaches in their studies of fathers. First, observational methods remain the central approach in the psychologists' methodological armature. For studies of process, this strategy continues to be the best approach. Observational studies of the interaction patterns of fathers and partners and/or children have provided important insights into the nature of the affective and social processes that characterize these relationships. Let me offer two examples. Recently, Carson and Parke (1996) found that reciprocity of negative affect (anger) was characteristic of the interaction patterns of fathers with sons who, in turn, were rejected by their peers. The discovery of the nature of the interactive exchange between fathers and children cannot be achieved with other methods.

Infants, under conditions of uncertainty, often turn to their parents for guidance. This phenomenon, social referencing, has been well documented in the infancy literature. Dickstein and Parke (1988) found that fathers in unhappy marriages are less likely to be the targets of social referencing on the part of their infants than fathers in happy marriages. This study illustrates the impact of marital relationships on the father-infant relationship in the first year of life. Moreover, it is again unlikely that this subtle effect of the marriage on infant behavior would have been uncovered without the use of sensitive observational methods.

The value of observational studies is important to underscore because they are often dismissed by other social scientists as "small-scale" studies, with the implication being that the sample sizes typical of these studies are too small for meaningful conclusions to be drawn. Furthermore, the claim is often made that samples used in these studies are generally non-representative of the general population. Despite such categories, however, it is generally the case that these small-scale studies are often replicated both within and across labs, a strategy (i.e., replication) that is important for two reasons. First, confidence in findings is increased by showing that the effects reported are robust across replications. Many times the replications involve variations in procedure and setting, so that the robustness of the effect is established in a more meaningful fashion. For example, Boyum and Parke (1995) found a similar relation between paternal negative affect directed toward children and their poor relationships with peers that Carson and Parke (1996) reported. However, in contrast to the structured lab play context used in the Carson and Parke (1996) study, the observations for the Boyum and Parke (1995) research took place at home during a regular family dinner. Second, replications across laboratories serve as a partial corrective to the issue of non-representativeness. When investigators in rural conservative Pennsylvania, urban liberal Berkeley, California, and central impoverished Baltimore produce similar findings, greater faith in the generalizability of the findings is warranted (see for example Belsky & Isabella, 1985; Cowan & Cowan, 1992).

At the same time, there is a movement toward multi-stage sampling approaches that combine the benefits of being able to gain a more representative sample with the advantages of work based on observation. Recent examples include the Hetherington, Reiss, and Plomin (1994) study on the effects of non-shared environments in step-families. After employing a representative national sampling strategy, these investigators subsequently videotaped the interactions of family members. Although extremely expensive and time-intensive, this multi-method strategy goes a long way toward resolving the issues involved. A more modest example of this approach was utilized by Beitel and Parke (1998) in their study of maternal gatekeeping. A large sample (n = 300) of mothers were surveyed concerning their attitudes toward and levels of paternal involvement, and a subsample of this larger group was chosen for observational analyses.

Other methods increasingly recognized as useful are focus groups, an approach that can help define the issues of importance for fathers (and mothers) in particular samples that are studied less frequently. Such a focus group strategy, for example, was used in a recent study concerning the effects of economic downturn on Latino families (Gomel, Tinsley, Clark, & Parke, 1998). Focus groups are a particularly useful strategy at the beginning of the research process during which variables are selected, study questions are refined, and the cultural equivalence of instruments is assessed.

Reliance on non-experimental strategies, however, may be insufficient to address the central issue of the direction of effects in work on the impact of fathers on children and families (Parke, 1995). Experimental studies have been underutilized in studies of fathers. By experimentally modifying either the father's type of behavior or level of involvement, firmer conclusions will be possible about the causative role that fathers play in modifying the development of their children and their wives/partners.

These experimental studies can be undertaken for several reasons. Thus, although the goal is generally to increase paternal involvement in the hope of improving the life chances of children, another central but often neglected reason for experimental interventions is to provide a test of a theoretical position (McBride, 1991; Parke, Power, Tinsley, & Hymel, 1979). This serves as a reminder that intervention–often viewed as an applied concern–and theory testing–often viewed as a basic research theme–are quite compatible. In fact, one could argue that the intervention strategy most likely to yield the highest payoff in terms of efficacy is an approach that is theory-based. Experimental interventions can assume a variety of forms and can be guided by the multi-level scheme outlined above. Individual interventions aimed at modifying fathering attitudes, beliefs, and behaviors is only one level of analysis. At the dyadic level, interventions targeting the marital couple or the spouse who is high in gatekeeping can provide a test of the importance of dyadic factors in determining father involvement. Other types of experimental interventions involve targeting neither individuals or dyads but focus on links across contexts. These strategies include programs (Epstein, 1989) that provide opportunities for parents to become involved in the activities of child-centered institutions (e.g., schools) by forming partnerships with other fathers and mothers. Another target of such programs is to focus on how changes in the workplace such as flextime, leave, reductions in job stress impact both fathering behavior and involvement (Levine & Pittinsky, 1988).

FINAL THOUGHTS

Fathers have shifted their level of involvement over the last 20 years but only in a slow, gradual manner. Back in the 1970s, however, some of my students, in a moment of youthful optimism, bought me a T-shirt that said "Fathers make better mothers." Although this claim, of course, was exaggerated, it did serve to capture feelings of optimism that some form of social revolution was underway, one in which fathers would soon be equal to mothers in their caregiving roles. As we now know, in turn, this social revolution did not happen and, instead, an evolutionary process proceeded to unfold (Parke & Brott, 1999). If we believe that increased paternal involvement has positive benefits for children, mothers, and the fathers themselves, then the search for better ways to measure father involvement and its determinants remains one of the important challenges for researchers throughout the social sciences.

REFERENCES

Allen, S.M., & Hawkins, A.J. (1999). Maternal gatekeeping: Mothers' beliefs and behaviors that inhibit greater father involvement in family work. *Journal of Marriage and Family, 61*, 199-212.

Barnett, R.C., & Baruch, G.K. (1987). Determinants of fathers' participation in family work. *Journal of Marriage and the Family, 49*, 29-40.

Bietel, A., & Parke, R.D. (1998). Maternal and paternal attitudes as determinants of father involvement. *Journal of Family Psychology, 12*, 268-288.

Belsky, J., & Isabella, R. (1985). Marital and parent-child relationships in family of origin and marital change following the birth of a baby: A retrospective analysis. *Child Development, 56*, 342-349.

Bhavnagri, N., & Parke, R.D. (1985, April). Parents as facilitators of peer-peer interaction. Paper presented at the Biennial Meeting of the Society for Research in Child Development, Toronto.

Bhavnagri, N., & Parke, R.D. (1991). Parents as direct facilitators of children's peer relationships: Effects of age of child and sex of parent. *Journal of Social and Personal Relationships, 8*, 423-440.

Boyum, L., & Parke, R.D. (1995). Family emotional expressiveness and children's social competence. *Journal of Marriage and Family, 57*, 593-608.

Carson, J. & Parke, R.D. (1996). Reciprocal negative affect in parent-child interactions and children's peer competency. *Child Development, 67*, 2217-2226.

Collins, W.A., & Russell, G. (1991). Mother-child and father-child relationships in middle childhood and adolescence: A developmental analysis. *Developmental Review, 11*, 99-136.

Coltrane, S. (1996). *Family man: Fatherhood, housework, and gender equity.* New York: Oxford University Press.

Coltrane, S. & Parke, R.D. (1999). Reinventing fatherhood: Toward a historical understanding of continuity and change in men's family lives. Commissioned paper. National Center on Fathers and Families.

Conger, R., & Elder, G. (1994). *Families in troubled times: Adapting to change in rural America.* New York, NY: Aldine de Gruyter.

Cowan, C.P., & Cowan, P. (1992). *When partners become parents.* New York: Basic Books.

Dickstein, S., & Parke, R.D. (1988). Social referencing: A glance at fathers and marriage. *Child Development, 59*, 506-511.

Doherty, W.J., Kouneski, E.F., & Erikson, M.F. (1998). Responsible fathering: An overview and conceptual framework. *Journal of Marriage and the Family, 60*, 277-292.

Dunn, J., & Plomin, R. (1991). Why are siblings so different? The significance of differences in sibling experiences within the family. *Family Process, 30*, 271283.

Elder, G. H. (1974). *Children of the great depression.* Chicago: University of Chicago Press.

Elder, G.H. (1998). The life course as developmental theory. *Child Development, 69*, 112.

Epstein, J.L. (1989). Family structures and student motivation: A developmental perspective. In C. Ames & R. Ames (Eds.). *Research on motivation in education.* Vol. 3 (pp. 289-293). New York: Academic Press.

Gadsden, V. (1999). Black families in intergenerational and cultural perspective. In M.E. Lamb (Ed.), *Parenting and child development in "nontraditional" families* (pp. 221-246). Mahwah, NJ: Lawrence Erlbaum Associates.

Gauvain, M. (1999). Family interaction, parenting style, and the development of planning: A longitudinal analysis using archival data. *Journal of Family Psychology, 13,* 75-92.

Gibbs, J.T. (1989). Black American adolescents. In J.T. Gibbs & L.N. Huang (Eds.), *Children of color: Psychological interventions with minority youth.* San Francisco, CA: Jossey-Bass.

Gomel, J., Tinsley, B.J., Clark, K. & Parke, R.D. (1998). The effects of economic hardship on family relationships among African-American, Latino, and Euro-American families. *Journal of Family Issues, 19,* 268-288.

Grossman, F. K., Pollack, W. S., & Golding, E. (1988). Fathers and children: Predicting the quality and quantity of fathers. *Developmental Psychology, 24,* 82-91.

Hartup, W. W. (1979). The social worlds of childhood. *American Psychologist, 34,* 944-950.

Hetherington, E.M., Reiss, D., & Plomin, R. (1994). *Separate social worlds of siblings: The impact of nonshared environment on development.* Hillsdale, NJ: Lawrence Erlbaum Associates, Inc.

Hossain, Z. & Roopnarine, J.L. (1994). AfricanAmerican fathers' involvement with infants: Relationship to their functioning style, support, education, and income. *Infant Behavior & Development, 17,* 175184.

Ishii-Kuntz, M. (1995). Paternal involvement and perception toward fathers' roles: A comparison between Japan and the United States. In W. Marsiglio (Ed.), *Fatherhood: Contemporary theory, research, and social policy* (pp. 102-118). Thousand Oaks, CA: Sage.

Isley, S., O'Neil, R., & Parke, R.D. (1996). The relation of parental affect and control behavior to children's classroom acceptance: A concurrent and predictive analysis. *Early Education and Development, 7,* 7-23.

Ladd, G. W., Profilet, S. M., & Hart, C. H. (1992). Parents' management of children's peer relations: Facilitating and supervising children's activities in the peer culture. In R. D. Parke & G. W. Ladd (Eds.), *Family-peer relationships: Modes of linkage* (pp. 215-254). Hillsdale, NJ: Erlbaum.

Lamb, M. E. (Ed.) (1987). *The father's role: Cross-cultural perspectives.* Hillsdale, NJ: Erlbaum.

Lamb, M.E. (Ed.) (1997). *The role of the father child development.* (3rd ed.). New York, NY: John Wiley & Sons.

Lamb, M.E., Pleck, J.H., Charnov, E.L., & Levine, J. A. (1987). A biosocial perspective on paternal behavior and involvement. In J. B. Lancaster, J. Altman, A. S. Rossi, & L. R. Sherrod (Eds.), *Parenting across the life span: Biosocial dimensions,* (p. 111-142). Hawthorne, NY: Aldine Publishing Co.

Lamb, M.E., Pleck, J.H., & Levine, J.A. (1985). The role of the father in child development: The effects of increased paternal involvement. In B. Lahey & E. E. Kazdin (Eds.), *Advances in clinical child psychology,* Vol. 8 (pp. 229-266). New York: Plenum.

Larson, R., & Richards, M.H. (1994). *Divergent realities: The emotional lives of mothers, fathers, and adolescents.* New York, NY: Basic Books.

Lerman, R.L., & Ooms, T.J. (1993). *Young unwed fathers: Changing roles and emerging policies.* Philadelphia: Temple University Press.

Levine, J.A. & Pittinsky, T.J. (1997). *Working fathers: New strategies for balancing work and family.* New York: Harcourt Brace.

Levy-Shiff, R., & Israelashvili, R. (1988). Antecedents of fathering: Some further exploration. *Developmental Psychology, 24,* 434-440.

MacDonald, K., & Parke, R.D. (1986). Parent-child physical play: The effects of sex and age of children and parents, *Sex Roles, 7-8,* 367-379.

McAdoo, J.L. (1993). The roles of African American fathers: An ecological perspective. *Families in Society, 74,* 2835.

McBride, B. A. (1989). Stress and fathers' parental competence: Implications for family life and parent educators. *Family Relations, 38,* 385-389.

McBride, B.A. (1991). Parental support programs and paternal stress: An exploratory study. *Early Childhood Research Quarterly, 6,* 137149.

McLanahan, S., & Sandefur, G. (1994). *Growing up with a single parent.* Cambridge, MA: Harvard University Press.

Mirande, A. (1991). Ethnicity and fatherhood. In F.W. Bozett & S.M.H. Hanson (Eds.). *Fatherhood and families in cultural context* (pp. 53-82). New York: Springer.

Mott, F.L. (1994). Sons, daughters, and fathers' absence: Differentials in father-leaving probabilities and in home environments. *Journal of Family Issues, 5,* 97-128.

Neville, B., & Parke, R. D. (1997). Waiting for paternity: Interpersonal and contextual implications of the timing of fatherhood. *Sex Roles, 37,* 45-59.

Palkovitz, R. (1997). Reconstructing "involvement:" Expanding conceptualizations of men's caring in contemporary families. In A.J. Hawkins & D.C. Dollahite (Eds.), *Generative fathering: Beyond deficit perspectives* (pp. 200-206). Thousand Oaks, CA: Sage.

Parke, R.D. (1978). Parent-infant interaction: Progress, paradigms and problems. In G. P. Sackett (Ed.), *Observing behavior: Vol. 1. Theory and applications in mental retardation.* (69-95). Baltimore: University Park Press.

Parke, R.D. (1988). Families in life-span perspective: A multilevel developmental approach. In E. M. Hetherington, R. M. Lerner, and M. Perlmutter (Eds.), *Child Development in Life-Span Perspective,* (pp. 159-190). Hillsdale, NJ: Erlbaum.

Parke, R.D. (1995). Multiple publications from a single data set: A challenge for researchers and editors. *Journal of Family Psychology, 8,* 384-386.

Parke, R.D. (1996). *Fatherhood.* Cambridge: Harvard University Press.

Parke, R.D., & Bhavnagri, N. (1989). Parents as managers of children's peer relationships. In D. Belle (Ed.), *Children's social networks and social supports.* (pp. 241-259), New York: Wiley.

Parke, R.D., & Brott, A. (1999). *Throwaway Dads.* Boston: Houghton-Mifflin.

Parke, R.D., & Buriel, R. (1998). Socialization in the family: Ecological and ethnic perspectives. In W. Damon (Ed.), *Handbook of Child Psychology,* (pp. 463-552). New York: Wiley.

Parke, R.D., Burks, V., Carson, J., Neville, B., & Boyum, L. (1994). Family-peer relationships: A tripartite model. In R.D. Parke & S. Kellam (Eds.), *Advances in family research, Vol. 4: Family relationships with other social systems* (115-145). Hillsdale, NJ: Erlbaum.

Parke, R.D., Power, T.G., Tinsley, B.R., & Hymel, S. (1979). The father's role in the family system. *Seminars in Perinatology, 3*, 25-34.

Parke, R.D., & Stearns, P.N. (1993). Fathers and child rearing. In G.H. Elder, J. Modell, & R.D. Parke (Eds.), *Children in time and place* (147-170). New York: Cambridge University Press.

Parke, R.D., & Tinsley, B.R. (1984). Fatherhood: Historical and contemporary perspectives. In K. McCluskey & H. Reese (Eds.), *Life span development: Historical and generational effects* (203-248). New York: Academic.

Pleck, J.H. (1981). Wives' employment, role demands and adjustment (final report). Unpublished manuscript, Wellesley College Center for Research on Women.

Pleck, J.H. (1997). Paternal involvement: Levels, sources, and consequences. In M.E. Lamb (Ed.), The role of the father in child development (3rd ed)., pp. 66-103). New York: John Wiley & Sons.

Power, T.G., & Parke, R.D. (1982). Play as a context for early learning: Lab and home analyses. In I.E. Sigel & L.M. Laosa (Eds.), *The family as a learning environment* (147-178). New York: Plenum.

Radin, N. (1993). Primary caregiving fathers in intact families. In A. Gottfried and A. Gottfried (Eds.), *Redefining families* (11-54). New York: Plenum.

Russell, G., & Russell, A. (1987). Mother-child and father-child relationships in middle childhood. *Child Development, 58*, 1573-1585.

Snarey, J. (1993). *How fathers care for the next generation.* Cambridge, MA: Harvard.

Stearns, P. (1991). Fatherhood in historical perspective: The role of social change. In F.W. Bozett & S.M. H. Hanson (Eds.), *Fatherhood and families in cultural context*, (pp.28-52). New York: Springer.

Tinsley, B.R., & Parke, R.D. (1988). The role of grandfathers in the context of the family. In P. Bronstein & C.P. Cowan (Eds.), *Fatherhood today: Men's changing role in the family.* (pp. 236-250) New York: Wiley.

Volling, B.L., & Belsky, J. (1991). Multiple determinants of father involvement during infancy in dual-earner and single-earner families. *Journal of Marriage and the Family, 53*, 461-474.

White, B.L., Kaban, B., Shapiro, B., & Attonucci, J. (1976). Competence and experience. In I.C. Uzgiris & F. Weizmann (Eds.), *The structuring of experience* (pp. 115-152). New York: Plenum.

Williams, E., Radin, N. & Coggins, K. (1993). Parental involvement in childrearing and the school performance of Ojibwa children: An exploratory study. *Merrill-Palmer Quarterly, 42*, 578-595.

Culture, History, and Sex: Anthropological Contributions to Conceptualizing Father Involvement

Barry S. Hewlett

SUMMARY. This paper provides a brief overview of anthropological approaches and studies of father involvement with the hopes of providing insights into how father involvement is conceptualized in the United States. The paper reviews four topics: (1) how our culture shapes how we feel about father-child relations; (2) factors cross-cultural studies have identified as being associated with high levels of father involvement; (3) the different roles of fathers during the past 120,000 years of human history; and (4) how biology and male reproductive interest influence father involvement. *[Article copies available for a fee from The Haworth Document Delivery Service: 1-800-342-9678. E-mail address: getinfo@haworthpressinc.com <Website: http://www.haworthpressinc.com>]*

KEYWORDS. Culture, Africa, father-child, evolution

A striking absence of anthropological literature is evident among the extensive bibliographies on fathering developed by the National Center on Fathers and Families as well as the Family and Child Well-Being Research Network. Excellent studies of fatherhood from the perspective of cross-cultural psychology are listed in these bibliographies, but anthropological studies of fatherhood are infrequently listed among these sources. Some may feel

Barry S. Hewlett is affiliated with Washington State University, Department of Anthropology, Vancouver, WA 98686 (e-mail: hewlett@vancouver.wsu.edu).

[Haworth co-indexing entry note]: "Culture, History, and Sex: Anthropological Contributions to Conceptualizing Father Involvement." Hewlett, Barry S. Co-published simultaneously in *Marriage & Family Review* (The Haworth Press, Inc.) Vol. 29, No. 2/3, 2000, pp. 59-73; and: *FATHERHOOD: Research, Interventions and Policies* (ed: H. Elizabeth Peters et al.) The Haworth Press, Inc., 2000, pp. 59-73. Single or multiple copies of this article are available for a fee from The Haworth Document Delivery Service [1-800-342-9678, 9:00 a.m. - 5:00 p.m. (EST). E-mail address: getinfo@haworthpressinc.com].

59

that good reasons exist for the exclusion of anthropological literature–what do anthropologists have to contribute to understanding fathers' involvement in the United States anyway? Perhaps it was Margaret Mead's statement that "Fathers are a biological necessity and a social accident" that has turned fatherhood researchers away from anthropology. Then again, this may result from the impressions that anthropologists often limit themselves to studies in "Bongo Bongo land" with research designs that are so qualitative and descriptive as to be neither reliable or relevant to policy decisions in the U.S. There is, of course, a grain of truth to these images, but this paper aims to dispel some of these misconceptions. Consequently, this article provides a brief overview of anthropological approaches and studies of father involvement, with the hope being to provide insights into how father involvement is conceptualized within the U.S. This is an important endeavor, because the way father involvement is conceptualized often influences how research is conducted and policy is developed.

CULTURE ETHNOCENTRISM AND EMOTIONS

The unifying concept in anthropology is culture, or a construct minimally defined as shared knowledge and practices that are transmitted non-biologically from generation to generation. A distinctive feature of culture is that it is by nature ethnocentric. Once one acquires cultural beliefs and practices and utilizes them for some time, there is a tendency to *feel* that these beliefs and practices are natural and universal. Routinization (how to eat, brush teeth, go to toilet, take care of infants) and the nature of regular interactions with others (called internal working models by Bowlby, 1969) pattern the emotional basis of culture. Individuals are usually unaware of the emotional basis of culture unless they see or experience something different (e.g., being asked to eat termites or caterpillars, seeing 8-month-olds using machetes or 5-year-olds smoking cigarettes).

A few examples of father involvement in other cultures are useful ways of demonstrating the emotional basis of our own culture. Among the patrilineal Fulani, divorce is relatively common, and the father always receives custody of the children after divorce; it is assumed that the "best interests of the child" are being served by being with the father's family. If a woman has a child by a man outside of marriage, the child is expected to stay with the woman's husband's family, not the mother or the biological father. Among the East African Kipsigis, fathers do not hold infants during the first year of life.

How would most U.S. fathers feel if they were not able to hold their infants for a year? How would U.S. mothers feel if their children always went to the father after divorce? The point here is that, by looking outside of our own culture, we come to better understand how our own culture affects how we *feel* what is right or wrong. We begin to evaluate our cultural assumptions about the roles of fathers and why paternal involvement is highly desirable. For instance, due to the assumption that father involvement is highly desirable, all of the papers in this collection and the national institutes that foster research on fathers (e.g., the National Center on Fathers and Families), are organized around the idea that father involvement should be increased. In addition, millions of dollars are spent every year in the U.S. to conduct research and develop policies and programs to increase father involvement. This reliance on strong moral authority reminds me of dairy commercials that say "milk is good for you"–which assumes that milk is universally good for all. The reality, of course, is that milk is not good for most lactose intolerant peoples of Mediterranean, African, and Asian descent where it can cause upset stomachs and diarrhea. This example, in turn, illustrates a type of nutritional ethnocentrism.

Another example is the current U.S. childbirth practice in which fathers are expected to have an active role–called "natural" childbirth–giving the impression that fathers around the world are involved in childbirth. In fact, cross-cultural studies have demonstrated that fathers seldom have an active role in childbirth, and in no culture do fathers direct the birthing process (Hewlett & Hannon, 1989). Father involvement and participation in childbirth appear to be especially important in the context of the middle-class American family which by cross-cultural standards is extremely atomistic. Other characteristics of middle-class American families that affect the context of father involvement are (1) low infant mortality rates, (2) the absence of regular warfare, (3) the fact that parents' time with children is limited due to work schedules, (4) that parents usually have no background in child-rearing until the first child is born, and (5) that children do not stay with parents when they get married.

Riesman's (1992) study of the Fulani points out another aspect of child-rearing that we tend to think of as universal and natural. He asked Fulani men about the important things fathers contribute to their children. "The father's first obligation" said the men, "is to seek out a good mother for the child." Given Riesman's Euro-American background he thought this meant a mother that was a good caregiver–attentive, loving, and supportive. What the Fulani men actually meant was a mother from a prestigious family with lots of kin. Fulani believe that parental care has very little impact on the child until he or she reaches the age of reason (7-8 years old). The child's character is determined by God; a father has a responsibility to correct a child who is doing something wrong, but God determines whether or not the child listens. Fulani fathers provide very little direct care to their children, yet, according to Riesman, their children are more vibrant and self-assured than most U.S.

children. Riesman points out that in the West, children are made, not born, as suggested by the title of Virginia Satir's book, *People-Making* (1972). Consequently, parents and teachers are regularly trying to shape young children's lives (e.g., make children eat something, make a child share with another, make a child go to bed). This does not happen among the Fulani and most African cultures with which I am familiar. This cultural view, according to Riesman (1992) and my ethnographic experience, takes away children's autonomous development.

Along these same lines, Western parents and researchers are interested in increasing father involvement, in part, because we believe this form of caregiving has significant social-emotional outcomes for the young later in life. This strong "future orientation" serves as a regular motivating force for the current conception of paternal behaviors with children, but from a cross-cultural standpoint, it is an uncommon arrangement. This people-making concept in Western cultures, however, has led researchers to focus almost exclusively on the role of fathers during childhood, whereas very little is known about the significance or dynamics of paternal roles in adulthood.

One anthropologist (Townsend, 1996) used a life course perspective to examine fathers' roles among the Tswana of Botswana, where the government of Botswana has adopted the American idea of "deadbeat dads." The government has adopted this stance because national demographic surveys indicate an increasing number of "illegitimate" births and female-headed households. Townsend finds that when men migrate to cities for work, the first child in a relationship is often born in the mother's family home. Male involvement during this period comes primarily from the child's maternal uncle rather than from the father. A man slowly pays the bride price to his wife's family and eventually, possibly years later, the family moves to live with the husband's family. This practice, with its roots in matrilocality, is not viewed as a problem by the local people. Government officials, however, have come to view this as a national problem because it shows up as "illegitimate" births on the national census. Townsend states:

> In the extended families I describe, "deadbeat brothers" may be as important a social problem as "deadbeat dads." . . . It may not be a contribution to the welfare of children to eliminate "deadbeat dads" at the expense of creating men who fail in their responsibilities as brothers, uncles, grandfathers, and social beings. (p. 128)

Americans, of course, are not the only ethnocentric people. When I describe the U.S. infant care practice of placing infants in cribs located within their own rooms, the Aka, with whom I have lived for several years, tend to view this as child neglect. A central aspect of good parenting for the Aka, therefore, is to hold the infant constantly.

Culture is by nature ethnocentric and it patterns emotional reality. National policy decisions regarding father involvement have to be made carefully and with sensitivity to the enormous cultural and ethnic diversity within the U.S. Although increased father involvement appears to be important in white middle-class families, in groups like the Aka, fathers can and do contribute to their children in several other ways that are poorly understood. That is, many cultures exist in which fathers provide very little or no direct care, but also where the children are mentally and physically healthy. Studies of African Americans by Furstenburg and his colleagues (this volume and Furstenburg & Harris, 1993) are instructive in this regard. They find important differences between male and female children, as well as between poor African American families and middle class white families when examining the relationship between paternal involvement and child well-being.

FACTORS ASSOCIATED
WITH INCREASED FATHER INVOLVEMENT

Since the focus of this collection of articles is to increase father involvement, I will briefly describe a few anthropological studies that have examined this topic. Anthropology is often characterized as being a holistic discipline, because researchers try to consider an array of factors that influence cultural beliefs and practices. My own study of Aka fathers (Hewlett, 1991) suggests the need to understand a complex web of factors in order to understand the extraordinarily high levels of paternal care (e.g., fathers are either holding or within an arm's distance of their infants for more than 50% of a 24-hour period). Factors which contribute to high father involvement include high fertility, no warfare, a non-violent ideology, flexible gender roles, male-female cooperative net hunting, and valuing both male and female children. Extensive husband-wife cooperation on net hunts and many other economic activities seem to be especially influential, but only within the context of these other features.

Although the Aka study refers to fatherhood in a society that is quite different from the United States, this research does have implications for our understanding of fatherhood roles in the contemporary U.S. society. For example, Aka children are very attached to their fathers, despite the fact that Aka fathers do not engage in vigorous rough and tumble play. This absence of behavior, in turn, contrasts with the U.S. context in which vigorous play has been identified as a key factor in understanding father-child attachment. Instead of rough and tumble play, however, it appears that Aka infants become attached to their fathers through regular communication and being held frequently. Consequently, data from the Aka study point to the importance of the amount of time spent with infants and contributes to the U.S. debate about the relative merits of quantity- versus quality-time devoted to the young. The primary reason that Aka fathers are not vigorous playmates is that they have spent considerable time with their infants, know them well, and know how to communicate with them in other ways.

The Aka data, as well as other cross-cultural studies, support the hypothesis of sociologist Nancy Chodorow (1974) that, when fathers are active in infant care, boys develop an intimate knowledge of masculinity, which makes them less likely to devalue those things identified as feminine. Consequently, greater gender egalitarianism and the status of women are fostered. In contrasting cultural circumstances, however, when fathers are not around very much, young men usually have not been exposed to a clear sense of masculinity. Consequently, their identities develop in opposition to those things that are feminine, which they, in turn, tend to devalue and criticize. Table 1 illustrates some of the cross-cultural support for Chodorow's hypothesis: as father involvement increases, the participation of women in political decisions increases (i.e., one measure of the status of women).

The Aka data are also consistent with other cross-cultural studies indicating that close husband-wife relations and relatively equal contribution by each spouse are linked to greater father involvement (Katz and Konner, 1981). Table 2 documents the fact that men are not always the primary breadwinners; in half of the societies studied the breadwinner role was shared about equally by men and women. Table 3 shows that societies in which husbands and wives share more activities such as eating, leisure time, and shared rooming arrangements, have higher scores on an index of father involvement with children.

Super and Harkness (1992) also utilize a holistic approach in their comparison of African Kipsigis fathers and middle-class U.S. fathers in Boston. They examine the "development niche" (physical and social setting, cultural practices, and parental ideology) of these two groups and point out how

TABLE 1. Father-Child Relations and the Status of Women

Number of Societies with:	Distant Father-Child Relations	Close Father-Child Relations
High female participation in public decisions	9	22
Moderate female participation in public decisions	5	14
Females excluded from participation in public decisions	15	4

Chi-square = 14.7; p < .001 (After Coltrans, 1988)

TABLE 2. Contribution of Women to Overall Subsistence–The Myth of the Male Breadwinner

Female's percentage contribution to family diet	Number of societies	Percent
0-20	4	4.4
21-40	37	41.1
41-60	45	50.0
70+	4	4.4

Note: Developed from data reported in "Cross-cultural codes dealing with the relative status of women," by M. K. Whyte, 1980, in H. Barry & A. Schlegel (Eds.), *Cross-Cultural Samples and Codes.* Pittsburgh, PA: University of Pittsburgh Press.

TABLE 3. Relationship Between Husband-Wife Relationship and Father Involvement in 37 Societies

Number of Societies with:	Low Father Involvement[b]	High Father Involvement
Husband-wife proximity[a]		
High	4	10
Low	17	6

Note: chi-square = 7.33; $p < .01$.
[a]Husband-wife eating arrangements, husband-wife rooming arrangements, and husband-wife leisure time activities were scored by Broude (1983) from 1-3; a score of 1 means husband and wife eat, sleep, or have activities together, while a 3 means they are not together for these activities. A "high" proximity means the culture had an average score of 1.0-1.5, while "low" proximity means the culture had an average score of 1.6-3.0.
[b]Fathers in each culture were scored by Barry and Paxson (1971) from 1-5 in terms of physical and emotional proximity. Low father involvement fathers received a score of 1-3, while fathers with high involvement received a score of 4 or 5.

parental ideology is central to understanding father's involvement in the two cultures. Although mothers provide more than half of the family subsistence, Kipsigis fathers emphasize their economic role (e.g., providing food and clothing, paying school fees, and medical bills) and their role as moral leader (e.g., teaching deference, respect, and obedience). Although they often are available to help out with children, Kipsigis fathers do not hold infants. These fathers were happy when their children were responsible and listened to elders. In contrast, Boston fathers emphasized the importance of establishing emotional relationships with their children, and of stimulating the cognitive and physical growth of the young. Kipsigis fathers, however, do not talk about establishing emotional relationships and Boston fathers do not talk about economic contributions. Such patterns of behavior indicate, in turn, that fathers talk about whatever worries them and fail to talk about things that are taken for granted.

This is consistent with Robert LeVine and associates' work (R. Levine, Dixon, S. Levine, Leiderman, Keefer & Brazelton, 1992), which suggests that parental goals for their children are linked to demographic and ecological factors. Kipsigis fathers are concerned with physical survival because infant mortality rates are between 10% and 20%. Infant mortality in Boston is less than 1%, so, in this case, fathers are less concerned about physical survival. Instead, fathers from Boston are more concerned that their children acquire the extensive knowledge and cognitive skills needed to survive in the U.S. labor market.

FATHER INVOLVEMENT IN HUMAN HISTORY

Anthropology is different from other social sciences in that the time periods investigated are often much broader. A sociological or psychological analysis of father involvement in history generally implies going back to the Victorian era or possibly the Middle Ages. By contrast, anthropologists are just as likely to be interested in patterns of father involvement that occurred thousands or millions of years ago. This is not surprising because archaeology and physical anthropology are subdisciplines of anthropology. Table 4 summarizes the relative importance of a variety of types of father involvement during the past 120,000 years of human history.

I am not going to describe the ways of life in each time period (see Hewlett, 1991, for more detail), but rather use the table as a means of demonstrating the following: (1) fathers contribute to their children in several ways, with the relative importance of different contributions varying dramatically in human history; (2) different ecologies and modes of production have a substantial impact on the contributions of fathers to their children; and (3) the father's role today is relatively unique in human history.

Fathers' roles as defenders and educators have declined, because the state has taken on a large proportion of these responsibilities. Furthermore, although the size of the typical father's family (i.e., kin resources) is no longer an important factor that influences the well-being of his children, his material wealth is central to their well-being. Direct caregiving seems to be especially important for current families as well as for such Holocene foragers as the Aka and !Kung. For these foraging cultures, men and women contribute

TABLE 4. Relative Importance of Different Dimensions of Father's Roles in Human History

Forms of father involvement	Late Pleistocene foragers (120,00-20,000 yrs. ago)	Holocene foragers (20,000 yrs. ago-present)	Simple farmers and collectors (10,000-present)	Intensive farmers and early industriali-zation on (5000 yrs ago-present)	Post-Modern (last 30 years in Anglo upper-middle class)
Provider of food and shelter	***	**	*	***	**
Caregiver of young children	*	**	*	NS	**
Transmit knowledge, primarily to sons	***	***	***	**	*
Defense of family	**	**	***	**	NS
Number of kin resources	***	***	***	**	NS
Inherited wealth and material resources	NS	NS	*	**	***

Note: Developed from *Intimate fathers*, by B.S. Hewlett, 1991, Ann Arbor, MI: University of Michigan Press.
NS = not important/significant. * = somewhat important. ** = important. *** = very important.

about equal amounts to the diet, whereas warfare and defense of resources is not important.

SEX, REPRODUCTION, AND FATHER INVOLVEMENT

Anthropologists are also somewhat different than other social scientists in that they are interested in how human nature, human biology, and the long evolutionary history of human populations influence culture and vice versa (e.g., Leakey's 1994 studies of human fossil evolution; Jane Goodall's 1991 studies of chimps). Consequently, anthropologists are active contributors to recent theoretical developments in evolutionary biology that are controversial.

There are two reasons I want to include a discussion of evolutionary approaches. First, father involvement is influenced by evolved propensities in both fathers and children, so it is essential to identify and understand these propensities if one is going to have a holistic understanding of involvement. Second, although biology is often viewed as a constraining factor, in actuality, biology is a generative or enabling factor in reference to father involvement. What actually seems to occur, in fact, is that biological propensities enable rather than constrain interactions by allowing fathers and children to engage in several important activities (e.g., father-child "bonding" and communication).

Because cultural perspectives commonly leave out biology and sex (i.e., an individual's reproductive interests), which include both mating and parenting, evolutionary theorists are generally critical of these approaches. From an evolutionary standpoint, men and women are expected to have different reproductive strategies, because men and women have different reproductive biologies. For example, the differences between men and women characterized in the book *Men Are from Mars, Women Are from Venus* (Gray, 1992) are not surprising to evolutionary biologists. Evolutionary researchers also expect men's relations with their children to be at least partially different from those of women because of different reproductive strategies. It is important to remember that reproductive strategies are complex and that their expression is dramatically shaped by demographic, ecological and cultural contexts. Evolutionary theorists tend to view individuals as active agents manipulating their ecological and cultural structures for their own benefit, whereas cultural models tend to view individuals as actors taking on roles from various cultural structures for the benefit of the group. The economic perspective described by Willis (1996) is consistent with an evolutionary perspective in the sense that economic interests and the strategies of husbands and wives should be examined separately.

Evolutionary biologists make an important conceptual contribution when they use the term male "investment" rather than "involvement," because they are interested in all of the ways in which fathers contribute to their children. Investment refers to anything a father does with a child that limits his ability to have another child. This includes both direct forms of investment (e.g., caregiving, proximity, protection, knowledge transmission, as well as providing food, shelter, and other resources) and indirect forms of investment that are not directly targeted for children, but from which the young benefit (e.g., social-emotional support of his wife, maintenance of the home or kin resources).

Social scientists have used the term "involvement" because their research focuses on how father-child interactions (or lack thereof) influence a child's development. Evolutionary ecologists tend to focus on child survival and fitness, but it is clear that the types of investment listed above dramatically influence the child's social, emotional, cognitive, and motor development. The concept "investment," however, is broad and does not have the morally or politically correct overtones of involvement. Although many fathers in the developing world from agricultural cultures are not very "involved" with their children, this does not mean, however, that they are "bad" fathers. Instead, they are investing in several other significant ways (e.g., the provision of food) that ensure the survival and social-emotional well-being of their children. Since developing areas of the world often have minimal state-level institutions for security and adjudication, fathers help provide family security/defense as well as contribute to community-based political decisions.

Moreover, the importance of a kin network is often overlooked in the West, but in some parts of the world kinship resources are viewed as *the* most important part of a father's investment in his children. Among some Australian Aborigines, for example, the most important wealth a man passes on to his children is the "wealth" that comes from the security of sufficient numbers of siblings (or half-siblings). Among the Aka the number of brothers a man has affects, in part, the amount of direct care he provides his infant. As a result, fathers with greater kinship resources provide less direct care.

Unfortunately, space does not allow an adequate review of all the studies of fathers with roots in evolutionary anthropology, but I would like to briefly describe some prominent contributions. Primate studies suggest that male care is often mating effort rather than parenting effort (Van Schaik & Paul, 1996), which means that male care is more a means of attracting females rather than investing in one's offspring. Male care in non-human primates is infrequent, but where it does occur the species have the most promiscuous mating systems. Consequently, males are likely to care for infants that are not genetically related (Smuts & Gubernick, 1992). Among humans, where hunting provides a substantial proportion of the diet, the meat that men have captured not only is consumed by the hunter's family, but also is distributed to many others for their survival and growth. That is, families with good hunters may not get any more meat than families with poor hunters.

Some suggest that this strategy is a means by which men try to increase mating opportunities with other women (Hawkes, 1990). Despite this distribution strategy, however, small-scale studies, e.g., Marlow's (in press) study of Hadza fathers, and studies of urban industrial societies, e.g., the Albuquerque Men's Study (Anderson, Kaplan, & Lancaster, 1996) demonstrate that men are more likely to spend time with and provide resources to biological rather than to step-children. Marlow also demonstrates that Hadza fathers provide less care to their biological children as their mating opportunities increase (i.e., the number of reproductive women around increases). These observations are consistent with Euro-American psychological and sociological literature which indicates that fathers are more likely to provide care to infants or children in public rather than private settings, for example in playgrounds and grocery stores (Mackey & Day, 1979). Men may be more likely to care for children in public settings because it provides a means of attracting another mate (for marriage or extra-marital relationship). Men display infant care in public because some females may view caregiving as an attractive and desirable feature in a mate.

This leads to another dimension of evolutionary theory–female choice. Men are predicted to compete with each other for resources that are important for survival (women also compete, but to a lesser degree; Hrdy, 1992). Women are predicted, in turn, to select the winners–males who control or can provide resources, including willingness to care, to the women and their offspring. The implication of female choice means that, if father involvement is important, women need to select men with these qualities along with their tendency to select men with material resources.

Kaplan and associates (Kaplan, Lancaster, Bock, & Johnson, 1995) have also taken an evolutionary approach in their study of over 7000 Anglo and Hispanic men in Albuquerque, New Mexico. They found that, while paternity certainly was important, about 25% of Anglo and Hispanic men said they were fathers of children whom they knew were not their biological children. They also found that father "loss" at any time before age 16 reduced child quality, a variable measured by adult income and education of the child. Results indicated, in turn, that the negative impact of father loss was stronger for education than for adult income. This observation led them to develop the "competitive labor market theory." Specifically, this perspective predicts that when paternal care increases a child's acquisition of "embodied capital" (i.e., knowledge and skills that allow an individual to procure resources and earn a living), parents with higher levels of embodied capital will invest more in their offspring than parents with less embodied capital. Their evidence providing support for this hypothesis is that, controlling for income, more highly educated men spent more time with their children than men who were less educated.

Another preliminary finding in the Albuquerque Men's Study is that men who identified themselves as homosexual or bisexual had about as many children as those who identified themselves as heterosexual (Bock, 1994). Bock suggests that homosexuality or bisexuality may be temporary life course adaptations to particular environmental contexts. Many gay men, therefore, may have already become parents earlier in the life course.

Finally, Hagen (1999) provides cross-cultural evidence to suggest that postpartum depression may be an evolved mechanism through which mothers withdraw investment and interest in a newborn, especially when the father or his family are not investing sufficiently in her and the infant. Evidence indicates that a young mother who lacks much paternal support is more likely to experience serious postpartum depression. Hagen suggests that this is an evolved mechanism through which mothers attempt to gain greater paternal investment.

IMPLICATIONS

This paper provides a general overview of anthropological contributions to conceptualizing father involvement. The culture and history sections indicate that caution is needed in developing national messages and images of fathers. President Clinton has pointed out that we are a nation of great diversity and that we should build upon this diversity. This observation also applies to the diverse ways in which fathers contribute to their children. We know relatively little about the complex nature of father's roles, and any national policy for fathers must respect the enormous socio-economic, cultural, and demographic diversity in the U.S.

U.S. conceptions of father involvement also limit and structure current research. Because "people-making" is a predominant schema in the U.S., research has focused on fathers' relations with young children. We know very little about the impact of fathers throughout the life course, especially in adulthood. As Townsend (1996) points out, our attempts to change policy toward increasing the involvement of fathers with children may have unintended repercussions for father-child relations later in life. That is, policies requiring greater father involvement in childhood may impact a man's role as stepfather or the father's ability to emotionally or economically assist and support children later in life.

Anthropologists have identified intracultural and intercultural factors that are linked to higher levels of father involvement: close husband-wife relations, equal male and female contribution to the diet, lack of regular warfare, lack of material wealth (i.e., father involvement is higher in cultures that do not accumulate wealth, such as hunting-gathering societies like the Aka). Increased father involvement in infancy also tends to increase gender equality cross-culturally.

The evolutionary approach also has policy implications. The embodied capital hypothesis implies that father involvement will increase if fathers are encouraged to obtain more education. The importance of female choice in shaping male behavior suggests women have a significant role to play in increasing father involvement. One reason why material wealth and consumerism are so important around the world (all cultures are moving towards increasing consumerism, none are moving in the opposite direction) is that men see wealth as important to attract a spouse, because women tend to select men with greater wealth.

Anthropologists who work in international development indicate that cultural change is most likely to occur if you build upon the beliefs and practices that already exist. If we want to encourage "involvement," then it is necessary to build upon what is there rather than creating negative images such as "deadbeat dads." Super and Harkness (1992) point out that Boston fathers have children for their own emotional enjoyment–children are fun. When divorce occurs, these views could be built upon to help encourage contact with their children. Many studies in this collection demonstrate the commitment by fathers after divorce to maintain contact with their children. New policies could be focused on efforts to make it financially, legally, and logistically easier for fathers to see their children.

REFERENCES

Anderson, K.G., Kaplan, H.S., & Lancaster, J.B. (1996 August). Determinants of paternal expenditures among Albuquerque men. Paper delivered at annual meetings of Human Behavior and Evolution Society Meetings, Evanston, IL.

Barry, H., & Paxson, L.M. (1971). Infancy and early childhood: Cross-cultural codes 2. *Ethnology, 10*, 466-508.

Bock, J. (1994 February). The frequency of homosexuality among new Mexican men. Paper presented at the annual meetings of the Society for Cross-Cultural Research, Santa Fe, NM.

Bowlby, J. (1969). *Attachment*. New York: Basic Books.

Broude, G.J. (1983). Male-female relationships in cross-cultural perspective: A study of sex and intimacy. *Behavior Science Research, 18*, 154-181.

Chodorow, N. (1974). Family structure and feminine personality. In M.Z. Rosaldo & L. Lamphere (Eds.), *Woman, culture and society* (pp. 43-66). Stanford, CA: Stanford University Press.

Coltrans, S. (1988). Father-child relationships and the status of women: A cross-cultural study. *American Journal of Sociology, 92*,160-1095.

Furstenberg, F. F., & Harris, K. M. (1993). When and why fathers matter: Impacts of father involvement on the children of adolescent mothers. In R. Lerman & T. Ooms (Eds.), *Young unwed fathers: Changing roles and emerging policies* (pp. 117-138). Philadelphia: Temple University Press.

Furstenberg, F.F. & Weiss, C.C. (2000). Intergenerational transmission of fathering roles in at risk families. *Marriage & Family Review, 29*, 2-3, 181-201.

Goodall, J. (1991). *Through a window: My thirty years with the chimpanzees of Gombe*. NY: Houghton Mifflin.

Gray, J. (1992). *Men are from Mars, women are from Venus: A practical guide for improving communication and getting what you want from your relationships*. NY: Harper Collins.

Hagen, E. (1999). The functions of postpartum depression. *Evolution and Human Behavior*. 20, 5, 325-359.

Hawkes, K. (1990). Why do men hunt? Benefits for risky choices. In E. Cashdan

(Ed.) *Risk and uncertainty in tribal and peasant economies* (pp. 145-166). Bolder, CO: Westview Press.

Hewlett, B.S. (1991). *Intimate fathers*. Ann Arbor, MI: University of Michigan Press.

Hewlett, B.S., & Hannon, N. (1989). *Myths about "natural" childbirth*. Paper delivered at annual meeting of the Society for Cross-Cultural Research, New Haven, CT.

Hrdy, S.B. (1992). Fitness tradeoff in the history and evolution of delegated mothering with special reference to wet-nursing, abandonment, and infanticide. *Ethology and Sociobiology, 13*, 409-442.

Katz, M.M., & Konner, M.L. (1981). The role of father: An anthropological perspective. In M.E. Lamb (Ed.), *The role of the father in child development* (2nd ed., pp. 155-181). NY: John Wiley & Sons.

Kaplan, H.S., Lancaster, J.B., Bock, J.A., & Johnson, S.E. (1995). Does observed fertility maximize fitness among New Mexican men? A test of an optimality model and a new theory of parental investment in the embodied capital of offspring. *Human Nature, 6*, 325-360.

Leakey, R. (1994). *The origins of humankind*. NY: Basic Books.

LeVine, R.A., Dixon, S., LeVine, S., Richman, A., Leiderman, P.H., Keefer, H., & Brazelton, T.B. (1992). *Child care and culture: Lessons from Africa*. Cambridge, UK: Cambridge University Press.

Mackey, W.C., & Day, R. (1979). Some indicators of fathering behaviors in the United States: A cross-cultural examination of adult male-child interaction. *Journal of Marriage and the Family, 41*, 287-299.

Marlow, F. (in press). Male care and mating effort among Hadza foragers. *Behavioral ecology*.

Mead, M. (1964). *Continuities in cultural evolution*. New Haven, CT: Yale University Press.

Riesman, P. (1992). *First find your child a good mother: The construction of self in two African communities*. New Brunswick, NJ: Rutgers University Press.

Satir, V. (1972). *Peoplemaking*. Palo Alto, CA: Science and Behavior Books.

Smuts, B. & Gubernick, D.(1992). Male-infant relationships in nonhuman primates: Paternal investment or mating effort? In B. Hewlett (Ed.), *Father-child relations: Cultural and biosocial contexts* (pp. 1-30). NY: Aldine de Gruyter.

Super, C.M., & S. Harkness (1992). The cultural foundations of father's roles: Evidence from Kenya and the United States. In B.S. Hewlett (Ed.), *Father-child relations: Cultural and biosocial contexts.* (pp. 191-212). NY: Aldine de Gruyter.

Townsend, N. (1996). Male fertility as a life time of relationships: Contextualizing men's biological reproduction in Botswana. In C. Bledsoe, J. Guyer, & S. Lerner (Eds.), *Fertility and the male life cycle in the era of fertility decline* (125-142). NY: Oxford University Press.

Van Schaik, C.P., & Paul, A. (1996). Male care in primates: Does it ever reflect paternity? *Evolutionary Anthropology, 5*, 152-156.

Willis, R.J. (1996). Economic Approaches to Understanding Nonmarital Fertility, *Population Development and Review Supplement, 22*, 67-86.

Contextualizing Father Involvement and Paternal Influence: Sociological and Qualitative Themes

William Marsiglio
Mark Cohan

SUMMARY. We clarify the basic features of a sociological perspective as it relates to the study of fathers' involvement with, and influence on, their children. Our analysis emphasizes the dynamic interplay between social structures and processes at the macro, meso, and micro levels while focusing on social psychological issues. We examine (a) the social, organizational, and cultural contexts for fathering, (b) fathers' social capital contributions, (c) the construction and maintenance of father identities, and (d) fathering as a co-constructed accomplishment. These foci draw attention to how father involvement is affected by race, gender, economic considerations and a father's relationships with his child's mother and others in the community. We also examine how reflected appraisals of others may affect how a man perceives himself as a father. Relying heavily on qualitative approaches such as in-depth interviews, discourse analysis, interpretive practice, narrative practice, and dramaturgy, we suggest a number of ways a sociological lens can inform our understanding of father involvement. *[Article copies available for a fee from The Haworth Document Delivery Service: 1-800-342-9678. E-mail address: getinfo@haworthpressinc.com <Website: http://www.haworthpressinc.com>]*

KEYWORDS. Father involvement, paternal influence, father identity

William Marsiglio (e-mail: marsig@soc.ufl.edu) and Mark Cohan (e-mail: mcohan@nersp.nerdc.ufl.edu) are affiliated with Sociology Department, University of Florida, PO Box 117330, Gainesville, FL 32611-7330.

[Haworth co-indexing entry note]: "Contextualizing Father Involvement and Paternal Influence: Sociological and Qualitative Themes." Marsiglio, William, and Mark Cohan. Co-published simultaneously in *Marriage & Family Review* (The Haworth Press, Inc.) Vol. 29, No. 2/3, 2000, pp. 75-95; and: *FATHERHOOD: Research, Interventions and Policies* (ed: H. Elizabeth Peters et al.) The Haworth Press, Inc., 2000, pp. 75-95. Single or multiple copies of this article are available for a fee from The Haworth Document Delivery Service [1-800-342-9678, 9:00 a.m. - 5:00 p.m. (EST). E-mail address: getinfo@haworthpressinc. com].

Sociologists have become increasingly active in the study of fatherhood in recent years. As we prepare to highlight sociological contributions to the study of father involvement in particular, we are mindful of the broad areas of overlap that sociology shares with other disciplines, including anthropology, child and family studies, economics, and psychology. Clearly, a sociological understanding of the topic of paternal involvement is only part of the larger picture–one that can be presented fully only by taking a multidisciplinary approach. Because disciplinary boundaries drawn too sharply are counterproductive, we avoid reifying those borders here. Rather our commentary accentuates some of the perspectives and methodologies that sociologists use, or could use, to investigate fathers' involvement with their minor children and the resources fathers contribute to them. In the process, we suggest that the analytic power of a sociological perspective is ultimately realized when it is integrated with other disciplinary perspectives.

For our purposes, we define father involvement broadly so as to include behavioral and affective dimensions as well as cognitive elements. This approach is consistent with recent efforts to expand conceptualizations of paternal involvement (Hawkins & Palkovitz, 1999; Marsiglio, Day, & Lamb, this issue; Palkovitz, 1997). By considering both direct and indirect paternal influences, our approach is also in line with recent calls to focus on the varied contributions that fathers can make to their children's well-being (Amato, 1998). Although we focus primarily on fathers' involvement with children eighteen years of age and younger, some of our observations can easily be applied to young adult children too.

Our project, then, is to show how particular sociological themes can be used to contextualize and examine various issues related to fathers' involvement with and influence on their children. We organize our discussion around sociologists' traditional concerns about social structure, social process, and the reciprocal relationship between them. Because our exploration is methodological as well as theoretical, we assess how survey and qualitative methodologies can uniquely advance a broad understanding of father involvement issues, many of which are related to scholars' concerns about "responsible" fathering (Doherty, Kouneski, & Erikson, 1998). We focus primarily on qualitative strategies because extensive reviews of issues associated with survey methodologies and research on father involvement can be found elsewhere (Federal Interagency Forum on Child and Family Statistics, 1998; Marsiglio, Amato, Day, & Lamb, 2000).

A major tenet of sociological thinking is that individuals' experiences are constrained and facilitated by various social patterns, structures, and group activities. Distinctive and interrelated features of the social landscape, existing on several analytical levels, influence fathers' opportunities and desires to be involved in their children's lives in particular ways. On the macro level, some of the structures of most interest to sociologists include the economy, the gender-segregated labor market, and public policies targeting families. Each of these is shaped by race and ethnic considerations. Organizational and cultural units, such as Fathers' Rights groups, the Promise Keepers, "corporate culture," and local support groups are key at the meso level; at the micro-level much attention centers on co-parental household arrangements. These structures and cultural milieus, coupled with demographic shifts in fathers' life course and residency patterns, provide the context within which multilevel social processes affect children's and fathers' development and well-being. These social processes can also be said to include identity-work individuals do "in their own heads," so to speak, because this intrapsychic activity incorporates individuals' awareness and interpretation of others (Mead, 1934).

Our commentary focuses on three interrelated domains: the social and cultural contexts for fathering, fathers' social capital contributions, and the social psychology of fathering with emphasis on identity issues and fathering as a co-constructed accomplishment. In each of these areas, we show how questions relevant to fathers' involvement with their children and influence in their lives are informed by a sociological emphasis on the connections between social structures and processes. Given our own theoretical and substantive interests, we devote considerable attention to the social psychology of father involvement. Our approach, consistent as it is with social ecological models that emphasize the multi-layered and interrelated systems affecting fathers' involvement with their children (Doherty et al., 1998), also underscores some of the organizational features of the social landscape that indirectly mold the context for father involvement.

Finally, we make no claim that our approach is either comprehensive or that it represents "the" sociological statement on father involvement and paternal influence. Other scholars could choose quite different yet equally legitimate organizing principles and research questions to map this terrain (for an extensive review of fatherhood research see Marsiglio et al., 2000). We do, however, expect that our particular means of delineating some of the key issues will help to identify common ground between sociologists and other scholars studying father involvement issues.

SOCIAL CULTURAL CONTEXT OF FATHERING

Demographic Features

For many sociologists, efforts to understand fathering are closely tied to the study of how the changing circumstances of fathers' life course and residency patterns are affecting the context within which fathers are involved with and can influence their children (Marsiglio et al., this volume; Marsiglio et al., 2000). Demographic and cultural changes related to the increase in nonresident, single resident, step, and gay fathers have implications for the cultural representations and normative understandings associated with fathering as well as the organized social responses to individuals' concerns about fatherhood. This fragmentation of fatherhood (Griswold, 1993) offers sociologically inclined researchers a rich setting to apply their trade as they explore the increasingly nebulous institutional and normative features of fatherhood.

While fatherhood has always been a social construction (Mead, 1969), in recent decades it has become an even more complicated and intriguing accomplishment that is intimately connected to demographic transitions and the micropolitics of family life. As the norms associated with different types of fatherhood have grown more diffuse, individuals have experienced greater leeway in constructing their own normative realities without relying on pre-existing templates.

Sociologists are keenly aware of how contemporary fathers' diverse and dynamic experiences provide intriguing opportunities to study the intersection between structural features of fatherhood and social processes directly and indirectly related to father involvement. Those committed to understanding the social psychology of fatherhood are particularly well equipped to examine how diverse structural circumstances affect the processes by which men and others negotiate paternal rights, obligations, and privileges in these changing times (Marsiglio, Day & Lamb, this collection). Issues such as these invite an interdisciplinary approach that is informed by sociologists' interest in the formal and informal group contexts within which people collaboratively invest situations with meaning and then act upon them–an issue we address in a subsequent section.

Key Sorting Variables

One distinct advantage of a sociological perspective is that it illuminates how social forces associated with economics, gender, and race contribute to sorting men and fathers into different sets of circumstances that in turn affect the way they think, feel, and act as fathers. Economics is clearly one of the most prominent of these structural sorting mechanisms. Given that the provider role remains a critical–if not the primary–hallmark of responsible fatherhood (Lamb, this collection; Wilkie, 1993), men's ability to provide materially for their children is related in complex ways to fathers' level and type of involvement with their children as well as their influence on them. Compared to men with greater resources, opportunities for positive involvement with offspring may in some instances be hindered for men who are un- or underemployed, have limited work skills and job prospects, or have a limited formal education. A child's mother or her parents may intentionally block the father's access to the child, having determined that they can provide better for the child than he can. Conversely, the man himself may believe that he cannot be an effective father with his limited resources, and he may cut ties with the child and her mother in order to avoid what he perceives as imminent failure at being a provider. If a father with limited work skills and a meager income does remain involved with his child, the provider role may swallow most opportunities the father has to fulfill other roles for his child. Hampered by obstacles like long working shifts (perhaps at more than one low-paying job), inflexible scheduling, and work at odd hours, a low-income father may see fathering reduced largely to "providing" simply as a matter of necessity. Meanwhile, fathers who earn better pay or have greater occupational prospects may have more freedom in balancing providing with other aspects of fathering, such as care and nurturing, play activities, and moral guidance. The sociological lesson here is that it is critical to consider how structural conditions influence specific forms of father involvement. Relatedly, this perspective leads us to ask questions about how structural conditions set the stage for the ways men judge themselves or find themselves judged by others. In turn, do these perceptions about men's fitness as fathers affect their commitment to and involvement with their children?

Macro-level economic factors, conditioned by race-based patterns, are clearly consequential in the micropolitics of family/union formation and household labor. Virtually all fathers are affected by the way gender structures the workforce. Among whites, the persistence of gender segregation in many occupations and industries results in gender inequities in wages and job prestige. This often has the effect of making the woman's job "expendable," or weakening her bargaining position when fathers and mothers negotiate how to divide workforce and household/child care responsibilities (Coltrane, 1996). The result is that women assume a "second shift" of unpaid household labor in conjunction with their work in the paid labor force (Hochschild, 1989), while men see opportunities to be involved fathers endangered by occupational demands. Even in those situations where economic disparities are not present among partners, fathers may still not be involved in domestic labor in an equal fashion (Brines, 1994).

When considering the experience of African Americans, the story is more confusing because college-educated black women are actually better off financially than their black college-educated male counterparts, and the overall gender gap in wages is smaller among blacks than whites (Roberts, 1994). This finding buttresses some black women's maternal gate-keeping role and can complicate some black men's efforts to be involved with their children. Because African American males have high rates of under- or unemployment, they are often perceived as poor marriage risks by black females and their parents (Furstenberg, 1995; Tucker & Mitchell-Kernan, 1995). Consequently, many black males may be discouraged from establishing paternity formally or participating in a co-resident household with or without marrying their partner.

Fathers and mothers do not simply succumb to the paths of least resistance created by market forces, however. Just as economic realities may exert pressure on families in the aforementioned manner, couples may negotiate arrangements that resist these trends, even if the parties involved are unaware of the way broad structural factors are shaping their opportunities. Some men, influenced by popular images of the new, nurturant father, may choose to express their identities as fathers over their occupational identities, irrespective of the financial consequences (Gerson, 1993). Others may have grown up fantasizing about being nurturing fathers, but found when they actually became fathers that their household arrangements were more conducive to their taking a more traditional role that emphasized breadwinning.

Organizational Contexts for Father Involvement

With ambiguity about the normative features of the fatherhood terrain running high in recent decades, some groups and organizations have surfaced with the intent to foster positive father-child relations. These organized responses provide sociologists with practical opportunities to study the broader organizational context and processes potentially associated with fathers' involvement with their children. Admittedly, many of the research questions in this area are a step removed from paternal involvement, and only a small (though growing) proportion of fathers are directly involved with the groups and organizations in question. Nevertheless, a broad sociological understanding of these collective efforts is consistent with our interest in understanding the social ecology of father-child relations.

A full accounting of this social ecology would also examine other groups that are not explicitly organized around fathering issues, but that raise them anyway (e.g., men's local support groups, court-mandated counseling sessions for wife batterers [Fox, Sayers, & Bruce, 1998]). One way to make sense of the varied and virtually endless research possibilities for sociological study in this area is to consider four broad domains of research: (a) groups as manifestations of collective behavior and, in rare cases, social movements; (b) group membership; (c) group ideology, rhetoric, and tactics; and (d) social impact.

Groups and organizations whose agendas may influence how fathers are involved with their children are quite heterogenous in terms of size, duration of existence, level of formal organization, degree of explicit attention to fatherhood issues, and identification or desire to be a recognizable collective. For example, the Million Man March was a one-day event that, nevertheless, delivered a coherent, direct message about fatherhood (in this case, African American fatherhood in a racialized society). In contrast, spokespersons for the Mythopoetic (Expressive) Men's Movement have never made such a deliberate, purposeful statement on fatherhood, even though their activities are often described as those of a social movement (Messner, 1997) and the movement identifies concerns about fathering as one of its unifying themes (Bly, 1990; Kimmel & Kaufman, 1994).

Community-based father responsibility programs have become increasingly popular in recent years (Levine & Pitt, 1995). While most emphasize fathers' active participation in their children's lives, these programs vary widely in their approaches, because they are developed within diverse local communities. Lastly, situations or organizations (e.g., boy scouts, school programs, sports) that bring fathers together in connection with their children's activities establish a context where men's awareness of themselves as fathers is heightened.

Sociological study of the collective tendencies and actions of these groups must be sensitive to this diversity. In fact, one way that sociologists can aid our understanding of these groups as social movements or collective actions is by studying the differences between single-event actions and collectives formed to act repeatedly over time. It may prove useful, for example, to study the symbolic, organizational, and practical trade-offs that accompany different forms of political actions in the name of involved fatherhood. Studies of these types would need to employ the widest range of research methods, from content and narrative analyses of the symbolic features of a group's public presentation, to interviews and surveys targeting the group's local or national influence on the type and level of father involvement.

Another important sociological question is whether or not any or all of these collectives can be said to be promoting a form of identity politics (Larana, Johnston, & Gusfield, 1994). For example, to the extent that organizations such as fathers' rights groups articulate their concerns not just for fathers but *as fathers*, they assume a likeness to other groups, such as NOW (women), NAACP (African-Americans), and ACT-UP (gays and lesbians), that have assembled to assert the rights of a particular class of people. Among other male groups (e.g., National Institute of Responsible Fatherhood and Family Revitalization in Cleveland, and Promise Keepers), a loose form of identity politics may develop around fathering "obligations" that are associated with concerns about jobs, schools, community crime, religious faith, and children's well-being. Given the debates about diversity that have arisen in some of the widely known identity-based movements (hooks, 1984; Collins, 1990), a group promoting the "rights" (or "obligations") of fathers provides a unique opportunity to investigate how different perspectives on masculinity may affect the stability of the alliances of men as fathers as well as the direction of the group's agenda.

Within particular groups, it can be useful to identify the relationships and commitments between participants that give a group its unique strengths, weaknesses, and character. This goal can best be achieved through analyses of the formal and informal social networks out of which the group is spun. For example, scholars should be attentive to how the Promise Keepers (PK) movement has been fostered by an infrastructure rooted in Christian-based ideology and social networks. This infrastructure has enabled PK fathers to solidify as a group and promote specific imperatives for Christian fathering. Learning about these networks can sensitize researchers to how larger structural entities are linked to the group's formation, growth, and messages about fathering.

Methodologically, studies designed to analyze these movements, groups, and events from a collective behavior perspective can take many forms. In the case of established, longstanding groups with broad-based membership, various survey techniques, such as mail-in questionnaires, telephone interviews, and even e-mail surveys can provide an effective means of collecting useful descriptive data. Meanwhile, some qualitative strategies may offer a more incisive look at the social psychological dynamics of collective behavior. Through ethnographic study, researchers can detail the day-to-day development, maintenance, and promotion of the group. Such participant observation can shed light on the ways in which group members construct a group identity through their interaction and how they influence each others' paternal involvement. Whether the research method is quantitative or qualitative, longitudinal and comparative projects can be especially effective because they avoid presenting the groups as static or isolated.

One element of understanding the emergence, appeal, and impact of a group is to identify its members. Collecting basic demographic data about the groups we study is virtually second nature to sociologists, but the disparate or regional nature of many of the groups that focus on fatherhood makes it a challenge to obtain data that are representative and reliable. For instance, estimates of the social composition of one-day events, such as the Million Man March or Promise Keepers demonstrations, must rely heavily on the reports of sociological observers and media outlets (see Kimmel & Kaufman, 1994; Messner, 1997). Similarly, what we know of fathers' rights groups has been derived from in-depth interviews and observation (Bertoia & Drakich, 1995; Coltrane & Hickman, 1992). Thus, while information about group membership is an important part of understanding the organized responses promoting fatherhood, gathering that information often involves some form of observational research to supplement whatever membership lists might be available.

Because these groups, organizations, and events have played a part in bringing fatherhood to the fore as a social issue, social scientists need to investigate the messages they are promoting. What sort of "fatherhood" do they advocate, what is the ideology on which that conception of fatherhood is founded, and what rhetoric and tactics do they employ to advance their cause? Previous sociological research in this area clearly demonstrates that there is little consensus among these groups as to what it means to be a father and how fathers should be involved with their children. Some groups agree that father involvement with families is a critical issue, but disagree about what constitutes positive involvement. To the Promise Keepers, for instance, fathers need to be involved by being the moral and spiritual leader as well as the primary breadwinner (Armato & Marsiglio, 1998). However, the directors of The Fatherhood Project, a program sponsored by the nonprofit Families and Work Institute, give involvement a somewhat different slant. They define positive involvement in terms of a man "sharing with the child's mother in the continuing emotional and physical care of their child, from pregnancy onwards" (Levine & Pitt, 1995: 5). Similarly, there are those who agree that men (and fathers) suffer gender-related problems in contemporary society, but they hold different conceptions of the nature of those problems. Mythopoetic men feel handicapped by the alienating, competitive, bureaucratic nature of modern life which they feel is exacerbated by the "father wound," an empty feeling created in their lives by physically absent or emotionally distant fathers. Fathers' rights advocates, in contrast, believe that they are oppressed by the legal system, which they say favors women in custody cases.

The meso level groups and organizations that address father involvement thus promote multiple, often contradictory messages and use a wide variety of means for pursuing their ends. Fathers' rights supporters employ a rhetoric of co-parenting and call for legal reform, while Promise Keepers (and participants in the Million Man March) eschew talk of equality to call for a return to father as spiritual leader, breadwinner, and head-of-household. Meanwhile, much of the advocacy for nurturant involvement has come from centers like the Family and Work Institute and community initiatives that confront the social and economic barriers to positive father involvement through education and mentoring (Levine & Pitt, 1995; see also Levine, Murphy, & Wilson, 1993).

The challenge for sociologists is to continue to deconstruct the rhetoric and tactics used by these (and other) groups and analyze the ideologies that drive them. A variety of methodologies are suited to the task, but three of particular interest are in-depth interviews, content analysis, and discourse analysis. In-depth interviews allow individual respondents to describe their thoughts, feelings, and actions in their own words, but they also allow researchers to see patterns in the individual stories that belie the commitments of the group. For example, Arendell's (1995) in-depth interviews with 75 divorced fathers allowed her to describe the "masculinist discourse" through which some of these men viewed their relationships with their former spouses and their experiences with the courts.

Content and discourse analysis represent the quantitative and qualitative sides of the same coin (see Silverman, 1993). In each case, the target of analysis is text, a form of data that is particularly important, since groups promoting fathers' involvement with children are likely to depend heavily on pamphlets, press releases, newsletters, and mass media programs to develop their public presence. Content analyses are appropriate for large secondary data sets because the goal is simply to count how many occurrences within the data fit into the researcher's preestablished categories. These sorts of analyses can tell us how much consistency there is in the rhetoric offered by different regional groups aligned with the same concern or national organization. Or, they can be used to identify changes in the rhetoric of one group over time.

Discourse analysis, being a qualitative approach, is designed for smaller amounts of text. The approach here is to treat the language usage in the texts as a form of action that is central to the social construction of reality (Potter & Wetherell, 1987; Berger & Luckmann, 1966). Instead of approaching the text with pre-established categories, the researcher's aim is to investigate how the author of the text constructs and utilizes categorization, contrast, metaphor and other rhetorical devices to construct particular meanings. In the realm of groups promoting father involvement, discourse analysis could shed light on the strategies that Promise Keepers use to create consistency between their ideology of family life and leadership by women in the public or private realm; investigate the rhetorical use of women in the texts presented by fathers' rights groups; or determine what are the practical criteria of "nurturant fathering" employed by those involved in The Fatherhood Project.

While the types of analyses described above can produce valuable insights, the most compelling questions regarding developmental and well-being outcomes for fathers and children address whether these organized responses actually make a difference in fathers' and children's everyday lives. By assessing the connection between group initiatives, father involvement, and child outcomes, sociologists can explore linkages between group and individual level activity. This is a topic of considerable interest to sociologists (Huber, 1991), but one that is seldom explored systematically in fatherhood research. The types of resources and support fathers acquire from participating in these groups, and the circumstances under which these resources lead to changes in the way fathers are involved with their children, should be of particular interest to sociologists. Ultimately, understanding how social movement and community-based initiatives influence paternal involvement and child outcomes will require evaluation research and longitudinal designs.

Fathering and Social Capital

Sociologists, by highlighting the importance of social capital for children's welfare, have lent their voice to the call for broader interpretations of father involvement and paternal influence (Amato, 1998; Furstenberg, 1998; Furstenberg & Hughes, 1995; Seltzer, 1998; see also Coleman, 1988; 1990). Social capital is a multidimensional concept and, when related to fathers' involvement in children's lives, indexes paternal contributions to family-based and community-based relations that typically benefit children's cognitive and social development. One set of relations involves the extent to which fathers maintain relationships with their children and their children's mother that are predicated on trust, mutual expectations, and a sense of loyalty. To what extent do fathers base their parenting roles on parental support mixed with authoritative control? To what extent do they share similar parenting values and conflict resolution strategies with their co-parent? Are they supportive of their co-parent in familial and nonfamilial areas? The other set of relations includes fathers' (and mothers') connections with individuals and organizations in their larger community, particularly the school and neighborhood. In this regard, fathers may maintain contacts with adults in the community who either interact with their children (e.g., teachers, coaches, employers, ministers, neighbors) or could provide them with resources and opportunities if called upon. Some of these contacts may include other men who are involved in male-oriented groups and organizations. Fathers can also develop social capital by establishing positive relationships with their children's friends and by incorporating their children into their own work or social networks.

Each of these approaches for developing different types of social capital are avenues for fostering positive father involvement (Furstenberg & Hughes, 1995). For instance, fathers can expose their children to healthy dyadic interaction processes, bring about closure in their children's social networks, and act as a liaison to valuable community resources for their children. Social capital can be viewed broadly, then, as a product of families, communities, and the connections between the two. When the social capital concept is conceptualized in this fashion, it is consistent with the basic sociological principle that recognizes that access to a wide variety of intangible social resources can enhance individuals' well-being. Consequently, analyses of social capital complement more traditional sociological and economic analyses that examine fathers' human and financial capital contributions to their children.

While social capital is measured at times at the individual level, it ultimately requires that families, inclusive of fathers' relations with their children, be studied as social systems that are embedded within a larger community system (Doherty et al., 1998; Furstenberg, 1998). If a family is conceived as a social and cultural entity, scholars can actually focus on parental figures' similarities or shared experiences in what they do and say as co-parents. This type of sociological approach to social capital is strikingly similar to how family systems theorists and growing numbers of developmental psychologists think about the social ecology of father-child relations and human development.

Sociologists are capable of enlisting survey and qualitative strategies as they face the challenge of studying social capital and fathers' unique contributions to it (Furstenberg, 1998; Seltzer, 1998). To date, survey approaches have taken stabs at collecting basic information that enables researchers to assess variables such as family cohesion and relationship quality, degree of similarity in parental values, and comparability in parental practices. Attempts have also been made to measure the degree and way in which parents are embedded in community institutions and social networks that involve their children. While survey or qualitative data can be used to assess fathers' contribution to the shared parental culture and their individual level of embeddedness in the community, qualitative strategies can best provide researchers with rich insights about the processes that either foster or constrain social capital development in specific contexts. These contexts may differ due to cultural values, demographic and legal arrangements, class-based resources, religious beliefs, or other contextual factors.

Sociological insights are of particular value when considering social capital issues in relation to key family transitions, such as relationship uncoupling and the formation of stepfamily households (Marsiglio, 1995a, 1995b; Seltzer, 1991; 1998). Concerns about shifting family structures, fathers' involvement, and paternal influence can prompt researchers to ask specific questions about the maintenance, modification, and dissolution of social capital. Longitudinal designs that explore the changes in men's connectedness to their biological or stepchildren as well as their community embeddedness are critical to understanding how children's quality of life and development may be influenced by how men and others adjust to family-based transitions. Qualitative approaches that explore how these contributions are negotiated with other relevant parties are critical to understanding social capital as both product and process. These considerations remind us that fathering is typically not done in isolation and it is more uniquely affected by contextual factors than mothering (Doherty et al., 1998).

FATHER IDENTITY AND CO-CONSTRUCTING FATHERING

Turning our attention now to issues of fathers' identity, and fathering as a co-constructed process, we focus on the micro-level of individual cognition, self-perception, and small group interaction. Rather than privileging the ways in which sociological forces seemingly act upon men by enabling and constraining their choices regarding father involvement, some sociologists reverse the looking glass by studying how men actively work to develop, manage, and sustain a sense of themselves as fathers. In taking up this perspective, however, we must not ignore that men's identities as fathers and their involvement as fathers are often intimately tied to the way fathers' current and previous romantic partners, most notably the mothers of their children, respond to them–and, indirectly, to their children. This perspective acknowledges fathering as a co-constructed process and, in turn, incorporates insights about how maternal perceptions and gatekeeping can help to shape father involvement patterns (Dienhart, 1998; Allen & Hawkins, 1999).

There are multiple ways of approaching "father" as an identity–approaches which each have unique consequences for how father involvement is studied. From the perspective of structural symbolic interactionists, who sometimes refer to their approach as identity theory, "father" represents one of multiple role identities that may be a part of a man's sense of self. All of the role identities that comprise a man's self are presumed to be arranged hierarchically in the man's psyche according to their salience and psychological centrality (Marsiglio, 1995c; Futris & Pasley, 1997; Ihinger-Tallman, Pasley, & Buehler, 1995; Stryker, 1980; Stryker & Serpe, 1994). The role identities may themselves have associated roles or sub-identities (e.g., breadwinner, caretaker, moral teacher), which are organized into similar hierarchies. These theorists are interested in the social factors that affect the positioning of the "father" role identity and its associated sub-identities in the man's overall sense of himself. For instance, it is well-established that a man's residency status vis-à-vis his children and the quality of his relationship with the children's mother is likely to influence the salience that being a father has for him (Furstenberg & Cherlin, 1991; Marsiglio, 1995b; 1995c). Researchers working within this theoretical tradition have recently studied identity structures among Promise Keepers (Armato & Marsiglio, 1998), role construction and adjustment among stepfathers (Fine, Ganong, & Coleman, 1997), and father-related sub-identity hierarchies of divorced and non-divorced nonresident fathers (Futris & Pasley, 1997).

Since identities are unavoidably social in nature, the influence that significant others (Berger & Luckmann, 1966), might have on a man's sense of himself as a father or on the importance that identity has for him are important questions. Fathers come to see themselves, at least in part, based on how they believe others see them. These reflected appraisals are often drawn from existing social or cultural beliefs and expectations. So, for example, fathers who enthusiastically co-parent are often treated as heroic by friends, coworkers, and others outside the family (Dienhart, 1998; Daly & Dienhart, 1997;

Gerson, 1993), even though the same level of involvement from a mother is rarely considered noteworthy. This is because cultural expectations for "hands-on" involvement are lower for fathers than for mothers. Cultural expectations may also affect the ways in which men of different races and social classes are appraised. Partners (and social service providers) of inner city black fathers may be more likely to support a positive appraisal of the men as fathers, even if they do not provide financial support, provided that they are involved with their children in some way. In contrast, middle-class fathers who do not provide financially for their children are likely to be judged harshly, even if they are actively involved in parenting in other ways.

Thus, both the persons with whom a father is interacting (e.g., the mother, a child, a social service agent) and the scale or mode of evaluation they employ affect how a father is appraised. In turn, these appraisals are likely to affect how a man thinks and feels about himself as a father, particularly when he is emotionally attached to the others or is a subordinate in some sort of power relationship with them.

Because the dynamics and influence of reflected appraisals extend beyond familial relations, identities are sometimes constructed and managed in less private sites, such as the corporate environment, father-related interest groups, and in school and recreational contexts. Sometimes the appraisals reflected back to men in these settings are that a father identity should remain secondary to some other, privileged identity. For example, some fathers working in corporate culture may choose or feel pressured to downplay their caregiving activities, because their superiors convey the message, either explicitly or subtly, that men's most pressing commitments should be to the company. From a social psychological standpoint, men who take liberal advantage of family leave policies may face the male equivalent of the chilly climate that women have experienced in the corporate world. Fathers devoted to the moral labor of parenting are in essence viewed as traitors for betraying their commitment to their companies. Not surprisingly, then, researchers have demonstrated that a "gendered culture of work organizations," in which men are expected to devote themselves to work while woman assume responsibility for domestic affairs, tends to inhibit men's use of family leave benefits even in countries with progressive family policies such as Sweden (Haas & Hwang, 1995).

People in other public settings may also seek to influence men's identity perceptions and paternal behavior. On the one hand, some men who routinely play sports with male friends may feel inclined to minimize certain features of their paternal identity so as not to jeopardize their image as carefree, fun-loving athletes. On the other hand, if several of the other men are fathers and begin to include their children in the sport activity, the men may actually encourage each other to act as playmates–and possibly mentors and teachers–

to their children. Meanwhile, in the context of an interest group focusing on fatherhood issues, fathers may be encouraged to politicize elements of their identity. For instance, men in fathers' rights groups can generate solidarity amongst themselves by rejecting the paternal breadwinner ideology that is seemingly fundamental to the courts. In the process, they can provide each other with support, at least rhetorically, to emphasize more hands-on forms of fathering.

Sociologists presume, all things being equal, that reflected appraisals on men's sense of themselves as fathers contribute to behavioral outcomes. Unfortunately, little research has investigated the factors and processes that influence the extent to which fathers' identities and their actual behaviors correspond. Since this link is a central feature of some social psychological approaches to father involvement, it clearly deserves more systematic study.

Two other social psychological approaches–dramaturgical analysis and interpretive practice–instruct us to take a less structured, more situated and conditional view of the father identity. In their own ways, each of these perspectives asserts that being a father is not a static position or set of roles that one fills, but rather an ongoing interactional accomplishment. Men may claim or be the subject of claims that they are a father or that they are a certain kind of father, but in the give and take of everyday life these claims may be questioned, qualified, or rejected by others as frequently as they are accepted.

Goffman's (1959) dramaturgical approach directs our attention to the techniques of self-presentation (impression management) that men use when they want their claims to a father identity to be honored. Essentially, we are reminded that if a man wants others (for example, his partner, his children, the legal system) to recognize him as a father, he must act like one. The difficulty is that the qualities of a convincing performance of a father identity vary across social situations and, as revealed by a social structural perspective, men vary greatly in the dramaturgical resources (abilities and tools for creating impressions) they bring to their performances. Obviously, middle and upper-class men have greater financial resources for acting as a provider than do poorer men. Similarly, nonresident fathers may have a difficult time convincing themselves and their children that they are involved or nurturant fathers because they lack frequent and appropriate opportunities to enact relevant performances. Indeed, some nonresident fathers cease to make claims to these identities not by choice, but because custodial arrangements or gatekeeping by mothers prohibits them from performing fatherhood in these ways (Braver & O'Connell, 1998). Implicit in this notion of the father identity as a performance is the belief that fathers and those with whom they interact have a stock of knowledge that references appropriate father behavior in various contexts (Milkie, Simon, & Powell, 1997). This presumed moral or normative order represents the standard against which the performer (the father) and his audience judge his performances.

With regard to the disparities that exist in men's resources for performing father identities, dramaturgy presents practical concerns to researchers and policymakers: How can the normative or moral order be altered such that those who judge fathers' everyday performances will be more sensitive to the differential resources that men bring to their performances? In essence, how can we best expand people's understanding of the conditions of fathering, such that men are less likely to be judged simply as "good dads" or "bad dads" (Furstenberg, 1988)? Researchers could conduct interviews to learn about creative ways that biological fathers and their children have worked together to facilitate effective performances of fathering despite limited dramaturgical resources (e.g., economic hardship, nonresidence, the presence of a stepfather or other father-figure in the child's life, poor relations with the child's mother). Other research opportunities related to dramaturgy involve the different ways fathers make use of the same or similar dramaturgical resources, as conditioned by the audience at hand. Given Goffman's insistence that analysis be situated (see Gubrium & Holstein, 1997), researchers might proceed by observing men acting as fathers in public places such as schools, playgrounds, restaurants, and sports facilities. These observations might then be coordinated with focus groups and in-depth interviews in which fathers, children, and mothers discuss their impressions of the quality of the fathers' performance in these settings. A study of this sort could aid our understanding of father involvement in a number of ways. First, it would allow us to document the different means by which different groups of people, such as children and mothers, evaluate the actual behavior of fathers. Second, it would allow us to decipher the ways in which the same person's scale or mode of evaluating father behavior might be circumstantially dependent. Third, we would get a glimpse of the creative aspects of impression management among fathers and children (including face-saving gestures by children that aid fathers' performances). And, finally, such a study could reveal fault lines in performances that might signal the existence of structural conditions or interactional dynamics that endanger the success of fathers' identity claims.

Like the dramaturgical approach, interpretive practice (Gubrium & Holstein, 1994; 1997) treats the identity "father" as an ongoing interactional accomplishment rather than a pre-existing role pattern or psychological structure. However, instead of focusing on behavior and talk as a performance that can be judged in terms of success or failure, those who study interpretive practice focus on the resources and strategies people use to make, maintain, or dispute identity claims in an interaction. In some instances, researchers focus specifically on instances of talk in an effort to explicate how meanings (and, implicitly, identities) are constructed in the stories people tell. Interpretive practice in this case becomes the study of narrative practice (Gubrium & Holstein, 1998; Cohan, 1997).

Whether the subject of analysis is talk or interaction, from this perspective identities are the tenuous result of the paradoxical combination of contested claims and co-construction. For instance, a mother who asserts her husband's legal paternity of their children on a survey or administrative form, might nonetheless tell the surveyor that, for all intents and purposes, the children are fatherless because of her husband's dedication to his work. In action, with a mark on the survey, the mother grants her husband a father identity, but simultaneously in word she withdraws it. From the perspective of interpretive practice, *both* identity claims are equally accurate, but they draw from different interpretive resources and speak to different frames of accountability. On the survey or administrative form, the mother responds to the need of an interviewer or organization to know the facts. In her comments, she refers to a practical domestic reality where, in her view, being a father means something other than biological paternity.

Though interpretive practice has been used to study family as a social and analytical category (Gubrium & Holstein, 1990), the construction of father identities has not, to our knowledge, been studied from this perspective. What sociologists stand to learn from applying it to father involvement are some of the conditions in which father identities become contested and the resources that are brought to bear in these arguments. On what grounds and in what contexts do mothers typically act as gatekeepers to fathers' involvement with children? Are these sometimes based on a denial of the father's claim to a father identity? How do children or their stepfathers talk about the identities that they assume for themselves and offer for one another? Do they recognize a kind of identity career vis-à-vis one another? Do members of separated families experience changes in the resources and strategies through which they make sense of one another as a result of their interaction with the procedures and discourse of the court system? Each of these questions can be fruitfully addressed from the perspective of interpretive practice.

CONCLUSION

We have provided a sampling of the diverse perspectives, methods, and analytic tools sociologists can contribute to the multidisciplinary study of father involvement and paternal influence. By focusing on the complex and interrelated ways in which gender, race, and economic factors shape the context for the practice of fatherhood, fathers' social capital contributions, and the social psychology of fathering, we underscored the utility of sociologists' traditional concerns about the interplay between social structure and process. Furthermore, our emphasis on qualitative methods supplements existing assessments and research associated with survey methodologies. Armed with a sociological lens, scholars are positioned to see more clearly that the way men ultimately perform their fatherhood role is a complex result of macro, meso, and micro-level activity. Sociologically informed analyses are therefore invaluable because they treat father involvement as an ongoing, negotiated process shaped by a range of socially constructed circumstances, including organized groups that espouse varied messages about fathering.

REFERENCES

Allen, S. M., & Hawkins, A. J. (1999). Maternal gatekeeping: Mothers' beliefs and behavior that inhibit greater father involvement in family work. *Journal of Marriage and the Family, 61*, 9-212.

Amato, P. (1998). More than money?: Men's contributions to their children's lives. In A. Booth & N. Crouter, (Eds.), *Men in families: When do they get involved? What difference does it make?* (pp. 241-278). Mahwah, NJ: Lawrence Erlbaum Associates.

Arendell, T. (1995). *Fathers & divorce*. Thousand Oaks, CA: Sage.

Armato, M., & Marsiglio, W. (1998). *Self structure, identity, and commitment: Promise Keepers? Godly man project*. Paper presented at the American Sociological Association Meetings, San Francisco, August.

Berger, P. L., & Luckmann, T. (1966). *The Social Construction of Reality: A Treatise in the Sociology of Knowledge*, New York: Anchor Books.

Bertoia, C. E., & Drakich, J. (1995). The fathers' rights movement: Contradictions in rhetoric and practice. In W. Marsiglio (Ed.), *Fatherhood: Contemporary Theory, Research, and Social Policy* (pp. 230-254). Thousand Oaks, CA: Sage.

Bly, R. (1990). *Iron John: A book about men*. Reading, MA: Addison-Wesley.

Braver, S. L. & O'Connell, D. (1998). *Divorced dads: Shattering the myths*. New York: Tarcher/Putnam.

Brines, J. (1994). Economic dependency, gender, and division of labor at home. *American Journal of Sociology, 100*, 652-660.

Cohan, M. (1997). Political identities and political landscapes: Men's narrative work in relation to women's issues. *The Sociological Quarterly, 38*, 303319.

Coleman, J. (1988). Social capital in the creation of human capital. *American Journal of Sociology, 94*, 95120.

Coleman, J. (1990). *Foundations of social theory*. Cambridge, MA: Harvard University.

Collins, P. H. (1990). *Black Feminist Thought: Knowledge, Consciousness, and the Politics of Empowerment*. New York: Routledge.

Coltrane, S. (1996). *Family man: Fatherhood, housework, and gender equity*. New York: Oxford University Press.

Coltrane, S., & Hickman, N. (1992). The rhetoric of rights and needs: Moral discourse in the reform of child custody and child support laws. *Social Problems, 39*, 401-420.

Daly, K., & Dienhart, A. (1997). *Stepping in time: The dance of father involvement.* Paper presented at National Council on Family Relations Conference, Crystal City: Virginia, November.

Dienhart, A. (1998). *Reshaping fatherhood: The social construction of shared parenting.* Thousand Oaks, CA: Sage.

Doherty, W. J., Kouneski, E. F., & Erikson, M. F. (1998). Responsible fathering: An overview and conceptual framework. *Journal of Marriage and the Family, 60,* 277-292.

Federal Interagency Forum on Child and Family Statistics (1998). *Nurturing fatherhood: Improving data and research on male fertility, family formation, and fatherhood.* Washington, DC.

Fine, M. A., Ganong, L. H., & Coleman, M. (1997). The relation between role constructions and adjustment among stepfathers. *Journal of Family Issues, 18,* 503525.

Fox, G. L. & Sayers, B. A., & Bruce, C. (1998). Beyond bravado: Themes of redemption and reconstruction in the fathering accounts of men who batter. Paper presented at the Southern Sociological Society, Atlanta.

Furstenberg, F. F., Jr. (1988). Good dads-bad dads: Two faces of fatherhood. In A. Cherlin (Ed.), *The Changing American Family and Public Policy.* Washington, DC: Urban Institute.

Furstenberg, F. F., Jr. (1995). Fathering in the inner city: Paternal participation and public policy. In W. Marsiglio (Ed.), *Fatherhood: Contemporary theory, research, and social policy* (pp. 119-147). Thousand Oaks, CA: Sage.

Furstenberg, F. F., Jr. (1998). Social capital and the role of fathers in the family. In A. Booth & N. Crouter (Eds.), *Men in families: When do they get involved? What difference does it make?* (pp. 295-301). Mahwah, NJ: Lawrence Erlbaum Associates.

Furstenberg, F. F. Jr. & Cherlin, A. J. (1991). *Divided families: What happens to children when parents part.* Cambridge, MA: Harvard University Press.

Furstenberg, F. F. Jr. & Hughes, M. E. (1995). Social capital and successful development among at-risk youth. *Journal of Marriage and the Family, 57,* 580-593.

Futris, T. G., & Pasley, K. (1997). *The father role identity: Conceptualizing and assessing within-role variability.* Paper presented at the 1997 NCFR Pre-Conference Theory Construction and Research Methodology Workshop, Crystal City, VA.

Gerson, K. (1993). *No man's land: Men's changing commitments to family and work.* New York: Basic-Books.

Goffman, Erving (1959). *The Presentation of Self in Everyday Life.* New York: Doubleday Anchor Books.

Griswold, R. (1993). *Fatherhood in America: A history.* New York: Basic-Books.

Gubrium, J. F., & Holstein, J. A. (1990). *What is Family?* Mountain View, CA: Mayfield.

Gubrium, J. F., & Holstein, J. A. (1994). Grounding the postmodern self. *The Sociological Quarterly, 35,* 685703.

Gubrium, J. F., & Holstein, J. A. (1997). *The New Language of Qualitative Method.* New York: Oxford University Press.

Gubrium, J. F., & Holstein, J. A. (1998). Narrrative practice and the coherence of personal stories. *The Sociological Quarterly, 39*, 163187.

Haas, L., & Hawng, P. (1995). Company culture and men's usage of family leave benefits in Sweden. *Family Relations, 44*, 28-36.

Hawkins, A. J., & Palkovitz, R. (1999). Beyond ticks and clicks: The need for more diverse and broader conceptualizations and measures of father involvement. *Journal of Men's Studies*, Vol. 8, no. 1, p. 11-32.

Hochschild, A., & Manning, A. (1989). *The second shift: Working parents and the revolution at home.* New York: Viking.

hooks, b. (1984). *Feminist Theory: From Margin to Center.* Boston: South End Press.

Huber, J. (1991). *Macro-micro linages in sociology.* Newbury Park, CA: Sage.

Ihinger-Tallman, M., Pasley, K., & Buehler, C. (1995). Developing a middle-range theory of father involvement postdivorce. In W. Marsiglio (Ed.), *Fatherhood: Contemporary theory, research, and social policy* (pp. 57-77). Thousand Oaks, CA: Sage.

Kimmel, M. S., & Kaufman, M. (1994). Weekend warriors: The new men's movement. In H. Brod & M. Kaufman (Eds.), *Theorizing Masculinities* (pp. 259-288) Thousand Oaks, CA: Sage.

Lamb, M. E. (1999). Research on father involvement: An historical overview. *Marriage & Family Review, 29*, 2-3.

Larana, E., Johnston, H. & Gusfield, J. R. (1994). *New social movements: From ideology to identity.* Philadelphia: Temple University Press.

Levine, J. A., Murphy, D. T., & Wilson, S. (1993). *Getting men involved: Strategies for early childhood programs.* New York: Scholastic.

Levine, J. A. & Pitt, E. W. (1995). *New expectations: Community strategies for responsible fatherhood.* New York: Families and Work Institute.

Marsiglio, W. (1995a). Stepfathers with minor children living at home: Parenting perceptions and relationship quality. In *Fatherhood: Contemporary theory, research, and social policy* (pp. 211-229). Thousand Oaks, CA: Sage.

Marsiglio, W. (1995b). Fathers' diverse life course patterns and roles: Theory and social interventions. In W. Marsiglio (Ed.), *Fatherhood: Contemporary theory, research, and social policy* (pp. 78-101). Thousand Oaks, CA: Sage.

Marsiglio, W. (1995c). Young nonresident biological fathers. *Marriage & Family Review, 20*, 325-348.

Marsiglio, W., Day, R. & Lamb, M. E. (2000). Exploring fatherhood diversity: Implications for conceptualizing father involvement. *Marriage & Family Review, 29*, 4, 269-293.

Marsiglio, W., Amato, P., Day, R., & Lamb, M. E. (2000). Scholarship on fatherhood in the 1990s and beyond: Past impressions, future prospects. *Journal of Marriage and the Family, 62*.

Mead, G. H. (1934). *Mind, self, and society: From the standpoint of a social behaviorist.* Chicago: University of Chicago Press.

Mead, M. (1969). *Male and female: A study of the sexes in a changing world.* New York: Dell. Originally published in 1949.

Messner, M. (1997). *Politics of masculinities: Men in movements.* Thousand Oaks, CA: Sage.

Milkie, M. A., Simon, R. W., & Powell, B. (1997). Through the eyes of children: Youth's perceptions and evaluations of maternal and paternal roles. *Social Psychology Quarterly, 60,* 218-237.

Palkovitz, R. (1997). Reconstructing "involvement:" Expanding conceptualizations of men's caring in contemporary families. In A. J. Hawkins & D. C. Dollahite (Eds.), *Generative fathering: Beyond deficit perspectives* (pp. 200-216). Thousand Oaks, CA: Sage.

Potter, J. & Wetherell, M. (1987). *Discourse and Social Psychology: Beyond Attitudes and Behaviour.* Newbury Park, CA: Sage.

Roberts, S. (1994). Black women graduates outpace male counterparts. *New York Times,* October 31, section A, pp. 12.

Seltzer, J. A. (1991). Relationships between fathers and children who live apart: The father's role after separation. *Journal of Marriage and the Family, 53,* 79-101.

Seltzer, J. A. (1998). Men's contributions to children and social policy. In A. Booth & N. Crouter (Eds.), *Men in families: When do they get involved? What difference does it make?* (pp. 303-314). Mahwah, NJ: Lawrence Erlbaum Associates.

Silverman, D. (1993). *Interpreting Qualitative Data: Methods of Analyzing Talk, Text, and Interaction.* Thousand Oaks, CA: Sage.

Styrker, S. (1980). *Symbolic interactionism: A social structural version.* Menlo Park, CA: Benjamin/Cummings.

Styrker, S., & Serpe, R. T. (1994). Identity salience and psychological centrality: Equivalent, overlapping, or complementary concepts? *Social Psychological Quarterly, 57,* 16-35.

Tucker, M. B. & Mitchell-Kernan, C. (1995). *The decline in marriage among African Americans: Causes, consequences, and policy implications.* New York: Russell Sage.

Wilkie, J. R. (1993). Changes in U.S. men's attitudes toward the family provider role 1972-1989. *Gender & Society, 7,* 261-279.

II. FATHERS IN INTACT FAMILIES

Putting Fathers Back in the Picture: Parental Activities and Children's Adult Outcomes

W. Jean Yeung
Greg J. Duncan
Martha S. Hill

SUMMARY. Drawing on over a quarter of a century of Panel Study of Income Dynamics data, this paper examines links between childhood home environment (as reported by fathers during those childhood years) and children's outcomes in early adulthood. The emphasis is on the role of fathers and the unique contribution of their activities and

W. Jean Yeung and Martha S. Hill are affiliated with the University of Michigan. Greg J. Duncan is affiliated with Northwestern University.

An earlier version of this paper was presented at the Conference on Father Involvement, October 10-11, 1996. Support from the National Institute for Child Health and Human Development through its Child and Family Well-being Research Network is gratefully acknowledged. The authors are also very appreciative of research assistance from Dave Knutson and Randy Herbison as well as comments from Cathleen Zick, Randal Day and Elizabeth Peters.

[Haworth co-indexing entry note]: "Putting Fathers Back in the Picture: Parental Activities and Chileren's Adult Outcomes." Yeung, W. Jean, Greg J. Duncan, and Martha S. Hill. Co-published simultaneously in *Marriage & Family Review* (The Haworth Press, Inc.) Vol. 29, No. 2/3, 2000, pp. 97-113; and: *FATHERHOOD: Research, Interventions and Policies* (ed: H. Elizabeth Peters et al.) The Haworth Press, Inc., 2000, pp. 97-113. Single or multiple copies of this article are available for a fee from The Haworth Document Delivery Service [1-800-342-9678, 9:00 a.m. - 5:00 p.m. (EST). E-mail address: getinfo@ haworthpressinc.com].

characteristics to children's development, measured in terms of the children's completed schooling, wage rates, and nonmarital childbearing in early adulthood. The paper shows that fathers' abilities add substantial predictive power to models based on maternal characteristics. Fathers' church attendance and the precautionary actions of parents are also strong predictors of children's adult outcomes, although differentially so for sons and daughters. *[Article copies available for a fee from The Haworth Document Delivery Service: 1-800-342-9678. E-mail address: getinfo@haworthpressinc.com <Website: http://www.haworthpressinc.com>]*

KEYWORDS. Fathers' roles, church attendance, education, nonmarital childbearing

In recent decades researchers concerned with the behavior and attainments of children have paid little attention to the role of fathers in children's lives. Although formulations of the Wisconsin intergenerational status-attainment model in the 1960s and 1970s included at least as many measures of fathers' characteristics (e.g., schooling, occupational prestige) as for mothers', more recent formulations of attainment models in economics and sociology and of developmental models in psychology have concentrated on mothers. Emphasis shifted to mothers' role as attention focused more on the early stages of childhood, when mothers are the primary caregivers, and as children became increasingly likely to spend portions of childhood living apart from their biological fathers. This shift toward more children with nonresident biological fathers plus a companion shift toward more children with resident nonbiological fathers (mostly step-fathers) have complicated the types of paternal inputs children receive as well as the conceptual and measurement challenges of research concerning paternal inputs.

Fathers' roles in children's development are largely unknown; most existing research focuses on benefits derived from fathers' labor force income and detriments derived from fathers' absence from the household. In this paper we seek to bring fathers back into the picture by investigating a wider range of routes through which fathers might influence children.

Our approach is to examine correlations between children's outcomes as young adults and fathers' characteristics, attitudes, and activities while children were growing up. We concentrate on two-parent families and on conditions that are potentially important to children's development. In examining the correlations between children's outcomes and the various attributes of fathers, we control for a number of characteristics and activities of mothers as well as conditions in the childhood home. Our list of possible influences of fathers is more comprehensive than that of other research.

Major theories in three social sciences–economics, sociology, and psychology–guide our selection of measures from the long-running Panel Study of Income Dynamics (PSID) (Hill, 1992a; 1992b). That study obtained self-reports from fathers about family conditions as their children were growing up and traced the children from childhood into adulthood. Motivated originally by a desire to test for attitudes and behavior that might account for poverty dynamics, the study provides measures of fathers' attitudes, cognitive skills, socio-economic status, and work and leisure-time activities, as well as many measures of mothers' characteristics and activities. Our analyses relate these measures to the socio-economic achievements (completed schooling and wage rates) and socio-demographic behavior (nonmarital childbearing) of the children when they are in their 30s.

We begin, in the second section, with a review of related background literature and theories. This is followed by a description of our general analytical approach, the data used in our analysis, and our results. In the final section we discuss the implications of these results.

BACKGROUND

Though the U.S. cultural image of fathers' role in families has fluctuated substantially during the 20th century, the reality of the role in everyday life has undergone more modest change. At the turn of the century fathers were expected to be providers of economic support and possibly bridge the gap between home and society; they were not expected to nurture children by providing day-to-day physical and emotional care. Since the 1930s societal expectations for fathers have expanded the role of provider to include child-rearing and nurturing as joint responsibilities along with mothers.[1] In reality, though, fathers still contribute much less than mothers to childrearing and the nurturance of children (Acock & Demo, 1994; Biller, 1993; Harris & Morgan, 1991, LaRossa, 1988). Fathers spend less time than mothers both in direct interaction with children and being available for children.[2] In addition, the nature of interaction with children differs by sex of the parent: fathers tend to engage children in play whereas mothers tend to be caretakers (Zick & Bryant, 1996; LaRossa, 1988; Lamb, Pleck Charnov, Levine, 1985; Lamb & Stevenson, 1978).

Economic, sociological and psychological theories posit differing ways in which parents influence their children, though all theories pay little attention to father-mother differences in the parenting role. Economic theories of the family emphasize the importance of resources as inputs to children's human capital development (Becker, 1981). Parents' income and time are viewed as important resources for providing goods (e.g., food and housing) and services (e.g., childcare, schooling, and health care) to build children's human capital. Several qualities of the parents, such as their education, cognitive skills, and orientation toward life, can shape the way resources are used in this human capital building endeavor.

Sociological theories suggest different mechanisms for parental family influences. Social capital theory emphasizes ties to others, inside and outside the family, as important resources and constraints (Coleman, 1988). Social interaction with others is seen as a means of building networks of potential assistance and obligations, and parents' social networks may assist or hinder children's prospects for obtaining jobs and meeting possible marriage partners. Socialization theories emphasize aspects of social interaction that involve socializing children. Children are viewed as learning most social behaviors from their parents, either through a process by which parents actively encourage or discourage children's behaviors or, as role model theory posits, by behaviors transmitted more passively as parents set examples with their behavior. According to role model theory, fathers serve as the prime example of adult male behavior upon which sons model themselves and upon which daughters build expectations about prospective husbands.

In combination, the different sociological theories posit a number of ways in which parents' activities in social networks could influence children (see Cochran, Larner, Riley, Gunnarsson, & Henderson, 1990, for a discussion). Activities such as attending cultural events, doing volunteer work, and socializing with friends could have positive influences on children by (a) providing emotional or instrumental support to the parents, (b) building connections that would help family members advance in their endeavors, or (c) building social skills in children if the children also participate in the activities. These same activities, on the other hand, could discourage attainment in children if they take the parents' time away from other activities that are more conducive to children's development.

Psychological theories of child development emphasize parenting orientation and style as key elements of the role of parents (Hetherington, 1983). These theories stress direct interaction between caregivers and children. Although the mother is generally the primary caregiver, the father can serve as a caregiver as well. Possible indicators of parenting orientation and style include parents' socio-economic background, cognitive ability, and beliefs about how the world operates.

General discussions in the literature (Pleck, 1997; Grossman, Pollack, & Golding, 1988) argue for taking account of both the quantity of parents' activities (amount of time) and its quality and content. Empirical research suggests that even when relatively uninvolved with the children, fathers' characteristics affect children (see Pleck, 1997). With limited measures of father-child interactions, some research suggests that only fathers' financial contributions to families, and not their nurturing behavior, influence the development and long-run attainments of children (see Harris & Marmer,

1996, for a discussion). However, research with more comprehensive measures of the nature of father-child interactions yields evidence of important roles for fathers' actions in children's development and later success.

Time fathers spend with children in several types of activities correlates strongly in the cross-section with children's academic performance, measured by grades (Cooksey & Fondell, 1996). Positive correlatations appear for shared meals, leisure activities, home activities, and reading or helping with homework (but not talking with children).

There is also evidence of strong associations between fathers' interactions with children and children's long-run behaviors. For children born just before the start of the Great Depression, research indicates that fathers' parenting behavior was an important mediator of financial loss and played a role in young children's development of defiant, aggressive behaviors (Elder, Liker & Cross, 1984). Income loss enhanced the arbitrariness of fathers' discipline, which encouraged explosive childhood behavior. These childhood problem behaviors, in turn, led to generally undercontrolled behavior in adulthood, as well as erratic work lives and unstable marriages for sons, and lower status marriages for daughters. For older children as well, fathers appear to play a crucial role in mediating the effects of financial hardship (Elder, Conger, Foster, & Ardelt, 1992).

Reviews of the ways fathers' interactions with children contribute to children's development (Harris & Marmer, 1996; Pleck, 1997) indicate that supportive parenting behaviors (e.g., physical affection, nurturance, interest, companionship, and sustained presence) are positively associated with desirable children's behaviors. These behaviors include self-control; self-esteem; life skills; life satisfaction as well as social and cognitive competence. Supportive paternal behavior also predicts reduced risk and problem behaviors, including delinquency, drinking, as well as fewer symptoms of externalizing and internalizing problems. Positive paternal interactions also appear to foster fewer behavior problems in school for boys and more self-direction by girls.

Regarding parents' activities in social networks, German data show that fathers' social activities relate strongly to children's educational achievements, whereas mothers' social activities do not (Büchel & Duncan, 1998). Children, especially boys, whose fathers frequently engaged in active sports and volunteer work were more successful in becoming enrolled in a university-track Gymnasium. These findings point to a need to consider not only direct interactions between parents and children but other activities of parents as well.

Suggestive evidence points to differences for sons and daughters in levels and influence of father's interaction (Bryant & Zick, 1996; Barber & Thomas, 1986; Lamb & Stevenson, 1978). Fathers tend to engage in more companionship and activities involving maintenance of the home, yard, and car with sons, but express more physical affection to daughters. For predicting children's self-esteem (potentially important to many adult outcomes), it is sustained contact with the father that matters for sons, but physical affection from the father that matters for daughters. Father's intellectual-academic support appears to be important for boys, whereas fathers' physical-athletic encouragement is what seems to be important for girls for predicting educational and wage outcomes (Snarey, 1993). These results suggest a need for special attention to possible differentials for sons and daughters in the influence of fathers on their adult skills and success.

ANALYTICAL APPROACH

The emphasis of our analytical approach is on assessing the power of fathers' characteristics, attitudes, and behaviors to predict children's social and economic outcomes as adults. Our measures of adult children's outcomes are years of completed schooling, hourly earnings (for sons) and nonmarital childbearing (for daughters). Our analytical framework derives from a basic model of the intergenerational influence of parents; it views adult outcomes as a function of childhood family circumstances without specifying the processes involved. Though no formal structure is given for the mechanisms, our analytical approach incorporates a wider variety of childhood circumstances than past research, with emphasis on potentially important but heretofore untested aspects of fathers' roles.

These aspects include measures of fathers' characteristics, attitudes, and behaviors thought to serve as indicators of the resources or preferences shaping children's human capital development. Fathers' activities are classified by type (e.g., church attendance vs. reading newspapers) and are calibrated in terms of the amount of time spent to reflect the saliency of the activity.

Because mothers' role could be at least as important as fathers', our analytical model includes comparable measures for mothers and fathers when available. Due to data limitations, however, the measures for mothers are less extensive. Measures of unpaid activities for mothers are limited to housework, whereas unpaid activities for fathers cover a broader range of activities. Paid work is measured for both.

Because some theories point to differences in the reactions of sons and daughters and because the applicability and measurability of some outcomes differ by sex, we estimate separate models for sons and daughters. Completed education, an indicator of adult socio-economic success, is examined for both. Hourly earnings, an indicator of adult economic success, is examined only for sons.[3] Nonmarital childbearing, an indicator of socio-demographic problems, is investigated only for daughters.

We begin our empirical analysis with the simple question "Do fathers' characteristics add predictive power over and above mothers' characteristics?" We address this by estimating two different specifications, one including essentially mothers' characteristics and one adding father's characteristics. Our next question is, "Are the activities and attitudes of fathers important factors independent of the parents' characteristics, and, if so, how relevant are activities with no direct parent-child interaction?" To address these issues, we add fathers' activities and attitudes as predictors.

We recognize that the interpretation of estimated influences of fathers' activities, in particular, could be affected by our omission of potentially relevant factors. Apparent relationships could be mere reflections of unmeasured characteristics (e.g., preferences, skills, aspirations, expectations, or constraints). Where possible, our empirical model includes measures of such characteristics. Where direct measurement is not possible, we interpret results with caution.

Data

Our data derive from 27 years of the Panel Study of Income Dynamics (1992a), a study that since 1968 has interviewed annually, a representative sample of about 5,000 families. The data follow children who leave home, couples who divorce, and family members who undergo even more complicated family changes. This procedure produces an unbiased sample of adult children tracked from childhood to adulthood.

Our measures of childhood conditions derive from in-person interviews with the household "head," defined as the father in the case of married-couple families. Our analysis is restricted to children living with their fathers during middle childhood and adolescence, when childhood circumstances were measured.

The PSID's original design focused on poverty by oversampling lower-income households, but sampling weights have been constructed to adjust for both differential sampling fractions and differential nonresponse. Our analysis uses the PSID's individual weight for the children's most recent observation (Hill, 1992a; 1992b)

Sample

We limited our sample to children born in the years 1956-62, who lived in intact families during their childhood.[4] Additional criteria for inclusion were that they had remained in the PSID from its initial wave in 1968, through or beyond the 1985 interviewing wave, when extensive information was gathered about parents' and children's educational and demographic histories.

The initial waves 1968-72 are crucial for measures of fathers' attitudes and activities because those measures were collected only during that period. With some further restriction due to missing data on variables in the regression models, our sample for the analysis consists of 1024 children, 505 males and 519 females.

Variables Used in the Analysis

Children's schooling and wages. Reports of years of *schooling completed by children* were taken, when possible, from self-reports in the 1995 interviewing wave. For children lost to attrition before 1995, we took the most recent report of completed schooling. Rare cases with no report available after age 21 were omitted. For each son, reports of *hourly earnings* were logged and averaged over the two most recent years prior to 1993 when he was present in the PSID, reported working at least 250 hours, and was age 21 or older. In most cases, the earnings data apply to ages 29 to 36.

To adjust for differences in the age and calendar year of reports of schooling and wage rate, we estimated a predicted level for these outcomes from a sex-specific regression of the outcome on the calendar year in which it was reported and the age of the child in that year. The outcome measures used in our schooling and wage-rate analyses are the differences between children's actual and predicted outcome.

Details concerning the predictor variables used in our final analysis are presented in the Appendix. Each variable is averaged across non-missing years from 1968 to 1972. For each measure there is a summary of question wording, 1968-72 cross-year correlations and alphas, and zero-order correlations between single-year items and children's completed schooling.[6]

Characteristics of children and families. Demographic measures include *race* of the father as observed by the interviewer (Black = 1, else = 0) and *child's birth cohort* (scored as birth year minus 1956). *Family size* is the average number in the family from 1968 to 1972. *City size/Location* reflects dummy variables in each year 1968-72 representing combinations of Census regions and whether the family resided in a city with a population of 100,000 or more.

Characteristics of mothers. Mothers' *years of schooling* derives, when possible, from self-reports in the 1985 wave. For mothers lost to attrition before 1985, we used the most recent (typically fathers') report of mothers' completed schooling. We used the PSID's demographic history data to measure mothers' *age at time of child's birth.* Questions typically asked of the fathers formed the basis of estimates of 1968-72 *average annual paid work hours* and *annual housework hours.*[7]

Characteristics of fathers. Fathers' achievement-related characteristics include measures of years of completed schooling, hourly earnings, occupation, disability status, and a verbal test score. *Years of schooling* is measured, when possible, from self-reports in the 1985 wave. For fathers lost to attrition before 1985, the most recent report of completed schooling is used. *Average hourly wage* was calculated by averaging self-reported wage data for all years 1968-72 in which the fathers worked at least 250 hours. Likewise, *occupation* was calculated by averaging the self-reported one-digit occupation code for all years from 1968-72 in which the fathers worked at least 250 hours. *Disability status* was created by averaging all available self-reports 1968-72 about having a health condition that limited the amount or type of work.

Word test score comes from the PSID's 1972-wave sentence-completion test, adapted from the Lorge-Thorndike intelligence test (as documented in Veroff, McClelland, & Marquis, 1971). The sample distribution of test scores indicates a degree of differentiation much greater at the low end than at the high end of the distribution.[8]

Fathers' attitudes and behaviors. A 1972 series of forced-choice questions comparing preferences for challenging as opposed to friendly situations formed the basis of the *challenge vs. affiliation* measure.[9] *Sense of personal control* was constructed by averaging (along the lines of Hill et al., 1985) 5-year mean scores on the questions concerning feelings about life working out as desired, plans working out as expected, and ability to finish things that are started.[10] *Trust/hostility* reflects the mean score on four dummy-variable measures concerning getting angry, feelings about life improving, concern about what others think, and trusting others.

Fathers' *precautionary behavior* reflects questions about parents, predominately fathers, avoiding unnecessary risks for the safety and economic security of the family. Indicators of risk avoidance include fathers' reports of: (a) having car insurance, (b) having health insurance, (c) using seat belts while driving, and (d) having at least two months' worth of precautionary savings.[12]

Measures of fathers' behaviors include time spent in major activities: *annual paid work hours, annual housework hours,* and *vacation time.* They also include measures of time spent in preference-revealing but less time-consuming activities: *frequency of newspaper reading* and *church attendance.*[13]

RESULTS

Descriptive Statistics

The descriptive statistics (Table 1, final column) show parental socio-demographic characteristics consistent with data from other sources. For example, fathers and mothers averaged around 13 years of schooling, and mothers

TABLE 1. Coefficients and Standard Errors for Regressions of Children's Adult Outcomes

	Years of Schooling		Wage Rate For Males	Risk of Nonmarital Birth For Females	Dependent Variable Means (std dev)
	Males	Females			
Intercept	−1.84* (.62)	1.59* (.53)	−.78* (.58)	−	−
Children and Family Characteristics					
Child's Birth Cohort	.01 (.02)	−.01 (.02)	.01 (.02)	.14 (.08)	4.02 (.92)
Whether Black	.11* (.05)	.05 (.04)	−.12* (.05)	.11 (.12)	.10 (.29)
Family Size	−.08 (.05)	−.09* (.04)	.04 (.05)	.60* (.14)	6.06 (1.93)
Mother's Characteristics and Behavior					
Years of Schooling	.00 (.05)	.14* (.04)	−.08 (.05)	−.23* (.13)	12.63 (2.13)
Age at Child's Birth	.04 (.05)	.02 (.04)	.07 (.04)	−.10 (.15)	27.21 (5.70)
Annual Market Work Hours (1,000s)	−.09 (.06)	−.07 (.05)	−.03 (.05)	.72* (.19)	.49 (.63)
Annual Housework Hours (1,000s)	−.06 (.06)	−.13* (.05)	.06 (.05)	.21 (.17)	1.98 (.69)
Father's Achievement-Related Characteristics					
Years of Schooling	.14* (.05)	.14* (.05)	.06 (.05)	−.40* (.11)	13.06 (3.05)
Hourly Wage	.10* (.05)	.10 (.06)	.08 (.05)	−1.00* (.43)	18.10 (1.87)
Disability Status	.03 (.05)	−.05 (.04)	−.05 (.05)	.07 (.16)	.11 (.25)
Word Test Score	.03 (.05)	.04 (.05)	.05 (.05)	.22 (.15)	9.97 (2.00)
Father's Attitudes and Behaviors					
Challenge vs. Affiliation	−.04 (.05)	.01 (.04)	−.05 (.04)	−.50* (.14)	1.46 (.90)
Sense of Personal Control	.10* (.05)	−.03 (.04)	.05 (.05)	−.18 (.14)	2.22 (.87)
Trust-Hostility Index	−.06 (.05)	.05 (.04)	−.04 (.04)	−.05 (.16)	2.24 (.92)
Precautionary Behavior	.23* (.06)	−.02 (.05)	.22* (.05)	.19 (.19)	2.73 (.80)
Annual Market Work Hours (1,000s)	.05 (.06)	.07 (.05)	−.10 (.05)	−.19 (.21)	2.35 (.63)
Annual Housework Hours (1,000s)	.05 (.05)	.03 (.04)	.04 (.05)	.14 (.15)	.09 (.19)
Annual Vacation Hours	−.02 (.05)	.06 (.05)	−.14* (.04)	.13 (.23)	1.92 (1.32)
Frequency of Newspaper Reading	.01 (.05)	−.04 (.05)	−.02 (.05)	−.26 (.15)	25.75 (7.91)
Church Attendance	.09* (.05)	.11* (.04)	−.01 (.04)	−.02 (.17)	.57 (.40)
Adjusted R-Square/Log-Likelihood	.233	.222	.119	−328.3	
Number of Observations	505	514	493	520	

Note. All predictors have been rescaled to produce a standard deviation of 1.0. All regressions include, but do not report dummy variables for city size/location and father's occupation.
* p < .05

were 27 years old, on average, when the child was born. The descriptive statistics also show a traditional division of labor: fathers averaged annually 2,350 hours of paid work but only about 90 hours of housework, whereas mothers averaged about 500 hours of paid work and nearly 2,000 hours of housework.

Regression Results

Coefficients and standard errors from the regressions are also presented in Table 1. To assist in evaluating the relative explanatory power of the predictors, we divide each by its whole-sample standard deviation. This produces coefficients in our regressions that can be interpreted as the change in the given dependent variable (e.g., years of schooling, log wage rates, probability of nonmarital childbearing) associated with a (whole-sample) standard deviation change in the given independent variable.[14]

Results regarding mothers' and family characteristics correspond well to those in the literature–generally positive effects of parental SES and some negative effects of larger family sizes. In our samples, beneficial effects of mothers' schooling and detrimental effects of family size are more apparent for daughters than sons. Mothers' paid work hours are a risk factor for daughters' nonmarital childbearing. Curiously, mothers' housework appears to have a negative effect on daughters' schooling, although a closer look at this relationship (results not shown) indicated that the negative effect comes from the situations in which the housework time is quite high (greater than 1,500 hours a year).

Fathers' achievement-related characteristics are clearly important predictors of both sons' and daughters' adult achievements. In results not shown here, the addition of characteristics such as fathers' schooling, wage rate, and occupation more than doubles the explained variance of the completed schooling models of sons and daughters, and increases explained variance of the wage-rate model of sons by more than 50%. Little used in the literature, fathers' hourly wage is seen to be a predictor of sons' schooling and daughters' out-of-wedlock childbearing, while fathers' schooling is a significant predictor for all but sons' wage rates.

In contrast, fathers' activities in terms of time allocated to paid work and housework have virtually no significant associations with children's outcomes. Fathers' vacation hours have a negative association with sons' wage rate (but not schooling), a result for which we have no ready explanation.

Fathers' time spent attending religious services appears to be beneficial for children's schooling, but does not affect sons' wage rates or daughters' probability of nonmarital birth. Since we were unable to control for the religious behavior of either the mother or the children, we cannot be confident that fathers' behavior is the key component of this result.

Interestingly, precautionary actions by (predominantly) fathers, as measured by our risk index, are associated with highly significant increments in both schooling and wage rates for sons, but have virtually no impact on the attainments of daughters. A look into the components of the risk index showed three elements to be most important–fathers' reports of using seat belts, having car insurance, and having precautionary savings equal to at least two months of income (data not shown).

The explanatory power of the saving component of this index may reflect the role of family assets in promoting children's attainment. But an asset-based explanation does not carry over to the other index components, nor does it account for the differential explanatory power for sons and daughters. Since adolescent boys generally engage in more overtly dangerous behavior than adolescent girls, the potential for parents' actions to affect children's risk-taking behavior may be greater for sons than for daughters.

The PSID's collection of fathers' psychological characteristics–orientation toward challenge, efficacy, and trust–produce one intriguing result: fathers' orientation toward challenge rather than affiliation (e.g., preferred a challenging job to friendly co-workers) is associated with a reduced probability of daughters' nonmarital childbearing. The lack of association of this characteristic with daughters' completed schooling, however, suggests caution in interpreting this result.

DISCUSSION

We have addressed several key questions regarding the nature of childhood influences on outcomes in early adulthood by children from intact families. A first issue was whether fathers' characteristics added predictive power to models based solely on the characteristics of children, mothers and families. We find considerable evidence that fathers' achievement-related characteristics are important predictors. Fathers' wage rate and completed schooling are important to children's schooling and to daughters' probability of nonmarital childbearing.

A second question was whether parental time allocation, especially to activities with little direct parent-child interaction, affects children's outcomes, independent of child, parental, and family characteristics. Here we found that measures of the time spent by fathers in paid work and in housework added little to the models; most important was the "quality" of time as measured by the wage rate and schooling.

But while the allocation of fathers' time to housework and paid work proved to be of modest importance, fathers' allocation of time to non-work activities, particularly certain types, was crucial. Fathers' reported church attendance was an important predictor in our analyses, though not for all outcomes. Children's completed schooling was the outcome most consistently associated with paternal church attendance; sons' wage rate was unrelated to paternal church attendance. This lack of association with a labor market outcome in conjunction with the strong association with schooling could reflect a decline in the importance of fathers' influence as children move farther into adulthood, or it may be that labor markets do not value the same thing that schools value in terms of what fathers' church attendance fosters in children. We cannot tell which, if either, explanation holds for the inconsistency. Also unanswered by our analysis is the question of mechanism: is this effect due to the fathers' religiosity, his promotion of the spiritual and moral development of his children, or a more basic willingness to involve himself in the lives of his children?

A third issue was whether the home environment mattered in other ways. Among the many measures we investigated, the most important was an indicator of the precautions parents took to ensure the safety and financial security of the family. Sons of fathers who reported using seat belts and having precautionary savings and car insurance were significantly more successful in both of the domains we studied. We speculate that this result reflects strategies parents adopt to reduce the risk-taking behavior of adolescents. That these effects are stronger for sons than daughters suggests more of a paternal role in reducing the generally riskier behavior of sons relative to daughters.

We should also note factors in our preliminary analyses that failed to matter. Our failure list includes the family's network of friends and relatives; various attitudinal measures, including components of the fathers' achievement motivation and orientation toward the future; and behavior measures such as fathers' reports of the frequency of going to bars or social clubs. Given the conventional wisdom regarding the importance of family schedules, it is also interesting to note that frequency of the family eating main meals together proved unimportant.

Taken together, our analysis of the adult outcomes of children raised in intact families reveals a major role for typically unmeasured conditions in the childhood home. Our approach considered the influence of fathers' characteristics, the time allocation patterns of parents, and qualities of the home environment produced by the actions of family members. That we found considerable explanatory power in a number of these measures should encourage research on the nature of father involvement and family organization.

NOTES

1. Much of the evidence about the changing cultural image of fathers comes from analyses of the way parents are portrayed with children in articles and cartoons published in popular magazines during the course of the past century (Atkinson & Blackwelder, 1993; LaRossa, Gordon, & Wilson., 1991; Day & Mackey, 1989). This

research indicates that during the 1930s, 1940s, 1970s, and 1980s the cultural image of fathers was likely to be that of nurturer as well as provider.

2. Time use diary-based data from the 1970s (Pleck, 1983) show that fathers' caretaking and shared activities with children amounted to about one-fourth or one-third that of mothers, depending on mothers' employment. Averaging across studies from the 1980s and 1990s, Pleck (1997) finds that fathers' time relative to mothers' was somewhat over two-fifths for time interacting with children and nearly two-thirds for time being available to children. He reports that these figures are somewhat higher than corresponding averages across studies in the 1970s and early 1980s (Lamb et al., 1985) and that fathers' absolute levels of interacting with or being available to children are higher when children are young than when they are adolescents.

3. Because non-participation in the labor market and part-time work due to family responsibilities are higher for females than males, wage rates are not as applicable to females as an indicator of economic success.

4. Potential problems of under-reporting of nonmarital fertility among males (Rendell, Clarke, Peters, Ranjit, & Verropoulou, 1999) argue for omitting analysis of that outcome for sons.

5. Children who lived in intact families were identified in two ways. In cases where both children and parents provided demographic history data in 1985, we could identify and select children who lived with both biological parents between birth and age 16 (N = 826). Children lacking 1985 parental demographic histories were classified as reared in "intact" situations if (a) they reported spending "most of the time until age 16 with both biological parents" and (b) at the time of an interview in 1968-72, they were residing in a household headed by a man with a co-resident wife (N = 226).

6. The cross-year correlations and alphas provide information about the reliability of the individual-year items as indicators of a multi-year latent construct. Since measurement models typically presume random errors in the items, the pattern of correlations between the annual items and our three dependent variables provides a check on the assumption of random variation across the five years.

7. Housework is defined as "time spent cooking, cleaning, and doing other work around the house." Mothers' annual housework hours are topcoded at 3,000 hours for the analysis.

8. A sample item is: "The ragged _____ may prove a good horse," with alternatives "Puppy," "Child," "Calf," "Lamb," and "Colt"; "Colt" was taken to be the correct response. As reported in Duncan, Duniforn, and Knutson, (1996), a parallel wage analysis using data on the PSID's sentence-completion test and NLSY's AFQT test score showed very similar results for young Black men but much weaker effects of the test score on earnings for Whites. They conclude that the PSID's sentence completion test is a decidedly error-prone measure of cognitive skills, with relatively greater reliability among some population subgroups.

9. The measure is the average of scores on the following two questions: "Would you like to have more friends, or would you like to do better at what you try?" and "Would you prefer a job where you had to think for yourself, or one where you work with a nice group of people?" (correlation = .19). The choices "like to do better"

and "think for yourself" were scored 1, indicating a preference for challenge over affiliation, while other choices were scored 0.

10. The questions are: "Have you usually felt pretty sure that your life will work out the way you want it to, or have there been more times when you haven't been sure about it?" "When you make plans ahead, do you usually get to carry out things the way you expected, or do things usually come up to make you change your plans?" and "Would you say that you nearly always finish things once you start them, or do you sometimes have to give up before they are finished?" (alpha = .80).

11. The questions forming the basis of the dummy variables are: "Do you get angry easily, or does it take a lot to get you angry?" "Do you think that the life of the average person is improving or getting worse?" "How much does it matter what other people think about you?" and "Do you trust most people, some, or very few?" (alpha = .83).

12. Each of these added one point to our index of risk avoidance. To adjust for the fact that fathers who did not own cars could report neither seat-belt usage nor car insurance, we added one point for non-owners.

13. Measures of fathers' activities that we eliminated from the final analysis because of their inability to account for differences in children's outcomes include time spent in social clubs, bars, watching TV, taking lessons, and spare time activities.

14. We present in the final column of Table 1 the standard deviations themselves, so that readers can easily convert our partially-standardized coefficients back to raw-score coefficients.

REFERENCES

Acock, A. C., & and Demo, D. H. (1994). *Family Diversity and Well-Being.* Thousand Oaks, CA: Sage.

Atkinson, M. P., & Blackwelder, S. P. (1993). Fathering in the 20th Century. *Journal of Marriage and the Family, 55,* 975-986.

Barber, B. K., & Thomas, D. L. (1986). Dimensions of Fathers' and Mothers' Supportive Behavior: The Case for Physical Affection. *Journal of Marriage and the Family, 48,* 783-794.

Becker, G. (1981). *Treatise on the family.* Cambridge, MA: Harvard University Press.

Biller, H. B. (1993). *Fathers and Families: Paternal Factors in Child Development.* Westport, CT: Auburn House.

Bryant, W. K., & Zick, C. D. An Examination of Parent-Child Shared Time. *Journal of Marriage and the Family, 58,* 227-237.

Büchel, F., & Duncan, G. J. (1998). Do Parents' Social Activities Promote Children's School Attainments? Evidence from the German Socio-Economic Panel. *Journal of Marriage and the Family, 60,* 1, 95-108.

Cochran, M., Larner, M., Riley, D. Gunnarsson, L. & Henderson, C. R. Jr. (1990). Extending families: The social networks of parents and their children. New York: Cambridge University Press.

Coleman, J. S. (1988). Social Capital in the Creation of Human Capital. *American Journal of Sociology, 94,* S95-S120.

Cooksey, E. C., & Fondel, M. M.(1996). Spending Time With His Kids: Effects of

Family Structure on Fathers' and Children's Lives. *Journal of Marriage and the Family, 58*, 693-707.

Day, R. D. & Mackey, W. C. (1989). An Alternate Standard for Evaluating American Fathers. *Journal of Family Issues, 10*(3), 401-408.

Duncan, Greg J., Dunifon, R., & Knutson, D. (1996). Vim Will Win: Long-Run Effects of Motivation and Other "Noncognitive" Traits on Success. Paper read at the Conference on Meritocracy and Inequality, September, 1996.

Elder, G. H., Conger, R. D., Foster, E. M., & Ardelt, M. (1992). Families Under Economic Pressure. *Journal of Family Issues, 13*, 5-37.

Elder, G.,H., Jr., Liker, J. K., & Cross, C. E. (1984). Parent-Child Behavior in the Great Depression: Life Course and Intergenerational Influences. *Life-Span Development and Behavior, 6*, 109-158.

Grossman, F. K., Pollack, W. S., & Golding, E.(1988). Fathers and Children: Predicting the Quality and Quantity of Fathering. *Developmental Psychology, 24*, 1, 82-91.

Harris, K. M., & Marmer, J. K. (1996). Poverty, Paternal Involvement, and Adolescent Well-Being. *Journal of Family Issues, 17*, 5, 614-640.

Harris, K. H. & Morgan, S. P. (1991). Fathers, sons, and daughters: Differential paternal involvement in parenting. *Journal of Marriage and the Family, 53*, 531-544.

Heatherington, M. (1983). *Handbook of child psychology, Vol. IV: Socialization, Personality and Social Development*. New York: Wiley.

Hill, M. (1992a). *The panel study of income dynamics*. Newbury Park, CA: Sage Publication.

Hill, M. (1992b). *The panel study of income dynamic: A users guide*. Newbury Park, CA: Sage Publication.

Jacobsen, L., & Edmondson, B. (1993). Father Figures. *American Demographics, 26*, 22-26.

Lamb, M. E., Pleck, J. H., Charnov, E. L., & Levine, J. A. (1985). Paternal Behavior in Humans. *American Zoologist, 25*, 883-894.

Lamb, M. E. & Stevenson, M. B. (1978). Father-Infant Relationships Their Nature and Importance. *Youth and Society, 9*, 3, 277-297.

LaRossa, R. (1988). Fatherhood and Social Change. *Family Relations, 37*, 451-457.

LaRossa, R., Gordon, B. A., Wilson, R. J. (1991). The Fluctuating Image of the 20th Century American Father. *Journal of Marriage and the Family, 53*, 987-997

Mackey, W. C. & Day, R. D. (1979). Some Indicators of Fathering Behaviors in the United States: A Cross-Cultural Examination of Adult Male-Child Interaction. *Journal of Marriage and the Family, 41*, 287-299.

Pleck, J. H. (1983). Husbands' paid work and family roles: Current research issues. In H. Lopata & J. Pleck (Eds.) *Research in the interweave of social roles: Vol 3. families and jobs* (pp. 231-333). Greenwich, CT: JAI.

Pleck, J. H. (1997). Paternal Involvement: Levels, Sources, and Consequences. In Lamb, M. (Ed.), *The Role of the Father in Child Development*, 3rd ed. New York: John Wiley & Sons

Rendall, M., Clarke, L., Peters, E., Ranjit, N., & Verropoulou, G. (1999). Incomplete

Reporting of Male Fertility in the United States and Britain: A Research Note. *Demography, 36*, 1, 135-144.
Snarey, John. (1993). *How Fathers Care for the Next Generation*. Cambridge, MA: Harvard University Press.
Veroff, J., McClelland, L., & Marquis, K. (1971) *Measuring Intelligence and Achievement Motivation in Surveys*. Final Report to HEW, OEO, Contract No. OEO4180.
Zick, C. D., & Bryant, W. K. (1996). A New Look at Parents' Time Spent in Child Care: Primary and Secondary Time Use. *Social Science Research, 25*, 260-280.

APPENDIX

Cross-year zero-holder correlations for various measures, and their correlations with children's education

	'68	'69	'70	'71	'72	5-year Alpha	Education
			Years				

Church Attendance: How many times a week do you attend religious services?

	'68	'69	'70	'71	'72	5-year Alpha	Education
1968	1.00					.92	.22
1969	.76	1.00					.20
1970	.71	.74	1.00				.20
1971	.65	.74	.72	1.00			.19
1972	.67	.65	.71	.73	1.00		.17

Read Newspapers: How often do you read a newspaper–every day, once a week, or what?

1968	1.00					.91	.24
1969	.71	1.00					.26
1970	.68	.73	1.00				.20
1971	.64	.72	.71	1.00			.22
1972	.61	.66	.66	.69	1.00		.22

Precautionary Behavior Index: Wearing seat belt, savings, car and medical insurance

1968	1.00					.90	.30
1969	.66	1.00					.29
1970	.63	.67	1.00				.27
1971	.57	.63	.70	1.00			.27
1972	.59	.62	.69	.70	1.00		.28

Personal Control Index: Carry out things as planned, feel life will work out, nearly always finish things

1968	1.00					.80	.18
1969	.43	1.00					.19
1970	.39	.52	1.00				.18
1971	.39	.50	.55	1.00			.20
1972	.33	.42	.47	.58	1.00		.17

Trust/Hostility Index: Get angry easily, think life is improving, trust people, important what others think

1968	1.00					.83	.10
1969	.49	1.00					.11
1970	.42	.52	1.00				.11
1971	.44	.50	.57	1.00			.13
1972	.44	.48	.53	.59	1.00		.14

Challenge/Affiliation Index (measures available only in 1972): Which of these is true for you, would you like to have more friends or would you like to be better at what you try? What kind of job would you want the most, a job where you had to think for yourself, or a job where the people you work with are a nice group?

1972							.07

Patterns and Determinants
of Paternal Child Care During
a Child's First Three Years of Life

Susan L. Averett
Lisa A. Gennetian
H. Elizabeth Peters

SUMMARY. This paper uses retrospective child care data from the NLSY79 to examine the patterns and determinants of paternal child care during a child's first three years of life. We focus on two-parent families with children whose mothers worked sometime between the child's birth date and the child's third birthday. We find that father care is a fairly stable form of care; the average number of months that father care is used during a year is similar to the duration of other forms of child care. In addition, we find that paternal care is often used in conjunction with other types of child care. We further find that different

Susan L. Averett is affiliated with the Department of Economics and Business, Lafayette College, Easton, PA 18042 (e-mail: averetts@lafvax.lafayette.edu).

Lisa A. Gennetian is affiliated with Manpower Demonstration Research Corporation, 16 East 34th Street, New York, NY 10016 (e-mail: lisa_gennetian@mdrc.org).

H. Elizabeth Peters is affiliated with Department of Policy Analysis and Management, Martha Van Rennselaer Hall, Cornell University, Ithaca, NY 14850 (e-mail: ep22@cornell.edu).

Address correspondence to: Susan L. Averett, Department of Economics and Business, Lafayette College, Easton, PA 18042.

Earlier versions of this paper were presented at the Conference on Father Involvement in Bethesda, MD, October 10-11, 1996 and at the annual meetings of the Population Association of America, March 27-29, 1997. The research was supported by NICHD grant #HD30944.

[Haworth co-indexing entry note]: "Patterns and Determinants of Paternal Child Care During a Child's First Three Years of Life." Averett, Susan L., Lisa A. Gennetian, and H. Elizabeth Peters. Co-published simultaneously in *Marriage & Family Review* (The Haworth Press, Inc.) Vol. 29, No. 2/3, 2000, pp. 115-136; and: *FATHERHOOD: Research, Interventions and Policies* (ed: H. Elizabeth Peters et al.) The Haworth Press, Inc., 2000, pp. 115-136. Single or multiple copies of this article are available for a fee from The Haworth Document Delivery Service [1-800-342-9678, 9:00 a.m. - 5:00 p.m. (EST). E-mail address: getinfo@haworthpressinc.com].

characteristics predict paternal child care according to the timing and extent of care. For those fathers who are the exclusive providers of child care during the first year of a child's life, the incidence of paternal child care is associated with race or ethnicity and a mother's identification with nontraditional gender roles. In contrast, for those fathers who provide some of total child care during the first three years of a child's life, the incidence of paternal child care is more highly associated with the flexibility of a mother's and father's work schedule. *[Article copies available for a fee from The Haworth Document Delivery Service: 1-800-342-9678. E-mail address: getinfo@haworthpressinc.com <Website: http://www. haworthpressinc.com>]*

KEYWORDS. Fatherhood, childcare

The dramatic increase in the labor force participation of mothers with young children has focused attention on the availability, cost, and quality of child care. Fathers are an important, but understudied, source of child care. In 1993, more than 1.5 million preschool children were cared for by their fathers while their mothers were at work (Casper, 1996). Understanding the patterns of this kind of father care can also contribute to the emerging literature on father involvement (Mosley & Thompson, 1995; Yogman, Kindlon, & Earls, 1995; Lamb, Pleck, & Levine, 1985).

Our paper uses retrospective information about child care from the 1979 cohort of the National Longitudinal Survey of Youth (NLSY79) (Center for Human Resource Research, 1997) to document the patterns and determinants of paternal care of young children while mothers are working. With these data we compare the use of father care to other types of non-maternal care, and we report results separately for care of infants versus toddlers. We also distinguish between families that use father care as the only form of child care versus those that use a mix of paternal and other types of child care arrangements during the hours the mother works.

We find that father care is a fairly stable form of care. The average number of months that father care is used during a year is similar to the duration of other forms of child care. Father care is often used in conjunction with other types of child care. We also find that both work schedules and personal characteristics such as race, ethnicity, and gender-role attitudes predict the use of father care. However, the importance of these different factors differs by the age of the child and by whether father care is the only type of care or is used with other types of care.

In the next section of the paper we briefly summarize the related literature and outline our conceptual framework. Additional sections describe the data used, sample criteria, and variable definitions; examine the patterns and determinants of father care; and present multivariate regression results of the determinants of paternal child care. A discussion and summary of results concludes the paper.

PREVIOUS LITERATURE AND CONCEPTUAL FRAMEWORK

We will briefly discuss two relevant strands of literature. The first relates to the choice of maternal versus non-maternal child care arrangements, in other words, the mother's choice about whether or not to work. The labor supply model in economics defines a person's wage rate as their opportunity cost of time. This literature generally finds that a mother's expected market wage is a significant (negative) predictor of whether she stays at home as the primary child care provider or, instead, enters the labor force and uses alternative types of child care (see Killingsworth & Heckman, 1986, for a survey of the literature on female labor supply). The literature shows that mothers are also more likely to work and use non-maternal forms of care when the cost of that care is lower (Averett, Peters, & Waldman, 1997; Blau & Robbins, 1988; Connelly, 1992 provide evidence on the responsiveness of female labor supply to child care costs).

A second literature has focused on how the price and quality of various non-maternal arrangements affect the choice of arrangement (Hofferth & Wissoker, 1992; Chaplin, Hofferth & Wissoker, 1996; Leibowitz, Waite, & Witsberger, 1988). These studies demonstrate that the age of the child and the price of the care are important determinants of which mode is chosen.

Both of these literatures can help us think about the factors that might predict father care while mothers are working. If we apply the insights about work versus child care obtained from the female labor supply model to fathers' child care choices, we would predict that a father with a higher wage would be less likely to provide child care, because he would forgo more money if he chose to work fewer hours in the labor market to provide care for his child. But we know from other evidence, however, that unlike women, most men work full-time, and men's labor supply is generally found to be unresponsive to changes in wages (see Pencavel, 1986). Thus we might expect that for fathers, the provision of child care would be less closely tied to hours worked and wages than for mothers.

A number of recent studies of father care focus on the father's availability for child care (Brayfield, 1995; Burchfield, 1996; Casper & O'Connell, 1996; 1998; O'Connell, 1993; Presser, 1988; 1989). These studies suggest that it is not the number of hours a father works, but rather the timing of his hours relative to the hours that are needed for child care. Most of these studies find that parental work schedules are an important determinant of father care. Fathers who work non-standard shifts are more likely to be available when child care is needed; mothers who work full-time are likely to need more hours of child care than fathers are able or willing to provide; and fathers are more likely to be available to provide care when mothers work non-standard shifts. Consistent with the labor supply model, some studies also find that fathers are more likely to provide child care when their opportunity costs are lower, for example, when they are unemployed (Casper & O'Connell, 1996; 1998).

The child care choice literature also provides insights into possible factors predicting father care. Specifically this literature suggests that father care would be more likely when the costs of alternative modes of child care are higher. Higher costs could be inferred for families living in areas that have higher child care worker wages or in states with stricter child care regulations. In addition, this literature highlights the importance of the child's age for child care choice, although plausible stories could be told to suggest either a positive or a negative correlation between the likelihood of father care and age of the child. For example, the demand for father care might fall as the child ages, because the cost of alternative modes of child care–especially center care–is lower for toddlers compared to infants. Also, parents may feel that the larger group settings of family day care and center care are more developmentally appropriate for toddlers. On the other hand, it is generally found that fathers prefer interacting with and caring for older children. Finally, the child care choice literature points out that the demand for different modes of child care depends on a family's preferences that may vary by factors such as race and ethnicity and attitudes about gender roles.

Our analysis of the determinants of father care provides evidence related to a number of the issues discussed above. Unlike most other studies, which focus on only one point in time, the nature of our data allows us to observe how child care choices change as children age. The data also allow us to use variation in child care costs and regulations for families living in different geographic areas to assess the importance of cost factors in childcare choice. Finally, the data contain information about work behavior of both the mother and father to evaluate the role of availability.

DATA DESCRIPTION

The NLSY79 is a nationally representative sample of approximately 12,000 individuals who were born between 1957 and 1964 (see Center for Human Resource Research, 1997, for more detail about the data). Black, Hispanic, and low-income White populations are oversampled in the data. Respondents were first interviewed in 1979 when they were between the ages of 14 and 22; they have been reinterviewed every year through 1994 and bi-annually after that date. The data include information about economic and demographic behavior and outcomes for the respondents and their families. What is particularly useful for our study is that the female respondents were asked retrospective questions about the types and duration of child care used for each of their children during the first three years of the child's life.

Sample Criteria

Our study focuses on the child care arrangements used for the children of the NLSY79 female respondents. We include children born between 1978 and 1987.[1] For a number of reasons including parental conflict, father detachment, and logistical problems, fathers in nonintact households are much less likely to provide childcare. To avoid confounding the use of father care with other variables that differ between intact and nonintact families, we limit our analysis to intact families. In addition, we eliminate children with disabilities since their child care needs may differ markedly from other children (Mott, 1991).

The final sample restriction relates to the mother's work behavior. Our purpose in this paper is to compare the patterns of care for children who were cared for by their fathers when their mothers worked with the patterns of care for children who had non-parental childcare when their mothers worked. Therefore we limit the data to children whose mothers worked at any time during the first three years of the child's life. At a minimum a mother may work only one week of the child's first three years of life. At a maximum a mother may work full time all three years of her child's life.

Given these sample restrictions and with the additional criteria that the values of the dependent and independent variables are not missing, our final sample is 1188 children of 863 mothers.

Mother's Employment

The data on mother's employment behavior comes from the NLSY79 work history file, which is a week-by-week accounting of a respondent's labor market activities. In each interview the respondent is asked about each job and employer during the year and the hours and weeks worked.[2] In our sample, 76.2% (74.3% unweighted) of mothers worked during their child's first year of life. In our sample, 76.2% (74.3% unweighted) of mothers worked during their child's first year of life. This number is much highter than the employment rates of mothers with infants reported in other national data sources for two reasons. First, we restrict our sample to mothers who worked sometime during the first three years of her child's life. Second, we measure mother's employment at any time during her child's first year of life rather than during the survey week. If we eliminate the first criterion, the employment rate for mothers with infants falls to 58.5% (57% unweighted), a number that is more comparable to national data sources. For example, in 1985, a time period which overlaps the time period of our data, 49.4% of mothers with infants were in the labor force (U.S. Bureau of the Census, 1997).

Child Care

The child care data come from retrospective reports by mothers about the types of regular care used for each child when the mother was working or engaged in some regular activity during the first three years of the child's life. The mothers were only asked for information about arrangements that lasted one month or more, and data were collected about the first three childcare arrangements in each year. The retrospective information about the type of care was asked in 1986, 1988, and 1992. Information about the duration of each arrangement was only asked in 1988 and 1992. The types of arrangements identified in the data include (a) the father; (b) relatives (grandparents, siblings, or other relatives); (c) non-relatives (both in the child's home and in another home); and (d) day care center, pre-school, or nursery school.

A substantial number of the women who were working in a particular year did not report any type of childcare in that year. For example, in year one, 40% of women did not report the childcare used, and in years two and three the figure is 30%. There are three primary reasons for this apparent inconsistency. First, the list of possible arrangements that the respondent was given did not specifically include "mother caring for the child while at work." Yet we know from other data that this type of care is used by about 15% of working mothers with infants and by 9 to 10% of working mothers with children ages 1 to 3 (Hofferth, Brayfield, Deich, & Holcomb, 1991).

This missing category accounts for some of the cases of working mothers who did not report any child care arrangement. A second explanation is that some of the employed women in our sample may have been on leave from a job with or without pay during the year. Klerman and Leibowitz (1994) estimate that this situation is common for employed mothers with very young infants, and by the time an infant is 12 months old, they find that 10% of employed mothers still report being on leave. The higher proportion of non-reports about child care in year one is consistent with the hypothesis that some of the employment reported by mothers of infants is, in fact, time on leave from a job, but not at work. Finally, it is possible that the missing child care information is due to recall error. The employment histories and child care histories were asked in different surveys or in different parts of the same survey. In general, employment histories were constructed from a one-year retrospective, while child care histories were collected about events that could have occurred up to eight years before. We describe in more detail below how our analysis accounts for the missing child care information.

In these data each child has up to three arrangements recorded for each of the child's first three years of life. We created mutually exclusive categories of child care arrangements in Year 1 and then separately for Years 2 and 3 combined to capture the various possibilities. For example, if a mother reported a child in father care and non-relative care during the first year, then this was coded as father and other childcare. If a mother is working and does not report child care, we code this as a separate category, since we cannot identify how the child is being cared for. The descriptive analyses that follow are conditional on information being reported about the child care arrangement, and the statistics we report use weights to account for initial sampling and attrition. In the multivariate analysis we include cases with and without information about childcare, and we control explicitly for the case where no childcare is reported. In addition, we use unweighted data for the multivariate analysis and include the variables that affect the weights (e.g., age, race, and sex) as regressors.

Explanatory Variables

Our analysis includes a number of variables that might be expected to affect the incidence of paternal childcare. First, we include variables that proxy for the cost of alternative modes of childcare and the demand for these other modes. Unfortunately, the NLSY79 data do not contain direct measures of the costs of the alternative child care arrangements in the relevant local market. Other data sources, however, have information about average childcare costs at the state level. We then merge this information into the NLSY79 data by matching with the respondent's state of residence. Given that personnel costs are a substantial fraction, about 65% of the total cost of providing center care (U.S. General Accounting Office, 1990), we use child care worker wages as a proxy for child care costs. From the Current Population Surveys (CPS), we calculate the average wages of child care workers by state and year.[3] In addition, we use a variable indicating whether the state required children in family day care to have a standard set of immunizations. This requirement would increase the cost of family day care for families who did not have access to affordable health care.[4]

At the family and individual level our proxies include the number of siblings under six years of age, father's nonearned income, and father's wage. Nearly all of the fathers in our sample are employed, so we used actual rather than estimated wages. We expect that an increase in the number of pre-school children in the family will increase the probability of father care, because other types of care–especially center care–do not provide price breaks for more than one child. An increase in nonearned income, which we define as total family income minus father's earned income, makes paid forms of child care more affordable. As discussed earlier, fathers with higher wages have higher opportunity costs of providing child care.

As proxies for family differences in preferences for childcare, we also include variables such as race, ethnicity, father's education, and the mother's identification with traditional gender roles. The gender role variable is constructed by summing the mother's responses (rated on a scale of 1 to 4, indicating strongly disagree to strongly agree) to a series of five questions about various dimensions of women's roles.[5]

Finally, we include variables such as the mother's and father's work schedules and the unemployment rate in the respondent's local labor market area to capture the father's potential availability to provide child care. Although we do not have a direct measure of the shift that the father works, we use data reported in Presser (1995) to calculate the percentage of persons in the father's occupation who work non-day shifts and match that back to the father's occupation. To measure aspects of the mother's work schedule we include variables indicating if she worked full time and if she worked a non-day shift. We measure full-time or part-time status of the mother as of the week she was surveyed.

The means of the variables used in our analysis are reported in Table 1.[6] These results show that families who used some father care were less likely to be Hispanic, Black, or live in the South, and the mothers were less likely to identify with traditional gender roles.

PATTERNS OF FATHER CARE

Much of the information that we know about national trends in childcare use over the past several decades comes from point-in-time data. For example, in the Survey on Income and Program Participation (SIPP), working mothers are asked about the type of child care arrangements used during the previous month. When more than one form of care is used at the same time, separate information is usually collected about the primary and secondary types of care. One advantage of the retrospective data from the NLSY79 is that it provides a history of the care used during the first three years of the child's life, rather than a snapshot of one point in time. One problem with the way that the child care history was collected in the NLSY79, however, is that information about the number of hours used is not available, and the timing of each childcare arrangement during the year is only available in 1992. Therefore, when more than one child care arrangement is used in a given year, we do not know whether the various arrangements are *sequential* (different arrangement used during different weeks in the year) or *concurrent* (analogous to the primary and secondary types of child care collected by

TABLE 1. Weighted Means for Children from Intact Households

| | Mother Employed Sometime Before Child's 3rd Birthday | |
	Father Provided Care	Father Did Not Provide Care
Mother Employed Year 1 (%)	88.2	74.0
Mother Employed Year 2 or 3 (%)	99.9	94.6
Mother's Identification with Traditional Gender Roles[a]	9.7 (2.2)	10.3 (2.8)
Father's Hourly Wage Rate (1990 $)[b]	13.1 (7.5)	13.3 (11.7)
Father's Education (years)[b]	12.5 (2.2)	12.6 (2.2)
Father's Age[b]	29.0 (4.1)	28.1 (4.2)
Family Non-Earned Income (1000s of 1990 $)[b]	1.8 (4.8)	2.2 (4.9)
Number of Siblings Less Than Age 6[b]	0.8 (0.8)	0.6 (0.6)
Hispanic (%)	6.0	8.6
Black (%)	5.5	8.0
Female (%)	47.0	47.3
Lives in the South (%)[b]	28.4	37.6
Child Care Worker Hourly Wage in State of Residence (1990 $)[c]	$4.74 (0.92)	$4.65 (0.91)
Family Day Care Requires Immunizations in State of Residence (%)[c]	67.0	54.9
Unemployment Rate in Local Labor Market (%)[c]	7.9	8.3
Sample Size	175	1013

Note. Standard deviations are in parentheses.
[a]Mother's Identification with Traditional Gender Roles is the sum of five scales ranging from 1 to 4, with higher scores reflecting identification with more traditional gender roles (see text for more details). [b]Variable is averaged over the first three survey years of the child's life. [c]Measured during year 1.

point-in-time data). We discuss the implications of this distinction in more detail below.

Figure 1 shows the frequency of childcare arrangements in our sample. Because some children are in more than one type of care, a simple accounting of the percent of children in each type of care would add up to more than 100%. To make our presentation more comparable to other data, in Figure 1 we count each child care arrangement as a separate observation. As has been reported by other studies (Hofferth et al., 1991), childcare arrangements differ substantially by the child's age. Younger children are more likely to be cared for by relatives, while older children are more likely to be in center-based day care. The percentage of children cared for by their fathers is similar across the child's age.

It is difficult to make a direct comparison between our numbers and data from other national surveys, because most published data report child care arrangements for all preschool children (e.g., ages zero to five), and, as just noted, child care arrangements differ substantially by the age of the child. Perhaps the closest match is to compare our data about child care arrangements in the third year with data from the SIPP about the type of arrangements used by the youngest child ages zero to five. The typical child in the latter sample might be expected to be about two and one-half years old. These data for married couple households with working mothers in 1988 (a year

FIGURE 1. Distribution of Child Care Arrangements by Year of Child's Life

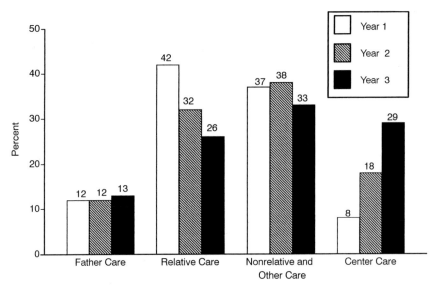

comparable to our sample) show that 19.7% of children have father care as the primary care arrangement while the mother works; 18.9% report care by relatives; 33.5% report care by non-relatives and other forms of care; and 27.9% are in center care (O'Connell, 1993:17). Because the NLSY79 does not include the category "mother cares for child at work," for comparability we also dropped those cases from the SIPP data and recalculated the frequencies. Comparing these numbers to the NLSY79 frequencies reported in Figure 1 for child care in the third year, we see that the frequency of center care and non-relative care is very similar in the two data sources. Relative care is higher in the NLSY79 data and the reports of father care are somewhat lower in our data. Despite the potential problems of recall error with retrospective data and the overcounting of secondary modes of child care; the data from the NLSY79 appear to be reasonably consistent with that reported in other data sets.[7]

In our data, about 25% (22% unweighted) of the children are in more than one arrangement during a given year, but only about 4% (3% unweighted) report three or more arrangements. For those children with more than one arrangement, we take the information about the number of months each arrangement was used to roughly classify the arrangements in a given year as concurrent or sequential. Specifically, we add up the total months reported by the respondent for all child care arrangements in a given year and compare that to the total number of months the she worked during the year. If the total reported for all children care arrangements is greater than the number of months that the mother worked in that year, we classify the arrangements as concurrent. For example, a mother who worked for nine months may report that her child was in center care for six months and that the grandmother cared for the child for nine months. It follows that there must have been some months during the year when both types of care were used simultaneously.[8]

In 1992 respondents were asked about the month and year in which the various child care arrangements began and ended. Thus for a small subsample, we can measure the prevalence of concurrent versus sequential arrangement more directly. A comparison of this 1992 data with the classifications obtained from our indirect method shows that our algorithm somewhat overstates the amount of sequential care. Figure 2 uses the subsample of data for which duration information is available to show the different patterns of child care use for various types of child care. With the exception of the first year, there is not much variation across childcare modes in the average number of months the arrangement was used in a given year (the average for each mode is about 9 months). We infer from these data that all modes of childcare are typically used for a long duration, and that no mode (including father care) is used primarily on a short-term basis just to fill in during a disruption in a more preferred mode of care.

FIGURE 2. Duration of Child Care by Type of Arrangement and Year of Child's Life

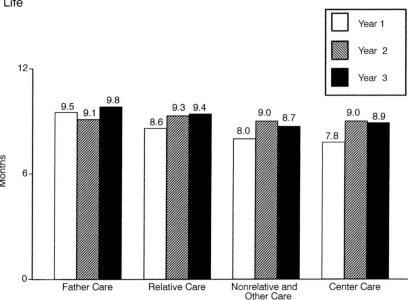

Although we do not know the number of hours per week that each arrangement is used, our classification of concurrent, sequential, or only one arrangement used during a year can help us interpret the duration data. Developmental psychologists have emphasized the importance of stability of care. Because sequential implies switching from one childcare provider to another, this classification is likely to represent a situation that is less stable.

Figure 3 shows that "center care" is the most stable type of arrangement. Compared to other modes of child care, "center care" is more likely to be the only care used in a year. "Father care" is more difficult to categorize with respect to stability. For example, compared to other modes of child care, "father care" is less likely to be the only type of care used in a year (45% in Year 1 compared to 68-83% for other modes), implying less stability. On the other hand, "father care" is more likely than other modes of care to be classified as concurrent (i.e., used over many months as a part-day arrangement in conjunction with other types of care), implying more stability. Overall, however, the higher probability of sequential care shown in Figure 3 (e.g., in Year 3, 34% of father care is sequential compared to 18-30% for other modes) implies that father care is, on net, somewhat less stable than other forms of care.

One consideration in whether or not father care is used is the timing of the

FIGURE 3. Frequency of Child Care Arrangements by Type of Arrangement

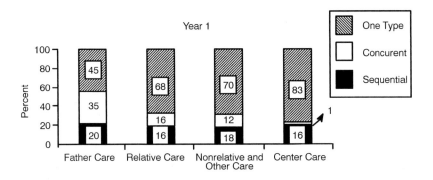

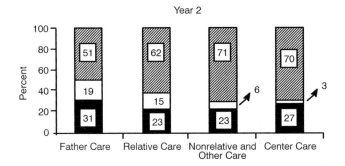

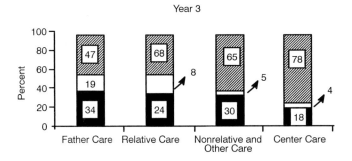

child care hours that are necessary and the quantity of those hours. Table 2 details the parents' work patterns and child care choices for each of the three years. Consistent with the results from other studies (Brayfield, 1995; Burch-field, 1996; Casper & O'Connell, 1996; O'Connell, 1993; Presser, 1988; 1989), we find that the mother's work schedule is related to the probability of father care. Table 2 shows that full-time working mothers, who need longer

TABLE 2. Selected Weighted Means by Mother's Employment Status for Children from Intact Households

	Mother Employed in Year 1		Mother Employed in Year 2		Mother Employed in Year 3	
	Father Provided Care	Father Did Not Provide Care	Father Provided Care	Father Did Not Provide Care	Father Provided Care	Father Did Not Provide Care
Number of Months Mother Employed During the Year	9.3 (2.6)	8.7 (3.2)	9.9 (3.0)	9.7 (3.2)	9.8 (3.2)	9.8 (3.2)
Mother Worked Full-Time (%)[a]	40.6	65.3	52.4	65.3	56.3	66.5
Mother Worked Day-Shift (%)[a,b]	49.6	76.6	47.7	73.8	70.9	77.5
Father Employed During the Year (%)	97.1	94.6	94.7	94.6	91.3	93.9
Father's Hourly Wage (1990 $)[a]	14.2 (13.9)	12.6 (11.1)	13.1 (13.1)	13.5 (10.2)	13.6 (13.3)	13.5 (11.4)
Percentage Who Work Non-day Shift in Father's Occupation	19.2 (12.0)	17.1 (12.8)	19.5 (15.1)	16.4 (11.5)	18.2 (12.9)	17.4 (12.5)
Sample Size	76	455	86	572	97	587

Note. Standard deviations are in parentheses.

[a]Measured at the time of the interview date during year 1, year 2 and year 3 of the child's life.
[b]Data regarding mother's day shift work status was not available between 1986 and 1989.

hours of care, are less likely to use father care. In contrast, mothers who work a non-day shift are more likely to use father care. Because we measured father employment annually, but the part-time/full-time distinction for mothers was measured as of the survey interview date, we cannot precisely compare work schedules of parents.

A father's schedule is also important in determining whether or not he provides child care.[9] We find that fathers in occupations in which a greater percentage of persons work a non-day shift are more likely to provide child care. Presser (1995) shows that while only 5% of accountants work a non-day shift, more than 60% of police work a non-day shift.

Casper and O'Connell (1986; 1998) suggest that a father may also be more likely to provide care if he is unemployed. Our data, on the other hand, show that employment rates for fathers who provide care are no lower than employment rates for fathers who do not provide care. Unfortunately the NLSY79 data do not provide any information about the timing of the various childcare arrangements during the year or any detail about which weeks the father may have worked. Thus there is no way to know for certain if a father who was employed at some time during the year provided child care only during weeks in which he was unemployed.

THE DETERMINANTS OF PATERNAL CHILD CARE

Table 3 reports the results from our multinomial logit analysis of the determinants of paternal care. We estimate two models to capture the determinants of "Father Care" separately for the first year of a child's life versus the second or third year of a child's life. In year 1, our dependent variable, mode of child care, depicts the mutually exclusive categories "Only Father Care," "Father Care With Other Care," and the reference category, any other combination of child care. Of the 883 children with working mothers during their first year of life, 4.2% are exclusively cared for by their fathers and 4.4% are cared for by their fathers and by some other type of child care arrangement. Because there are no children who are exclusively cared for by their fathers in both years 2 and 3, our second model estimates only the determinants of "Father Care With Other Care" with the same reference category as year 1. In years 2 or 3, 12.5% of the 1132 children with working mothers experienced some paternal childcare. Note that in both models the dependent variable, mode of child care, also includes the category "Child Care Not Reported." Because the focus of this paper is on the determinants of father care, we do not show these results in Table 3.

The coefficients reported in Table 3 can be interpreted as the effect of a one-unit change in the independent variable on the log odds of "Only Father Care" (or "Father Care With Other Care") relative to the reference category, other combinations of child care. In Year 1, our results show that "Only Father Care" is significantly more likely for families living in states with higher costs of child care (i.e., higher child care worker wages and where immunization is required for family day care). "Only Father Care" is significantly less likely for Hispanics, and significantly less likely when mothers identify with traditional gender roles. Column 2 shows that a different set of factors is significant in predicting the use of father care with other care. While the cost of childcare is still important in increasing the use of some father care, traditional gender role identification is no longer significant, and the work schedule variables, in particular the father's work schedule, become

TABLE 3. Multinomial Logit Estimation of the Probability of Father Care Conditional on the Mother Being Employed

		Year 1	Year 2 and/or 3
	Only Father Care	Father Care with Other Care	Father Care with Other Care[a]
Father's Education[b]	0.01 (0.13)	0.14† (1.73)	−0.09† (1.93)
Father's Hourly Wage (1990 dollars)[b,c]	−0.04 (1.24)	0.01 (0.77)	−0.003 (0.24)
Proportion Who Work Non-Day Shift in Father's Occupation[b,c,d,]	0.01 (0.50)	0.03† (1.96)	0.02* (2.17)
Mother Worked Full-Time[c]	−0.49 (1.26)	−0.16 (0.42)	−0.28 (1.33)
Mother Worked Day-Shift[c]	−0.18 (0.44)	−0.65 (1.58)	−0.67* (2.53)
Family Nonearned Income (in 1,000s of 1990 $)[b,c,e]	−0.08 (1.04)	−0.03 (0.55)	−0.81 (0.31)
Number of Siblings Under 6[b]	−0.04 (0.12)	−0.36 (1.11)	−0.05 (0.33)
Mother's Identification with Traditional Gender Roles[f]	−0.16* (2.01)	−0.07 (0.95)	−0.01 (0.36)
Child Care Worker Hourly Wage Rate in State of Residence (1990 $)[b]	0.45† (1.88)	0.46* (2.01)	0.08 (0.67)
Family Day Care Requires Immunizations in State of Residence[b]	1.55* (3.27)	0.89* (2.09)	0.40† (1.74)
Female Child	−0.16 (0.44)	0.72† (1.96)	−0.17 (0.87)
Unemployment Rate in Local Labor Market[b,c]	0.03* (2.50)	−0.004 (0.62)	−0.22 (0.48)
Unemployment Rate * Hispanic	0.04* (2.93)	−0.02 (0.78)	0.02* (2.57)
Unemployment Rate * Black	0.01 (0.37)	−0.06† (1.90)	0.003 (0.27)
Hispanic	2.69* (2.32)	0.61 (0.41)	−1.76* (2.74)
Black	−0.14 (0.10)	3.47† (1.90)	−0.39 (0.52)
Lives in South[b,c]	−0.57 (1.22)	−0.96* (1.97)	−0.43† (1.75)

	Year 1		Year 2 and/or 3
	Only Father Care	Father Care with Other Care	Father Care with Other Care[a]
% Urban in County of Residence	−0.02*	−0.02†	0.0005
	(2.03)	(1.93)	(0.11)
% of Population with Income below Poverty in County of Residence	−0.11*	−0.06	−0.03
	(2.10)	(1.12)	(1.36)
Constant	0.67	−4.47*	0.33
	(0.30)	(2.12)	(0.28)

Note. Absolute value of t-statistics are in parentheses. All models also include but do not report variables to control for missing values on *Mother Worked Day-Shift* and *Mother's Identification with Traditional Gender Roles.* The multinomial logit models in this table also estimated the determinants of the additional dependent variable category *Child Care Not Reported Year 1* and *Child Care Not Reported Year 2/3.* However, we do not report those results in this table.

[a]This category includes any report of father care during either the second or third year. Note that there are no observations with only father care during both the second and third year. [b]Missing observations were replaced with data from the closest survey possible.[c] For the Year 2 and/or 3 column, variable is averaged over the second and third survey year of the child's life. [d]Percentage Who Work a Non-Day Shift in Father's Occupation is relevant for the civilian labor force only. Approximately 4.5% of the fathers in our sample worked in the military sometime during the first three survey years of the child's life. Due to severe collinearity problems, we cannot control separately for this occupation. Instead, for all fathers in the military we code the non-day shift variable as zero. [e] Family nonearned income is family income minus father's and mother's earnings. [f]Mother's Identification with Traditional Gender Roles is the sum of five scales ranging from 1 to 4, with higher scores reflecting identification with more traditional gender roles (see the text for more details).

† $p < 0.10$. * $p < 0.05$.

significant. In addition, we find that families living in the South are less likely to use some father care. Similarly, in year 2-3 (column 3), mixing father care with other child care is significantly associated with parents' work schedules (both mothers' and fathers'), high child care costs, and living in the South.

Together the results in Table 3 suggest that the determinants of father care vary with the extent of care provided (father care only versus father care with other care) and with the age of the child. Children with working mothers who identify more closely with traditional gender roles are less likely to be cared for exclusively by their fathers during their first year of life, but this effect is not significant if the child is in a mix of father care and other care arrangements. In contrast, parental work schedules do not determine the probability of a child being exclusively cared for by the father during the mother's work hours in the first year of life, but work schedules are important in predicting the use of father care with other care.

Finally, these results highlight how the incidence of father care differs by race and ethnicity and, in particular, how the effect of macroeconomic conditions on the incidence of father care differs by race. For example, in both columns 1 and 3 we see that Hispanics generally are less likely to provide father care, but those living in areas with high unemployment rates are *more* likely to provide care. In contrast, in the first year both whites and Blacks living in high unemployment areas are less likely to provide father care. One possible explanation for the differences in the effect of macro conditions on the probability of father care is that higher unemployment rates may cause some fathers to become unemployed, while other fathers may have to work longer hours to keep from becoming unemployed. If high unemployment rates differentially affect the probability of unemployment across race and ethnic groups, the effect of higher unemployment rates on the probability of father care will differ by race and ethnicity. An alternative explanation relates to the experience of unemployment across race and ethnic groups and the importance of the economic provider role to a man's identity as a father. For groups such as African Americans who experience high rates of long term unemployment, being unemployed can undermine the economic provider role and could lead to a decrease in father involvement and father care. Others who experience unemployment more as a short-term phenomenon may be able to use the experience to increase the time they can spend with their children. Our data are not detailed enough to be able to identify which processes have produced the patterns we report. Our findings pose questions for future research.

CONCLUSION

The dramatic increase in the labor force participation of mothers with young children has focused attention on the availability, cost, and quality of child care, and fathers are one source of child care. In addition, there is an emerging interest in the consequences for children of increased involvement by their fathers. Our paper contributes to what we know about paternal child care as one aspect of father involvement by examining the patterns and determinants of paternal child care during the mother's work hours in the child's first three years of life.

We find that father care is often used with other forms of child care and that the number of months father care is used in a given year is similar to the use of other types of childcare. Our results highlight the role of race and ethnicity. We also confirm the findings in previous literature about the relationship between parental work schedules and paternal childcare. However, we find that the determinants of father care vary with the extent of care provided and with the age of the child. For those fathers who are the exclusive providers of child care during the first year of a child's life, paternal childcare is less likely when mothers identify with traditional gender roles. In contrast, for those fathers who provide some of total child care during the first three years of a child's life, the incidence of paternal child care is more highly associated with the flexibility of a mother's and father's work schedule. Our results suggest that if we want to increase this kind of father involvement, supporting flexible work schedules such as alternative work shifts or flex-time is one method that will help achieve this goal.

NOTES

1. Although the mothers originally come from a nationally representative sample, the children are not representative of the group of all children who will ever be born to these women, because many of the women have not yet completed their childbearing. Specifically, children who are born to older mothers will be underrepresented in this sample. In 1992 the women in the sample were between the ages of 27 and 34. The Center for Human Resource Research (1995, p. 2) estimates that about 70% of the children who will ever be born to these women have already been born by the 1992 survey.

2. Note that a woman is counted as employed even if she was not at work during a particular week, as long as she was on vacation, sick leave, unpaid leave of less than one month, or maternity leave of less than 90 days (Center for Human Resource Research, 1993, p. 62). Thus, as Klerman and Leibowitz (1994) note, the number of weeks employed is likely to overstate the actual duration of work, especially during the first year of the child's life, when some mothers may take paid or unpaid maternity leave.

3. The occupational categories used to identify child care workers in the CPS include (a) prekindergarten and kindergarten teacher (1978-82: occupation code 143; 1983-91: occupation code 155); (b) child care workers except private household (1978-82: occupation code 942; 1983-91: occupation code 468); and (c) child care workers in private households (1978-82: occupation code 980; 1983-91: occupation code 406). To circumvent the problem of small sample sizes in some states, we calculate a three-year moving average.

4. All states require children in center care to be immunized, but only about 60% of our sample lived in states that required immunization for children in family day care. Note that other child care regulations such as group size, teacher education, and adult-child ratios would also affect average child care costs. However, these types of regulations are also closely associated with child care quality. We chose not to include these regulations in our analysis of the determinants of father care, so as to avoid confounding cost and quality issues. We obtained the data on immunization regulations from a number of different data sources including Hayes, Palmer and Zaslow (1990) and the RAND Corporation, Santa Monica, CA.

5. Our scale includes responses about agreement with the following statements: (a) "A woman's place is in the home, not in the office or shop." (b) "A wife who carries out her full family responsibilities doesn't have time for outside employment." (c) "The employment of wives leads to more juvenile delinquency." (d) "It is much better for everyone concerned if the man is the achiever outside the home and the woman takes care of the family." (e) "Women are much happier if they stay

at home and take care of their children." The summed index ranges from 1 to 20, with higher scores reflecting more traditional gender role attitudes. Using a similar aggregation method, the Center for Human Resource Research (1993, p. 55-56) reports inter-item correlations ranging from .40 to .56 and a reliability coefficient of .74. The respondents were asked this same set of questions in three different interviews: 1979, 1982, and 1987. To reduce the possibility of reverse causation or ex-post rationalization (i.e., reported sex role attitudes may be affected by actual employment experiences and family conditions rather than the reverse), we used the responses from the survey that was closest, but prior to the birth of the child.

6. Throughout the paper, when we report frequencies or means, we use weighted data, so that the reader can more easily compare to other sources. For each child we use the weight calculated in the survey from which the assessment is taken. The weights adjust for child attrition and for the oversampling of blacks, Hispanics, and economically disadvantaged whites. Our regressions all use unweighted data, and the age, race, and ethnicity variables upon which the weights are based are included as regressors.

7. Another kind of consistency check is to compare the retrospective data from a given mother with point-in-time data reported by the same mother. Questions about child care use during the past four weeks were asked in the NLSY79 in several different interview years. Only the information collected in 1986 and 1988 can be linked to a specific child, and a comparison can only be made for children who were less than three years old in those two survey years. Somewhat less than 200 matched observations are available for each of the three ages. The results from the matched comparison are similar to what we found when comparing our frequencies to another data source: although there is a great deal of agreement between the two sources of data, there is somewhat less correspondence when the point-in-time data report using father care or relative care. Mott (1991) and Baydar and Brooks-Gunn (1991) also report that father care is underreported in the NLSY79. In addition, we find that a large proportion of working mothers who did not report using any care in the retrospective data reported that they cared for their child while at work in the point-in-time data. These mothers were also disproportionately likely to report father and other relative care in the point-in-time data.

8. In 1992, respondents were asked about the month and year in which the various child care arrangements began and ended. Thus for a small subsample, we can measure the prevalence of concurrent versus sequential arrangement more directly. A comparison of this 1992 data with the classifications obtained from our indirect method shows that our algorithm somewhat overstates the amount of sequential care.

9. Although it is possible that both the mother's and father's work schedules may be endogenous, incorporating this joint decision making is beyond the scope of this study. In addition, Presser (1989) provides evidence that child care was rarely the primary reason given by fathers for working a non-day shift.

REFERENCES

Averett, S., Peters, E., & Waldman, D. (1997). Tax Credits, Labor Supply, and Child Care. *The Review of Economics and Statistics, 79*, 125-135.

Baker, P., & Mott, F. (1989). *NLSY handbook 1989: A Guide and Resource Document for the National Longitudinal Survey of Youth 1986 Child Data*. Columbus, OH: Center for Human Resource Research, Ohio State University.

Blau, D. M., & Robins, P. K. (1988). Child Care Costs and Family Labor Supply. *The Review of Economics and Statistics, 70*, 374-381.

Blau, D. M., & Robins, P. K. (1989). Fertility and Employment, and Child Care Costs. *Demography, 26*, 87-299.

Brayfield, A. (1995). Juggling Jobs and Kids: The Impact of Employment Schedules on Fathers' Caring for Children. *Journal of Marriage and the Family, 57*, 321-332.

Burchfield, D. C. (1996). Determinants of Fathers as Primary Child Care Providers in Working Families. 42nd Annual Conference of the American Council on Consumer Interests, Nashville, Tennessee.

Casper, L. M. (1996). *Who's Minding Our Preschoolers?* Washington, DC: U.S. Bureau of the Census.

Casper, L. M., & O'Connell, M. (1996). *Couple Characteristics and Fathers as Child Care Providers.* Washington, DC: U.S. Bureau of the Census.

Casper, L.M., & O'Connell, M. (1998). Work, Income, the Economy, and Married Fathers as Child-Care Providers. *Demography, 35*, 2, 243-50.

Center for Human Resource Research. (1993). *The NLSY Child Handbook.* Columbus: Ohio State University.

Center for Human Resource Research. (1997). *NLSY79 Users' Guide: A Guide to the 1979-1996 National Longitudinal Survey of Youth Data.* Columbus, OH: Ohio State University.

Chaplin, D., Hofferth, S. & Wissoker, D. (1996). Price, quality and income in child care choice: A revision. *The Journal of Human Resources, 31*, 703-706.

Connelly, R. (1992). The effect of child care costs on married women's labor force participation. *Review of Economic and Statistics, 74*, 83-90.

Hofferth, S. L., Brayfield, A., Deich, S., & Holcomb, P. (1991). *National Child Care Survey, 1990.* Washington DC: The Urban Institute Press.

Hofferth, S. L., & Wissoker, A. (1992). Price, Quality and Income in Child Care Choice. *Journal of Human Resources, 27*, 70-111.

Killingsworth, M. R., & Heckman, J. J. (1986). Female Labor Supply: A Survey. In O. C. Ashenfelter & R. L. (Eds.), *Handbook of Labor Economics* (pp. 103-204). Amsterdam: Elsevier Science Publishers.

Klerman, J.A., & Leibowitz, A. (1994). The Work-Employment Distinction Among New Mothers. *Journal of Human Resources, 29*, 277-303.

Lamb, M. E., Pleck, J. H., & Levine, J. A. (1985). The Role of the Father in Child Development: The Effects of Increased Paternal Involvement. In B. Lahey & E. E,. Kazdin (Eds.), *Advances in clinical child psychology*, Vol. 8. (pp. 229-266) New York: Plenum.

Leibowitz, A., Waite, L. & Witsberger, C. (1988). Child Care For Preschoolers: Differences by Child's Age. *Demography, 25*, 205-20.

Mosley, J. & Thompson, E. (1995). Fathering Behavior and Child Outcomes: The Role of Race and Poverty. In M. William (Ed.), *Fatherhood: Contemporary Theory, Research, and Social Policy.* (pp. 148-165). Thousand Oaks, CA: Sage Publications.

Mott, F. L. (1991). Developmental Effects of Infant Care: The Mediating Role of Gender and Health. *Journal of Social Issues, 47*, 139-159.

O'Connell, M. (1993). Where's Papa? Fathers' Role in Child Care. *Population Trends and Public Policy.* Washington, DC: U.S. Bureau of the Census.

Pencavel, J. (1986). Labor Supply of Men: A Survey. In O. C. Ashenfelter & R. Layard. (Eds.), *Handbook of Labor Economics* (pp. 3-102). Amsterdam: Elsevier Science Publishers.

Presser, H. (1988). Shift Work and Child Care Among Young Dual-Earner American Parents. *The Journal of Marriage and the Family, 50,* 133-48.

Presser, H. (1989). Can We Make Time for Children? The Economy, Work Schedules, and Child Care. *Demography, 26,* 523-43.

Presser, H. (1995). Job, Family, and Gender: Determinants of Nonstandard Work Schedules Among Employed Americans. *Demography, 32,* 577-598.

U.S. Bureau of the Census. (1997). *Statistical Abstract of the United States: 1997.* (117th ed.). Washington, DC.

U.S. General Accounting Office. (1990). Early Childhood Education: What Are the Costs of High-Quality Programs? (GAO/HRD 90-43BR). Washington, DC: Human Resource Division.

Yogman, M. W., Kindlon, D., & Earls, F. (1995). Father Involvement and Cognitive/ Behavioral Outcomes of Preterm Infants. *Journal of the American Academy of Child and Adolescent Psychiatry, 34,* 58-66.

III. SINGLE FATHERS AND FATHERS WITH NONMARITAL CHILDREN

Father Involvement with Their Nonmarital Children: Patterns, Determinants, and Effects on Their Earnings

Robert Lerman
Elaine Sorensen

Robert Lerman is Professor of Economics, American University, and Director, Human Resources Policy Center, Urban Institute.

Elaine Sorensen is Principal Research Associate at Urban Institute.

The authors are grateful for the support for this research from the Ford Foundation. The authors thank Nikki Blasberg for excellent research assistance and Steve Bell for thoughtful comments. The views expressed in this paper are those of the authors and do not necessarily reflect those of the Urban Institute or its funders.

The authors presented previous versions of this paper at the Population Association of America Meetings in March 1997 and at the NICHD Conference on Father Involvement, sponsored by the NICHD Family and Child Well-Being Network, held in October 1996.

[Haworth co-indexing entry note]: "Father Involvement with Their Nonmarital Children: Patterns, Determinants, and Effects on Their Earnings." Lerman, Robert, and Elaine Sorensen. Co-published simultaneously in *Marriage & Family Review* (The Haworth Press, Inc.) Vol. 29, No. 2/3, 2000, pp. 137-158; and: *FATHERHOOD: Research, Interventions and Policies* (ed: H. Elizabeth Peters et al.) The Haworth Press, Inc., 2000, pp. 137-158. Single or multiple copies of this article are available for a fee from The Haworth Document Delivery Service [1-800-342-9678, 9:00 a.m. - 5:00 p.m. (EST). E-mail address: getinfo@haworthpressinc.com].

137

SUMMARY. The expanding consensus about the advantages of two-parent families, together with the rising number of children growing up without the presence of both parents, has stimulated policy-makers to look for ways of increasing fathers' involvement. This paper examines two sets of questions relevant to these policy initiatives. The first concerns the patterns of involvement between fathers and children born outside of marriage. The paper defines father involvement as a continuum ranging from no visitation, to frequent visitation, to co-residence with the child, and to co-residence along with marrying the mother. We examine this involvement in specific years and over time. One key finding is that most fathers of nonmarital children in their late twenties and early thirties are highly involved with at least one of their nonmarital children. In addition, we find that cohabiting relationships and frequent visitation are often unstable, sometimes changing toward lower involvement, while in other cases changing toward higher degrees of involvement. A second question we address in this paper is whether father involvement leads to increased earnings. We find a positive relationship between increased involvement of fathers and their subsequent hours of work and earnings. *[Article copies available for a fee from The Haworth Document Delivery Service: 1-800-342-9678. E-mail address: getinfo@ haworthpressinc.com <Website: http://www.haworthpressinc.com>]*

KEYWORDS. Father involvement, nonmarital children, father's earnings

Concern over the absence of fathers in the lives of their children is now widespread among the public and leaders from across the political spectrum. Today, nonmarital births constitute about one of every three births and over four in ten children live away from at least one natural parent. Certainly, the dramatic growth in the proportion of American children born outside marriage and not living with their natural father has contributed to child poverty and welfare dependency (Lerman, 1996). Yet, inadequate incomes of single-parent families and the nonpayment of child support are only parts of the problem. Research shows that even after controlling for the lower incomes of single parent families, children growing up without a father present will perform more poorly in school, commit more crimes, use more drugs, have more teenage pregnancies, and create other social problems (McLanahan & Sandefur, 1994).

New perceptions about the importance of having fathers present and contributing more financially have stimulated the development of demonstration projects. The goal of these programs is to assist noncustodial fathers in (1) obtaining jobs, (2) providing counseling, and peer support so they can earn additional income, (3) increasing their child support payments, and (4) taking more of an interest in their children (Achatz & MacAllum, 1994; Bloom & Sherwood 1994). Community-based programs, such as that developed by Charles Ballard, try to break the cycle of fatherlessness in which boys without fathers subsequently become absent fathers. These programs persuade mothers to involve the fathers in raising their children, and by convincing unwed fathers that they can and should play a vital role in the lives of their children. One hope underlying these initiatives is that, when children develop a good relationship with their fathers, their well-being will increase and help them become more constructive adults. Yet researchers (Furstenberg & Harris, 1993; King, 1994) have found only mixed empirical evidence that closer father involvement will improve child outcomes.

Father involvement can also affect fathers themselves. Ballard contends that once fathers become closely involved with their children, their lives in general begin to turn around. They become more energetic in finding and holding a job, and they engage in less risky behavior. Other evidence suggests that marriage itself may generate an earnings premium over otherwise similar workers (Korenman & Neumark, 1991). Despite the *potential* impact of increased father involvement on the earnings of unwed fathers, we know little about whether an actual relationship exists or its pattern over time. Sorting out the actual linkages is difficult because causation runs in both directions. Fathers who happen to find a good job may suddenly have the resources and confidence to visit their children more frequently and provide more child support. Alternatively, the decision to take on a more serious parenting role may induce fathers to become more energetic in seeking employment.

These issues have direct policy consequences. Raising the earnings of fathers and their financial support for their children, as well as improving father-child relationships, are all positive outcomes. The question is: Should the interventions initially focus on jobs or on promoting a more active and constructive fathering role?

This paper investigates the relationship between earnings and the involvement of one group of fathers–those with at least one child born outside marriage. Before examining the earnings-fatherhood relationship, we analyze in detail the patterns and dynamics of childbearing, visitation, and residence with children. We consider whether various types of father visitation and residence patterns are stable, erode, or strengthen over time. The complexity and variability of patterns offer a good opportunity to identify the nature of the linkages between father involvement and earnings. Next we summarize the few existing relevant studies. In Section 3 we provide a description of the data used in the study; Section 4 analyzes the dynamics of father involvement based on visitation and residence patterns. Finally, in Section 5, we present simple measures of the relationship between father involvement and earnings, followed by summary of our findings and a discussion of their implications.

THE LITERATURE

Much of our understanding of nonresident fathers' involvement with their children who are born out of wedlock has been provided by ethnographic studies, analyses of small samples, or data from programs to assist low-income, noncustodial fathers. As far as the authors are aware, the only national survey large enough to examine this population is the National Longitudinal Survey of Youth, 1979 (NLSY79).

The basic theme of this research is that nonresident fathers of children born out of wedlock are more involved with their children than one might have thought. Using the NLSY79, Lerman (1993) found that nearly half of young unwed fathers in 1988 said they visited their youngest child at least once a week. Although noncustodial fathers tend to report more visitation than do custodial mothers, research by Mott (1990) suggests that fathers' reports are only somewhat higher than that reported by custodial mothers. For example, Mott found that young mothers of children born out of wedlock reported that nearly two out of five noncustodial fathers visited at least once per week. Seltzer (1991), who examines nonmarital mothers of all ages, finds that these mothers report that 30% of nonmarital fathers visited their children at least once a week during the past 12 months.

This research, however, has tended to define father involvement narrowly to include only visitation and has tended to overlook the fact that men who begin as nonresident fathers could end up living with or marrying the mother of their nonmarital child. Later in this study, we show that, once father involvement is more broadly defined to include marriage and cohabitation, an even larger percent of initially nonresident fathers of nonmarital children remain involved with their children.

A few studies have attempted to identify correlates of nonmarital fathers' involvement. Most studies, for example, find that nonmarital fathers' involvement declines as children age (Lerman, 1993; Seltzer, 1991). Physical distance between the father and child is also negatively related to fathers' involvement (Lerman, 1993; Seltzer, 1991). Other studies have shown that poor relations with the mother and a lack of authority over childrearing decisions are negatively related with fathers' involvement (Furstenberg, 1995; Seltzer, 1991).

The exact relationship between father involvement and these correlates is difficult to ascertain because, in most cases, causality can proceed in both directions. Very few studies have attempted to disentangle these causal relationships (for an exception, see Seltzer, 1991). Moreover, none of these causal models have dealt with nonmarital fathers, but, instead, have focused on divorced or separated fathers who were previously married to the child's mother.

One relationship that has received surprisingly little research attention is the causal linkage between fathers' involvement and their employment. Several ethnographic and small-scale studies have argued that a lack of employment leads to reduced father involvement (Achatz & MacAullum, 1994; Anderson, 1993; Danziger & Radin, 1990; Furstenberg, 1995). They find that mothers are less inclined to allow fathers access to their children when they are out of work, and fathers are less likely to seek access because they do not feel that they are living up to their own expectations of a "good father." Many practitioners propose, on the other hand, that fathers' involvement can influence employment behavior, with the argument being that, once fathers establish a relationship with their children, they will find work (Levine & Pitt, 1995). Thus, these findings suggest that causality between fathers' involvement and their employment patterns can proceed in either direction.

DATA DEVELOPMENT

The data for this analysis come from the National Longitudinal Survey of Youth, 1979, a nationally representative sample of men and women who were first interviewed in 1979, when they were between the ages of 14 and 22. Respondents were re-interviewed annually between 1979-1994. The NLSY79 does not ask men directly whether they have had children out of wedlock. This information, however, can be ascertained through the marital and birth history variables which the NLSY79 creates for each year starting in 1982. To identify whether births were marital or nonmarital, we compared the dates of each child's birth with the man's marital history. We assumed that any birth that occurs during a marriage is a product of that marriage.

The NLSY79 also asks men detailed questions about the living arrangements of their children as well as the contact they have with children who do not live with them. The data include detailed information about the residence of each child in every year. In addition, in 1984, 1985, 1986, 1988, 1990, and 1992, the NLSY asked several questions about children living outside of the home, including how far away each child lives, how often the father visits each child, and the duration of these visits. For each child living in the household, the father is also asked whether the child's mother lives in the household.

We utilized this information and the marital status variables for the corresponding years to construct a variable detailing a father's contact with each of his nonmarital birth children. For each nonmarital child who appears in any of these survey years (and has not died or been adopted by that time), we note whether the child lives with the father, and if so, if that child's mother also lives in the household. If this is the case, we then utilize the marital status variable to determine whether he is currently married to the mother or not (we assume that, if the child and the child's mother are in the household and the father is married, that he is married to the child's mother). If the nonmarital child does not live in the household, we use the corresponding visitation information to determine the amount of contact the father had with the child in that year.

This information is used to construct our father involvement scale. Fathers who have no contact with their children in the past 12 months are considered the least involved. Involvement increases with the number of times a father visits his children. Visitation is divided into those who visited their children less than once per month in the past year, those who visited 1 to 3 times a month in the past year, and those who visited at least weekly in the past year. Fathers who live with their children are considered to be the most involved with their children. We identify three living arrangements for these fathers: (a) those who live with their nonmarital children and the biological mother is not present; (b) those who live with their nonmarital children and the biological mother, but the parents have never married; and (c) those who are living with their nonmarital children and the biological mother, and the parents subsequently got married.

This contact information is used to track a father's involvement with his first nonmarital child over time. We use the year that the first nonmarital child first appears in the survey (either 1984, 1986, 1988, 1990, or 1992) as the initial year of observation for this variable. Then we code the contact information for this same child 2 years later, 4 years later, 6 years later, and 8 years later.

Using the same contact scale, we also create a variable indicating a father's maximum involvement with any of his nonmarital children in a given year. This variable is created by coding the involvement of a father with each of his nonmarital children in each of the relevant years. The maximum is then simply the closest contact with any such child in a particular survey year.

Errors due to misreporting could affect the results in two major ways. First, some young men who have fathered children outside marriage may report they had no children. Second, noncustodial fathers may exaggerate the frequency of their visits. To examine the potential magnitude of these errors, we also present information about the number of mothers with children born outside marriage, their subsequent co-residence with and/or marriage to their child's father, and their reports of visitation by fathers.

THE PATTERNS OF NON-MARITAL CHILDBEARING AND FATHER INVOLVEMENT

The patterns of childbearing and father involvement are complex. There are several possibilities even at one point in time. Some men have had one child born outside marriage, have married the mother, and remained married for any subsequent children. Others have fathered several children outside marriage and are not currently visiting any of them. Still others have had one child and are visiting frequently.

The situation becomes even more complex when we take account of patterns over time. The involvement of fathers with children born outside marriage may erode, strengthen, or stay the same. Fathers may go from visiting frequently to moving in with the mother of their children. Or they may move away and visit less frequently. Of those whose involvement with one child erodes, some may marry and become closely involved with a second child, while others may remain unmarried.

We examine several aspects of father involvement with their children, the first of which is to describe patterns of childbearing. How many men become fathers of children outside marriage? How many fathers have both marital and nonmarital children? We check the consistency of reports by males and females, but the comparison is not straightforward. Males in a particular age range (say, 21-28) might report fathering fewer children born outside of marriage than do females of the same ages. This may be merely because males become parents at older ages than females. Consequently, we take this factor into account by comparing men's reports of childbearing with the reports of women who are in an age group two years younger than the males.

Second, we classify father involvement with nonmarital children in a way that takes account of living arrangements, marriage, and visitation. We assume that the closest involvement occurs when fathers live with their children. Marrying and living with the mother generally results in a longer term relationship than cohabitation; thus we assume it reflects a higher degree of involvement than cohabitation. Next comes visiting the children at least weekly, visiting them at least once per month, and visiting less often. Of course, those who do not visit at all are assumed to be the least involved.

The third element recognizes that fathers may be closely involved with one child but not with another. Thus, we present measures that show the maximum involvement a father has with any of his nonmarital children. For this concept of involvement, we compare the reports by males with those of females. We also examine father involvement with his first nonmarital child. Because this paper deals with how father involvement interacts with earnings, it is appropriate to make the father the primary unit of analysis. Policymakers who are often more concerned with the current plight and future of children should recognize that patterns of father involvement, from the perspective of children, could differ from those that fathers report. For example, one child may not have any contact with his father, while the same father could, simultaneously, have a substantial amount of involvement with another of his nonmarital children. Finally, we examine several of these patterns over time, with particular attention to what proportion of fathers become more or less involved as their children age.

Non-Marital and Marital Children Fathered by Young Men

Estimates (weighted to population totals) drawn from reports by males from the 1992 interview of the NLSY79 show that about 2.5 million of the 17 million 27-34-year-old males (about 15%) had fathered at least one child outside marriage. These 2.5 million males reported fathering 3.9 million children outside marriage, or an average of about 1.6 children per father.[1] About 37% of fathers with nonmarital children also had a child born within a marriage; another 39% fathered only one child outside marriage and no others. The remaining 24% fit a common stereotype of young men fathering several children outside marriage and not having any children within a marriage.

African American males show a much higher incidence of nonmarital fathering than other groups, as well as a smaller interaction with marital fathering.[2] Nearly one in two (47%) African American males reported fathering a child outside marriage by their late 20s or early 30s. Of these, about 32% also had a child within marriage and about 35% had only one nonmarital child and no marital children. The remaining 33% had multiple nonmarital births and no marital births. In contrast, about 41% of white fathers of children outside marriage had a marital child, 42% had only one nonmarital child and no other children, and 16% had multiple nonmarital children with no marital children.

Less than half (45%) of the fathers with nonmarital children by 1992 had started their nonmarital fathering by 1984, when their ages ranged from 19-26. In fact, the median age at which young men first fathered a child outside of marriage was 22. Only about 10% had their first nonmarital child before reaching age 18 and only 22% had done so before age 20.

Patterns of Father Involvement

Once young men father a child outside marriage, they can remain closely involved by living with the child or visiting frequently, less involved by visiting infrequently, or uninvolved by not seeing the child. We examine father involvement from three perspectives or measures, the first of which captures the father's maximum involvement with any child born outside marriage in specific years. The second measure assesses the involvement with the father's first nonmarital child, whereas the third set of measures captures the dynamics of the father's involvement.

We begin by examining the maximum involvement of fathers with any of their nonmarital children as of 1984, 1988, and 1992. Table 1 shows that, in 1988, nearly half (48.6%) of the fathers with nonmarital children reported living with at least one child born outside marriage. An additional 21.6% reported visiting at least one nonmarital child once per week or more frequently. Of the 32.3% of fathers in 1992 who were not living with a nonmarital child or visiting a nonmarital child frequently, about half were married to someone other than the biological mother of their nonmarital children and two-thirds had a subsequent *marital* birth. The striking reality is that about two of three fathers (under 35 years old) who have fathered a child out of wedlock have a close involvement with at least one of their nonmarital children. Many of those who do not have a close relationship with at least one of their nonmarital children have married someone else and are living with a marital child.

To assess the quality of the data reported by men, we compare fathers' and mothers' reports about the number of children born and the fathers' involvement with their nonresident children. The men and women in the NLSY79 data are not mothers and fathers of the *same* children.[3] Thus any comparison between mothers' and fathers' reports is only valid at the aggregate population level. An appropriate comparison of these aggregated reports requires an assumption about the average age gap between fathers and mothers. We make the simple assumption of a two-year age gap, a difference which yields similar weighted numbers of males and females.

The responses by mothers suggest that fathers may understate the number

TABLE 1. Maximum Involvement of a Father with Any Child Born Outside of Marriage

	1984		1988		1992	
	(19-26 Year Olds)		(23-30 Year Olds)		(27-34 Year Olds)	
	Number	*Percent*	*Number*	*Percent*	*Number*	*Percent*
Did Not Visit	113,466	10.7	164,607	9.4	308,967	13.2
Visited Less Than Once per Month	142,941	13.5	204,635	11.7	288,712	12.4
Visited 1-3 Times per Month	91,403	8.6	149,855	8.6	156,282	6.7
Visited at Least Once per Week	297,951	28.1	377,511	21.6	457,972	19.6
Lived with Child but Not Mother	30,881	2.9	70,245	4.0	120,552	5.2
Not Married, Lived with Child, Mother	116,906	11.0	261,408	15.0	320,570	13.7
Married, Lived with Child, Mother	266,717	25.2	516,269	29.6	685,411	29.3
Total	1,060,265	100	1,744,530	100	2,338,466	100

Source. National Longitudinal Survey of Youth, 1979.

of nonmarital children they have and overstate their involvement with the children they report. Our analysis shows that virtually identical (weighted) numbers of men and women report a marital birth, about 4.9 million. However, far fewer men than women report having a nonmarital child. There are 1.36 mothers with a nonmarital birth for every father reporting a nonmarital birth. Of course, if some men fathered children with several women, then it is possible that the numbers are accurate. However, it is also plausible that men underreport having nonmarital births at a greater rate than do women (see Rendall, Clarke, Peters, Ranjit, & Verropoulou, 1999, for similar results).

Table 2 compares the reports of males, ages 30-34, with females, ages 28-32. According to mothers, the proportion of fathers who never or only rarely visited a nonmarital child was 35.9%, or 11 percentage points higher than the reports by fathers. Perhaps the more appropriate distinctions are the differentials in absolute numbers of fathers by visitation category (column 5). In the top three visitation categories, the numbers of fathers based on their own responses are within about 15% of the numbers based on responses by mothers. Fathers reporting themselves in the "did not visit" category, however, represent less than half (47.2%) the number reported in this category by

TABLE 2. Reports by Men and Women on the Maximum Involvement of Fathers with Any Child Born Outside of Marriage, 1992

	As Reported by Fathers		As Reported by Mothers		Absolute Number of Fathers Compared to Mothers (col 1 ÷ col 3)
	Number	Percent	Number	Percent	Percent
Did Not Visit	217,116	13.5	460,000	22.5	47.2
Visited Less Than Once per Month	186,940	11.6	273,513	13.4	68.3
Visited 1-3 Times per Month	124,556	7.8	155,994	7.6	79.8
Visited at Least Once per Week	314,173	19.6	375,868	15.4	83.6
Not Married, Lived with Child and Mother	255,452	15.9	269,909	13.2	94.6
Married, Lived with Child and Mother	507,705	<u>31.6</u>	508,102	<u>24.9</u>	99.9
		100		100	

Source. National Longitudinal Survey of Youth, 1979.

Note. We restrict the sample of men to those who report that the child lives with the mother.

mothers. The most plausible explanation is that men who never visit a nonmarital child may simply never report having the child. Among men who report their fathering of a nonmarital child, on the other hand, the responses appear reasonably close to reports by mothers.

In Table 3, we examine the evolution of father involvement by focusing on a particular nonmarital birth and following the father's involvement with that child. We pool observations on all those who become nonmarital fathers, but focus on their first nonmarital birth.[4] We then observe the patterns of involvement for the next 2, 4, 6, and 8 years. Because all cases are included from

TABLE 3. Patterns of Father Involvement by Year Since First Observation of Visitation

	Initial Year	Two Years After	Four Years After	Six Years After	Eight Years After
Percent Who:					
Did Not Visit at All in Prior Year	7.6	12.0	12.6	17.0	17.0
Visited Less Than Once per Month	10.8	12.0	13.7	18.2	15.8
Visited 1-3 Times per Month	7.5	9.8	11.3	11.4	11.3
Visited at Least Once per Week	27.5	22.1	22.3	19.5	22.4
Lived with Child but Not Mother	2.7	3.6	4.3	5.0	5.9
Not Married, Lived with Child and Mother	22.0	15.7	9.9	5.6	5.4
Married, Lived with Child, Mother	22.0	24.8	25.9	23.4	22.2
Total	100.0	100.0	100.0	100.0	100.0
Number of Fathers	1092	867	737	606	406
Percent Who:					
Lived with Child	46.6	44.1	40.2	34.0	33.5
Lived with Child or Visited Once per Week	74.1	66.2	62.4	53.5	55.9
Infrequent or No Visitation	18.4	24.0	26.3	35.1	32.8

Source. National Longitudinal Survey of Youth, 1979.
Note. Initial year represents the first year in which visitation data are available for the father's first non-marital child. The columns two, four, six, and eight years later show patterns of father involvement in the respective years after the initial year.

their year of initial visitation information (usually within one to two years of the child's birth) and since men become fathers at different periods relative to the end of the sample period, the composition of fathers changes by year. Thus, although Table 3 shows erosion in the relationship with the child does occur,[5] some of the patterns we observe could relate to the changing mix of fathers rather than to the changes in involvement over time. Still, the data in Table 3 indicate that the proportion of fathers who rarely or never visit rises sharply over time from only 18.4% at the first observation to 29.6% only six years later. The category of involvement defined as living with the child but not married to the mother declines most sharply (from 22% in the initial year to 5.6% six years later). Similarly, the share of fathers visiting at least once per week falls from 27.5% to 19.5%.

Using Table 4, we analyze the types of transitions in father involvement from the initial year to 6 years later. Since we follow a panel of 559 fathers, the composition problem does not arise. Not surprisingly, those who married the mother of their nonmarital child had the most stable involvement with their children. About two-thirds of these fathers continued to live with their child and another 11% visited at least once per week. Again, the erosion in father-child relationships was substantial among two groups of fathers–those initially observed to be living with their children but not married and those visiting at least once per week. At a point six years after the initial observation, 33% to 39% of these two groups were neither living with the first

TABLE 4. Father Involvement with First Nonmarital Child Six Years Later by Initial Level of Involvement

	Six Years Later			
Initial Year	Few or No Visits	Visits At Least Once a Week	Lives with Child	Total
Did Not Visit at All in Prior Year	85.4	4.9	9.8	100
Visited Less Than Once per Month	78.4	10.8	10.8	100
Visited 1-3 Times per Month	64.8	18.5	16.7	100
Visited at Least Once per Week	38.9	33.1	28.0	100
Lived with Child but Not Mother	20.0	33.3	46.7	100
Not Married, Lived with Child and Mother	32.5	13.3	54.2	100
Married, Lived with Child and Mother	22.2	11.1	66.7	100
Total	45.1	19.1	35.8	100
Number of Fathers	252	107	200	559

Source. National Longitudinal Survey of Youth, 1979.
Note. Only cases in which children were under age three when first observed are included.

nonmarital child nor visiting at least once per week. At the same time, 28% of the fathers initially observed to be visiting once per week or more were living with the child six years later. Of those living with the child but not initially married, about half (54.2%) continued to live with the child and about one in five also married the mother (not shown in the table). Evidence of both erosion and strengthening of involvement shows up when we track those who initially visited 1-3 times per month. Nearly two-thirds (64.8%) of this group reduced their visitations substantially, while just under 17% were subsequently living with their child.

The patterns of father involvement (as reported by fathers) differed by race and Spanish origin in ways that depend on the amount of time after the birth of the child. Note in the top panel of Table 5, which covers the period 2-6 years after the first nonmarital birth, that Hispanic fathers show the highest rates of father involvement: they are most likely to live with the child and least likely to visit infrequently or not at all. African American fathers are least likely to live with the mother and child but most likely to visit at least once per week. The bottom panel of Table 5 shows that four years later, father involvement, especially in terms of nonmarital residence with mother and child, has eroded considerably for the first nonmarital child among Hispanic and White fathers and somewhat less so for Black fathers.

Determinants of Father Involvement

The multivariate approach attempts to explain the factors influencing two aspects of father involvement: the maximum involvement in 1992 with any child born outside marriage and father's involvement with his first nonmarital child within two years after the child's birth. Although the data come entirely from reports by fathers, as discussed above the patterns of visitation and living arrangements among the men in this sample appear reasonably accurate. At the same time, however, it is important to note limitations in the generalizability of the results, in particular, with respect to men who have children but do not report this in the data.

Table 6 reports the results from multinomial logit regression models estimating the determinants of father involvement. The categories of involvement that are estimated are the same as those used in the univariate analysis. In panel A, the dependent variable is the maximum involvement in 1992. The explanatory variables for that model include (a) age of the child, (b) age of the father, (c) race or Spanish origin of the father, (d) the local unemployment rate, (e) father's highest grade completed as of 1992, (f) the number of nonmarital children, (g) whether the father lived with his own father when growing up, and (h) performance on the math and verbal portions of the Armed Forces Qualification Test (AFQT). In panel B the dependent variable is the first observed involvement; in that model we add the child's sex as an

TABLE 5. Nonmarital Father Involvement by Race and Ethnicity

	Hispanic	Black	White	Total
2-6 Years After First Nonmarital Birth				
Did Not Visit at All in Prior Year	9.3%	10.8%	9.5%	10.0%
Visited Less Than Once per Month	8.1%	11.5%	15.1%	12.8%
Visited 1-3 Times per Month	4.4%	13.5%	4.4%	8.4%
Visited at Least Once per Week	13.9%	30.0%	14.8%	21.3%
Lived with Child but Not Mother	2.5%	4.5%	2.1%	3.2%
Not Married, Lived with Child and Mother	31.9%	12.7%	18.2%	17.2%
Married, Lived with Child, Mother	30.0%	17.1%	36.0%	27.2%
Total	100.0%	100.0%	100.0%	100.0%
Weighted Number of Fathers	159,135	682,250	727,156	1,568,541
Number of Observations	140	417	197	754
6-10 Years After First Nonmarital Birth				
Did Not Visit at All in Prior Year	17.5%	10.3%	31.3%	19.4%
Visited Less Than Once per Month	12.5%	20.1%	13.3%	16.6%
Visited 1-3 Times per Month	10.9%	13.3%	6.7%	10.4%
Visited at Least Once per Week	10.5%	24.6%	11.4%	17.9%
Lived with Child but Not Mother	4.0%	6.0%	3.7%	4.9%
Not Married, Lived with Child and Mother	10.4%	5.1%	3.7%	5.1%
Married, Lived with Child, Mother	34.2%	20.6%	29.9%	25.7%
Total	100.0%	100.0%	100.0%	100.0%
Weighted Number of Fathers	105,168	519,512	419,020	1,043,700
Number of Observations	87	309	98	494

Source. National Longitudinal Survey of Youth, 1979.

explanatory variable and drop the age of the child, since nearly all are 1-2 years old when first observed.

In broad terms, we expect attitudes, family background, educational attainment, and earnings opportunities all to influence father involvement. Because the father's own earnings can be a cause and effect of father involvement, we use the local unemployment rate as an exogenous measure of earnings opportunities. Separate regressions with these data demonstrate that the unemployment rate variable does indeed exert significant, negative effects on earnings. The father's age and educational level are exogenous, but their impact on father involvement may occur as a result of the man's maturity and knowledge or as a result of the positive effects of age and education on earnings. The presence of one's own father when growing up is a background indicator that could influence attitudes about parenting.

To provide an intuitive interpretation of the findings, Table 6 shows the

TABLE 6. Determinants of Maximum Father Involvement in 1992 and Initial Father Involvement

	Not Involved or Few Visits	Visits Frequently	Lives with Child Not Married	Lives with Child Married Mother
Panel A: Maximum Involvement as of 1992				
Predicted Involvement at Mean Values	0.327	0.201	0.164	0.308
Percentage Point Change in Involvement with:				
Black Relative to White	− 0.066	0.128†	0.023	− 0.086
Hispanic Relative to White	− 0.018	0.007	− 0.007	0.018
High (10%) vs. Low (6%) Unemployment	− 0.167	0.076†	0.040†	0.051†
Highest Grade Completed (14 vs. 10)	0.064	0.064	− 0.073†	− 0.055
Age of Youngest Child (Age 12 vs. Age 4)	0.198	− 0.049†	− 0.195†	0.046†
Age of Father (Age 27 vs. Age 19)	− 0.065	− 0.003	0.064†	0.004
Number of non-marital births (2 vs. 1)	− 0.062	− 0.016	0.093†	− 0.014
Father Absent at Age 14	0.142	0.055	− 0.050†	− 0.147†
High vs. Low Math Score (15 vs. 5)	− 0.023	− 0.125†	0.007	0.141†
High vs. Low Verbal Score (50 vs. 30)	− 0.078	0.023	0.003	0.052
Panel B: First Observed Involvement				
Predicted Involvement at Mean Values	0.204	0.311	0.305	0.179
Percentage Point Change in Involvement with:				
Black Relative to White	− 0.060	0.294†	− 0.049	− 0.185†
Hispanic Relative to White	− 0.107	− 0.039	0.185	− 0.039
High (9%) vs. Low (5%) Unemployment	0.014	0.003	0.017	− 0.034
Highest Grade Completed (14 vs. 10)	0.007	− 0.057	− 0.070	0.120†
Child is Male	− 0.061	0.018	0.011	0.032
Age of Father (28.5 vs. 22.5)	− 0.134	− 0.020†	0.192†	− 0.038
Father Absent at Age 14	−0.106	− 0.078	0.072†	0.111†
High vs. Low Math Score (15 vs. 5)	− 0.104	0.053†	− 0.011	0.061†
High vs. Low Verbal Score (50 vs. 30)	− 0.004	− 0.020	0.014	0.010

Source. National Longitudinal Survey of Youth, 1979.

Note. In most cases the change in the continuous variable represents the difference between one standard deviation above and below the mean.

† $p < 0.10$.

percentage point change in each father involvement category induced by a specific independent variable, assuming mean levels of all the remaining independent variables. For dummy variables, the changes represent movements from one status (e.g., non-Hispanic White) relative to another status (e.g., Hispanic). In the case of a continuous independent variable, the percentage point change captures the effect of a specified increase in the level of a variable, such as an increase in completed education from 10 years to 14 years. In general, the specified changes in independent variables measure the difference between one standard deviation above and one standard deviation below the variable's mean. Note that an independent variable may have a statistically significant impact on one involvement category but not on another category.

The racial impacts mirror the univariate tabulations in Table 5. Even after controlling for educational attainment, local unemployment rates, age of children, test scores, and the father's age and prior family history, Black young men were much more likely than Whites to visit at least once per week in 1992, but much less likely to live with a nonmarital child. They essentially substitute frequent visitation for co-residence involving marriage to the child's mother. The pattern of involvement by Hispanic fathers differed little from Whites in 1992. However, soon after the birth of the first nonmarital child, Hispanic fathers were significantly more likely to live with their child than Whites, albeit without marrying the child's mother.

Surprisingly, high unemployment exerted no significant effect on first involvement and led to *higher* father involvement for the maximum involvement measure. This is a striking finding because it casts doubt on the idea that improved earnings opportunities will lead to increased visitation, co-residence, and marriage to the child's mother. Although low unemployment raises earnings, those fathers in low unemployment areas in 1992 were actually less likely than other fathers to become closely involved with their children.

Achieving high levels of schooling did little to reduce the proportion who rarely or never visit their children. Education levels lowered co-residence in the case of maximum involvement. However, in the case of first involvement, education increased co-residence linked to marriage and lowered the rate of frequent visitation. Test scores also varied in their effects. None of the effects associated with verbal scores were statistically significant, but for both the maximum and initial involvement measures, higher math scores tended to raise involvement, especially through marriage to the mother. This positive effect of higher math scores could be partly linked to the increased earnings capacity of fathers. However, verbal scores were also positively associated with earnings, but had no effect on father involvement.

Fathers with other nonmarital births were more likely to reside with at least one child, though not in a marriage to the child's mother. The positive link between involvement and other nonmarital births is perhaps expected, since more nonmarital births give the father more opportunities to become closely involved with at least one child. A conceivable idea, on the other hand, is that young men who fathered more than one child out of wedlock would be less responsible in regard to any of their children.

Growing up away from one's own father significantly weakened maximum involvement in 1992, while significantly raising initial involvement. Apparently, men who did not live with their own fathers were initially more involved with their first nonmarital child and were more likely to reside with the child both with and without marriage to the mother. However, as of 1992, the pattern had reversed itself; at that point, growing up without a father present had become associated with significantly less co-residence.

The ages of fathers and children were significant determinants of father involvement. Older fathers were much less likely than younger fathers to isolate themselves from their children. As of 1992, fathers at age 27 were 6 percentage points less likely to never or infrequently visit and were 6 percentage points more likely to live with their children without marrying the child's mother. The impact of father's age on initial involvement was even more substantial. Infrequent visitation was about 13 percentage points lower and co-residence about 15 percentage points higher among older fathers than among younger fathers. As of 1992, fathers were much less likely to visit older children than younger children. The rate of noninvolvement or infrequent visitation was almost 20 percentage points higher among fathers with older children than fathers with younger children.

The equations also tested the possibility that fathers were initially more closely involved with boys than with girls. The observed effects run in this direction, though none are statistically significant.

Finally, we performed other analyses that included lagged earnings as a determinant of maximum involvement in 1992. In general, higher earnings in a previous year was associated with higher father involvement in all categories though the direction of causation is not clear. Fathers with higher earnings in 1990 were significantly more likely to visit frequently, to co-reside with their children, and to marry the child's mother.

Overall, we find substantial involvement of fathers in the lives of children born outside marriage. A strikingly high proportion live with their children or visit frequently. The relationships between father involvement and race and ethnic origin were significant, even after accounting for such variables as local unemployment rates, test scores, school attainment, and the age of fathers. Growing up without a father present initially increased father involvement, but as of 1992, these men had become much less involved with any nonmarital child. The ages of the father and the child often showed significant coefficients. Generally, the older the father and the younger the child, the more likely were fathers to exhibit a close involvement with their children. This result suggests an additional advantage for children of delays in parenthood.

FATHER INVOLVEMENT AND EARNINGS

The relationship between father involvement and earnings is no doubt complex. Positive external shocks to income, such as reductions in unemployment, could encourage fathers to participate more in the lives of their children. But, causation can flow in the other direction. Once fathers decide to become more involved with their children, they may become more active in taking advantage of available opportunities. Another possibility is that as fathers devote substantially more time to raising their children, they will have lower earnings because they have less time for market work.

One way of dealing with the simultaneity is to focus on timing. If increased father involvement leads to subsequent increases in earnings (holding constant prior earnings), then one might conclude that father involvement motivates men to do more to succeed in the job market. While the timing approach has merit, it is not definitive because fathers may become more involved once they *anticipate* their ability to earn more. For example, they may increase their involvement (say, marry the mother of their child) because they obtain a job with excellent growth prospects. Alternatively, if added earnings came before the increased involvement, their interest in becoming more involved with their children in the future may have motivated fathers to work harder in the present. One can envisage a range of dynamic processes at work. Close involvement may stimulate a father to gain valuable work experience that subsequently raises earnings even when the father becomes less involved with his children. Steady father involvement over the years may lead to higher earnings or may produce no higher earnings than those involved on a contemporaneous basis.

This section analyzes the father involvement-earnings relationship by estimating how *changes* in father involvement affect the *level* of fathers' subsequent employment and earnings, holding constant prior employment and earnings. Specifically, we estimate ordinary least squares models of hours worked in 1993 and earnings in 1993 as functions of changes in father involvement between 1988 and 1992, holding constant race, age, highest grade completed as of May 1994, local 1993 unemployment rates, AFQT scores, and prior hours worked or earnings (1987, 1989, and 1990). On a contemporaneous basis, increased earnings could induce more involvement, but more involvement could stimulate increased labor market activity. By including hours worked and earnings during the 1988-92 period as separate independent variables, we end up measuring the effect of changes in father involvement on subsequent earnings net of any involvement effects on contemporaneous earnings.

The analyses use an ordinal measure of maximum father involvement with any nonmarital child, rising from 0 when fathers never visit to 6 when fathers marry the mother of their nonmarital child and live with both mother and child. The other categories are visiting less than once a month (1), visiting once a month but not weekly (2), visiting at least once a week (3), living with the child but not the mother (4), and living with mother and child in an unmarried state (5). Change in involvement is equal to the involvement level (0 to 6) in the final year minus the involvement level in the base year. This measure may understate the role of involvement since it treats as zero both continuing involvement and continuing non-involvement.

The results in Table 7 show large and statistically significant impacts of father involvement on both hours worked and annual earnings. Each unit increase in involvement between 1988 and 1992 was associated with about 53 1/2 additional hours of work and almost $800 in additional earnings in 1994. Both effects are significant at the 1% level. The role of changes in father involvement looks large in comparison with the effects of other variables. Moving up one unit on the involvement scale exerted a larger impact than having an additional year of schooling. Moreover, the effects of change in father involvement were robust to a range of specifications involving different time periods, the inclusion of a measure of initial involvement, and whether the change in involvement was toward more or less involvement. While these findings do not prove that becoming more involved as a father leads to improved labor market outcomes, they document a close relationship between changes in involvement and subsequent employment and earnings.

CONCLUSION

The most striking results from this paper are the high rates of father involvement with children born outside marriage observed for a large sample of men in their mid- to late twenties and early thirties. Nearly half the fathers lived with at least one nonmarital child and about two-thirds either lived with the child or visited once a week or more. Thus, the vast majority of fathers reported a close involvement with at least one nonmarital child.

Fathers who marry the child's mother generally retain close involvement over time. However, the relationship with the nonmarital child erodes for about one in three fathers who initially visited at least weekly or who initially lived with the child but did not marry the mother. Nonetheless, father involvement among nonmarital fathers does not always erode. In fact, 30% of fathers who started out as frequent visitors of their nonmarital child eventual-

TABLE 7. Impact of Changes in Maximum Father Involvement Between 1988 and 1992 on Hours Worked and Earnings in 1993

Independent Variables	Hours Worked in 1993		
	Coefficient	T-statistic	Means
Change in Maximum Involvement, 1988-92	53.46	3.20†	−0.10
Black	−101.75	−1.18	0.48
Hispanic	−45.05	−0.41	0.09
Age in 1988	−11.89	−0.80	27.29
Highest Grade Complete (1994)	31.61	1.51	12.07
AFQT Percentile (missing = 0)	3.50	1.73†	27.18
AFQT Score Missing	265.15	2.21	0.05
Unemployment Rate (1994)	22.96	0.87	2.67
Hours Worked in 1990	0.28	4.14†	1,720
Hours Worked in 1989	0.07	1.07	1,730
Hours Worked in 1987	0.29	5.79†	1,681
In School in 1994	−299.72	−1.28	0.03
Constant	404.38	0.93	−
R-square	0.37		
Sample Size	635		
Mean Hours Worked in 1993			1,652

Independent Variable	Earnings in 1993		
	Coefficient	T-statistic	Means
Change in Maximum Involvement, 1988-92	790.30	2.94†	−0.10
Black	−808.36	−0.68	0.48
Hispanic	−786.76	−0.48	0.09
Age in 1988	163.53	0.80	27.29
Highest Grade Complete (1994)	699.31	2.29†	12.07
AFQT Percentile (missing = 0)	30.95	1.02	27.18
AFQT Score Missing	1670.60	0.56	0.05
Unemployment Rate (1994)	−459.45	−1.50	2.67
Earnings in 1990	0.46	6.28†	16,175
Earnings in 1989	0.16	1.84†	16,129
Earnings in 1987	0.21	2.32†	13,408
In School in 1994	−2067.38	−0.76	0.03
Constant	−7415.57	−1.16	−
R-square	0.50		
Sample Size	577		
Mean Earnings in 1993			$17,057

Source. National Longitudinal Survey of Youth, 1979.

† $p < 0.10$.

ly moved in with the child and mother. Although the approximately 13% of fathers who did not visit their children initially rarely return to close contact, some of the infrequent visitors do increase their involvement over time.

Earnings and father involvement have a direct, though not necessarily monotonic relationship in both directions. Higher earnings seemed to lead to a higher extent of marriage and coresidence and to reduce the likelihood that a father would visit his child only rarely. At the same time, more father involvement appeared to lead to higher subsequent earnings and higher amounts of hours worked over an entire year.

Increasingly, policymakers are promoting efforts aimed at encouraging non-custodial fathers to participate more in raising their children. Their motivation is partly the hope that children will do better if they interact with their fathers and partly the expectation that involved fathers are more likely to pay child support. Given the findings in this paper, stimulating increased involvement is likely to generate better labor market outcomes for fathers.

NOTES

1. The unweighted NLSY79 sample contains 1,052 such fathers.

2. Fathers are divided into three racial/ethnic categories–Hispanic, Black non-Hispanic, and other–which we refer to as Hispanic, African-American (or Black), and White.

3. The men and women in the NLSY79 data are independent nationally representative samples of their respective age-sex cohorts.

4. Fathers with children who were born before 1984 are included so long as the child is less than age 4 in 1984. Fathers with children born after 1984 are usually observed within the first 3 years of the child's life.

5. Figures that include information from more than one year are not weighted (i.e., Tables 3, 4, 5, and 6). Data from a single year are weighted by the appropriate annual weight.

REFERENCES

Achatz, M., & MacAllum, C. (1994). *Young unwed fathers, report from the field.* Philadelphia, PA: Public/Private Ventures.

Anderson, E. (1993). Sex codes and family life among poor inner-city youths. In R. Lerman & T. Ooms (Eds.), *Young unwed fathers: Changing roles and emerging policies* (pp. 74-98). Philadelphia, PA: Temple University Press.

Bloom, D., & Sherwood, K. (1994). *Matching opportunities to obligations: Lessons for child support reform from the parents' fair share pilot phase.* New York City, NY: Manpower Demonstration Research Corporation.

Danziger, S., & Radin, N. (1990). Absent does not equal uninvolved: Predictors of fathering in teen mother families. *Journal of Marriage and the Family, 52,* 636-642.

Furstenberg, F., Jr., & Harris, K. (1993). When and why fathers matter: Impacts of father involvement on the children of adolescent mothers. In R. Lerman & T. Ooms (Eds.), *Young unwed fathers: Changing roles and emerging policies* (pp. 117-138). Philadelphia, PA: Temple University Press.

Furstenberg, F., Jr. (1995). Fathering in the inner city: Paternal participation and public policy. In W. Marsiglio (Ed.), *Fatherhood: Contemporary theory, research, and social policy* (pp. 119-147). CA: Sage Publications, Inc.

King, V. (1994). Nonresident father involvement and child well-being: Can dads make a difference? *Journal of Family Issues, 15*, 1, 78-96.

Korenman, S., & Neumark, D. (1991). Does marriage really make men more productive? *Journal of Human Resources, 26*, 2, 282-307.

Lerman, R. (1993). A national profile of young unwed fathers. In R. Lerman & T. Ooms (Eds.), *Young unwed fathers: Changing roles and emerging policies* (pp. 27-51). Philadelphia, PA: Temple University Press.

Lerman, R. (1996). The impact of the changing U.S. family structure on child poverty and income inequality. *Economica, 63*, S119-139.

Levine, J.A., & Pitt, E.W. (1995). *New expectations: Community strategies for responsible fatherhood.* New York, NY: Families and Work Institute.

McLanahan, S., & Sandefur, G. (1994). *Growing up with a single parent: What hurts, what helps?* Cambridge, MA: Harvard University Press.

Mott, F. (1990). When is a father really gone? Paternal-child contact in father-absent homes. *Demography, 27*, 4, 499-517.

Rendall, M. S., Clarke, L., Peters, H. E., Ranjit, N., &Verropoulou, G. (1999). Incomplete Reporting of Men's Fertility in the United States and Britain: A Research Note. *Demography, 36*, 1, 135-144.

Seltzer, J. (1991). Relationships between fathers and children who live apart: The father's role after separation. *Journal of Marriage and the Family, 53*, 79-101.

Seltzer, J., & Brandreth, Y. (1994). What fathers say about involvement with children after separation. *Journal of Family Issues, 15*, 1, 49-77.

Nonresident Father Involvement and Child Well-Being Among Young Children in Families on Welfare

Angela Dungee Greene
Kristin Anderson Moore

SUMMARY. This study uses early descriptive data from the National Evaluation of Welfare to Work Strategies (NEWWS) Child Outcome Study, a sub-study of the larger random assignment evaluation of the Federal JOBS program, to answer two timely and important questions. First, what factors predict father involvement among nonresident fathers of young children who receive welfare? And second, is nonresident father involvement associated with better outcomes for these children? The three measures of nonresident father involvement examined are father-child visitation, formal child support payments received through the welfare office, and informal child support, such as money given directly to the mother, groceries, clothes, or other items. Findings reveal that while only 16.6% of fathers provided child support through the formal system during the past year, a considerably larger proportion, 42.3%, provided informal child support, and 67% visited at least once in the past year. Informal support and father-child visitation are the most highly correlated forms of involvement, and they share many of the same predictors. Only two

---

Angela Dungee Greene and Kristin Anderson Moore are affiliated with Child Trends, Inc., Washington, DC.

Support for this research was provided by the National Institute of Child Health and Human Development through its Family and Child Well-Being Research Network and its Minority Research Supplement Program. Primary support for data collection was provided by ASPE, ACF, and DHHS.

[Haworth co-indexing entry note]: "Nonresident Father Involvement and Child Well-Being Among Young Children in Families on Welfare." Greene, Angela Dungee, and Kristin Anderson Moore. Co-published simultaneously in *Marriage & Family Review* (The Haworth Press, Inc.) Vol. 29, No. 2/3, 2000, pp. 159-180; and: *FATHERHOOD: Research, Interventions and Policies* (ed: H. Elizabeth Peters et al.) The Haworth Press, Inc., 2000, pp. 159-180. Single or multiple copies of this article are available for a fee from The Haworth Document Delivery Service [1-800-342-9678, 9:00 a.m. - 5:00 p.m. (EST). E-mail address: getinfo@haworthpressinc.com].

159

predictors are significant and in the same direction for all three measures of nonresident father involvement. Father's residence in the same state as the focal child and the provision of support for the child from the father's family are associated with a higher likelihood of his involvement. In general, findings for the child well-being measures show that monetary and material contributions from the father, especially contributions provided informally, are positively associated with more positive child well-being outcomes. *[Article copies available for a fee from The Haworth Document Delivery Service: 1-800-342-9678. E-mail address: getinfo@haworthpressinc.com <Website: http:// www.haworthpressinc.com>]*

KEYWORDS. Welfare, non-resident fathers, visitation, informal support, well-being

Welfare reform has focused attention on the fathers of children who receive welfare, with the goal of reducing public outlays by more strictly enforcing child support obligations of nonresident fathers. Yet, there is surprisingly little empirical research on the involvement of these fathers in the lives of their children. Most research on nonresident father involvement has focused on middle-class fathers; little is known about involvement among nonresident fathers of children in families that receive welfare, and patterns may differ. For instance, the guidelines for Aid to Families with Dependent Children (AFDC), the predecessor of the present Temporary Assistance for Needy Families or TANF program, stipulated that only $50 of child support could be disregarded and passed through to the family. Thus, fathers of children on welfare may have been more likely to contribute informally by giving money directly to the mother or providing items, such as groceries, clothes, and toys. These contributions may be as important as formal child support payments to the home environment and general well-being of children on welfare. Yet, few studies have examined the effects of nonresident involvement, particularly informal child support, on child outcomes.

This study uses data from the Descriptive Survey of the National Evaluation of Welfare to Work Strategies (NEWWS) Child Outcome Study to address two timely and important questions. First, what factors predict various forms of father involvement among nonresident fathers of young children who receive welfare? Second, is nonresident father involvement associated with more positive outcomes for these children?

BACKGROUND

The Salience of Informal Child Support for Families on Welfare

For more than a decade, welfare legislation has emphasized the role of the Child Support Enforcement program, which locates nonresident fathers, arranges for the establishment of paternity, facilitates the granting of child support awards, and collects payments. Under Aid to Families with Dependent Children (AFDC), recipients were required to sign over their child support benefits to the state providing AFDC and to cooperate with efforts to locate absent fathers and establish paternity. However, despite concerted attempts to recoup public outlays to welfare recipients, the child support collection rates for this group remain low. Many if not most of the nonresident fathers of children on welfare are in dire or marginal circumstances themselves (Mincy and Pouncy, 1997). A recent analysis of national data on the ability of young non-custodial fathers to pay child support showed that about half of the 67% of fathers who fail to pay support are poor. Attempts to make them pay are referred to as "squeezing blood from a turnip" (Mincy & Sorensen, 1998).

Another disincentive for establishing paternity and cooperating with the formal child support system may be the stipulation that only the first $50 of monthly child support is passed on to the family: the remainder is used to reimburse the state for welfare expenditures to the family.[1] This stipulation is considered one reason these fathers may opt for alternative means of contributing to the support of their children. Even fathers in marginal or economically unstable conditions have been found to contribute food, diapers, clothing, and some financial assistance informally (Hardy, Duggan, Masnyk, & Pearson, 1989).

The main contention of the present study is that in the context of welfare regulations, child support provided through informal, cooperative arrangements may be a more common and potentially beneficial resource for families on welfare. Flexible, informal arrangements allow fathers with intermittent employment to contribute when they choose or are able to contribute. Mothers and fathers may agree on arrangements that are acceptable for both of them. The child support enforcement system may be deemed the last resort in instances when the father is uncooperative or unreliable. For instance, an ethnographic study of young, African American fathers in a low-income neighborhood reveals that in most cases, couples established paternity through informal acknowledgment by the male before the birth of the child and then made plans for the child's care and support. After the birth of the child, young fathers were likely to find sporadic "off the books" employment so that their financial contributions to the mother could not be traced and deducted from her AFDC benefits.

Available research on informal support is sparse. However, a couple of recent studies involving mothers on welfare in inner cities show that, although overall father involvement is low, fathers assume more responsibility for their children informally than through the formal child support system (Edin & Lien, 1997; Rangarajan & Gleason, 1998). According to qualitative data from a small pilot project, some fathers contend that they prefer to maintain control over how their money is spent by purchasing items and services for their children rather than paying money directly to the mother or the child support or welfare office. They view these tangible contributions as symbols of responsible fatherhood that gain them respect in their community (Achatz & MacAllum, 1994).

As the present study proposes, informal child support and father-child contact may be complementary forms of involvement, in that fathers who provide monetary and in-kind support are more likely to remain in contact with their children (Rangarajan & Gleason, 1998). Mothers may be more likely to allow access to children when fathers contribute financially. Also, fathers who have informal child support arrangements are more likely to spend time with their children and in so doing discover that their children need items like shoes or clothing which they agree to purchase (Edin & Lien, 1997).

Factors Associated with Nonresident Father Involvement

Studies focusing on support provided through formal child support agreements find a strong correlation between father-child contact and child support. Fathers who maintain contact with their children are more likely to pay child support and vice versa (Arditti & Keith, 1993; Furstenberg, Nord, Peterson, & Zill, 1983; King, 1994a; Rangarajan & Gleason, 1998; Seltzer, Schaeffer, & Charing, 1989). For example, findings from the National Survey of Families and Households show that in the absence of financial support, contact is especially low, and the important factor is the provision of support rather than the amount of support (Seltzer et al., 1989).

Both small- and large-scale studies find lower rates of child support payment and visitation for never married fathers compared to previously married fathers (Cooksey & Craig, 1998; Furstenberg & Harris, 1993; King, 1994a; Seltzer, 1991; Seltzer & Bianchi, 1988). It is also clear that there are significant declines in nonresident father involvement over time (Furstenberg et al., 1983; Lerman, 1993; Mott, 1990; Seltzer, 1991). Also, fathers' residential proximity to their children increases the likelihood of father-child visitation (Arditti & Keith, 1993; Cooksey & Craig, 1998; Furstenberg et al., 1983; Lerman, 1993; Seltzer, 1991). Other factors associated with increases in the likelihood of nonresident father involvement are a positive relationship between the mother and father, involvement of the father's family, father's financial resources, father's work experience, father's education, and mother's education (a proxy for father's education) (Cooksey & Craig, 1998; Danziger & Radin, 1990; Seltzer, 1991). Factors associated with decreasing father involvement include geographic mobility, a new spouse or partner, conflicts between the mother and father, and insufficient financial resources

(Furstenberg & Harris, 1993; Rangarajan & Gleason, 1998; Seltzer & Bianchi, 1988).

Nonresident Father Involvement and Child Well-Being

Findings from national data provide limited support for an association between nonresident father involvement and child well-being; however, involvement indicators are usually limited to the amount of child support paid and the frequency of father-child contact. The effect of informal child support on child outcomes, the focus of the present study, has not been examined.

Many large-scale studies find no association between frequency of father-child contact and child well-being measured by cognitive test scores, academic achievement measures, behavior ratings, perceptions of scholastic competence, and self worth (Baydar & Brooks-Gunn, 1994; Furstenberg, Morgan, & Allison, 1987; King, 1994b; McLanahan, Seltzer, Hanson, & Thomson, 1994). However, a few studies have found evidence of a negative effect of father-child contact on child outcomes (Furstenberg et al., 1987; King, 1994a).

These mixed findings may reflect the inadequacy of the contact measure most commonly used. Until quite recently, most surveys contained only a measure of the frequency of father-child contact in the past year. Findings from some small-scale studies suggest that the nature and quality of the involvement or interaction or the level of attachment between the father and child affects child outcomes. This research also suggests that involvement quality is more important than the frequency of father-child contact (Furstenberg & Harris, 1993; Hess & Camara, 1979; Nord, Brimhall, & West, 1997; Perloff & Buckner, 1996).

The most compelling evidence of an association between non-resident father involvement and child well-being involves the provision of child support. According to several large-scale studies, there is a positive association between child support and child outcomes, particularly in the domain of cognitive development and academic achievement among school-age children (Graham, Beller, & Hernandez, 1994; King 1994b; Knox & Bane, 1994). In addition, the provision of child support appears to be related to fewer school-related problems and general behavior problems (Furstenberg et al., 1987; McLanahan et al., 1994).

A study that disaggregated the child support measure and analyzed the effects of both cooperative and court-ordered awards revealed that the beneficial effects of child support appear to be greater when the child support agreement is reached cooperatively rather than by court order (Argys, Peters, Brooks-Gunn, & Smith, 1998). This finding is consistent with the contention of the present study that voluntary informal child support may be more important than formal child support payments to the well-being of children on welfare.

In sum, based on prior research, the provision of child support, both formal and informal but particularly informal, are expected to be positively associated with children's well-being.

DATA

Early descriptive data from the NEWWS Child Outcomes Study are used to explore the correlates of formal child support, informal child support and father visitation. We also examine these forms of nonresident father involvement as correlates of child outcomes for a sample of preschool-age children in African-American families that receive welfare.

The NEWWS Child Outcomes Study is a sub-study of the larger random assignment evaluation of the Federal JOBS program, conducted by the Manpower Demonstration Research Corporation in seven sites around the country and involving 55,000 individuals. The NEWWS Child Outcomes study is a longitudinal investigation designed to assess the effects of the mandatory welfare-to-work program on children who were ages three to five when their mothers entered the program. The study involves about 3,000 mothers and children in three sites: Fulton County, Georgia; Riverside County, California; and Kent County, Michigan. At each site, those eligible for the JOBS program were randomly assigned to either a control group or one of two program groups, called the human capital development and the labor force attachment groups (Moore, Zaslow, Coiro, Miller, & Magenheim, 1995). The Descriptive Survey, a component of the Child Outcomes Study, was conducted in Fulton County, Georgia. The sample is comprised of 790 mother-child pairs from all three research groups (Moore et al., 1995).

The present study focuses on children from the Descriptive Survey sample who were living with their biological mothers and had a father living elsewhere, excluding those in prison for whom child support and visitation are impossible. About 96% of the Descriptive Survey sample are African American women and their children, and the sample for this study has been limited to African American respondents. The resultant sample consists of 693 mostly never-married mothers and their children. The Descriptive Survey data are comprised of information collected from mothers on various topics including father involvement, interviewer observations of the home environment and mother-child interactions, and achievement and school readiness assessments given to the children by the interviewers. The NEWWS evaluation was not intended to study child support or fatherhood per se. However, mothers were asked several limited questions about the biological father of the focal child. While data reported by the father on his involvement would be a very desirable addition, such information is not available; reporting by biological mothers is common and considered a relatively conservative appraisal of father involvement (Seltzer & Brandreth, 1994).

An advantage of these data is that they not only include the conventional measures of child support and visitation but also indicators of informal support, as well as measures of child well-being, which allow for an assessment of the relative associations of these three forms of involvement with child outcomes.

The Child Outcomes Study data were weighted to adjust for differential sampling across the human capital development, labor force attachment, and control groups. Although program participation may directly or indirectly affect father involvement, these data were collected about three months after random assignment, too soon for long-term program effects to surface and bias the estimates reported here.

MEASURES

Father Involvement Variables

The three measures examined here represent separate dimensions of involvement. Formal child support refers to the cash payments that mothers who have voluntary or court-ordered award agreements receive from fathers through the formal child support enforcement system. Informal child support, however, is not contingent on the existence of an award agreement and indicates cash and or in-kind contributions fathers offer directly to mothers in addition to or in lieu of formal child support payments. Formal and informal child support may be complements in some cases, but may also be substitutes for each other. Visitation is the third measure. Informal child support and visitation are expected to be more closely associated since they are both more likely to be voluntary forms of involvement. It was anticipated that these variables would be interval or ordinal level measures. However, initial analyses indicated that presence/absence was more important than level or frequency in these data. Therefore, dummy variables were created and used in all analyses.

Formal child support. This measure indicates whether the mother received at least one child support payment in the past year through the welfare office. Unfortunately, data were not collected on the amount of child support received through the welfare office.

Informal child support. Informal child support is comprised from three items: how often the father gave money directly to the mother in the past year (regularly = 2, at least once = 1, never = 0), how frequently he bought groceries, and how frequently he bought clothes and or toys (often = 2, sometimes = 1, never = 0). Scores were summed (range = 0 to 6), and a dichotomous variable was created to indicate whether the father contributed any one type or combination of types of informal support at least once in the past year.

Father visitation. Paternal visitation is operationalized by an item that asks how often the child has seen his or her father in the past year. Response categories are coded from lowest to highest frequency and include: never, once in the past 12 months, two to 11 times, one to three times per month, about once a month, two to five times per week, or almost every day. The item (range = 0 to 6), was collapsed into a dichotomous variable indicating whether the father has seen the child at least once in the past year.

Child Outcome Variables

The Caldwell Preschool Inventory (PSI). The PSI is a measure of the school readiness of preschool children (Caldwell, 1970). This interviewer-administered inventory consists of 32 items designed to assess skills and concepts, such as the ability to follow directions, knowledge of the meaning of common words, and knowledge of colors, shapes, and numbers. High PSI scores indicate high levels of school readiness, according to this definition of school readiness. Age corrected norms are not available, therefore PSI scores are expected to vary according to the child's age, and age is controlled in all analyses.

Personal Maturity Scale (PMS). The second outcome measure is the *PMS* and it measures each child's emotional and behavioral development based on the mother's report on 14 items, including whether the child fights, is creative, is loving and affectionate, or has a strong temper. The higher the score, the greater the level of perceived maturity.

HOME. The short form of the *Home Observation for Measurement of the Environment* (the HOME-SF; Baker & Mott, 1989) serves as our measure of the quality of the child's home environment. The scale consists of 25 items that are based on maternal report and interviewer rating and tap the level of emotional and cognitive support available to the child in the home. An item that related to the child's father was excluded from the HOME-SF scale for these analyses; the adapted version includes 24 items. The HOME-SF scale consists of socioemotional and cognitive stimulation sub-scales, comprised of 10 items and 14 items respectively. Researchers note that the HOME-SF is sensitive to small increments in family income, particularly for the home environments of poor children (Garret, Ng'andu, & Ferron, 1994; Moore, Glei, Driscoll, & Zaslow, 1999). Therefore, formal and informal child support are expected to have positive effects on the home environment.

Table 1 shows the means and standard deviations of the predictors in-

TABLE 1. Means and Standard Deviations of Variables Used in Regression Models*

	Mean	(S.D.)
Child's Characteristics		
1 = Child's gender is male	0.50	
Child's age in months (ranges = 38 to 76)	55.84	(8.40)
Father's Characteristics		
1 = Father lives in same state as child	0.75	
1 = Father has other children	0.44	
1 = Not known whether father has other children	0.26	
0 = Omitted category = Father does not have other children		
Mother's Characteristics		
1 = Mother was married to father or legal paternity established	0.26	
1 = Mother was age 19 or younger at child's birth	0.16	
1 = Number of mother's own children (range = 1 to 5)	2.30	(1.10)
1 = Mother is in Education/Training Group	0.38	
1 = Mother is in Labor Force Group	0.39	
0 = Omitted category = Mother is in the Control group		
1 = Mother on welfare less than 2 years	0.20	
1 = Mother on welfare 5 or more years	0.43	
0 = Omitted category = Mother on welfare 2-4 years		
1 = Mother has less than 12 years of education	0.33	
Mother's literacy level (range = 1 to 5)[a]	2.46	(0.87)
Sources of Support		
1 = Child's father figure is mother's partner or friend[b]	0.36	
1 = Child's father figure is a relative or someone else[b]	0.17	
0 = Omitted category = no father figure		
1 = Family of child's father provides some help[c]	0.38	
1 = Mother receives some help from own parents[d]	0.68	
* Sample = 690		

Source. Child Trends, Descriptive Survey, Atlanta, National Evaluation of Welfare to Work Strategies, 1992

[a]This measure is based on the Test of Applied Literacy Skills (TALS) developed by the Educational Testing Service. It measures a broad range of math and reading skills used in everyday life. There are five levels, and scores in levels one or two indicate low levels of basic literacy. [b]In two separate questions mothers were asked if the focal child has a father figure other than his or her biological father, and if so, whether the father figure is the mother's current partner or friend, former husband/boyfriend, father, brother, a relative of the child's birth father, or someone else. [c]Mothers were asked to indicate whether in the past 12 months anyone in the family of the focal child's father, such as his mother or sister, ever: (a) bought clothes, toys, or presents for the child; (b) babysat for the child; or (c) cared for the child overnight. The "yes" responses were coded 1 and summed. A dichotomous measure was created where a score of one or more (a "yes" response to one or more items) was coded 1. [d]This dichotomous variable is a combination of two items. Each mother was asked whether her own mother helps to take care of her children a lot, quite a bit, just a little, or not at all. The same question was asked regarding the mother's own father. Responses for the two items were combined and then collapsed into some help (1) versus no help (0) from own parents.

cluded in the regression models. Selected predictors include the age and gender of the focal child and information about the mother's educational attainment, literacy level, duration of welfare receipt, and whether she was a teen at the birth of the focal child. Characteristics related to the father include whether he was ever married to the child's mother or has established legal paternity, whether he lives in the same state as the focal child, and whether, to the mother's knowledge, he has other children. Other predictors are support from the father's family in the form of clothing, toys, presents, or child care; support for the mother from her own parents; and whether the child has a father figure other than his or her biological father. All models also control for whether the mother is in the labor force attachment group, the human capital development group, or the control group.

METHODS

The analyses are divided into two sections. The first section addresses the question posed regarding predictors of father involvement among nonresident fathers of young children who receive welfare. Logistic regression equations were estimated to identify predictors of each dichotomous form of father involvement. OLS regression equations were also estimated to identify predictors of the ordinal measures of informal child support and visitation.

The second section consists of a series of OLS regression equations in which formal child support, informal child support, and visitation are independent variables. The primary aim of these analyses is to observe the relative importance of the three measures as predictors of selected child well-being measures. These regressions address the second research question by examining whether the economic or personal investments made by fathers who live apart from their children affect the cognitive and behavioral outcomes or the home environments of their children, net of other factors.

FINDINGS

Descriptive Results

Table 2 shows the percent distribution of the three forms of father involvement in the past year based on the mother's report. Only 16.6% of the fathers made at least one child support payment through the formal system in the past year. As expected, the provision of informal support is much more common; 42.3% of fathers provided informal support such as money directly to the mother, groceries, or clothes for the child. As Table 2 reveals, visitation is

TABLE 2. Detailed Distribution of Formal Child Support, Informal Child Support, and Visitation Variables (in the Past Year)

Formal Child Support	%	Informal Child Support[a]	%	Visitation	%
No Formal Child	83.4	None	57.7	Never	33.0
Some Formal Child Support	16.6	Sometimes one type of informal support	19.5	Once in past 12 months	9.8
		Sometimes two types; or often one type	9.7	About 2 to 11 times in past 12 months	21.3
		Sometimes three types; or sometimes one type and often one type	6.1	About 1-3 times a month	14.6
		Sometimes two types and often one type or often two types	3.9	About once a week	6.5
		Sometimes one type and often two types	1.0	About 2-5 times a week	9.1
		Often all three types	2.0	Almost daily	6.0
Total	100	Total	100	Total	100
Sample Size	686	Sample Size	682	Sample Size	684

Source. Child Trends, Descriptive Survey, Atlanta, National Evaluation of Welfare to Work Strategies, 1992

Note. Table values (except sample sizes) are based on weighted data.

[a]The three types of informal support are: (a) gives money directly to the mother; (b) buys groceries, (c) buys clothes, toys or presents, possible combinations for each level of the informal support summary variable are shown above with corresponding percentages

the most common form of involvement for this sample. Sixty-seven percent of the children saw their father at least once in the past year.[2]

For descriptive purposes, correlations between the forms of involvement were also analyzed. The correlation between formal child support and visitation ($r = .19$) and between formal child support and informal child support ($r = .17$) is modest in comparison to the correlation between informal child support and visitation ($r =. 53$). Thus the two voluntary forms of involvement are positively related as expected.[3]

Multivariate Results

Table 3 presents the odds ratios for separate logistic regression models predicting formal child support, informal child support, and visitation. Two predictors are significant and in the same direction for all three forms of

TABLE 3. Odds Ratios for Models Predicting Three Forms of Father Involvement in the Past Year

	Formal Child Support	Informal Child Support	Visitation
Child's Characteristics			
Child's gender (1 = male)	0.86	1.25	0.90
Child's age in months	0.97*	0.99	1.00
Father's Characteristics			
Father lives in same state as child	4.86***	3.43***	5.87***
Father has other children	1.79*	0.95	0.70
Not known whether father has other children	1.12	0.53*	0.28***
Mother's Characteristics			
Mother was married to father or legal paternity established	2.88***	1.03	1.44
Mother was age 19 or younger at child's birth	1.61	0.67	0.50*
Number of mother's own children	1.17	1.07	1.14
Mother is in Education/Training Group	1.01	1.09	1.00
Mother is in Labor Force Group	0.80	1.04	0.85
Mother on welfare less than 2 years	0.41*	1.79*	1.75†
Mother on welfare 5 or more years	0.87	0.53**	0.69
Mother has less than 12 years of education	1.19	1.36	1.07
Mother's literacy level	1.07	1.13	1.23
Sources of Support			
Child's father figure is mother's partner or friend	1.63*	0.65*	0.63*
Child's father figure is a relative or someone else	1.15	1.08	0.48*
Family of child's father provides some help	1.56†	6.10***	6.35***
Mother receives some help from own parents	1.40	0.92	1.13
−2 Log Likelihood	536.44	721.89	620.19
Sample Size	686	682	684

Source. Child Trends, Descriptive Survey, Atlanta, National Evaluation of Welfare to Work Strategies, 1992

Note: Table values (except sample sizes) are based on weighted data; means substituted for missing values on independent variables.

† $p < .10$. * $p < .05$. ** $p < .01$. *** $p < .001$.

involvement. Fathers' residence in the same state as the focal child dramatically increases the likelihood of his involvement. The residence factor is associated with nearly a five-fold increase in the odds of formal child support, a three-fold increase in informal child support provision, and nearly a six-fold increase in the odds of visitation. In addition, compared to fathers with uninvolved family members, fathers whose family members provide support for the child such as clothes, toys, and child care, are more likely to be involved with their children. These fathers are 56% more likely to pay formal child support, and over six times more likely to visit and to provide informal child support.

Most of the predictors that affect informal support affect visitation in the same direction. For instance, mothers were asked whether the father has other children. This measure appears to be a proxy for ongoing contact between the mother and father. Mothers who are uncertain whether the father has other children, compared with mothers who were certain the father does not have other children, are 47% less likely to receive informal support and 72% less likely to visit. On the other hand, the likelihood of formal child support receipt *increases* by 79% among mothers who know the father has other children. Perhaps mothers are more aggressive about securing child support when they know the father of their child has other children elsewhere who may be competing for his limited resources.

As Table 3 further indicates, paternity establishment through marriage or legal judgment is associated with a threefold increase in the likelihood of formal child support, but has no association with the other two forms of involvement. This finding is logical since paternity establishment is a prerequisite for obtaining a formal child support award agreement; whereas neither of the voluntary forms of involvement are contingent on legal status.

The focal child's age is predictive of formal child support only. The probability of receiving formal child support declines with age. Another association, limited to only one form of involvement, shows that children who were born to teen mothers were 50% less likely than children born to older mothers to have seen their fathers at least once in the past year.

Father involvement is also associated with the length of time mothers have received welfare. Among mothers who have received welfare for less than two years (as compared to the middle range of two to four years) the odds of formal child support decreased by 59%, but the odds of informal child support and father-child visitation increased 79% and 75% respectively. Interestingly, among mothers on welfare five or more years, the odds of receiving informal child support declined by 47%.

Finally, Table 3 reveals that compared to children with no father figure (other than the biological father), the odds of father-child visitation decline for children whose reported father figure is a relative or someone else. Moreover, for children whose father figure is the mother's partner or friend, the likelihood of receiving formal child support increases by 63%, while the likelihood of informal child support receipt and father-child visitation decreases by about a third. Perhaps nonresident fathers are less likely to remain involved with their children voluntarily when the mother has a new partner; alternatively, when fathers are not involved, a substitute father figure may help with childrearing, and mothers may be more likely to seek child support through the formal system.

Father involvement and child outcomes. Table 4 presents unstandardized regression coefficients for models predicting the five child outcome measures. The first column shows the model for the Caldwell Preschool Inventory (PSI), a school readiness indicator. Although an association between child support payments and cognitive outcomes was hypothesized, none of the measures of father involvement are associated with this child outcome in this sample. The main predictors of the PSI are the child's gender and age. Females score significantly higher than males, and, not surprisingly given the age sensitive nature of the assessment, scores improve with increases in age.

The second column indicates that both formal and informal child support are associated with this measure of emotional and behavioral development, suggesting that children benefit from the monetary and material support fathers provide. Even controlling for many factors, children who received formal or informal support from their fathers at least once in the past year received significantly higher (better) ratings from their mothers on the Personal Maturity Scale than their peers whose fathers did not contribute formally or informally.

Column three shows a marginally significant association between one father involvement measure, informal child support, and the HOME-SF. In partial support of this study's hypothesis regarding material resources, informal child support, but not formal child support, is associated with a more supportive home environment. This finding suggests that informal monetary and non-monetary contributions may improve the quality of the child's home environment.

Findings for the two sub-scales of the HOME-SF (columns 4 and 5) reveal that informal child support exerts its positive effect on the cognitive aspect of the home environment. The cognitive stimulation sub-scale includes items related to the overall safety and organization of the home environment, the availability of books and magazines in the home, whether someone helps the child learn basic academic skills, and whether someone takes the child on outings to church, the library, museums, and other places. Informal child support is the only father involvement indicator associated with this outcome. Children who receive informal support from their fathers have more cognitively stimulating environments than their peers who do not receive such support.[4]

Socioemotional sub-scale items refer to the emotional tone of the mother's interactions with her child, physical punishment of the child observed by the interviewer or reported by the mother, and the structuring of the child's day to provide choices, supervision, and support. There is no association between the father involvement measures and this sub-scale. Children who receive

TABLE 4. Unstandardized OLS Regression Coefficients for Models Predicting Child Outcomes

	PSI[a]	PMS[b]	HOME-SF Total	HOME-SF Cognitive	HOME-SF Socio-emotional
Intercept	−7.07	84.11	15.72	9.22	6.48
Father Involvement In Past Year					
Formal Child Support (1 = some)	0.30	4.90*	0.07	0.10	−0.17
Informal Child Support (1 = some)	0.54	4.02*	0.43†	0.39*	0.04
Visitation (1 = some)	−0.10	−1.35	−0.14	−0.08	−0.02
Child's Characteristics					
Child's gender (1 = male)	−1.45***	−3.60*	−0.52**	−0.31*	−0.28*
Child's age In months	0.46***	0.11	0.01	0.01	0.00
Mother's Characteristics					
Mother was married to father or legal paternity established	0.15	−1.17	0.54*	0.46**	0.16
Mother was age 19 or younger at child's birth	0.25	1.84	−0.25	−0.07	−0.14
Number of mother's own children	−0.53**	0.85	−0.34**	−0.21**	−0.16*
Mother is In Education/Training Group	0.20	0.03	−0.32	−0.20	−0.08
Mother is In Labor Force Group	0.94†	2.60	0.20	0.20	−0.09
Mother on welfare less than 2 years	0.80	6.28**	0.63*	0.31	0.28†
Mother on welfare 5 or more years	−0.44	−2.56	−0.09	0.08	−0.18
Mother has less than 12 years of education	−0.85†	−2.72	−0.47*	−0.46**	−0.04
Mother's literacy level	0.50*	6.76***	0.56***	0.35***	0.20**
Sources of Support					
Child's father figure is mother's partner or friend	−0.61	−4.46**	−0.06	0.11	−0.23†
Child's father figure is a relative or someone else	0.52	−2.70	0.26	0.18	0.03
Family of child's father provides some help	−0.03	−4.41*	0.41†	0.38*	−0.04
Mother's parents provide some help	−0.34	−1.81	0.40†	0.19	0.20
R^2	0.42	0.16	0.16	0.15	0.08
Sample Size	652.00	668.00	675.00	660.00	654.00

Source. Child Trends, Descriptive Survey, Atlanta, National Evaluation of Welfare to Work Strategies, 1992

Note. Table values (except sample sizes) are based on weighted data; means substituted for missing values on independent variables.

[a] Caldwell Preschool Inventory.

[b] Personal Maturity Scale.

† $p < .10$. * $p < .05$. ** $p < .01$. *** $p < .001$.

formal support, informal support, or visits from their fathers are at no greater or lesser advantage relative to their peers in terms of the socioemotional circumstances of their homes.

To determine whether father involvement is of greater or lesser importance for boys than girls, interaction terms of child's gender by each form of involvement were included with covariates in equations for the five outcomes (results not reported in tables). The three forms of involvement were then combined in a variable indicating no father involvement versus some father involvement and interacted with child's gender in regressions for each outcome. According to the significant findings that emerged, the receipt of informal child support is associated with improvements in the overall home environment and the socioemotional facets of the home environment for boys more than for girls. Similarly, the complete absence of father involvement appears to be more detrimental for boys in terms of their overall home environment, particularly the cognitive stimulation features of their home.

Policymakers and program administrators often predicate their efforts to increase nonresident father involvement on the assumption that both child support and father-child visitation are beneficial to children. The merits of formal child support and especially informal child support are reflected in the findings described above. To further analyze the relationship between visitation and selected child outcomes, two additional measures of father-child visitation, babysitting and overnight care, were also examined. However, analyses consistently failed to uncover associations between even these measures of father-child contact and child well-being. Indicators that capture the nature and quality of father-child contact may provide more insight.

DISCUSSION

Among these mothers on welfare in Atlanta in the early nineties, many nonresident fathers of children who receive welfare are involved with their children at least minimally. For example, while only 16.6% of fathers provided child support through the formal system during the past year, a considerably larger proportion (42.3%) provided informal child support, and 67% visited at least once in the past year. The most striking finding, given the premise of this study, is the relatively large proportion of fathers who made informal monetary and in-kind contributions directly to the mother in addition to, or more often, in lieu of payments through the welfare office. Clearly, a focus on formal child support alone as a measure of economic involvement may grossly underestimate the support provided by fathers of children on welfare.

Of the three forms of involvement examined here, informal support and visitation are most closely associated. Most of the predictors that are positively associated with informal child support are associated with visitation in the same direction. In fact, father's residence in the same state as the focal child and support from the father's family are the only two predictors associated with all three forms of involvement.

Other research using more precise measures of distance also shows that residential proximity is associated with increases in father involvement (Seltzer, 1991; Furstenberg et al., 1985). However, the direction of causation is unclear. Fathers who want to remain involved (and want to contribute informally and visit) may choose to live near their children to facilitate contact and support. On the other hand, proximity may *lead to* greater involvement, because it is much less difficult and costly to visit their children when fathers live nearby.

In terms of formal child support, it may be that mothers can report accurate information about fathers to the child support enforcement office, because they are more likely to know the address and employment status of fathers who live nearby. In addition, it is administratively easier for state child support enforcement agencies to collect from in-state fathers compared to out-of-state fathers.

Additionally, all three forms of involvement are more likely among those fathers whose family members also provide support for the child, such as clothes, toys, and child care, than among fathers with uninvolved family members. Again the direction of causation is unknown; however, prior research suggests that in many cases, the father's family assists in the care and support of the child and encourages the father to remain involved (Anderson, 1993; Sullivan, 1993).

Of keen interest to policymakers and researchers, is whether nonresident father involvement is beneficial to children. Overall, findings for the child well-being measures show, as hypothesized, that both formal and informal child support are positively associated with better ratings on the Personal Maturity Scale. Mothers who receive formal or informal support from fathers report fewer behavior problems and higher levels of social and emotional adjustment for their children. This finding is consistent with prior research showing that the payment of child support is associated with declines in school-related and general behavior problems (Furstenberg et al., 1987; McLanahan et al., 1994). In addition to the economic benefits of child support, some researchers propose that child support may be a proxy for unmeasured characteristics of the father. These can include a sense of responsibility for and commitment to the child, that enhance child well-being and are unique to fathers who are able and willing to provide for their children (King, 1994b; McLanahan et al., 1994). Given that this is a mother-report measure, better child behavior may also reflect a more positive perspective on the part of the mother, as well as improved behavior on the part of the child. Even small or inconsistent contributions from fathers through the formal system or directly to the mother may have both tangible and symbolic significance for mothers and children in this sample.

The informal child support measure provides the strongest evidence of an association between father involvement and child well-being. Informal child support is positively associated with the Personal Maturity Scale, as well as the HOME-SF and its cognitive stimulation sub-scale. Although both formal and informal child support were hypothesized to exert positive effects, these findings reveal that only informal child support is associated with improvements in the child's home environment, particularly the level of cognitive stimulation available. The lack of association between formal child support and outcomes in this domain suggests that the payments received through the formal system matter less than the money given directly to mothers or the value of the in-kind contributions fathers provided. Again, consider that at most only $50 of the father's formal child support payment is passed on to the mother and child. Edin and Lien (1997) note that among families on welfare, flexible arrangements were made around informal support. Nonresident fathers increase their monetary contribution or purchase specific items for the child when needed and then lower the amount of their contribution at less crucial times and when fathers were unable to assist. Perhaps the mothers in this sample made similar arrangements with the fathers of their children, which resulted in this positive association with the quality of the home environment.

This association between informal child support and the home environment is especially important because a cognitively stimulating home environment has positive effects on children's intellectual development (Mott, 1993). Over time, informal support from the father may be associated with improvements in cognitive assessment scores and academic achievement for these children.

As prior research has shown, in the absence of a more detailed measure of the nature and quality of father-child contact, no association between visitation and child well-being was observed. As noted, although the data offer new insights, the NEWWS evaluation was not designed to study fathers or father involvement, so information regarding fathers is limited.

In addition, all of the NEWWS evaluation data are mother-reported. For a variety of reasons, the mother may choose to under-report both the receipt of assistance from the father and father-child contact. Such under-reporting would inevitably undermine the strength of any associations. In recognition of the need for more and better data on fathers, several new and emerging surveys have plans to incorporate more items reported by and about fathers that may enhance future investigations (Federal Interagency Forum on Child And Family Statistics, 1998).

If the findings regarding formal and informal child support among low income and welfare samples were replicated in other, more representative populations, they might suggest varied policy approaches to this problem. These policy suggestions might range from increased efforts to help families leave welfare so they could receive child support payments directly from the father to passing a larger amount of the formal child support payment to the mother and child. The cooperative, voluntary, and non-punitive aspects of informal child support appear salient, and suggest that policy and programmatic efforts to assist fathers to become compliant may be more effective than punitive approaches. Mincy and Pouncy (1997) suggest that child support enforcement may be more effective for men in marginal situations when combined with assistance in finding conventional employment, strengthening ties with their children, and forging cooperative relations with the mothers of their children.

These data were collected before AFDC had been replaced with TANF. The new law strengthens provisions for paternity and establishment of a child support order and authorizes strict penalties for non-cooperation with these efforts. In addition, states are no longer required to, and many states have opted not to, pass through the first $50 of each child support payment to the family, and automated tracking procedures of delinquent child support accounts are being upgraded. On the other hand, the present welfare law allows states to use welfare-to-work grants, formerly restricted to custodial parents, for programs and services for non-custodial parents, usually fathers (Knitzer & Page, 1998). How these new provisions will interact to affect fathers' payment of formal child support, their provision of informal child support, their visitation with their children, and child well-being is unknown but worthy of future investigation.

NOTES

1. Under the new welfare legislation, states have the option to give all of the collected child support to the family; pass through an amount greater than, less than; or equal to $50; or discontinue the pass through whereby the family receives nothing. Results of a recent survey of states indicate that 30 states have opted to discontinue the pass through, 13 states plan to continue to pass through and disregard $50, six states will give families more than $50, one state plans to pass through less than $50, and one state plans to pass through the entire amount of child support collected and count it as earnings when considering TANF grant eligibility and receipt (Bernard, 1998).

2. Table 2 displays a detailed percent distribution of the father involvement variables. The available data only allowed for a dichotomous measure of formal support but a more detailed distribution of informal child support and visitation shows, for instance, that 21.3% of children saw their father about two to eleven times in the past

year, 14.6% saw him one to three times a month and 15% of children saw their father more than once a week.

3. In unpublished analysis (available from the authors on request) we find that about 70% of fathers were involved with their preschool children at least minimally in the past year; about 10% of fathers provided some formal child support and informal child support and also visited at least once. Only about 2.0% of fathers provided formal child support alone. Instead, fathers that paid formal child support were likely to have provided some informal child support and to have visited as well. However, the largest category of involvement, 30.6%, indicates that the combination of two forms, informal child support and visitation, was most common among these fathers. Yet, while only about 1% of fathers contributed informal child support alone, a full 21.7% visited without providing formal or informal support. These two findings suggest that fathers visit with their children when they bring items like money, groceries, clothes, or toys; however, when fathers visit with their children, they do not necessarily offer monetary or in-kind contributions.

4. There was only one instance in which the level or frequency of father involvement was significant. High informal support but not low informal support is associated with the cognitive sub-scale of the HOME-SF. Apparently, the occasional or one-time contribution of money, groceries, or other items is not substantial enough to significantly affect the cognitive aspects of the child's home environment.

REFERENCES

Achatz, M., & MacAllum, C. A. (1994). *Young unwed fathers, report from the field.* Philadelphia, PA: Public/Private Ventures.

Anderson, E. (1993). Sex codes and family life among poor inner-city youths. In R. I. Lerman & J. T. Ooms (Eds.), *Young unwed fathers* (pp. 27-51). Philadelphia: Temple University Press.

Arditti, J. A., & Keith, T. Z. (1993). Visitation frequency, child support payment, and the father-child relationship post-divorce. *Journal of Marriage and the Family, 55,* 699-712.

Argys, L.M., Peters, H.E., Brooks-Gunn, J., & Smith, J.R. (1998). The impact of child support on cognitive outcomes of young children. *Demography, 35,* 159-174.

Baker, P.C., & Mott, F.L. (1989). *NLSY child handbook.* Columbus, OH: Center for Human Resource Research.

Baydar, N., & Brooks, G. J. (1994). The dynamics of child support and its consequences for children. In I. Garfinkel, S. S. McLanahan, & P. K. Robins (Eds.), *Child support and child well-being* (pp. 257-279). Washington, DC: The Urban Institute Press.

Caldwell, B. M. (1970). *Cooperative preschool inventory.* Monterey, CA: CTB/McGraw-Hill.

Caldwell, B.M., & Bradley, R.H. (1984). *Home observation for the measurement of the environment.* Revised edition. Little Rock, AR: University of Arkansas.

Cooksey, E.C., & Craig, P.H. (1998). Parenting from a distance: The effects of paternal characteristics on contact between nonresidential fathers and their children. *Demography, 35,* 187-200.

Danziger, S. K., & Radin, N. (1990). Absent does not equal uninvolved: Predictors of fathering in teen mother families. *Journal of Marriage and the Family, 52,* 636-642.

Edin, K., & Lien, L. (1997). *Making ends meet: How single mothers survive welfare and low-wage work.* New York: Russell Sage Foundation.

Federal Interagency Forum on Child and Family Statistics (1998). *Nurturing fatherhood: Improving data and research on male fertility family formation and fatherhood.* Washington, DC: Author.

Furstenberg, F. F., & Harris, K. M. (1993). When and why fathers matter: Impacts of father involvement on the children of adolescent mothers. In R. I. Lerman & T. J. Ooms (Eds.), *Young unwed father: Changing roles and emerging policies.* (pp. 117-140). Philadelphia: Temple University Press.

Furstenberg, F. F., Morgan, S. P., & Allison, P.A. (1987). Paternal participation and children's well-being after marital dissolution. *American Sociological Review, 52,* 695-701.

Furstenberg, F. F., Nord, C. W., Peterson, J. L., Zill, N. (1983). The lifecourse of children of divorce: Marital disruption and parental contact. *American Sociological Review, 48,* 656-668.

Garrett, P., Ng'andu, N., & Ferron, J. (1994). Poverty experiences of young children and the quality of their home environments. *Child Development, 65,* 331-345.

Graham, J. W., Beller, A. H., & Hernandez, P. M. (1994). The determinants of child support income. In I. Garfinkel, S. S. McLanahan, & P. K. Robins (Eds.), *Child support and child well-being* (pp. 317-333). Washington, DC: The Urban Institute Press.

Hardy, J. B., Duggan, A. K., Masnyk, K., & Pearson, C. (1989). Fathers of children born to young urban mothers. *Family Planning Perspectives, 21,* 159-163.

Hess, R. D., & Camara, K. A. (1979). Post-divorce family relationships as mediating factors in the consequences of divorce for children. *Journal of Social Issues, 35,* 79-96.

King, V. (1994a). Variation in the consequences of nonresident father involvement for children's well-being. *Journal of Marriage and the Family, 56,* 963-972.

King, V. (1994b). Nonresident father involvement and child well-being. *Journal of Family Issues, 15,* 78-96.

Knitzer, J., & Page, S. (1998). *Map and track: State initiatives for young children and families.* New York: National Center for Children in Poverty.

Knox, V. W., & Bane, M. J. (1994). Child support and schooling. In I. Garfinkel, S. S. McLanahan, & P. K. Robins (Eds.), *Child support and child well-being* (pp. 285-310). Washington, DC: The Urban Institute Press.

Lerman, R. I. (1993). A National Profile of Young Unwed Fathers. In R. I. Lerman & J. T. Ooms (Eds.), *Young unwed fathers* (pp. 27-51). Philadelphia: Temple University Press.

McLanahan, S. S., Seltzer, J. A., Hanson, T. L., & Thomas, E. (1994). Child support enforcement and child well-being: Greater security or greater conflicts. In I. Garfinkel, S. S. McLanahan, & P. K, Robins (Eds.), *Child support and child well-being* (pp. 239-254). Washington, DC: The Urban Institute Press.

Mincy, R. B., & Pouncy, H. (1997). Paternalism, child support enforcement, and fragile families. In L.M. Mead (Ed.), *The new paternalism: Supervisory approaches to poverty* (pp. 130-160). Washington, DC: Brookings Institution Press.

Mincy, R. B., & Sorensen, E. (1998). Deadbeats and turnips in child support reform. *Journal of Policy Analysis and Management, 17,* 44-51.

Moore, K.A., Glei, D. A., Driscoll, A. K. & Glei, D.A. (1999. *Poverty and welfare patterns: Implications for children.* Washington, DC: Child Trends, Inc.

Moore, K.A., Zaslow, M.J., Coiro, M., Miller, S.M., & Magenheim, E.B. (1995). *The JOBS Evaluation: How well are they faring? AFDC families with preschool-aged children in Atlanta at the outset of the JOBS evaluation.* Washington, DC: U.S. Department of Health and Human Services, U.S. Department of Education.

Mott, F. L. (1990). When is a father really gone? Paternal-child contact in father-absent homes. *Demography, 27,* 499-517.

Mott, F.L. (1993). *Absent fathers and child development: Emotional and cognitive effects at ages five to nine.* (Report for the National Institute of Child Health and Development). Columbus: Ohio State University, Center for Human Resource Research.

Nord, C.W., Brimhall, D., & West, J. (1997). *Fathers' involvement in their children's schools.* Washington, DC: U.S. Department of Education, National Center for Education Statistics.

Perloff, J.N., & Buckner, J.C. (1996). Fathers of children on welfare: Their impact on child well-being. *American Journal of Orthopsychiatry, 66,* 557-571.

Rangarajan, A., & Gleason, P. (1998). Young unwed fathers of AFDC children: Do they provide support? *Demography, 35,* 175-186.

Seltzer, J.A. (1991). Relationships between fathers and children who live apart: The father's role after separation. *Journal of Marriage and the Family, 53,* 79-101.

Seltzer, J. A., & Bianchi, S. M. (1988). Children's contact with absent parents. *Journal of Marriage and the Family, 50,* 663-677.

Seltzer J. A. & Brandreth Y. (1994). What fathers say about involvement with children after separation. *Journal of Family Issues, 15,* 49-77.

Seltzer, J.A., Schaeffer, N.C., & Charing, H. (1989). Family Ties after divorce: The relationship between visiting and paying child support. *Journal of Marriage and the Family, 51,* 1013-1032.

Sullivan, M. L. (1993). Young fathers and parenting in two inner city neighborhoods. In R. T. Lerman & T. J. Ooms (Eds.), *Young unwed fathers* (pp. 52-73). Philadelphia: Temple University Press.

Intergenerational Transmission
of Fathering Roles
in At Risk Families

Frank F. Furstenberg
Christopher C. Weiss

SUMMARY. The purpose of this article is to examine the long-term consequences of paternal involvement for a sample of young men, with the intent being to examine whether patterns of fatherhood are transmitted across generations. Initially, a theoretical framework is discussed that has led researchers to expect that patterns of fatherhood will be produced across generations. Data from the Baltimore Parenthood Study were used, a 30-year longitudinal study that has followed the reproductive patterns of teenage parents and their children. A subsample of 110 males were examined with an occasional reference made to a subsample of females. Results indicated that a strong link existed between the stable presence of a biological father in the histories of the young men and the timing of their own family formation. Early fatherhood, both during the teen years and early twenties, is much more likely

Frank F. Furstenberg is the Zellerbach Family Professor of Sociology, University of Pennsylvania, Department of Sociology, 3718 Locust Walk, Philadelphia, PA 19104-6299 (e-mail: fff@pop.upenn.edu).

Christopher C. Weiss is affiliated with the University of Michigan, School of Education, 610 E. University, Ann Arbor, MI 48109-1259 (e-mail: ccweiss@umich.edu).

An earlier version of this paper was presented at the NICHD Family and Child Well-Being Network's Conference on Father Involvement, National Institute of Health, Bethesda, MD, October 10-11, 1996. This research was supported by a grant from The William T. Grant Foundation No. 94-1619-94. The authors would like to thank Laura Carpenter for her editorial assistance.

[Haworth co-indexing entry note]: "Intergenerational Transmission of Fathering Roles in At Risk Families." Furstenberg, Frank F., and Christopher C. Weiss. Co-published simultaneously in *Marriage & Family Review* (The Haworth Press, Inc.) Vol. 29, No. 2/3, 2000, pp. 181-201; and: *FATHERHOOD: Research, Interventions and Policies* (ed: H. Elizabeth Peters et al.) The Haworth Press, Inc., 2000, pp. 181-201. Single or multiple copies of this article are available for a fee from The Haworth Document Delivery Service [1-800-342-9678, 9:00 a.m. - 5:00 p.m. (EST). E-mail address: getinfo@haworthpressinc.com].

to occur if young men did not grow up living with their own fathers. Moreover, early fatherhood is somewhat more likely to occur if the young men did not have a stepfather in the past who was a stable presence in the home. Young fathers also were less likely to be living with their children if their own fathers had not lived in residence with them throughout childhood. *[Article copies available for a fee from The Haworth Document Delivery Service: 1-800-342-9678. E-mail address: getinfo@ haworthpressinc.com <Website: http://www.haworthpressinc.com>]*

KEYWORDS. Fatherhood, intergeneration, single parent

After a long period of neglect, fatherhood has begun to attract the attention of social scientists. With a few notable exceptions (Lamb, 1987; Liebow, 1967; Lynn, 1974; Parke, 1981; Pleck, 1981; Schultz, 1969), developmental and sociological researchers paid scant notice to the role of men in families except as breadwinners until the 1980s. More recently, studies on the causes and consequences of paternal participation have appeared.[1] This research has examined both the benefits conferred by "good dads"–the men who attend the childbirth classes and are present in the delivery room, change diapers, read books on child development, and come home early to pick up their children from nursery school–and at the costs incurred for children by those "bad dads" who not only fail to participate in these sorts of activities but absent themselves from the home altogether (Furstenberg, 1988).

Most social scientists have confirmed that fathers have a noticeable effect on their children's well-being; some would go even further to say that they have a distinctive role in the child's life and they matter in ways that are different from the ways that mothers matter for the developing child. (Popenoe, 1996, summarizes this argument in his recent volume, *Life Without Father.*)

This paper pursues these issues by examining the long-term consequences of paternal involvement for young men's own parenting behaviors, a topic that has generated much speculation but very little hard data. (See, for example, the reviews of Amato, 1994; Marsiglio, 1995a; Gadsden & Hall, 1995.) It is widely assumed that patterns of fathering are reproduced across generations (Cowan & Cowan, 1987; Gerson, 1993; Popenoe, 1996). At the same time, it is widely acknowledged that styles of fatherhood are changing historically: some men are becoming more and others less connected to their children than were their fathers (Demos, 1982; Griswold, 1993). Prospective data that might permit us to explore the continuities and discontinuities in fathering is difficult to come by partly because of the absence of interest in paternal relations in ongoing longitudinal studies.

A few investigations have surmounted this problem by following up studies that had questions on men's relationships with their children, but there is not yet a large enough body of research from which to reach any general conclusions. Elder's (1974) work on the Berkeley and Oakland cohorts shows that relations with fathers have distinctly different impacts for girls and boys, but the small size of the samples and the complex and contingent findings necessitate replication. Moreover, Elder's work did not focus on the question of how styles of fathering may have persisted across generations. The same can be said of the intergenerational study by Rossi and Rossi (1990), who primarily attend to relationships of parents and children over time. (See also Hill's intergenerational study, 1993.) The most relevant recent work on this issue was produced by Snarey (1993), who looked at the ways that men in adulthood profited by close attachments to their fathers. He finds strong hints of continuity in gender roles and men's sense of identity. The focus of this study is somewhat different, however: the timing of parenthood and co-residence among men and their children.

In this respect, the data that we will examine in this study chart new ground even though they come from a select population–the families of teenage parents. Although the findings reported here cannot be generalized to other populations, they provide information on a highly relevant and strategic group to social scientists who seek to understand the so-called "cycle of poverty" and to policy makers who want to break that cycle. The initial section of the paper lays out in more detail the theoretical framework that has led researchers to expect that patterns of fatherhood would be reproduced across generations. To test the theory, we use data from the Baltimore Parenthood Study–a 30-year longitudinal study that has followed the reproductive patterns of teenage parents and their children. The study, briefly described in the second part of this paper, extends findings from previous analyses on the males in the study (Furstenberg & Harris, 1993; Furstenberg, 1995). In the third part we begin the discussion of the results by showing the patterns of fathering provided to 110 males in the study for whom we have data from birth. We will also occasionally refer to comparable data from the 116 females in the Baltimore study, though they will serve more as a contrast than a principal focus of this analysis. Finally, we take up the main question of whether the fathering provided to the children influenced their patterns of family formation, looking specifically at the timing of first births and whether those who became fathers were residing with their children. The summary of the paper considers some of the implications of our results for further research and efforts at intervention.

WHY FATHERS MATTER

An important line of sociological research on men in the family is rooted in a theory of marriage. Matrimony is viewed as a social mechanism for connecting men to their offspring. Without this invention, children would lose the economic and social advantages conferred by patrimony (Davis, 1985; Goode, 1960; Malinowski, 1930). The benefits of legitimacy are obvious in a family system whereby men provide status and economic assets to their children and connect them to a wider kinship network that confers material and social benefits. The social value of marriage becomes less obvious, as Goode (1960) noted some years ago, among those at the lower rung of the social ladder in modern societies (see also Rodman, 1963; Rainwater, 1970; Schultz, 1969; Stack, 1974). Nonetheless, most previous research has demonstrated that paternal involvement by biological or surrogate fathers is linked to a set of discrete outcomes. First, it has been predominately associated with long-term economic success (Aldous, Osmond & Hicks, 1979; Amato, 1996; Haveman & Wolfe, 1994; McLanahan, 1988). Long-term economic prospects, in turn, are linked to timely family formation and conjugal stability (Cherlin, 1981; Sullivan, 1989; Testa, 1992; Wilson, 1987). Thus, men's presence in families is likely to be reproduced indirectly via status attainment across generations which, in turn, is linked to marriage and greater prospects of marital stability across generations.

Various theorists from both social and developmental psychology contend that a more direct path exists between the presence of fathers in one generation and the next (Lamb, 1987; Parke, 1981). Ample evidence exists that a father's presence in the home may promote a positive gender identification and his absence may undermine such an identification. A long tradition in developmental and sociological research explores the ways that males introduce an element of social control in the family by lending authority to their partners or exercising it directly to regulate behavior (Hetherington, 1987; McLanahan & Sandefur, 1994). The mere presence of another stable figure in the family creates the sense of parental unity and, in contemporary sociological parlance, increases family-based social capital by creating normative consensus within the household (Coleman, 1988; Furstenberg, 1998; Furstenberg & Hughes, 1995; Sampson, 1992). By the same token, of course, the father's presence in the home potentially creates conflict between parental figures and undermines the child's acquisition of social norms (Amato & Booth, 1991; Arendell, 1986; Maccoby & Mnookin, 1992; Seltzer, 1991). The developmental benefits of having two parents in the home are thus conditional: enhanced when the parents can successfully collaborate and diminished when they cannot (Amato, 1996). Thus, it would seem that a child who develops a close attachment to his father will benefit over and above the attachment he may form with his mother. Indeed, children should especially profit when they form a close bond with both of their parents (Ahrons & Miller, 1993; Furstenberg & Cherlin, 1991).

Much less agreement exists among researchers on whether the contribution of fathers outside the home is likely to improve children's developmental prospects and hence improve the chances of paternal involvement in the succeeding generation (Marsiglio, 1995b; Amato, 1996). Previous findings from research that my colleagues and I conducted show little evidence for this proposition (Furstenberg & Harris, 1992; 1993). Other investigators find mixed evidence for the premise that children do better in the long run when biological fathers remain involved in their children's lives (Barber, 1994; King, 1994; Wallerstein & Blakeslee, 1989). The problem, it seems, is that most fathers become rather marginal figures in their children's lives, even when they do continue to see them.

The role of surrogate fathers, stepfathers in particular, is even more ambiguous. Most research indicates that, on average, stepfathers do not improve children's long-term prospects despite the fact that they appear to lift their economic status (Booth & Dunn, 1994; Cherlin & Furstenberg, 1994; Hetherington & Arasteh, 1989; Zill, 1978). Many researchers have concluded that the step-parent role promotes conflict and normative confusion within the household and possibly competition with the biological parent outside the home. Still, we do not fully understand when step-parents improve the child's life prospects and when they do not, as step-parents typically assume parental responsibilities after a divorce has occurred. No study as yet has effectively separated the presumably adverse impact of remarriage from the presumably adverse impact of divorce (Morrison, 1995).

The various reasons why the stable presence of a father in the home, especially when he effectively co-parents with his partner, produces positive developmental outcomes for children are related and mutually reinforcing when clustered together. Similarly, the reasons why the absence of a father or his withdrawal from childrearing can be detrimental are also often packaged together. Indeed, the configuration of advantages or disadvantages can be expected to produce a powerful difference between children who enjoy a positive relationship with a father who resides continuously in the home compared to those whose fathers have withdrawn from their lives or who do not play a stable and positive role in their upbringing.

A number of theories might also lead us to predict that the absence of fathers is particularly hard for boys who miss out not only on fathers as models and mentors but also on fathers as agents of social control and sponsorship in the outside world (Amato, 1993; Hetherington, 1987, Patterson, DeBaryshe, Ramsey, 1989; Wallerstein & Blakeslee, 1989). From Moynihan (1965) to Wilson (1987) to Anderson (1990), many commentators on African American and inner-city families have referred to the pernicious consequences of paternal absence for perpetuating disadvantage from one generation to the next. It has also been noted in prior research that girls may be vulnerable to the absence of a father in the home, though possibly the effects of his absence might differ (Wallerstein & Blakeslee, 1989).

Previous analyses on prior phases of the Baltimore study have provided some evidence that the stable presence of a male in the home improves the chances of children doing well in late adolescence (Brooks-Gunn, Guo & Furstenberg, 1993; Furstenberg, Brooks-Gunn & Morgan, 1987; Furstenberg & Harris, 1993). A small-scale case study of the male offspring who themselves had children early in life revealed that most had limited contact with their fathers or father surrogates (Furstenberg, 1995). Despite passionate pledges not to repeat the pattern exhibited by their dads, they seemed all but destined to reproduce what had happened to them. However, this previous research considered only a small number of cases and did not include youth who postponed parenthood. This analysis follows up the leads from the earlier qualitative case study, comparing young men who grew up with a stable father in the home with those who lived apart from their father and who experienced varying degrees of investment and involvement from him. It draws on new survey data from the most recent wave of the Baltimore study which was completed in 1996.

THE BALTIMORE SAMPLE

In 1966-1968, as part of one of the nation's first comprehensive prenatal programs for adolescent mothers, 323 (out of an initial sample of 398 eligible cases) women were followed from pregnancy through the first five years after delivery. The initial objective of the study was to evaluate the impact of a pre-natal intervention, and these interviews collected only a minimal amount of information about the father and his participation in the family. The topics covered in these early study waves centered on the mother and child. At the three-year follow up, we attempted to interview the fathers of the children, but nearly half simply could not be located. As time went on, however, the focus of the study shifted to tracing the life course of the family and the well-being of the children. Accordingly, we began to collect more data about the involvement of the biological fathers and/or the surrogates who had assumed parental responsibilities.

Interviews with the mothers and their children who had reached mid-adolescence were conducted in 1984 and again in 1987, when the children were in their late teens and early twenties. The 1983 and 1987 interviews included a life-history calendar that was recorded for each year for the parents and firstborn child. The calendar provided information on whether children were living with their biological fathers, and if not, whether surrogate fathers were present in the home. In addition, we asked the mother (or mother surrogate when the mother was not residing with the child) about contact with the biological father and financial support provided by him. The children were asked several questions about their relationship with their biological father–when contact occurred at least on a monthly basis–and also about the quality of relations with any male who was in the child's judgment "like a father" to him or her. In 1995-96 we completed a 30-year follow up of the mothers, their children, and the offspring of the children–the grandchildren of the original sample of teen mothers. The children of the teen mothers were in their late twenties, and many had begun to establish families. These new data allow us to examine how the involvement of their fathers during their formative years has affected their own patterns of family formation.

Table 1 provides a summary of the study design and sample loss. In the early stages of the study, we followed teen mothers who remained in Baltimore and who kept their children. We lost a disproportionate number of white women (originally 20% of the sample) who moved away or who remained unmarried and gave up their children for adoption. At the one-year follow up, we managed to interview 339 of the mothers who had children with whom

TABLE 1. Design of the Baltimore Study

Interview Schedule	Interview Dates	Participants	Completed Interviews
Time 1: During Pregnancy	1966-1968	Adolescent Mothers	404
		Mothers of Adolescent Mothers	350
Time 2: 1 Year After Delivery	1968-1970	Adolescent Mothers	382
Time 3: 3 Years After Delivery	1970	Adolescent Mothers	363
Time 4: 5 Years After Delivery	1972	Adolescent Mothers	331
		Children of Adolescent Mothers	306
Time 5: 16-17 Years After Delivery	1983-1984	Adolescent Mothers or Surrogates	289 35
		Children of Adolescent Mothers	296
Time 6: 20 Years After Delivery	1987	Adolescent Mothers or Surrogates	243
		Children of Adolescent Mothers	252
Time 7: 29 Years After Delivery	1995-1996	Adolescent Mothers or Surrogates	228 19
		Children of Adolescent Mothers	226
		Grandchildren of Adolescent Mothers	92

they were residing. Mortality among the mothers and children was another significant source of attrition. By the 30-year follow up, 5% of the mothers and 3% of the children were no longer living. Of the 308 children who were still living (as far as we could ascertain), we managed to interview 226 in 1995-96, representing two-thirds of the children who were in the mother's household at the one-year follow up. Since most attrition occurred among whites and women who married, we did particularly well in re-interviewing the black households. Surprisingly, we managed to locate and interview roughly the same proportion of young men and women. This was accomplished by interviewing 20 males and 2 females who were in jail at the time of the interview.

PATERNAL CONTACT AND RELATIONS DURING CHILDHOOD

Previous research has shown that the early years of parenthood may not provide a good indication of continued paternal co-residence, especially for young parents (Furstenberg, Nord, Peterson, & Zill, 1983; Mott, 1990; Seltzer, 1991). Young fathers may not move in with the mothers prior to or even right after birth because they lack the means to set up an independent household and may not be welcomed in the maternal home. Others who are able to establish a separate residence or move into the mother's household tend to stay only for a short time. Consequently, an informative way of examining this issue is through a distribution of time that biological fathers co-reside with their sons throughout the entire duration of childhood up to age 15 (see Table 2). The survey data presented in Table 2 show that more than half of the biological fathers (the teen mother's partners) never lived with their sons for as long as a full year (a few of these men may have spent a brief spell living

TABLE 2. Males' Residential Experiences with Fathers During Childhood and Adolescence

Years Lived With Biological Father, Birth to Age 15	0 Years	1-5 Years	6-10 Years	11-14 Years	15 Years
	52% (n = 57)	25% (n = 27)	10% (n = 11)	3% (n = 3)	11% (n = 12)
Amount of Contact With Biological Father at Mid-Adolescence (If Not Living With Father and Father Not Deceased)	Weekly	Monthly	Occasionally	None	
	22% (n = 20)	14% (n = 12)	30% (n = 27)	33% (n = 30)	

with their children before moving out), while 11% lived with them continuously following delivery. The others resided with the child for 1 to 14 years (the median was four years), but were not living with him by the time he reached mid-adolescence. Most of the men who were not residing with the child did not have regular contact with him. Few (22%) saw their sons as often as weekly or even monthly (14%); most were in touch on an occasional basis (30%) or had no contact at all (33%).

As we reported earlier, qualitative interviews conducted in 1987 and 1993 indicated that the children were anything but casual about the absence of their fathers. It was common for children to speak of their biological father with pain, bitterness, or a sense of resignation.

> When I was younger I didn't have any positive role models, males around . . . I hadn't seen my father since I was 5 years old . . . I wanted him so bad in my life that by the time I got out of high school I didn't think about him anymore. I didn't want to think about him anymore.

> [When he left] I can't remember [him]. I guess I was between the age of three to four. Far as I can see it he is not my father. A father is not the person that bears the child, it's the person that raises the child . . . A father's not somebody who's not going to be there for you.

> He stays with his mother and I go to my grandmother's house quite a bit. I see him . . . Sometime I don't think he know I am talking to him. His head will nod off and you know. Really I don't pay any attention. If I take friends over there I don't introduce him as my father, I just introduce him as a person. I never did call him daddy, so I don't introduce him as my father. In other words, I am ashamed of him.

We found no indication in the qualitative study that these sentiments were altered by the presence of a stepfather or surrogate father in the home. Almost all of the males who had not lived with their fathers–and even most who did–had lived with a stepfather or with a partner of their mother during part of their childhood. Nearly half the children who had resided with a surrogate father spent nine or more years living with him, and one-third of these children were living with a father during their mid-teens. Many of the males retained some contact with these men who had been "daddies" to them, though the day-to-day involvement of non-residential surrogate fathers in the child's life was typically limited. Whether they were biological or non-biological fathers, the day-to-day role of these men was largely ritualistic. From time to time they were consulted on problems, helped out in emergencies, and provided a presence at celebratory occasions. But they were often not around as a steady presence in the child's life and generally could not be counted on regularly to meet the child's needs.

In sum then, fewer than a quarter of the males had experienced the continuous in-home presence of any father into their adolescent years. Many others had spent relatively long spells residing with a male in the home, though only rarely was this male their biological father. (Parenthetically, these results apply equally to the female offspring, who were no more or less likely to have lived with their fathers than the males in the study.) Although ethnographers have made much of the presence of non-residential fathers in the lives of African American children, evidence from surveys–especially those taken when the children are older–demonstrates that few fathers, living apart from their children, play an active role in their lives (Furstenberg, 1995; Seltzer, 1991; Teachman, 1991).

Perhaps the limited role of fathers is most clearly indicated in the data on the quality of the relationship between men and their sons which was collected in 1983 when the male offspring were in their mid-teens. Table 3 displays an index of the quality of the father-son relationship constructed from two interrelated items measuring the degree of closeness and the extent that sons wanted to be like their fathers when grown up. The results are striking, showing as they do the paucity of boys who had both a close relationship with their father and said that they wanted to be like him when they grew up. Indeed, we could not ask most boys the questions as they saw their fathers too infrequently for the questions to be appropriate. (It seemed insensitive to ask the children how close they felt to their fathers when they

TABLE 3. Males' Relations with Fathers During Childhood and Adolescence, by Their Residential Experience

Males' Experience with Father Figures (Biological Father or Someone Else "Like a Father" to Them)	Avg. Number of Years Lived with Any Father	% Living with Any Father at 1983 Interview	% Close to Father and Want to Be Like Rim
"Little Fathering" Less than 5 years with any father (n = 32)	2.3 years	16%	13%
"Sporadic Fathering" 6-9 years with any father (n = 53)	8.6 years	42%	18%
"Step-Fathering" 10 or more years with any father (n = 10)	13.7 years	100%	30%
"Biological Fathering" 10 or more years with biological father (n = 14)	14.9 years	100%	79%

had not seen them in the past year.) Although nearly four in five of the boys (79%) who were living with their biological fathers felt very close to them and wanted to be like them when grown up, fewer than one in five (17%) of those who were not living with them provided this response. Only rarely, then, do biological fathers living outside the home sustain an intimate relationship with their adolescent sons.

Even more striking than the results on the biological fathers is the absence of close ties to men who may have taken the father's place in the home. Overall, few of the males report a very close relationship with a stepfather or surrogate father. Few of these boys felt very close to their stepfather or wanted to be like him when they grew up. Remarkably, this result applied even to the non-biological father figures who had lived with the males for at least 10 years; only 30% of these boys felt very close to him and wanted to be like him when they grew up. Contrast these findings to the relationships reported by the sons with their mothers, the vast majority of whom (79%) were coresidents with their biological moms (data not shown in table). Specifically, 58% said that they felt very close to their mothers and wanted to be like them when they grew up, more than twice the proportion that felt that way about their fathers.

The skewed distributions of these findings (i.e., the large number of males living apart from their fathers) poses some problems for examining the intergenerational influence of fathers. Just 14 boys lived with their biological fathers throughout childhood, eleven of whom reported a close relationship with their male parent. About an equal number of males who were living apart from their fathers stated that they were close to them and wanted to be like their fathers when they were older. Ten males had been living with a stepfather, but only a few of these had a very strong relationship with him. Such a diversity of patterns among a small sample obviously presents some challenges for drawing conclusions about inter-generational influences. The analysis that follows must be considered exploratory and the findings provisional. Nonetheless, they point to some interesting directions for further research.

PATTERNS OF FAMILY FORMATION AMONG YOUNG ADULT MALES

Many different indicators could be examined to assess the possible influence of paternal involvement on young men's development. We selected two of obvious policy importance which, according to the theoretical positions described in the first part of this paper, seem to be plausibly connected to the active presence of a father in the young man's life. The first is whether the young man had a child by the time of the interview; the second, whether those who have become fathers are residing with their child. Neither of these outcomes necessarily represents "responsible" or "irresponsible" family formation; however, when examined together, they do provide a reasonable assessment of whether patterns of paternal involvement are recurring. Essentially, these two indicators serve as good starting points for exploring the mechanisms whereby fathering may be reproduced.

By their late twenties, 65% of the males reported having at least one child, with 22% having their first child before the age of 20.[2] These levels are only slightly higher than the birth timing for all African American men, but much earlier than the birth timing for whites (Alan Guttmacher Institute, 1994).

Judging from previous studies, some under-reporting of parenthood is likely to have occurred (Marsiglio, 1987). Men who fail to remain in contact with their offspring may fail to report them in social surveys, perhaps out of denial of responsibility, doubts that they were the actual fathers, or in order to avoid claims of child support. We know from in-depth interviews of men and reports from women that, in all likelihood, the figures reported above are understatements. For example, 7% of the young women in the Baltimore study who were mothers said that their child's father did not acknowledge paternity. Moreover, 28% of the males in the study replied affirmatively to the question when asked in 1987: Have you ever had a girlfriend who said you had gotten her pregnant but you didn't know for sure? However, once children were acknowledged, all but 3% were reported in subsequent interviews.

At the time of the 1996 interview, the firstborn children of the men were 7 years old on average. Just 30% of the men who had become fathers were living with their child at the time of the 1996 interview. Of course, they may later move in with their child or could become supportive and involved non-residential parents. Still as we argued earlier, most non-residential fathers will not play an active role in their children's lives, whether through seeing them on a regular basis, having overnights with them, or providing significant amounts of child support throughout their lives. It appears that absent fatherhood was in most instances reoccurring for the men who had already become fathers.

Now we turn to the central question of this paper: whether father absence seems to be implicated in the inter-generational persistence of low paternal participation. We will attempt to answer a series of related questions: (1) Did men who experienced limited fathering from their biological fathers become parents earlier in life and withdraw attentions from their own children? (2) How much did it matter whether a surrogate father entered the men's lives and provided persistent attention? and, (3) To what extent did close and continuous relationships with their mother mitigate the absence of paternal involvement?

CONTINUITIES IN PATERNAL PARTICIPATION

In view of the small number of cases, the models used to examine these questions are quite restricted. In separate models, we calculate the likelihood of becoming a father by the late twenties for men with varying patterns of co-residence with either biological or surrogate fathers. We then introduce closeness to biological and non-biological fathers to determine whether the quality of the relationship with a father inside or outside the home accounts for the relationship of outcomes to patterns of co-residence. We also consider whether the results are altered when closeness with mothers is included in the model. The analysis permits us to get some purchase on the initial question of whether paternal presence affects what Marsiglio (1987) refers to as "the stockpile of ideas related to the expression of fatherhood roles."

We then recapitulate this analysis just for men who have ever had a child by looking at whether they are co-residing with their offspring, which researchers have considered to be an indication of assuming a high level of paternal responsibility for offspring. This measure of "responsible fatherhood," however, excludes men who have postponed childbearing. We can solve this limitation by combining the previous measures in a single outcome that determines whether men either waited to have children or had a child with whom they were residing. Obviously, such a measure is taken at a single point in time and, as such, may overstate the extent of "responsible fatherhood" given that some men may have children and subsequently not reside with them or move away from children with whom they are currently living. Conversely, a small number may yet live with children with whom they are not currently residing or take an active role in raising their children though they will never live with them. Our earlier analysis of these men's own fathers suggests these cases will be relatively rare.

Table 4 shows the results of the first analysis, which considers whether the male offspring had a child by their late twenties. Clearly, the absence of a resident biological father greatly increased the odds of fatherhood among both the males who had not resided with their fathers for more than 5 years as well as those whose fathers had resided with them for longer periods, but no longer did so by mid-adolescence. Despite the small sample, both groups were significantly different from the males who were still living with biological fathers in their mid-teens. The young men who had grown up with stepfathers and were still living with them in adolescence were somewhat more likely to have had a child by their late twenties, but the increased likelihood was not statistically significant.

We were not able to run the regression model to ascertain if this pattern of fathering was related to teen births because none of the men with in-home biological fathers and only one male who had a stable surrogate father had become a father before age 20. By comparison, there was nearly a quarter of

TABLE 4. Logistic Regression Estimates of Fatherhood Patterns Among Youth, by Fathering Received During Childhood

	Has Child			Lives with Child			Composite		
	1	2	3	1	2	3	1	2	3
Father Type[a]									
Little Fathering	1.376* (.68)	1.031 (.75)	1.419* (.68)	−1.168 (1.02)	−1.556 (1.23)	−1.173 (1.03)	−1.667* (.84)	−1.555 (.91)	−1.691 (.84)
Sporadic Fathering	1.453* (.63)	1.143 (.70)	1.543* (.64)	−1.693 (1.00)	−2.018 (1.16)	−1.699 (1.01)	−2.015* (.81)	−1.914* (.87)	−2.069 (.82)
Step-Fathering	.993 (.85)	.686 (.91)	1.043 (.86)	−.405 (1.22)	−.731 (1.36)	−.409 (1.23)	−.944 (1.03)	−.845 (1.07)	−.972 (1.03)
Father Closeness	—	−.540 (.52)	— —	— —	−.505 (.87)	— —	— —	.171 (.53)	— —
Mother Closeness	— —	— —	.368 (.42)	— —	— —	−.024 (.56)	— —	— —	−.232 (.41)
N	110	110	110	70	70	70	110	110	110

Note. Standard errors are reported in parentheses. [a]Omitted Category is Biological Fathering. *p < .05

the men in the other groupings. Clearly, growing up without a stable father figure in the home is strongly related to having a child early in life.

How much does closeness with the father account for the difference? The second column of Table 4 shows that the quality of the father-son relationship does not change the association between the timing of first birth and paternal presence. Similarly, in the third column we found closeness to mothers does not modify the relationship of paternal presence. A son's relationship to either parent does not appear to be significantly related to the timing of his first birth.

The second stage of our analysis examined the fathering patterns of the males who had become fathers. The results presented in the middle three columns of Table 4 show a strong association with the presence of a father in the home throughout childhood. Sons whose biological fathers were absent were significantly less likely to be living with their own children, compared to those who lived with their fathers through adolescence. Males who grew up with a stepfather in the home were somewhat, but not significantly, less likely to live with their children as well. As before, closeness to either parent in adolescence did not modify the likelihood that a son would reside with his child later in life.

Our final measure of "responsible fatherhood," shown in rightmost three columns of Table 4, combines both of the previous measures by distinguishing the males who either defer fatherhood or live with the child whom they have conceived. Not surprisingly, we see the same pronounced differences between the males who grew up with a father in the home and those who did not. The sharpest differences occur among the small number of boys who lived with their biological father through mid-adolescence. They were substantially more likely either to defer parenthood or to be living with their child as the men whose fathers were not in the home when they were in their middle-teens. Males who had spent considerable time with resident fathers, but were no longer living with them during the 17-year follow up, were no more likely to practice "responsible" patterns of family formation than were males who had spent little time with residential fathers. Males who had grown up with stepfathers in the home also were less likely to be responsible fathers. Specifically, the difference between men who had grown up with stepfathers and those who lived with their biological father at age 17 was not statistically significant. It appears that these men are at moderate risk for both premature and non-residential fatherhood, but the small number of cases precludes a clear-cut conclusion.

As observed in the earlier analysis, the quality of relationships with parents does not account for these findings. Closeness to biological or non-biological fathers does not lessen the risk of "irresponsible" fatherhood for either the men whose fathers lived outside the home or those whose fathers lived with them during their formative years. Whatever the benefits of a stable paternal presence, it does not seem to derive from merely being close to a responsible father figure or wanting to be like him in later life.

We examined whether the pattern of paternal presence is merely a proxy for the socio-economic status of the family. As expected, the two-parent families in the Baltimore study–especially when both are the biological parents–are much better off than the single-parent households. They are also more likely to have the accouterments of middle-class life–a savings account, a credit card, a car, and so on. In a separate analysis not shown here, we discovered that the economic well-being of the family was, as predicted, related to "responsible fatherhood" among the male offspring of the teen parents (though the magnitude of the relationship was modest). However, the introduction of the economic measures into the model did not greatly reduce the effect of paternal presence. In other words, the impact of the father's presence in the home on perpetuating "responsible parenthood" could not merely be explained by the material resources he provided.

Finally, we examined whether long-term residential fathers provided a source of authority, regulation, and perhaps social capital contributing to the sense of responsibility that developed among their offspring. We constructed an index of items reported by the mother on how much influence the father had over the child and whether he collaborated successfully with the mother on childrearing practices. None of the items, separately or combined into a single index, predict patterns of family formation. Nor, when entered into the model, did they account for the association between paternal presence during childhood and responsible parenthood.

Our analysis also considered the impact of fathering on family formation among the female offspring of Baltimore Study mothers. We used the early timing of the first birth as the relevant outcome since three-fourths of the women were mothers and virtually all were living with their child. The patterns described above for the males were not replicated for the females. The father's presence in the home was unrelated to the timing of first birth. Closeness with the father was also unrelated to early parenthood for all the groupings. Thus, the effect of the father's presence appears to be gender-specific.

CONCLUSION

This analysis has explicitly focused on the males in the Baltimore study–a longitudinal study of the offspring of families created by a teenage birth–to explore a question that has both theoretical and policy relevance: whether family formation patterns are linked to the active involvement of fathers, biological or surrogate. We discovered a strong link between the stable presence of a father–especially if he is the child's progenitor–and the timing of family formation among the males in the study. Early fatherhood, both during the teen years and in the early twenties, is much more likely to occur if men did not grow up living with their fathers and is somewhat more likely to occur if they did not have a stepfather who was a stable presence in the home. Young fathers were also less likely to be living with their children if their father did not reside with them throughout childhood.

We explored several sources that might account for the observed link between paternal responsibility across generations. The child's relationship with his father (or, for that matter, his mother) was not implicated in this link. Men who had been close to fathers and wanted to be like them when they grew up were over-represented in the families where fathers were a stable presence in the home, but the quality of relations with fathers did not mediate the association with paternal responsibility nor was it a strong independent predictor of paternal responsibility. Similarly, we found no evidence that the link could be explained by the economic advantages associated with a two-parent household. Households were better off when two biological parents were present, and economic resources increased the probability of responsible fatherhood; however, economic resources did not substantially lessen the association between paternal presence and responsible parenthood among the male offspring. Finally, we examined a series of questions that tapped the father's involvement in childrearing and ability to collaborate with the mother. None of these questions separately or combined in an index was strongly related to responsible family formation. They did not reduce the strength of the relationship between paternal presence and the male offspring's pattern of family formation.

These findings appeared to be confined to the males in the Baltimore study. When examined separately, early timing of motherhood is unaffected by the presence of a father in the home or by a girl's closeness to either her residential or non-residential father. Apparently, the results reported in this paper showing that the presence of a stable father figure in the home affects the likelihood of responsible parenthood (as defined by postponement of first birth until a father can live with his child) is limited to males in this study. We are aware that this finding conflicts with evidence from several large-scale studies showing that girls in mother-headed families initiate sex earlier and enter parenthood sooner. However, these studies are not based on populations of inner-city African Americans. We are currently examining information from the National Longitudinal Survey of Youth to determine the robustness of our results.

This study presents an intriguing finding and a puzzle for future research: How does the presence of a stable male figure in the home shape the pattern of family formation in the next generation of males? We were unable to account for the relatively strong association by recourse to some of the popular explanations invoked for the reproduction of fathering across generations. It seems that stable fathers make a difference, but how and why they do remains something of a mystery. In the near future, we intend to look closely at both the qualitative and quantative interviews for clues. We are on the right trail, but we are still not quite certain where it will eventually lead us.

NOTES

1. A number of excellent edited volumes contain this research work: Hanson & Bozett, 1985; Kimmel, 1987; Lamb, 1987; Lamb & Sagi, 1983; Lerman & Ooms, 1993; Marsiglio, 1995a, as well as volumes summarizing primary research such as Coltrane, 1996; Gerson, 1993; Marsiglio, 1998; and Parke, 1996.

2. By contrast, three-quarters of the female offspring were mothers by their late twenties and 38% had borne their first child by age 20.

REFERENCES

Ahrons, C. R., & Miller, R. B. (1993). The effect of the postdivorce relationship on paternal involvement: A longitudinal analysis. *American Journal of Orthopsychiatry, 63,* 441-450.

Alan Guttmacher Institute. (1994). *Sex and America's teenagers.* New York: Alan Guttmacher Institute.

Aldous, J., Osmond, M. W., & Hicks, M. W. (1979). Men's work and men's families. In W. R. Burr, R. Hill, F. I. Nye & I. L. Reiss (Eds.), *Contemporary theories about the family*, (Vol. 1, pp. 227-256). New York: The Free Press.

Amato, P. R. (1993). Children's adjustment to divorce: Theories, hypotheses, and empirical support. *Journal of Marriage and the Family, 55*,1, 23-38.

Amato, P. R. (1994). Father-child relations, mother-child relations, and offspring psychological well-being in early adulthood. *Journal of Marriage and the Family, 56*, 1031-1042.

Amato, P. R. (October 1996). More than money? Men's contributions to their children's lives. Paper presented at the Men in Families Symposium, The Pennsylvania State University, State College, PA.

Amato, P. R., & Booth, A. (1991). The consequences of divorce for attitudes toward divorce and gender roles. *Journal of Family Issues, 12*, 306-322.

Anderson, E. (1990). *StreetWise*. Chicago: University of Chicago Press.

Arendell, T. (1986). *Mothers and divorce: Legal, economic, and social dilemmas*. Berkeley: University of California Press.

Barber, B. L. (1994). Support and advice from married and divorced fathers: Linkages to adolescent adjustment. *Family Relations, 43*, 433-438.

Booth, A., & Dunn, J. (Eds.). (1994). *Stepfamilies: Who benefits? Who does not?* Hillsdale, NJ: Lawrence Erlbaum.

Brooks-Gunn, J., Guo, G., & Furstenberg, F. F. (1993). Who drops out of and who continues beyond high school? A 20-year follow-up of Black urban youth. *Journal of Research on Adolescence, 3*, 3, 271-294.

Cherlin, A. J. (1981). *Marriage, divorce, remarriage*. Cambridge, MA: Harvard University Press.

Cherlin, A. J., & Furstenberg, F. F. (1994). Stepfamilies in the United States: A reconsideration. *Annual Review of Sociology, 20*, 359-381.

Coleman, J. S. (1988). Social capital in the creation of human capital. *American Journal of Sociology, 94* (Suppl. 95), S95-S120.

Coltrane, S. (1996). *Family man: Fatherhood, housework, and gender equity*. New York: Oxford University Press.

Cowan, C. P., & Cowan, P. A. (1987). Men's involvement in parenthood: Identifying the antecedents and understanding the barriers. In P. W. Berman & F. A. Pedersen (Eds.), *Men's transitions to parenthood: Longitudinal studies of early family experience* (pp. 145-174). Hillsdale, NJ: Lawrence Erlbaum.

Davis, K. (1985). *Contemporary marriage: Comparative perspectives on a changing institution*. New York: Russell Sage Foundation.

Demos, J. (1982). The changing faces of fatherhood: A new exploration in American family history. In S. H. Cath, A. R. Gurwitt, & J. M. Ross (Eds.), *Father and child: Developmental and clinical perspectives* (pp. 425-445), Boston: Little, Brown.

Elder, G. H., Jr. (1974). *Children of the Great Depression: Social change in life experience*. Chicago: University of Chicago Press.

Furstenberg, F. F. (1988). Good dads-bad dads: The two faces of fatherhood. In A. J. Cherlin (Ed.), *The changing American family and public policy* (pp. 193-218). Washington, D.C.: Urban Institute Press.

Furstenberg, F. F. (1995). Fathering in the inner-city: Paternal participation and public policy. In W. Marsiglio (Ed.), *Fatherhood: Contemporary theory, research, and social policy* (pp. 119-147). Thousand Oaks, CA: Sage Publications.

Furstenberg, F. F. (1998). Social capital and the role of fathers in the family. In A. Booth & N. Crouter (Eds.), *Men in families: When do they get involved? What difference does it make?* (pp. 295-301). Mahwah, NJ: Lawrence Erlbaum, Assoc.

Furstenberg, F. F., Brooks-Gunn, J., & Morgan, S. P. (1987). *Adolescent mothers in later life.* New York: Cambridge University Press.

Furstenberg, F. F., & Cherlin, A. J. (1991). *Divided families: What happens to children when parents part.* Cambridge, MA: Harvard University Press.

Furstenberg, F. F., & Harris, K. M. (1992). The disappearing American father? Divorce and the waning significance of biological parenthood. In S. J. South & S. Tolnay (Eds.), *Demographic perspectives on the American family: Patterns and prospects* (pp. 197-223). Boulder, CO: Westview Press.

Furstenberg, F. F., & Harris, K. M. (1993). When and why fathers matter: Impacts of father involvement on the children of adolescent mothers. In R. Lerman & T. Ooms (Eds.), *Young unwed fathers: Changing roles and emerging policies* (pp. 117-138). Philadelphia: Temple University Press.

Furstenberg, F. F., & Hughes, M. E. (1995). Social capital and successful development among at-risk youth. *Journal of Marriage and the Family, 57*(3), 580-592.

Furstenberg, F. F., Nord,C. W., Peterson, J. L., & Zill, N. (1983). The life course of children of divorce: Marital disruption and parental conflict. *American Sociological Review, 48, 5,* 656-668.

Gadsden, V., & Hall, M. (1995). Intergenerational learning: A review of the literature. Paper commissioned by the National Center for Fathers and Families, University of Pennsylvania.

Gerson, K. (1993). *No man's land.* New York: Basic Books.

Goode, W. J. (1960). A deviant case: Illegitimacy in the Caribbean. *American Sociological Review, 25,* 21-30.

Griswold, R. L. (1993). *Fatherhood in America: A history.* New York: Basic Books.

Hanson, S. M. H., & Bozett, F. W. (1985). *Dimensions of fatherhood.* Beverly Hills, CA: Sage Publications.

Haveman, R., & Wolfe, B. (1994). *Succeeding generations.* New York: Russell Sage Foundation.

Hetherington, E. M. (1987). Family relations six years after divorce. In K. Pasley & M. Ihinger-Tallman (Eds.), *Remarriage and stepparenting: Current research and theory* (pp. 185-205). New York: Guilford Press.

Hetherington, E. M., & Arasteh, J. (Eds.) (1989). *The impact of divorce, single parenting and stepparenting on children.* Hillsdale, NJ: Lawrence Erlbaum Assoc.

Hill, R. (1993). *A research on the African American family.* Westport, CT: Auburn House.

Kimmel, M. S. (Ed.) (1987). *Changing men: New directions in research on men and masculinity.* Newbury Park, CA: Sage Publications.

King, V. (1994). Nonresident father involvement and child well-being: Can dads make a difference? *Journal of Family Issues, 15, 1,* 78-96.

Lamb, M. E. (Ed.) (1987). *The father's role: Cross-cultural perspectives.* Hillsdale, NJ: Lawrence Erlbaum Assoc.

Lamb, M. E., & Sagi, A. (Eds.) (1983). *Fatherhood and family policy.* Hillsdale, NJ: Lawrence Erlbaum Assoc.

Liebow, E. (1967). *Tally's corner.* Boston: Little, Brown.

Lerman, R. I., & Ooms, T. J. (1993). *Young unwed fathers: Changing roles and emerging policies.* Philadelphia: Temple University Press.

Lynn, D. (1974). *The father: His role in development.* Monterey, CA: Brooks and Cole.

Maccoby, E. E., & Mnookin, R. H. (1992). *Dividing the child: Social and legal dilemmas of custody.* Cambridge, MA: Harvard University Press.

Malinowski, B. (1930). Parenthood, the basis of social structure. In R. L. Coser (Ed.), *The family: Its structures and functions* (pp. 51-63). New York: St. Martin's Press.

Marsiglio, W. (1987). Adolescent fathers in the United States: Their initial living arrangements, marital experience and educational outcomes. *Family Planning Perspectives, 19,* 6, 240-251.

Marsiglio, W. Ed. (1995a). *Fatherhood: Contemporary theory, research, and social policy.* Thousand Oaks, CA: Sage Publications.

Marsiglio, W. (1995b). Fatherhood scholarship: An overview and agenda for the future. In W. Marsiglio (Ed.), *Fatherhood: Contemporary theory, research, and social policy* (pp. 1-20). Thousand Oaks, CA: Sage Publications.

Marsiglio, W. (1998). *Procreative man.* New York: New York University Press.

McLanahan, S. (1988). Family structure and dependency: Early transitions to female household headship. *Demography, 25,* 1-16.

McLanahan, S., & Sandefur, G. (1994). *Growing up with a single parent.* Cambridge, Mass.: Harvard University Press.

Morrison, D. R. (1995). The effects of postmarital unions on child well-being. Research proposal.

Mott, F. (1990). When is a father really gone? Paternal-child contact in father-absent homes. *Demography, 27,* 4, 499-517.

Moynihan, D. P. (1965). *The Negro family: The case for national action.* Washington, DC: U. S. Department of Labor, Office of Policy Planning and Research.

Parke, R. D. (1981). *Fathers.* Cambridge, Mass.: Harvard University Press.

Parke, R. D. (1996). *Fatherhood.* Cambridge, MA: Harvard University Press.

Patterson, G. R., DeBaryshe, B. D, & Ramsey, E. (1989). A developmental perspective on antisocial behavior. *American Psychologist, 44,* 2, 329-335.

Pleck, J. H. (1981). *The myth of masculinity.* Cambridge, MA: MIT Press.

Popenoe, D. (1996). *Life without father.* New York: Martin Kessler Books.

Rainwater, L. (1970). *Behind ghetto walls.* Chicago: Aldine Publishing Co.

Rodman, H. (1963). The lower-class value stretch. *Social Forces, 42,* 3, 205-215.

Rossi, A. S., & Rossi, P. H. (1990). *Of human bonding: Parent-child relations across the life course.* New York: Aldine de Gruyter.

Sampson, R. J. (1992). Family management and child development: Insights from social disorganization theory. In J. McCord (Ed.), *Advances in criminal theory* (pp. 63-93). New Brunswick: Transaction Books.

Schultz, D. A. (1969). *Coming up Black: Patterns of ghetto socialization.* Englewood Cliffs, NJ: Prentice-Hall.

Seltzer, J. (1991). Relationships between fathers and children who live apart. *Journal of Marriage and the Family, 53,* 79-101.

Snarey, J. (1993). *How fathers care for the next generation: A four decade study.* Cambridge, MA: Harvard University Press.

Stack, C. (1974). *All our kin.* New York: Harper and Row.

Sullivan, M. (1989). Absent fathers in the inner city. *Annals, American Academy of Political and Social Science,* xx, 501.

Teachman, J. D. (1991). Contributions to children by divorced fathers. *Social Problems, 38,* 358-371.

Testa, M. F. (1992). Racial and ethnic variation in the early life course of adolescent welfare mothers. In M. K. Rosenheim & M. F. Testa (Eds.), *Early parenthood and coming of age in the 1990s* (pp. 89-112). New Brunswick, NJ: Rutgers University Press.

Wallerstein, J. S., & Blakeslee, S. (1989*). Second chances: Men, women, and children after divorce.* New York: Ticknor and Fields.

Wilson, W. J. (1987). *The truly disadvantaged.* Chicago: University of Chicago Press.

Zill, N. (1978). Divorce, marital happiness, and the mental health of children: Findings from the FCD National Survey of Children. Paper prepared for the National Institute of Mental Health Workshop on Divorce and Children.

The Single-Father Family:
Demographic, Economic,
and Public Transfer Use Characteristics

Brett V. Brown

SUMMARY. This paper examines the demographic and economic characteristics of single-father families, with particular attention to public transfer receipt. Cohabiting and non-cohabiting single fathers are examined and compared to fathers in married-couple families. Estimates from the 1997 March, Current Population Survey (CPS) are featured. Selected trend data for 1984, 1989, and 1996 are also presented. The analyses show that single fathers earn substantially less than married fathers, have lower household incomes, are less educated, and are substantially more likely to be receiving public transfers. Further, the socioeconomic gap between single and married fathers has been increasing since 1984. *[Article copies available for a fee from The Haworth Document Delivery Service: 1-800-342-9678. E-mail address: getinfo@ haworthpressinc.com <Website: http://www.haworthpressinc.com>]*

KEYWORDS. Single fathers, public transfers, trends, children, single parent, EITC

Brett V. Brown is Senior Research Associate, Child Trends, Inc., Washington, DC.

An earlier version of this paper was delivered at the *Conference on Father's Involvement*, Bethesda, MD at the Natcher Conference Center, October 11, 1996. Funding for this paper was provided by the NICHD Child and Family Research Network. The author would also like to thank Charles Halle and Sharon Vandivere for providing research assistance in the production of the paper.

[Haworth co-indexing entry note]: "The Single-Father Family: Demographic, Economic, and Public Transfer Use Characteristics." Brown, Brett V. Co-published simultaneously in *Marriage & Family Review* (The Haworth Press, Inc.) Vol. 29, No. 2/3, 2000, pp. 203-220; and: *FATHERHOOD: Research, Interventions and Policies* (ed: H. Elizabeth Peters et al.) The Haworth Press, Inc., 2000, pp. 203-220. Single or multiple copies of this article are available for a fee from The Haworth Document Delivery Service [1-800-342-9678, 9:00 a.m. - 5:00 p.m. (EST). E-mail address: getinfo@haworthpressinc.com].

For the past several decades, there has been a substantial and continuous increase in families headed by single fathers, both absolutely and as a percentage of all families with children (Bianchi, 1995; Casper & Bryson, 1998; Eggebeen, Snyder, & Manning, 1996; Garasky & Meyer, 1996). The Census Bureau estimates that there were over 2.1 million such families in the United States in 1998, an increase of over 50% since 1990. They now represent 18% of all single-parent families with children under age 18 (Casper & Bryson, 1998).[1]

Until very recently, little was known about single-father families beyond the most basic demographic information offered in government reports. Their rapid growth, however, has prompted scientists and policy-makers to begin to ask questions about the social forces driving the trend. How do such families differ from two-parent and single-mother families in their social dynamics, socioeconomic circumstances and need for social supports? What are the consequences for the children who grow up in such families?

Basic descriptive information on the demographic and socioeconomic circumstances of single-father families is provided in this article, with particular attention being given to the receipt of public transfers. Such information is much needed in an era of dramatic changes in the nation's social safety net–changes that have taken place in ignorance of the likely consequences for single-father families. Time trend data from 1984 to 1996 are also examined to document how the characteristics of these families have changed during this period of rapid growth.

PREVIOUS LITERATURE

Literature on the characteristics of single-father families is limited with much of the work having been produced in the last seven years. Estimates on selected characteristics of single-father families, however, have been regularly published for a long time by the Bureau of the Census based on analyses of the March, Current Population Survey (CPS). Characteristics covered include race and Hispanic origin of the father, number and age of children, marital status, educational attainment, and metropolitan/nonmetropolitan residence. In general, because these data have been published in tables that also include estimates for two-parent and single-mother families, they received little individual attention. Data from these series have been culled and presented as time trends in several published articles and a book, revealing that substantial increases have occurred in the number of such families over the last several decades (Bianchi, 1995; Hernandez, 1993; Meyer & Garasky, 1993).

The interpretation of trends based on these estimates, however, is problematic, because single-father families are defined as including fathers who are actually cohabiting with the mother of their children. Bumpass and Raley

(1995) point out that much of the observed increase in single-father families may, in fact, reflect increases in cohabitation rather than increases in single parenthood among fathers. In response to such conclusions, Garasky and Meyer used a decomposition technique to assess the independent contributions of cohabiting and non-cohabiting fathers to the overall growth in single-father families. Using 1960 through 1990 decennial census data, they demonstrate that cohabitation accounts for about one-half of the observed increase in single-father households during the specified period. However, the number of non-cohabiting single-father families also increased throughout the period. During the 1980s, the rate of increase accelerated for this group, surpassing the rate of growth for non-cohabiting single-mother families. The increase in non-cohabiting single fathers was about evenly split between ever-married and never-married fathers.

Eggebeen et al. (1996) use 1990 census data to examine the characteristics of the single-father families from the perspective of the child. These child-based analyses systematically compare demographic and socioeconomic characteristics for children in nine distinct types of single-father families defined by marital status (divorced, widowed, and never married) and, within marital status, by living arrangements (cohabiting, lone father, and complex household).[2] The characteristics examined included father's education and employment patterns, poverty status, income, and adult-to-child ratios.

DATA AND METHODS

Most of the data for the analyses in this article come from the March 1997 CPS. The data are recent and provide a benchmark of characteristics prior to, and immediately following, the 1996 welfare reform legislation.[3] In addition, estimates for 1984, 1989, and 1996 were produced to examine changes in selected characteristics of single-father families, also using March CPS data.

The unit of analysis is a father who is living with his own child or children under age 18. Three types of fathers are systematically compared: married fathers, non-cohabiting single fathers, and cohabiting single fathers. For the 1997 data, cohabitants are limited primarily to those who have been identified as the "unmarried partner" of the father, though it is not possible to tell whether that partner is also the mother of the father's resident children.[4] Prior to 1995, it was not possible to distinguish between partners and housemates. For that reason, in the time trend analyses, cohabiting fathers include those living with partners and some who are living with housemates. The inclusion of those living with housemates is minimized by including only those who are opposite sex, unmarried, age 15 or older, and within 10 years of age of the father.[5] While sample sizes for single years of data were adequate to support the analyses of the 1997 data, they were not adequate for earlier years when single-father families were less prevalent. To conduct the time trend analyses, then, it was necessary to combine two years of data for each time period covered. The March CPS is designed so that estimates for adjacent years are based on samples with approximately a 50% overlap. To avoid problems on nonindependence associated with combining data from overlapping samples, I chose to combine data from nonadjacent years. Estimates were produced for 1984, 1989, and 1996 based on the samples from March CPS data adjacent to those years. The resulting sample sizes are listed in the tables that follow.

Simple descriptive statistics are offered across three broad areas: demographic characteristics, socioeconomic characteristics, and public transfer receipt. The demographic measures include the age, race, and marital status of the father, and several measures related to the composition of the household. Socioeconomic measures include educational attainment, earnings and income, employment level, and insurance coverage. Public transfers include the Earned Income Tax Credit (EITC), food stamps, public assistance (primarily Aid to Families with Dependent Children, AFDC), public health insurance (Medicare and Medicaid), and free or reduced price lunches for children at school.

CHARACTERISTICS OF CONTEMPORARY SINGLE FATHER-FAMILIES

Demographic Characteristics

Table 1 presents demographic characteristics of fathers and their families and households for 1997. One in twenty fathers who are residing with their children is a non-cohabiting single father. Among all single fathers, three-quarters are non-cohabiting.

Age, Race, Ethnicity, and Marital Status

Cohabiting fathers, with a mean age of 32, are considerably younger than either married fathers or non-cohabiting single fathers with a mean age of 39. Cohabiting fathers are the most likely to be from a minority group[6] (41%), followed by non-cohabiting single fathers (33%) and married fathers (25%). In other analyses, not shown, nearly 16% of all black fathers living with their own children were single fathers of one type or the other, more than twice the overall rate of 7%.

By examining the marital status of cohabiting and non-cohabiting single fathers, one can shed light on the paths leading to these family arrangements. The estimates show that separation or divorce is the primary path to non-co-

TABLE 1. Demographic Characteristics of Married and Single Fathers Residing with Own Children: 1997

	Married	Single	
		Non-Cohabiting	Cohabiting[a]
Father Characteristics			
Total (%)	93.0%	5.2%	1.8%
Age of Father (Mean)	39	39	32
Race/Ethnicity(%)			
White (non-Hispanic)	75%	67%	59%
Black (non-Hispanic)	8%	19%	19%
Hispanic	12%	10%	18%
other	5%	4%	4%
	100%	100%	100%
Marital Status (%)			
widowed	--	5%	1%
separated or divorced	--	71%	38%
never married	--	24%	61%
		100%	100%
Relation to Household Head			
head or spouse	98%	84%	85%
child	1%	11%	4%
other relative	1%	3%	2%
unmarried partner	0%	0%	7%
other	0%	2%	1%
	100%	100%	100%
Household and Family Characteristics			
Other Relatives in Household (%)			
Any Adult Relative[b]	5%	18%	8%
Parent	1%	13%	4%
Mean Number of Persons in Household	4.2	3.4	4.3
Families with Only One Child (%)	37%	61%	60%
Families with Children < age 2 (%)	19%	10%	34%
Sample Size	13,065	704	261

[a]Includes unmarried partners, does not include housemates.
[b]Does not include spouse or children.

habiting single fatherhood (71%), while nonmarital fertility is the primary path for cohabiting single fathers, 61% of whom have never been married. What is interesting, though, is the fact that a quarter of all non-cohabiting fathers have never been married, indicating a willingness among a significant number of never-married fathers to take primary parental responsibility for their own children. In addition, more than one in three cohabiting fathers were separated, divorced, or widowed. This may mean that a substantial proportion of single fathers bring their children into cohabiting relationships, and that cohabiting fathers are not exclusively those living with the mother of their children.[7]

Headship and Family Structure

The vast majority of single fathers (around 85%) are head of their own household. However, 14% of all non-cohabiting single fathers live in households headed by their parents or another relative. This arrangement is less common among cohabiting fathers at 6%, and only 2% of married fathers live in such arrangements. Nearly one in five (18%) non-cohabiting fathers lives with adult relatives other than their adult children. Such living arrangements may serve to enhance the material well-being of the father's family, and may offer opportunities to share child care and supervision duties. Recent research by Eggebeen et al. (1996) indicates that non-cohabiting single fathers who are living in such complex households are considerably less educated and have lower earnings than those who live only with their children.

Child Characteristics

Where the majority (63%) of married fathers live with two or more of their own children, most single fathers live with only one child (about 60%). The children of cohabiting fathers are more likely to be infants or young toddlers. Specifically, 34% of such fathers have a child under age two, compared to only 10% among non-cohabiting fathers, and 19% among married fathers. These characteristics imply substantially different child care needs across the three groups.

Socioeconomic Characteristics

Education and income. Single fathers of either type are less educated and have much lower incomes than married fathers (see Table 2). Married fathers are much more likely to have received post-high school education and are less than half as likely to be poor. Moreover, fathers who are married earn at least $14,000 more per year than single fathers and have total household incomes of at least $20,000 more per year.

TABLE 2. Socioeconomic Characteristics of Married and Single Fathers Residing with Own Children: 1997

	Married	Single	
		Non-Cohabiting	Cohabiting[b]
Educational Attainment			
less than 12 years (%)	12%	19%	23%
12 years (%)	32%	44%	50%
more than 12 years (%)	55%	37%	27%
	100%	100%	100%
Income and Related Measures			
Poverty (%)	8%	17%	24%
Father's Earnings (in 1,000s)[a]	$41.7	$27.5	$23.1
Total Income (in 1,000s)[a]			
family	$62.9	$32.4	$24.9
family + partner	–	–	$37.3
household	$63.7	$40.7	$39.8
Child Support Receipt (%)	0%	7%	3%
Health Insurance Coverage			
Youngest Child (% covered)	88%	78%	71%
Father (% covered)	87%	74%	56%
Employment			
Full-Time/Full-Year Worker (%)	82%	68%	64%
Non-worker (%)	4%	11%	7%
Worked 45+ hours in previous week (%)	32%	21%	16%
Sample Size	13,065	704	261

[a]Reported in 1996 dollars.
[b]Includes unmarried partners, does not include housemates.

Comparisons between the two single father types are more complex. Co-habiting fathers are less educated than non-cohabiting fathers, with 27% versus 37% receiving post-high school education. They are also more likely to be poor (24% versus 17%) and to have lower earnings and family incomes. Both of these groups of single fathers, on the other hand, have very similar mean household incomes ($39,750 and $40,652, respectively). Most of the difference between father's income and household income is due to income from the unmarried partners of cohabiting fathers who add, on average, over $12,000 to the household income. Although this still leaves the households of cohabiting fathers with less income per person ($9,244 versus $11,956), it does substantially close the income gap between the two family types.

Receipt of Child Support

Child support receipt plays at most a modest role in the economic life of single fathers. Only 7% of non-cohabiting and 3% of cohabiting single fathers receive any child support at all.

Health insurance coverage. Rates of health insurance coverage for the youngest child were highest among married fathers at 88%, followed by non-cohabiting single fathers at 78% and cohabiting single fathers at 71%. Coverage for the fathers themselves exhibited a similar pattern, except that rates of coverage were considerably lower for cohabiting single fathers at 56%.

Employment. Single fathers are less likely to work full-time and full-year than married fathers, and less likely to be working long hours. Among married fathers, 32% worked 45 or more hours during the week prior to the CPS survey compared to 21% and 16% of non-cohabiting and cohabiting single fathers, respectively. In addition, single fathers were more likely than married fathers to report not working at all (11% and 7% for non-cohabiting and cohabiting single fathers, versus 4% for married fathers).

These patterns undoubtedly reflect age- and education-related differences in employment patterns, but may also reflect additional time spent in parenting activities by single fathers. The fact that one in nine non-cohabiting single fathers did not work at all during the previous year is particularly striking, suggesting the possibility that some fathers are adopting a full-time caretaker role for their children.

Public Transfer Receipt

An issue of substantial importance to contemporary policy is the extent to which single-father families depend on public transfers for their material well-being, and the types of transfers on which they depend. Table 3 presents rates of receipt for the EITC, Food Stamps, public health insurance, public assistance (AFDC and general assistance), and free or reduced-price lunch. Average annual dollar amounts for recipients are also presented for the EITC, Food Stamps, and public assistance. The data indicate that a large percentage of single-father families depend to some extent on public transfers, far in excess of the receipt rates of married father families.

EITC. The Earned Income Tax Credit (EITC) is a Federal program that uses the tax system to subsidize the earnings of low wage workers. While 14% of married fathers receive EITC funds, 46% of non-cohabiting and 64%

TABLE 3. Public Transfer Receipt Among Married and Single Fathers Residing with Own Children: 1997

| | Married | Single | |
		Non-Cohabiting	Cohabiting[a]
Percent Receiving Public Transfers			
Earned Income Tax Credit (father)	14%	46%	64%
Food Stamps (household)	6%	14%	23%
Public Assistance			
family	3%	7%	2%
family & partner	–	–	15%
Public Health Insurance Coverage			
youngest child			
(Medicaid/Medicare)	11%	22%	30%
father (Medicaid)	4%	12%	5%
Free or reduced price lunch (household)	16%	29%	26%
Average Annual Amount Received Among Recipients			
Food Stamps (household, 1996 $)	$1,983	$1,744	$2,122
Public Assistance (household, 1996 $)	$4,239	$3,906	$3,762
Earned Income Tax Credit (father, 1996 $)	$1,607	$1,566	$1,639
Sample Size	13,065	704	261

[a]Includes unmarried partners, does not include housemates.

of cohabiting single fathers received money from the EITC. The average amount received among recipients was around $1,600 for all three father types, making this both a common and a significant source of support for single fathers and their families.

Food stamps. The Food Stamp Program is a Federal program that provides vouchers to low income households for food purchases. Cohabiting single fathers had the highest rate of household food stamp receipt at 23%, followed by non-cohabiting single fathers at 14%, and married fathers at 6%. Among recipient households, the average cash value of food stamps received during the previous year was between $1,700 and $2,100 among the three father types, again a substantial level of support.

Public assistance. Public Assistance includes AFDC and general assistance programs. AFDC is a state administered program that provides income to low income families with children. The program is generally targeted for low income children with only one-resident parent.[8] Rates of public assistance receipt in 1996 claimed by the fathers themselves are modest across all three father groups, with a high of 7% among non-cohabiting single fathers, 2% among cohabiting fathers, and 3% among married fathers. However, when public assistance receipt claimed by the unmarried partner is included, the rate of receipt for families with cohabiting fathers rises to 15%. Among recipients, the annual average level of support is quite substantial, between about $3,700 and $4,200 among the three father types.

Public health insurance coverage. Public health coverage plays a significant role in the lives of children living with all three father types, but especially for those living with single fathers. One in five non-cohabiting fathers (22%) had a youngest child covered by Medicaid or Medicare, as did three in ten cohabiting fathers. This compares to a rate of 11% for married fathers, a much smaller though still substantial rate of coverage. Non-cohabiting single fathers were also more likely to be dependent on Medicaid for their own health coverage, with coverage rates of 12% versus 4% for married fathers and 5% for cohabiting fathers.

Free or reduced-price lunch. Single fathers were more likely than married fathers to have children in the household receiving a free or reduced price lunch at school, with receipt rates of 26% and 29% for the single father groups versus 16% for married fathers.

THE CHANGING CHARACTERISTICS
OF SINGLE-FATHER FAMILIES

Trend data are presented in Appendix Tables I, II, and III on characteristics of single- and married-father families for the years 1984, 1989, and 1996. The characteristics included in these tables are a selected set of measures included in the first three tables of the paper. The text below highlights those characteristics that have changed substantially during that identified time period.

In order to obtain acceptable sample sizes for the earlier years, trend estimates are based on the combined samples of two years of data: 1983 and 1985 are used to create "1984" estimates, and so on. In addition, the operational definitions of "cohabiting" and "non-cohabiting" single fathers are somewhat different. As discussed earlier, prior to 1995 one could not distinguish between unmarried partners and housemates. In order to have comparable father-type definitions across the time period, any woman who is identified as a partner/housemate and who is age 15 or older, unmarried, and within 10 years of the age of the father is assumed to be a cohabitant of the father.[9]

Changes in Demographic Characteristics

The total number of single-father families (cohabiting plus non-cohabiting) increased by 370,000 between 1984 and 1989, and by an additional

510,000 between 1989 and 1996 to 1.77 million (see Appendix Table I). Cohabiting fathers accounted for about 60% of the increase in the first time period, and about 50% in the later time period. Single-father families as a percentage of all families containing fathers increased steadily from 3.6% to 6.5% over those time periods.

The racial and ethnic diversity of all three father types increased over this time period as it did for the population as a whole. The proportion of single fathers who were never married rose for both types between 1984 and 1996, from 12% to 18% for non-cohabiting single fathers, and from 48% to 61% among cohabiting single fathers.

Changes in Socioeconomic Characteristics

Trends in educational achievement and income show that married fathers have been pulling away from single fathers while the latter stagnate or lose ground (see Appendix Table II). Between 1984 and 1996, the percentage of married fathers who completed more than 12 years of education increased from 46% to 56%, while rates for single fathers were stagnant. During that same time period the household income of married fathers rose by 19%, while the incomes of both types of single-father families stayed virtually the same. Receipt of child support/alimony has risen modestly for non-cohabiting single fathers from 3% in 1984 to 7% in 1996.

Changes in Public Transfer Receipt

Between 1984 and 1989, participation rates in public transfer programs were fairly stable for all three father groups, with modest increases in public health insurance coverage for children across the three groups (see Appendix Table III). Between 1989 and 1996, however, participation in public health insurance and free or reduced-price lunch programs increased substantially for all three groups, as did receipt of food stamps for single fathers. During that period, rates of public health coverage for the youngest child increased from 5% to 11% for married fathers, from 10% to 20% for non-cohabiting fathers, and from 19% to 30% for cohabiting fathers. Participation in the free or reduced-price lunch program by one or more children in the household increased from 10% to 15%, 16% to 29%, and from 18% to 27%, respectively, for married, non-cohabiting single, and cohabiting single fathers. Food stamp receipt increased from 9% to 14% for non-cohabiting single fathers, from 19% to 25% for co-habiting single fathers, and from 5% to 7% for married fathers. Rates of public assistance receipt (mostly AFDC), on the other hand, were fairly stable for all three father groups across both time periods.

DISCUSSION

This paper has highlighted several features of single-father families that have important implications for social policy and for the lives of the fathers and children who live in such families. The continued and rapid growth in the 1990s of both cohabiting and non-cohabiting single-father families suggests that these family forms may well become increasingly common in the coming decade. This is the time to begin considering more systematically the relationship of social policy to single-father families, and to identify the considerable research needs and the data needed to fulfill them.

First and foremost, it is clear that a substantial proportion of both non-cohabiting and cohabiting single-father families depend on public transfers to enhance their well-being. Receipt of the EITC is the most widespread, affecting 46% of cohabiting and 64% of non-cohabiting single-father families in 1996. One in five non-cohabiting single fathers rely on public health insurance to cover their youngest child, and one in seven rely on food stamps to help feed their families. The percentages are even larger for cohabiting single fathers.

Rates of public assistance receipt are relatively modest among non-cohabiting single-father families at 7%, but play a larger role in cohabiting father households where 15% receive public assistance, and where the average annual amount received exceeds $3,700. Most of the public assistance does not come directly to the father in such families, however, but through the father's partner.

The public transfer programs on which non-cohabiting and cohabiting single-father families are most reliant (the EITC, Medicaid/Medicare, Food Stamps, and free or reduced-price school lunches) have all experienced significant expansions in recent years (Committee on Ways and Means, 1998), and are still substantially controlled at the Federal level. There was talk during the 1996 Congress about reducing most of these programs and giving the states more control over them, though by and large that has not happened. The welfare reform legislation of 1996 had the largest impact on the AFDC program. Thus we may infer that welfare reform will have little impact on the financial well-being of non-cohabiting single-father families (who are less likely to receive this kind of public assistance) and a modest impact on cohabiting single-father families (whose partners are moderately likely to receive this kind of public assistance).

The analyses of the socioeconomic characteristics of these father-headed families confirm previous findings that single fathers have less education and considerably less earnings and income than their married counterparts (Eggebeen et al., 1996; Meyer & Garasky, 1996). In addition, the results show that the socioeconomic gap between single and married fathers has been getting larger since 1984; married fathers have had substantial gains in educational attainment and household income, while income and education levels for both types of single-father families have stagnated. The children growing up in single-father families are finding themselves increasingly financially disadvantaged relative to children in two-parent families, though their resources remain high relative to single-mother families (U.S. Department of Health and Human Services, 1998).

The findings regarding living arrangements and employment patterns are suggestive of strategies that single fathers may be adopting regarding income maximization, parenting, and child care arrangements. Nearly one in five non-cohabiting single fathers live with an adult relative compared to one in twenty married fathers. A parent of the father is present in about two-thirds of those cases. Of particular interest are the one in nine non-cohabiting single fathers in 1997 who had not worked at all during the previous year. It may be that many of these fathers have opted to become full-time caretakers for their children. Fathers who are awarded custody of their children may in part be awarded custody because of a willingness or desire to perform such a role. Alternatively, it may be that single fathers who do not have good employment prospects have opted for the caretaker role, perhaps within the context of an extended household. Research on patterns of child care and caretaking within such families would yield important insights into the social dynamics of such extended family situations.

One important area of research that has received very little attention to date is the nature of the parent/child relationship within single-father families as well as the larger social dynamics that exist in such households. Research has shown that mothers and fathers do act differently in fulfilling their parenting roles in two-parent families and as non-custodial parents (see Lamb, 1997; Marsiglio, 1995). Very little research exists, however, on the nature of parenting in single-father families. It is likely that many such fathers are taking on a wider range of parenting activities than they would undertake if a spouse were present. As single-father families become more common, their example might feed back into our more general notions of what it is to be a father, affecting the parenting practices of married fathers as well.

Researchers interested in analyzing these and other important issues related to single-father families are severely limited by existing national data sources. The National Longitudinal Study of Adolescent Health is a promising resource for such analysis, but is limited by the small number of participants living in single father families. The CPS and the Decennial Census have large enough samples of single fathers to support such research, but are limited by the lack of parent/child and child well-being measures. Moreover, both are further limited by an inability to cleanly distinguish between cohabiting parents and fathers who are cohabiting with someone other than the mother of their children.

The latter problem can be solved by adopting a more rigorous set of household relationship questions that identify exact relationships between each child and adult in the household. This is done in another national survey, the Survey of Income and Program Participation (SIPP), though the small number of single-father families in that survey will support only limited analyses.

Recently, however, The Federal Interagency Forum on Child and Family Statistics (1998) launched an initiative to improve the breadth and amount of national data available to study male fertility, family formation, and fatherhood. Although there was no specific mention of father-only families, there is a strong general commitment to identify and develop new measures of father-child interaction and add them to federal surveys. Before this effort can benefit the study of single-father families, however, it would be necessary to add new questions measuring parent/child relationships and child well-being to the CPS. An alternative way, in turn would be to design smaller national surveys that both include such measures and oversample single-father families. Potential candidates for oversampling include the SIPP, the National Health Interview Survey, and the National Household Education Survey. With the commitment of the Federal Interagency Forum to improving national data resources for research on fathers, there is reason to hope that we may soon have the data needed to pursue more in-depth research on the growing phenomenon of single-father families.

NOTES

1. This includes related and unrelated subfamilies as well as family households.

2. "Cohabiting" consists of those living with an acknowledged unmarried partner; "lone father" consists of fathers living only with their children; and "complex households" consist of the father, his children, and related or unrelated adults other than partners.

3. The income, employment, and public transfer receipt data in the 1997 March CPS refer to prior calendar year, 1996. Welfare reform legislation was enacted in late summer of that year.

4. In all cases where the single father or his partner is head of household, partner status can be unambiguously identified. This was the case for over 85% of all single fathers.

5. This definition may somewhat overstate cohabitants as a component of total growth.

6. A minority is defined here as all persons other than non-Hispanic whites.

7. From these data it is not possible to tell what proportion of divorced fathers actually brought children into the cohabiting relationship.

8. Under some circumstances the AFDC-UP program provides benefits to low income families with two resident parents when one parent is unemployed.

9. This is essentially the same technique used by Garasky and Meyer (1996) for their trend analyses of decennial census data. Analyses using 1995 CPS data revealed that about two-thirds of the fathers identified in this way were in fact cohabiting with a partner; the remainder were living with female house mates. A comparison of single father characteristics using the alternative definitions using data from the March 1995 CPS indicates that this mis-identification results in slightly higher education and income for cohabiting fathers, and modestly lower education and income for non-cohabiting fathers.

REFERENCES

Bianchi, S.M. (1995). The changing demographic and socioeconomic characteristics of single parent families. *Marriage and Family Review 20*, 71-97.

Bumpass, L.L., & Raley, R.K. (1995). Redefining single-parent families: Cohabitation and changing family reality. *Demography 32*, 425-36.

Casper, L., & Bryson, K. (1998). *Household and family characteristics:* March 1998. Current Population Reports, P20-5 15 and P20-515u. Washington, DC: U.S. Census Bureau.

Committee on Ways and Means. (1998). *1998 Green book.* Washington, DC: U.S. G.P.O.

Eggebeen, D.J., Snyder, A.R., & Manning, W.D. (1996). Children in single-father families in demographic perspective. *Journal of Family Issues 17*, 441-465.

Federal Interagency Forum on Child and Family Statistics. (1998). *Nurturing fatherhood: Improving data and research on male fertility, family formation and fatherhood.* Washington, D.C.

Garasky, S., & Meyer, D.R. (1996). Reconsidering the increase in father-only families. *Demography 33*, 385-393.

Hernandez, D.J. (1993). *America's children: Resources from families, the government, and the economy.* New York: Russell Sage.

Lamb, M.E. (Ed) (1997). *The role of the father in childdevelopment: 3rd ed.* New York: John Wiley and Sons, Inc.

Marsiglio, W. (Ed.) (1995). *Fatherhood: contemporary theory,* research, and social policy. Thousand Oaks: Sage Publications.

Meyer, D.R., & Garasky, S. (1993). Custodial fathers: myths, realities, and child support policy. *Journal of Marriage and the Family 55*, 73-89.

U.S. Department of Health and Human Services. (1998). *Trends in the well-being of American children and youth: 1998.* Washington, D.C.: U.S. Department of Health and Human Services/Assistant Secretary for Planning and Evaluation.

APPENDIX TABLE 1. Demographic Characteristics of Married and Single Fathers Residing with Own Children: Selected Years, 1984-1996

	Married			Single					
				Non-cohabiting			Cohabiting[a]		
Father Characteristics	1984	1989	1996	1984	1989	1996	1984	1989	1996
Total									
number (millions)	24.29	24.97	25.70	0.77	0.92	1.17	0.12	0.34	0.60
As a percent of all living with child	96.5%	95.2%	93.6%	3.1%	3.5%	4.3%	0.5%	1.3%	2.2%
Age of Father (mean)	38	38	39	39	39	39	30	31	32
Race/ethnicity (%)									
White non-Hispanic	82%	79%	76%	75%	74%	67%	71%	66%	60%
Black non-Hispanic	8%	8%	8%	16%	16%	19%	19%	17%	20%
Hispanic	8%	9%	12%	8%	8%	11%	7%	14%	16%
other	3%	4%	4%	2%	3%	3%	3%	3%	4%
	100%	100%	100%	100%	100%	100%	100%	100%	100%
Marital Status (%)									
widowed	--	--	--	11%	10%	7%	2%	1%	1%
separated or divorced	--	--	--	77%	75%	75%	50%	50%	39%
never married	--	--	--	12%	15%	18%	48%	49%	61%
				100%	100%	100%	100%	100%	100%
Relation to Household Head									
head or spouse	98%	98%	98%	84%	86%	83%	92%	90%	88%
child	1%	1%	1%	13%	11%	12%	5%	2%	3%
other relative	1%	1%	1%	3%	3%	3%	3%	0%	1%
non-relative	0%	0%	0%	0%	1%	2%	0%	8%	8%
	100%	100%	100%	100%	100%	100%	100%	100%	100%
Household and Family Characteristics									
Any adult relative in household[b]	5%	5%	5%	21%	26%	20%	9%	5%	7%
Mean number of persons in household	4.3	4.2	4.2	3.4	3.3	3.3	3.8	4.0	4.2
Families with only one child	39%	39%	37%	64%	60%	61%	74%	72%	62%
Families with children < age 2	21%	21%	19%	4%	9%	8%	22%	35%	33%
Sample size	35,058	32,908	28,167	1105	1175	1233	177	443	653

[a]Includes housemates as well as unmarried partners.

[b]Does not include spouse.

APPENDIX TABLE II. Socioeconomic Characteristics of Married and Single Fathers: Selected Years, 1984-1996

| | Married | | | Single | | | | | |
| | | | | Non-cohabiting | | | Cohabiting | | |
	1984	1989	1996	1984	1989	1996	1984	1989	1996
Educational Attainment									
less than 12 years (%)	17%	14%	12%	25%	19%	18%	31%	28%	35%
12 years (%)	37%	36%	32%	35%	40%	41%	42%	44%	51%
more than 12 years (%)	46%	49%	56%	39%	41%	41%	27%	29%	25%
Income and Related Measures (Previous Years)									
Poverty (%)	10%	80%	80%	20%	15%	17%	32%	22%	27%
Father's Earnings (in 1,000s)	$35.4	$38.6	$39.2	$28.3	$29.8	$26.8	$22.3	$24.8	$22.5
Total Income (in 1,000s)									
family	$50.2	$56.4	$59.6	$34.1	$37.1	$32.2	$25.0	$27.6	$24.2
family & partner	–	–	–	–	–	–	$36.3	$41.0	$35.1
household	$50.8	$57.1	$60.3	$40.6	$43.6	$39.5	$40.1	$43.4	$39.1
Child Support/ Alimony Receipt (%)	0%	0%	0%	3%	4%	7%	0%	1%	2%
Health Insurance Coverage[b]									
Youngest Child (% covered)	–	89%	88%	–	78%	79%	–	73%	72%
Father (% covered)	90%	89%	87%	79%	77%	76%	70%	65%	59%
Employment									
Full-Time/Full Year (%)	73%	79%	81%	59%	65%	66%	51%	64%	63%
Non-Worker	5%	4%	5%	14%	11%	13%	10%	5%	8%
Sample Size	35,058	32,908	28,167	1,105	1,175	1,233	177	443	653

[a]Reported in 1996 dollars.
[b]Health insurance measures for 1984 are not comparable to later years.

APPENDIX TABLE III. Public Transfer Receipt Among Married and Single Fathers: Selected Years, 1984-1996

	Married			Single					
				Non-cohabiting			Cohabiting[a]		
Percent Receiving Public Transfers	1984	1989	1996	1984	1989	1996	1984	1989	1996
Food Stamps (household, previous year)	7%	5%	7%	12%	9%	14%	18%	19%	25%
Public Assistance (previous year)									
household	3%	3%	3%	10%	9%	9%	20%	18%	17%
family + partner	3%	3%	3%	6%	7%	8%	20%	18%	17%
Public Health Insurance Coverage									
youngest child (Medicaid/Medicare)	4%	5%	11%	8%	10%	20%	13%	19%	30%
father (Medicaid)	3%	3%	5%	9%	7%	12%	11%	6%	8%
Free or Reduced Price Lunch (household)	11%	10%	15%	18%	16%	29%	11%	18%	27%
Sample Size	35,058	32,908	28,167	1,105	1,175	1,233	177	443	653

[a]Includes housemates as well as unmarried partners.

IV. MARITAL DISRUPTION AND PARENT-CHILD RELATIONSHIPS: INTERVENTIONS AND POLICIES ON FATHERHOOD

The Impact of Marital Quality, Divorce, and Remarriage on the Relationships Between Parents and Their Children

Terri L. Orbuch
Arland Thornton
Jennifer Cancio

Terri L. Orbuch is affiliated with the Oakland University Department of Sociology, and the University of Michigan Institute for Social Research.

Arland Thornton and Jennifer Cancio are affiliated with the University of Michigan Department of Sociology, Institute for Social Research.

Address correspondence to: Terri L. Orbuch, Department of Sociology, Oakland University, 520A Varner Hall, Rochester, MI 48309.

The research in this paper was supported by a grant from NICHD (5 U01 HD30928). An earlier version of this paper was presented at the NICHD Conference on Father Involvement, Washington, DC, October 10-11, 1996. The authors would like to thank Linda Young-DeMarco, Judy Baughn, Annette Dentel and the Survey Research Center at the University of Michigan for assistance with data analysis and the presentation of tables.

[Haworth co-indexing entry note]: "The Impact of Marital Quality, Divorce, and Remarriage on the Relationships Between Parents and Their Children." Orbuch, Terri L., Arland Thornton, and Jennifer Cancio. Co-published simultaneously in *Marriage & Family Review* (The Haworth Press, Inc.) Vol. 29, No. 4, 2000, pp. 221-246; and: *FATHERHOOD: Research, Interventions and Policies* (ed: H. Elizabeth Peters et al.) The Haworth Press, Inc., 2000, pp. 221-246. Single or multiple copies of this article are available for a fee from The Haworth Document Delivery Service [1-800-342-9678, 9:00 a.m. - 5:00 p.m. (EST). E-mail address: getinfo@haworthpressinc.com].

221

SUMMARY. This paper examines data from a panel study on the long-term effects of parental marital quality and divorce on relationships between parents and adult children. Attention is focused on whether these effects vary by age and gender of child as well as the theoretical explanations linking mother-father and parent-child relations. The relational quality between adult children (18-31 years old) and both mothers and fathers is examined from the perspective of both children and parents. Among intact families, parental marital quality has long-term effects on father-child relations, regardless of gender, whereas short-term effects are characteristic of mother-child relations and only perceived by mothers. Further, although divorce without remarriage hurts sons' relationships with both fathers and mothers, it hurts father-daughter relations even more. Mother-daughter bonds appear to be improved by divorce, with declines in income explaining a large portion of the tendency for divorce to affect father-child relations. *[Article copies available for a fee from The Haworth Document Delivery Service: 1-800-342-9678. E-mail address: getinfo@haworthpressinc.com <Website: http:// www.haworthpressinc.com>]*

KEYWORDS. Parent-child relations, divorce, remarriage, parental marital quality

Parent-child relationships are formed early in children's lives and are vital to their development, adjustment, well-being, and educational attainment throughout the life course (Amato & Booth, 1991; Grych, Seid, & Fincham, 1992; Rossi & Rossi, 1990; Thornton, Orbuch, & Axinn, 1995). Given the importance of parent-child relations, a growing interest has emerged in the interrelatedness between mother-father and parent-child relationships. Recent studies indicate that low marital quality and divorce by parents have adverse effects on parent-child relations, especially for father-child ties (Aquilino, 1994a, 1994b; Booth & Amato, 1994; Erel & Burman, 1995; Kerig, Cowan, & Cowan, 1993). However, whether these effects are long-term, consistent across a child's life course, and how they are explained remain unclear.

The primary goal of this paper is to understand the long-term effects of parental marital quality and disruption on children's relationships with parents. Children may learn overall interpersonal patterns of relating within families that are carried over the life course and across familial relationships (Amato, 1993; 1999; Elder & Caspi; 1988; Webster, Orbuch, & House, 1995). Although most parent-child studies have focused on early periods of children's lives and reports from only mothers, we examine the relational quality between 18-31-year-old children and both their mothers and fathers. This is a time when children are transitioning into adulthood and forming their own marital/intimate relationships. Special attention is devoted to whether the effects of parents' marital histories differ with the gender of the child and over the life course of the parent-child relationship. Since there is evidence for the idea that parent-child relationships are evaluated differently by parents and children, both perspectives are assessed in this study (Gronvold, 1988; Thornton, Orbuch, & Axinn, 1995).

BACKGROUND

Parental Marital Quality

Studies on the effects of parental marital quality on parent-child relationships find that the well-being of parental bonds has a significant effect on parenting styles, parent-child interactions, resource exchanges, and contact between parents and children (Amato, Rezac, & Booth, 1995; Kerig, Cowan, & Cowan, 1993). With few exceptions, however, this research is limited to cross-sectional data, reports from only one member of the dyad, and children who are young.

Two theoretical frameworks that *directly* discuss the impact of parental marital quality on the quality of parent-child relations are identified (Erel & Burman, 1995). Both frameworks claim that the quality of mother-father and parent-child dyads are interrelated, but the underlying mechanism and the direction of effect differs between the two perspectives. The first of these frameworks, the spillover perspective (Easterbrooks & Emde, 1988; Erel & Burman, 1995), argues that when parental relationships are positive, this emotion carries over and positively affects the quality, behaviors, and interactions within parent-child bonds (Bolger, DeLongis, Kessler, & Wethington, 1989). Strong support exists for this perspective (Erel & Burman, 1995). Alternatively, the compensatory framework hypothesizes a negative effect of parental marital quality on parent-child relations (Erel & Burman, 1995). When the parental marital bond lacks positive affect, this deficit is counterbalanced in the parent-child relationship. Some findings confirm this perspective (Belsky, Youngblade, Rovine, & Volling, 1991; Gutek, Repetti, & Silver, 1988), but other results have not supported this perspective (Erel & Burman, 1995).

Both the spillover and compensatory frameworks can operate in multiple directions, with the quality of parental relationships affecting parent-child bonds and the quality of parent-child relationships influencing marital quality. The association between marital quality and parent-child bonds can be the product of reciprocal and mutually reinforcing causal mechanisms (Cowan & Cowan, 1992; Kerig, Cowan, & Cowan, 1993). Although evidence suggests a positive relationship between parental marital quality and parent-child quality (Booth & Amato, 1994; Cooney, 1994; Erel & Burman, 1995), little is known about whether the effects are consistent across the life course. Moreover, little is known about whether this intergenerational link affects parent-child relationships as viewed by both parents and children.

Parental Marital Disruption

A number of studies have examined the effects of parental divorce on children (Amato & Keith, 1991; Cherlin, Furstenburg, Chase-Lansdale, Kierman, Robins, Morrison, Teitler, 1991; Furstenberg & Teitler, 1994; McLanahan & Sandefur, 1994), with results generally suggesting that parental divorce has negative consequences for young children's well-being, achievement, and social/interpersonal relationships (for reviews see Amato, 1993; Amato & Keith, 1991; Hetherington, 1999a). Research also suggests that the consequences of divorce for children may occur before the divorce itself (Cherlin et al., 1991; Furstenberg & Teitler, 1994; Rossi & Rossi, 1990). Some studies also find that parental divorce is related negatively to frequency of parental contacts, parent-child interactions, parenting styles, and future economic support from parents, but these effects are more significant for young children's relationships with fathers than mothers (Amato, 1993; Seltzer & Bianchi, 1988; White, 1992).

A more limited number of studies have asked the question of whether the effects of parental divorce on parents' relationships with children are constant across the life course of the child (Amato, 1999; Amato & Booth, 1996; Cooney, Hutchinson, & Leather, 1995; Zill, Morrison, & Coiro, 1993). Does divorce affect parent-child relations when children are older, more mature, and able to make their own decisions about contact and the quality of parent-child relationships? Research suggests that parental divorce has a negative effect on relationships between parents and adult children, but the effects are strongest for father-daughter relationships (Amato & Booth, 1996; Aquilino, 1994a; 1994b; Cooney, 1994; Zill, Morrison, & Coiro, 1993).

Theoretical Explanations Linking Divorce and Parent-Child Quality

Several theoretical explanations have been proposed for why parental divorce has negative consequences for children's well-being (Amato, 1993; McLanahan, 1999; Webster, Orbuch, & House, 1995). Most of these perspectives focus on how parental divorce may deprive children of economic, community, or parental resources (McLanahan & Sandefur, 1994). Although none of these perspectives refer *directly* to the effects of parental divorce on parent-child bonds, many have related implications for the parent-child relationship.

One perspective focuses on how the loss of economic and financial resources, economic instability, or long-term poverty following divorce may be detrimental for children's educational, occupational, and emotional well-being (McLanahan, 1999; McLanahan & Sandefur, 1994; Teachman, Paasch, Day, & Carver, 1995). Economic hardship and stress can also affect directly the quality of both parent-child and marital relations (Conger, Ge, Elder, Lorenz, & Simons, 1994; Hashima & Amato, 1994; Hustin, 1995). Another framework claims that divorce can be stressful to children because it weakens their attachments to community institutions such as religion (McLanahan & Sandefur, 1994). Many religious institutions value the family and discourage divorce, with the result being that messages sanctioning divorce and advocating marriage may not be satisfying to divorced families. These families may then decrease their involvement in religious activities (Thornton, 1985) which, in turn, may negatively influence parent-child relationships. Religious commitment has been shown to have significant positive effects on parent-child relationships (Pearce & Axinn, 1998). However, studies do not examine how religious participation or involvement intervenes in the association between divorce and children's parent-child relationships.

A third framework maintains that divorce typically reduces the number of parental figures who can supervise and direct children in reference to such issues as school involvements and extracurricular activities (Avenevoli, Sessa, & Steinberg, 1999; McLanahan, 1999). Given the multiple demands and responsibilities of single parenthood, these conditions may lead to lower levels of support, enjoyment, and understanding between parents and their children. However, if remarriage occurs and a second parental figure contributes time and energy to the family, the adverse effects of family structure on parent-child quality may be greatly reduced.

Another explanation concentrates on the affective tone of the family system or parental marital dyad, with particular focus on the level of parental conflict prior to divorce or separation (Amato, Loomis, & Booth, 1995). Studies have indicated that children whose parents were unhappily married demonstrated the lowest psychological well-being when compared to children whose parents experienced either low stress divorces or happy intact marriages (Amato and Booth, 1991). These findings support the idea that divorce is correlated with children's outcomes, even before the divorce occurs (Amato & Booth, 1996; Cherlin et al., 1991; Hetherington, 1999b). Moreover, this is consistent with both the spillover perspective and the view that children develop overall relationship patterns by watching or experiencing the relationships presented and displayed by their parents. Children who experience low parental marital quality may learn and develop interactional styles that are repeated later in other relationships as adults.

This study assessed the long-term effects of divorce on parent-child relations, testing specific hypotheses that correspond with several of these frame-works. Specifically, the focus is on how parent-child bonds are influenced by several resources that children may be deprived of following a divorce: (a) parental supervision/guidance, assessed as the lack of one parental figure in the home; (b) financial resources; and (c) religious participation or com-mitment. For example, the negative effects of divorce on parent-child rela-tions may be reduced when mothers remarry and an additional parental figure helps to supervise and socialize children. Further, although evidence is some-what mixed, remarriage can decrease the tension between biological mothers and fathers, leading to greater parent-child relationship quality (Booth & Dunn, 1994; DeGarmo & Forgatch, 1999). The majority of studies suggest, however, that the issues are quite complex and that the effects of remarriage depend on such factors as the following: (1) the age of the child, (2) how long the stepparents have been together, (3) parenting practices, (4) consistency in perceptions of the stepparent role, and (5) the quality of relations between ex-spouses. These factors have all been linked to the adjustment of the step-family and the quality of parent-child bonds after remarriage (Fine, Coleman, & Ganong, 1999; Ganong & Coleman, 1994; Hetherington & Clingempeel, 1992; Kurdek & Fine, 1993). Given the available research, it remains unclear whether parental divorce and mother's remarriage in childhood has long-term effects on parent-child bonds in young adulthood.

The negative effects of divorce on parent-child relationships are also ex-pected to diminish with greater financial resources and religious participa-tion. A particular focus of this study concerns the role of financial resources and religious participation or commitment in the association between divorce and parent-child relations. Although our substantive interest is in the role of economic and religion factors as intervening variables that may transmit the effects of divorce to parent-child relations, the possibility also exists that divorce is selective of people who are less financially affluent and less in-volved in religion. Our empirical analysis, therefore, is designed to evaluate whether parental finances and religious commitment influence divorce and parent-child relationships–thereby making the latter correlation spurious–or whether divorce influences finances and religious involvement, which in turn, affect parent-child relations.

Because parent-child relationship quality is not assessed in this study until children are 18, our empirical analyses are not capable of testing the long-term effects of childhood parental divorce on parent-child changes during the growing-up years. However, other analyses are conducted using a sample subgroup (those who experienced parental divorce in early adulthood) that examine the effects of parental divorce on *changes* in parent-child relation-ships from the child's age of 18 to 31. These additional analyses must be interpreted with caution because of the small number of sampled children who experienced parental divorce between these ages (N = 55). Finally, it is argued that the overall affective tone of the parents' marital relationship is an important influence on children's bonds with their parents after divorce. However, direct tests of this argument were not conducted, because we do not have measures of marital quality for those mothers who divorce.

The Effects of Gender and Age of the Child

Another interest of this study is the extent to which the effects of parents' marital quality and divorce on children's relationships with parents will vary by the gender and age of children. Previous research suggests that marital unhappiness and disruption are associated with less close and negative parenting styles within father-child relations (Cooney, 1994; Howes & Markman, 1989; Kerig, Cowan, & Cowan, 1993). The negative influence of divorce on father-child relationships is likely to be exacerbated because most children live with their mothers following divorce. Children may also reduce contact and withdraw from fathers after divorce because they blame them for the divorce (Cooney, 1994). Similarly, fathers may withdraw from children when confronted with marital distress (Howes & Markman, 1989), since they behave similarly with their wives (Christensen & Heavey, 1990). For many men, the meaning and expectations of fatherhood may be so closely linked to those of the husband/spouse role (Furstenberg & Cherlin, 1991; Lamb & Elster, 1985) that fathers are unable to differentiate these relationships from each other. When the role of husband is disrupted because of divorce, fathers may have difficulty maintaining close ties with their children. This effect of marital discord and divorce may be less important for father-son relationships than for father-daughter relationships because of the greater shared interests and activities that may occur between fathers and sons. This is consistent with the evidence that fathers and sons are more likely to maintain contact than fathers and daughters following divorce (Amato & Keith, 1991; Cooney, 1994).

The literature is less clear regarding the implications of marital quality and divorce on mother-child relations (Cooney, 1994; Kerig, Cowan, & Cowan, 1993), though it is likely that negative effects would be less for mothers than for fathers.[1] That is, most children of divorce continue to live with mothers rather than fathers, and thereby disrupt mother-child bonds less than father-child bonds. Moreover, mothers tend to demonstrate greater involvement and commitment to the parental role, with even non-custodial mothers having more contact with children than non-custodial fathers. Yet another possibility is that divorce and maternal custody could improve the relationship between mothers and children. As Weiss (1979) has argued, an echelon structure may exist within intact families in which mothers and fathers maintain a family hierarchy that reinforces parental authority and distance between parents and children. However, this echelon structure may be weakened through divorce and allow custodial parents, usually mothers, to develop even closer parent-child ties, with the strongest being with daughters rather than with sons.

Whether the link between mother-father and parent-child relations persists over time, as children and parents grow older, is not clear in the existing literature. Current research indicates that children's paternal contact declines significantly over time after a divorce, especially for daughters (Amato and Keith, 1991). In contrast, the experience of fatherhood (or parenthood more generally) may be closely linked to the father-mother relationship only when children and parents are young. These two relationships may become distinct and separate from one another as children develop their own identities and as parents become less responsible financially and psychologically for their children.

METHOD

Sample

The data are part of an intergenerational panel study of mothers and children (drawn from the July 1961 birth registrations of the Detroit Metropolitan Area) that used a probability sample of women who gave birth to first-, second-, and fourth-born white children. Mothers were first interviewed in 1962 and then again in 1963, 1966, and 1977. In 1980, when the target child turned 18 years old, interviews also were conducted with the children. For the purposes of this study, mothers and children were interviewed three times between 1980 and 1993 during which the children were 18, 23, and 31 years old, respectively. Response rates remained high for the data collection periods, with (1) 92% of the original sample of mothers being interviewed in 1962, (2) 85% of the original mother-child pairs being interviewed in 1980 (916 pairs; children were included), (3) 82% of the original mother-child pairs being interviewed in 1985 (867 pairs), and (4) 80% (803) of these pairs being interviewed in 1993. Two cases were deleted because the mothers were unable to answer the survey themselves and proxy respondents were used. Consequently, the sample was confined to 801 cases in which both mother and child were interviewed at each of the three data collection periods between 1980 and 1993. Cases were then omitted in which the parents experienced marital disruption through the death of the child's biological mother or father (n = 31). Although data from both mothers and fathers would be desirable, fathers were not interviewed.

Measures

The measures of parental marital history are examined using data from two different time periods. Mothers' marital quality reports are based on data from 1980-1993. For the analyses on marital disruption, mothers are classified based on data from 1962-1980 and 1980-1993.

Marital quality. During 1980, 1985, and 1993, mothers were asked to report on the quality of their marital relationships. These analyses are confined to 517 mother-child pairs in which the mothers have remained married to the child's biological father from 1962-1993.[2]

Marital quality was measured by averaging mothers' answers to five questions: (a) "How well do you think your husband understands you, your feelings, your likes, and dislikes." (b) "How well do you think you understand your husband." (c) "Generally speaking, would you say that the time you spend together with your husband is extremely enjoyable, very enjoyable, enjoyable, or not enjoyable." (d) "Taking things all together, how would you describe your marital happiness." and (e) "How often do you have problems getting along with each other." High scores on this scale represent high marital quality; low scores represent low marital quality. The same five items were used to measure marital quality in all three time periods. Cronbach's alphas for the marital quality measure are .79 (child age 18), .79 (child age 23), and .80 (child age 31), respectively. The means and standard deviations are reported in Table 1.

Marital disruption. During each interview, data were collected on the nature of the relationship between the child's biological father and mother. For those mothers who were no longer married to the child's biological father, information about divorce and remarriage dates was obtained. The

TABLE 1. Means and Standard Deviations of Relationship Variables

	Child at Age 18[a]	Child at Age 23[a]	Child at Age 31[a]
Marital Quality as Reported by Mother	3.05 (0.52)	3.02 (0.55)	2.97 (0.56)

	Child at Age 18[b]	Child at Age 23[c]	Child at Age 31[d]
Parent-Child Relationship Quality			
Mother-Child from Mother's Perspective	3.11 (0.56)	3.25 (0.52)	3.35 (0.54)
Mother-Child from Child's Perspective	2.98 (0.61)	3.09 (0.58)	3.13 (0.63)
Father-Child from Child's Perspective	2.81 (0.67)	2.87 (0.64)	2.87 (0.69)

[a]Sample consists of children who have two continuously married parents through child's age 31 (*n* = 515). [b]Sample consists of children who reported on two biological parents at age 18 (*n* = 702). [c]Sample consists of children who reported on two biological parents at ages 18 and 23 (*n* = 676). [d]Sample consists of children who reported on two biological parents at ages 18, 23, and 31 (*n* = 676).

mothers (768) were classified for analysis into three categories based on the data from 1962 to 1980: (a) continuously married 1962-1980 (N = 617), (b) divorced and remarried (N = 72), and (c) divorced and not remarried (N = 79).[3] The three groups of mothers were recoded for the regression analyses into a mutually exclusive set of two dummy variables, with "continuously married" being the omitted category for all the analyses. Analyses also were conducted in which the omitted category is divorced and remarried to examine whether a mother's remarriage has significant effects on mother-child and father-child relationships. These results are reported in the text. Other analyses classified mothers into the same three categories based on data from 1980-1993: (a) n = 517, (b) n = 18, and (c) n = 37.

Parent-child quality. Another focus of this study is the quality of the parent-child relationship from the perspective of both parent and child. Three measures of parent-child quality are analyzed in this study, with two being based on the child's report (one of father-child quality, one of mother-child quality) and one being based on the mother's perception of her relationship with the child. Across all three panels, seven items assessed the quality of parent-child bonds from the child's perspective, with versions of the same items being used for both mothers and fathers. Children were asked to report on their agreement with the following statements: (a) "My mother's/father's ideas and opinions about the important things in life are ones I can respect." (b) "My mother/father respects my ideas and opinions about the important things in life." (c) "My mother/father accepts and understands me as a person." (d) "I enjoy doing things together with my mother/father." (e) "My mother/father makes it easy for me to confide in her/him." (f) "My mother/father gives me the right amount of affection." and (g) "When something is bothering me I am able to talk it over with my mother/father."

Five items assessed the parent-child relationship from mothers' perspectives by asking them to agree/disagree with the following statements: (a) "CHILD's ideas and opinions about the important things in life are ones you can respect." (b) "CHILD respects your ideas and opinions about the important things in life." (c) "You find it easy to understand CHILD." (d) "You enjoy doing things together with CHILD." and (e) "You enjoy talking to CHILD." Note that considerable similarity and overlap exist between the mother-child and child-parent questions.

Three summary measures of parent-child relationships were created for each year of the study, with parent-child quality being obtained by averaging the answers to each set of questions. A 4-point scale was used in which 1 represents low relationship quality and 4 indicates high quality. These questions were evaluated previously using LISREL and found to have high reliability and consistency across time (Thornton, Orbuch, & Axinn, 1995). The means and standard deviations for the three indices are reported in Table 1.

During all three data collection times, children of parents with intact marriages were asked to report on their relationships with their biological mothers and fathers. When children were 31 years old in 1993, children of divorced parents also were asked about biological parents. However, in 1980 (child age 18) and 1985 (child age 23) children of parents who had divorced were asked "Which female parent or guardian do you think has had the most influence in your life?" A similar question was asked to ascertain the most influential male parent or guardian, They were then instructed to report on their relationship with the male and female parent who had the most influence on their lives. Although almost all of these children indicated that their biological mother had been the most influential female parent or guardian, a significant number reported someone other than the biological father as the most influential male parent or guardian. Data are reported in this study only for biological mothers and fathers, with the advantage being to limit the analysis to biological fathers throughout. However, this procedure both reduces the sample size available for analysis and introduces potential bias. Children who report their most influential male parent or guardian to be an adoptive, step, or foster father may have less positive relationships with their biological father than children who designate their biological father as the most influential. If this is true, our procedures may underestimate the correlation between divorce and relationships with biological fathers.

Control and Intervening Variables

Several variables are included which prior research suggests are related to either marital disruption/quality or parent-child relationships. The first group of controls includes variables which are personal attributes of the target child or the marital situation in 1962: (a) gender (0 = male, 1 = female), (b) birth order (first: 36%; second: 32%; or fourth: 32%), and (c) whether the mother was premaritally pregnant at the time of marriage (0 = no; 1 = yes). Research finds that intergenerational relationships may be more central to daughters' rather than sons' psychological health (Umberson, 1992). The association between marital history and parent-child relationship quality also may vary by the gender of the child (Erel & Burman, 1995; Kerig, Cowan, & Cowan, 1993). The birth order of the child may influence the quality of the husband-wife relationship and whether they remain married over time (Erel & Burman, 1995).[4] Prior research also suggests that marriages are of lower quality and less likely to remain stable over time if children are born or conceived before the marriage (Thornton & Rodgers, 1987). Approximately 18.4% of the mothers were pregnant at the time of their marriage.

The second group of variables includes family variables: (a) household income, (b) mother's and father's educational attainment, (c) religious denomination, and (d) religiosity. *Income* was coded as a continuous variable (in dollar units) in 1980 and 1985, assessing the mothers' reports of total household income from all sources prior to the survey year. Given that 1962 and 1993 income was originally reported in income ranges that closely represented total household income, these data were recoded into midpoints to approximate a continuous variable. Mother's and father's *educational attainment* were assessed using a 6-category variable in 1962 and 1980: (a) 0-4 years, (b) 5-8 years, (c) 9-11 years, (d) 12 years, (e) 13-15 years, and (f) 16 or more years. These categories were recoded into their approximate midpoints. *Religious denomination* was reported by the mother and coded as a mutually exclusive set of dummy variables: fundamentalist Protestant, non-fundamentalist Protestant, Catholic, Jewish or other/no preference. *Religiosity* was measured by mothers' answers to the question: "How often do you usually attend religious services?" The response categories were several times a week, once a week, a few times a month, once a month, less than once a month, or never.

Analysis Strategy

The first analyses examined the short- and long-term effects of maternal marital quality on parent-child bonds for those mothers who have been married continuously from 1962 to 1993 (see Table 2). In all of these models, mothers' and fathers' education are assessed in 1980, whereas religious denomination, religiosity, and annual income are assessed the same year that the parent-child quality dependent variable is measured. Given that these effects may vary by gender of child, interactions were calculated for marital quality by gender and entered into the equations.

Another focus is the link between parental divorce during 1962 to 1980 and parent-child relations in 1980, when the child is 18 years of age. The particular interest is whether a significant negative relationship exists for father-child and mother-child bonds from the perspective of both parent and children. The two marital history dummy variables are entered into each regression equation and then examined as to whether the relationship between marital disruption and parent-child quality is diminished as sets of predictor variables are entered. The results from these analyses are presented in Table 3. Since good reason exists to believe that these effects may vary by gender of the child, interaction terms are calculated for each marital history dummy variable by gender and entered into our models (see Table 4). Next, the link was examined between parental divorce in young adulthood (when the children's ages range from 18 to 31) and the change in parent-child relationships during these years (see Table 5).

RESULTS

Mother's Marital Quality and Parent-Child Quality

Table 2 addresses the issue of whether the effects of marital quality on parent-child relations persist over time. The characteristics of the child (gen-

TABLE 2. Effects of Parental Marital Quality Parent-Child Relationships for Continuously Married Mother Sample

	Dependent Variables: Parent-Child Relationship		
Independent Variables	Mother-Child/Mother[a] at Child's Age 18	Mother-Child/Mother[a] at Child's Age 23	Mother-Child/Mother[a] at Child's Age 31
Marital Quality at Child's Age 18	0.19*** (0.05)	0.11* (0.04)	0.09* (0.05)
Marital Quality at Child's Age 23		−0.02 (0.04)	0.00 (0.05)
Marital Quality at Child's Age 31			0.04 (0.04)
	Mother-Child/Child[b] at Child's Age 18	Mother-Child/Child[b] at Child's Age 23	Mother-Child/Child[b] at Child's Age 31
Marital Quality at Child's Age 18	0.09* (0.05)	−0.02 (0.05)	0.00 (0.05)
Marital Quality at Child's Age 23		0.00 (0.05)	−0.05 (0.05)
Marital Quality at Child's Age 31			0.00 (0.05)
	Father-Child/Child[c] at Child's Age 18	Father-Child/Child[c] at Child's Age 23	Father-Child/Child[c] at Child's Age 31
Marital Quality at Child's Age 18	0.20*** (0.06)	0.13* (0.05)	0.13* (0.06)
Marital Quality at Child's Age 23		0.16** (0.05)	0.10† (0.05)
Marital Quality at Child's Age 31			0.16** (0.05)

Note. These effects are estimated from an unstandardized regression equation that has as predictor variables parental marital quality plus child's gender, birth order, premarital pregnancy, mother's and father's education in 1980, religious denomination, religiosity, and income. Religious denomination, religiosity and income are measured in the same year as the parent-child relationship dependent variable. For the sake of conciseness, coefficients are only shown for the effects of parental marital quality on parent-child relationship quality. Only one marital quality measure and one parent-child dependent variable are included in each equation.

[a]Quality of mother's relationship with child from mother's perspective. [b]Quality of mother's relationship with child from child's perspective. [c]Quality of father's relationship with child from child's perspective.

† $p < 0.10$. * $p < 0.05$. ** $p < 0.01$. *** $p < 0.001$.

TABLE 3. Additive Multivariate Equation of Father-Child Relationship Quality at Age 18 from Child's Perspective

	Model 1	Model 2	Model 3	Model 4
Divorced and Not Remarried	−0.17†	−0.21*	−0.18†	−0.08
	(0.09)	(0.09)	(0.10)	(0.10)
Divorced and Remarried	−0.04	−0.40	0.00	0.01
	(0.13)	(0.13)	(0.13)	(0.13)
Child's Gender (F = 1, M = 0)	−−	−0.13**	−0.13**	−0.15**
		(0.05)	(0.05)	(0.05)
Birth Order	−−	−0.05*	−0.05*	−0.05*
		(0.02)	(0.02)	(0.02)
Premarital Pregnancy	−−	0.02	0.03	0.02
		(0.07)	(0.07)	(0.07)
Mother's Education	−−	−0.03*	−0.04*	−0.05**
		(0.02)	(0.02)	(0.02)
Father's Education	−−	0.02*	0.03*	0.02
		(0.01)	(0.01)	(0.01)
Fundamental Protestant	−−	0.19*	−0.17†	0.16†
		(0.09)	(0.09)	(0.09)
Non-Fundamental Protestant		0.02	0.01	0.02
	−−	(0.07)	(0.07)	(0.07)
Jewish		0.18	0.22	0.21
	−−	(0.16)	(0.16)	(0.16)
Other	−−	−0.06	−0.06	−0.12
		(0.19)	(0.19)	(0.20)
Religiosity at Child's Age 0	−−	0.02	0.00	0.00
		(0.02)	(0.02)	(0.02)
Income at Child's Age 0	−−	0.01	0.01	0.00
		(0.01)	(0.01)	(0.01)
Religiosity at Child's Age 18	−−	−−	0.04*	0.05**
			(0.02)	(0.02)
Income at Child's Age 18	−−	−−	−−	0.004**
				(0.002)
Sample Size	694	694	694	663
R^2	0.01	0.04	0.05	0.06

Note. Numbers in the table are unstandardized regression coefficients with their standard errors in parentheses.

† $p < 0.10$. * $p < 0.05$. ** $p < 0.01$.

TABLE 4. Multivariate Equation of Parent-Child Relationships at Child's Age 18 with Marital Disruption-Gender Interactions

	Mother-Child/Mother[a]		Mother-Child/Child[b]		Father-Child/Child[c]	
	1a	1b	2a	2b	3a	3b
Child's Gender	0.09*	0.10*	0.02	0.01	−0.11*	−0.14**
	(0.04)	(0.05)	(0.05)	(0.05)	(0.05)	(0.06)
Divorced and Not Remarried	−0.15	−0.13	−0.16	−0.12	−0.15	0.00
	(0.10)	(0.11)	(0.11)	(0.12)	(0.12)	(0.13)
Divorced and Remarried	−0.11	−0.12	−0.22	−0.23	0.01	−0.02
	(0.16)	(0.16)	(0.18)	(0.18)	(0.20)	(0.20)
Gender * Divorced Not Remarried	0.32*	0.33*	0.40*	0.37*	−0.14	−0.19
	(0.15)	(0.15)	(0.17)	(0.17)	(0.19)	(0.19)
Gender * Divorced and Remarried	−0.08	−0.02	0.11	0.19	−0.09	−0.05
	(0.22)	(0.22)	(0.24)	(0.25)	(0.26)	(0.27)
Birth Order	−0.02	−0.02	−0.03	−0.03†	−0.05*	−0.05*
	(0.02)	(0.02)	(0.02)	(0.02)	(0.02)	(0.02)
Premarital Pregnancy	0.07	0.08	0.07	0.08	0.02	0.02
	(0.06)	(0.06)	(0.06)	(0.06)	(0.07)	(0.07)
Mother's Education	0.00	−0.01	−0.01	−0.02	−0.03*	−0.05**
	(0.01)	(0.01)	(0.02)	(0.02)	(0.02)	(0.02)
Father's Education	0.01	0.01	0.02	0.02	0.02*	0.02†
	(0.01)	(0.01)	(0.01)	(0.01)	(0.01)	(0.01)
Fundamental Protestant	−0.07	−0.09	0.03	0.02	0.19*	0.16†
	(0.07)	(0.07)	(0.08)	(0.08)	(0.09)	(0.09)
Non-Fundamental Protestant	−0.01	0.00	−0.05	−0.04	0.02	0.02
	(0.06)	(0.06)	(0.06)	(0.06)	(0.07)	(0.07)
Jewish	−0.16	−0.14	−0.13	−0.08	0.18	0.20
	(0.13)	(0.13)	(0.14)	(0.15)	(0.16)	(0.16)
Other	0.18	0.22	−0.14	−0.17	−0.06	−0.11
	(0.15)	(0.17)	(0.17)	(0.19)	(0.19)	(0.20)
Religiosity at Child's Age 0	0.02	0.01	−0.01	−0.02	0.02	0.00
	(0.02)	(0.02)	(0.02)	(0.02)	(0.02)	(0.02)
Income at Child's Age 0	0.012†	0.012†	0.001	0.001	0.012	0.005
	(0.007)	(0.008)	(0.008)	(0.009)	(0.009)	(0.002)
Religiosity at Child's Age 18	− −	0.04**	− −	0.06**	− −	0.05**
		(0.02)		(0.02)		(0.02)
Income at Child's Age 18	− −	0.001	− −	−0.001	− −	0.004**
		(0.001)		(0.002)		(0.002)
Sample Size	694	663	694	663	694	663
R^2	0.05	0.07	0.02	0.04	0.04	0.07

[a]Quality of mother's relationship with child from mother's perspective. [b]Quality of mother's relationship with child from child's perspective. Quality of father's relationship with child from child's perspective.

† $p < 0.10$.   *$p < 0.05$.   **$p < 0.01$.

TABLE 5. Additive Multivariate Equations of Parent-Child Relationship Quality at Age 31

	Mother-Child/Mother 1			Mother-Child/Child 2			Father-Child/Child[c]		
	1a	1b	1c	2a	2b	2c	3a	3b	3c
Divorced and Not Remarried	−0.06 (0.08)	−0.05 (0.08)	−0.05 (0.09)	−0.10 (0.10)	−0.10 (0.10)	−0.09 (0.11)	−0.50** (0.10)	−0.49*** (0.10)	−0.46*** (0.11)
Divorced and Remarried	−0.40*** (0.12)	−0.38*** (0.12)	−0.40*** (0.12)	−0.24† (0.14)	−0.25† (0.14)	−0.28† (0.15)	−0.23 (0.15)	−0.20 (0.15)	−0.19 (0.16)
Parent-Child Relationship at age 18	0.46*** (0.04)	0.46*** (0.04)	0.45*** (0.04)	0.37*** (0.04)	0.37*** (0.04)	0.37*** (0.04)	0.49*** (0.04)	0.49*** (0.04)	0.48*** (0.04)
Gender	0.04 (0.04)	0.04 (0.04)	0.04 (0.04)	−0.09† (0.05)	−0.09† (0.05)	−0.08 (0.05)	−0.09† (0.05)	−0.09† (0.05)	−0.09† (0.05)
Includes Religiosity at Child's Age 31		X	X		X	X		X	X
Includes Income at Child's Age 31			X			X			X
Sample Size	539	539	520	537	537	518	531	531	513
R^2	0.26	0.26	0.26	0.16	0.16	0.15	0.30	.30	.30

Note. In addition to the variables listed, all models control for birth order, mother's education, father's education, religious denomination, and the child's income and religiosity at age 18. These are not reported for the sake of conciseness.

1 Quality of mother's relationship with child from mother's perspective. 2 Quality of mother's relationship with child from child's perspective.[c] Quality of father's relationship with child from child's perspective.

† $p < 0.10$. **$p < 0.01$. ***$p < 0.001$.

der, birth order), premarital pregnancy, and family factors (mother's and father's education, religious denomination, religiosity, and income) that were discussed previously are controlled for in all the models. Table 2 includes coefficients only for the effects of mother's marital quality (for conciseness) and does not report the coefficients for the control variables.[5] Note that each coefficient reported in Table 2 is estimated in a separate equation, with only one marital quality measure and one parent-child measure being included in each equation. The coefficients for the interaction terms of gender by mother's marital quality are not shown in Table 2, because they are nonsignificant in all of the models. Nonetheless, the general pattern of results by gender are discussed below.

The results in Table 2 indicate that mothers' marital quality at children's age 18 is significantly and positively related to mothers' perceptions of parent-child relational quality at children's age 18. However, the strength of mother's marital quality diminishes as children and parents grow older; with the effect being .19 at child's age 18, .11 at age 23, and .09 at age 31. Evidence from the second panel, however, indicates that the effect of mother's marital quality on adult children's view of their relationship with mother is generally weak and short-term.

These results suggest that as children become adults, mothers and children are better able to differentiate maternal from spousal ties. Perhaps as children leave home and begin the transition to adulthood, mothers are less "burdened" with parental role responsibilities and strains. Such changes in expectations may allow mothers to affectively and cognitively differentiate their motherhood from spousal roles. Children are also better able to make distinctions between how they feel toward their mother and their parents' marital bond as they grow older. Further, although none of the gender interaction terms were significantly related to mother-child relations, the general pattern of results suggests that mother-son relations are more strongly influenced by parental marital quality than mother-daughter relations. This pattern of results was consistent at ages 18, 23 and 31 and from the perspective of both mother and child.

The results presented in Table 2 (panel 3) also demonstrate that adult children's relationships with fathers are consistently and significantly related to mother's marital quality. This relationship remains significant and positive throughout the years observed in our study, suggesting that the affective nature of the parental bond spills over to the father-child relationship, even when that child is 31 years old. Although adult children may differentiate the parental bond from the relationship with their mother as they grow older, they are less able to make these distinctions in their relationships with fathers. Contrary to previous research and our expectations, the effect of marital quality on father-child relations was not significantly different for daughters and sons. However, the general pattern for a child ages 18, 23, and 31 suggests that father-daughter relations are more strongly influenced by maternal marital quality than are father-son relations.

Divorce and Parent-Child Quality

Another interest is whether childhood divorce has consequences for parent-child relationships when adult children are beginning the transition to adulthood.[6] These findings indicate that parental divorce between 1962-1980 is not predictive of mother-child relationship quality in 1980 (when the child is age 18) as perceived by both mothers and children. Neither of the marital history variables was significantly related to mother-child relationship quality, nor was the association between divorce and mother-child quality significantly changed when any of the child and familial factors were added to the equation.

In contrast, the results in Table 3 (Model 1) demonstrate a tendency for divorce to be significantly related to children's perceptions of father-child relational quality. Children with divorced mothers who are not remarried tend to report lower quality relationships with fathers than children with continuously married parents. In other analyses in which the omitted category was divorced and remarried mothers, results indicate that no significant differences existed in father-child quality between divorced and remarried and divorced and not remarried groups.

In Model 2, the results indicate that the characteristics of the child and family prior to the divorce (measured in the child's year of birth) do not account for the negative link between having a divorced and not remarried mother and father-child relational quality. This suggests that the relationship between parental divorce and father-child relations is not spurious in the sense of being a product of pre-existing factors, including income and religious commitment.

In Models 3 and 4, we consider the effects of intervening variables that occur after the parental divorce. When we account for mother's religious commitment at child's age 18 (Model 3), the relationship between having a divorced and not remarried mother and father-child quality is reduced only slightly from Model 1. This is true despite the expected positive and statistically significant influence of religiosity on father-child relations. Not until income at child's age 18 is included (Model 4) does the relationship between a divorced and not remarried mother and father-child quality become substantially reduced (by one-half) to non-significance. The financial resources of the mother, rather than her commitment and religious participation, account for most of the negative relationship between divorce and father-child bonds.

The results in Table 4 indicate that the effects of divorce on parent-child relations vary by gender of the child. The main effect of divorce and not remarrying on mother-child relations from the mother's perspective is $-.15$ (Model 1a), which means that divorce and no remarriage decreases the quality of mother-child relations for sons. However, the significant interaction term for gender by divorce without remarriage is a positive .32, which when combined with the main effect, signifies a positive effect of .17 for divorce on mother-child relations involving daughters.

These results suggest that divorce may benefit mothers' relationships with daughters, but only if mothers do not remarry. These results are also consistent with our expectation that, in comparison to continuously married mothers, mothers who are divorced and not remarried become closer to their daughters. In contrast, divorce without remarriage negatively influences mothers' relationships with their sons. Neither the additive nor the interactive effects of divorce and remarrying are significant.

Such results are very similar when we examine children's perceptions of their relationships with their mothers (Models 2a and 2b). Again, divorce without remarriage reduces the quality of mother-child relations among sons, while improving them among daughters. Note that religiosity and income at age 18 explain only a small fraction of the additive and interactive effects of divorce on mother-child relations (compare Models 1a vs. 1b and 2a vs. 2b).

The additive and interactive effects of divorce on father-child relationships are considered in Models 3a and 3b. Although gender differences were not significant, the general pattern of results suggests that the effect of divorce without remarriage on sons is similar for father-child relations as for mother-child relations (as indicated by the main effect of $-.15$ in Model 3a). However, unlike with the mother-child relations dependent variable, the interactive effect of gender by divorce/not remarry is negative for father-child relations. This means that divorce has an even greater negative influence on father-child relations for daughters than for sons. Thus, while divorce without remarriage hurts sons' relationships with both fathers and mothers, it hurts father-daughter relations even more, while at the same time improving mother-daughter bonds. Mother's income when the child is 18 explains most of the negative effect of divorce on father-child relations among sons, and a moderate part of it for daughters.

A problem is that this study cannot assess the long-term effects of childhood divorce on change in parent-child bonds during the child's years of growing up. However, what can be examined is the extent to which parental divorce in a child's early adulthood is predictive of change in parent-child relational quality during young adulthood (see Table 5). The pattern of results for mothers who divorce without remarriage is similar to the earlier findings for childhood divorce. Specifically, when children are young adults, a mother's divorce without remarriage is not predictive of change in the quality of the mother-child relationship from either the mother's or adult child's perspective. These children do, however, report a significant decrease in father-child relationship quality ($p < .001$), a negative effect that does not change with the addition of mother's religious involvement and income (measured at child's age 31) to the equation. Perhaps since children who are young adults tend to leave the parental home, the community and financial resources (as reported by mothers) may not have the same consequences for father-child ties as when children are 0 to 18 years old. Given the small sample size of children who experienced divorce during these ages, gender differences in these effects could not be tested.

The results follow a different pattern for those mothers who divorce and remarry during a child's young adulthood. In Model 1, the results indicate that mothers report a significant decrease in mother-child relational quality if they divorce and remarry during a child's young adulthood ($p < .001$). Similarly, from the perspective of the child, a mother's divorce and remarriage is marginally associated with a decrease in mother-child relational quality. These results do not change with the addition of mother's religious involvement and income to the equation (Models 1b and 1c). The advent of a new spousal relationship for mothers when children are young adults negatively influences mothers' relationships with their children, as perceived by both mothers and adult children. An interesting point, however, is that, children's perceptions of father-child bonds demonstrates a negative effect, but not large enough to be statistically significant.

CONCLUSION AND DISCUSSION

A primary interest of this paper has been to understand more fully the long-term effects of mother-father relations on parent-child relationships. The focus was on the interrelatedness of these two family dyads during the child's transition to adulthood, a time when children are forming their own marital/intimate relationships. Using data from an intergenerational panel study of mothers and children, the work of previous studies was extended by examining whether the effects of parental marital quality and disruption: (a) differ for father-child and mother-child relations, (b) are long-term and consistent across the adult child's life course, and (c) differ with gender of the child. Given previous theoretical expectations, we also focus on whether factors such as financial resources, religious participation or commitment, and remarriage account for the negative effects of parental divorce on parent-child relations.

The effects of parental marital quality and divorce on parent-child relations were found to differ substantially depending on gender of the parent and child. First, for mother-child relations, these results indicate that parental marital quality (when the child is 18) has short-term significant consequences for mother-child relations, but only for quality as perceived by mothers. As children and mothers grow older, parental marital quality is not significantly related to mother-child bonds from either perspective. Gender of the child did not significantly differentiate the effect of mother's marital quality on mother-child relations.

Although parental divorce without remarriage negatively influences mothers' relationships with sons, it improves their relationships with daughters. Mothers who do not remarry following a divorce may compensate for the lack of a spousal bond by becoming closer to their daughters. Consistent with Weiss's argument (1979), it appears that under some conditions, divorce can lead to positive outcomes for mother-daughter relations. However, if mothers divorce and remarry when children are young adults, both mothers and children report a decrease in mother-child relational quality.

By contrast, father-child relationships are influenced by mother's reports of marital quality and parental divorce. Among intact families, contrary to expectation, parental marital bonds had consistent long-terms effects on children's relationships with their fathers. Thus, fathers may be less likely to maintain close ties with children when marital problems are prevalent. Similarly, husbands may feel less close to their wives when they are having problems with their children. Equally probable is that children may withdraw or feel less close to their fathers when the parental dyad is stressed. Consequently, the quality of the parental dyad appears to have important consequences for father-child relations independent of the child's gender.

Children with mothers who are divorced and not remarried tend to report relationships with their fathers that are of lower relational quality than children with continuously married parents. This finding is statistically significant when an examination is made of the effect of mother's divorce and remarriage during young adulthood on change in relationship quality within the father-child dyad. The general pattern of cross sectional results also suggests that both father-son and father-daughter relationships are negatively influenced by divorce, but the consequences may be more adverse for father-daughter ties when the mother does not remarry. Thus, when mother and father live in the same household, the emotions and interactional nature of the parental dyad influence both father-daughter and father-son relations. However, when marital disruption occurs and fathers no longer live in the household, the negative effects may be greater for father-daughter than for father-son relations. Given shared interests and activities, in turn, fathers and sons may make special efforts to maintain contact with each other. Consequently, additional research is needed on fathers' expectations of parenthood, how they are linked to the expectations of spouse, and if these expectations vary depending on whether fathers live in the same household as their children.

Declines in financial resources after the divorce also were found to explain a large portion of the effect of childhood parental divorce on father-child bonds at child's age 18. A decrease in religious involvement following the divorce, as reported by mothers, also explains a small portion of the negative consequences on father-child relations. Consequently, these findings support the perspective that both economic and religion factors are intervening variables which transmit the effects of childhood divorce to father-child relations, rather than factors which influence divorce. These same factors, however, did not explain the effects of parental divorce in young adulthood on change in father-child bonds. When children become more mature, financial and religious factors do not have the same consequences for father-child relations. In general, the results also indicate that the effects of divorce on father-child bonds are reduced when mothers remarry.

Despite such robust findings, this study has several limitations. The measure of marital quality was only assessed from the perspective of the mother/

wife. Because wives and husbands often disagree on the subjective and objective details of marriage, it would be valuable to have husbands' reports of marital quality as well as fathers' reports of father-child relational quality. More diverse measures of marital and parental interactions might also illuminate the processes by which children learn overall patterns of relating or interacting with others that remain with them over the life course and across different familial relationships.

An analysis was not conducted on children's age at the time of divorce or mother's remarriage in childhood. Zill, Morrison, and Coiro (1993), for example, have found that children who experience divorce early, rather than later in life, may have poorer relationships with their fathers. Moreover, data were not available on whether fathers remarried after divorce. Future research should also examine the processes by which mother's remarriage reduces the effect of parental divorce on children's paternal relationships, with more attention being devoted to post-divorce custody arrangements.

Most of these results have been interpreted in fairly bi-directional terms. Nonetheless, it must be emphasized that the association between parental marital quality and divorce and parent-child relations is reciprocal and influenced by mutually reinforcing causal mechanisms. The intent here is to understand a process that occurs over time (a process leading to divorce and then its consequences on parent-child relations), whereas parental divorce, in most of our analyses, was measured as an event occurring sometime before the child's eighteenth birthday. More careful attention needs to be given, therefore, to those conditions leading up to and following divorces for their effects on parent-child relations. Further, many argue (Cherlin et al., 1991; Furstenberg & Teitler, 1994) that the consequences of divorce may occur for children before the divorce itself.

The bonds that children develop with their parents early in life are important to children's overall well-being and adjustment throughout their lives. As a result, the association between parental relations and adult children's relationships with their parents should become more central to research efforts that focus on marriage and family issues.

NOTES

1. Zill et al. (1993) found that daughters were more likely than sons to develop negative mother-child relationships after divorce, however, this gender interaction was only marginally significant. Further, the measure of parent-child quality assessed in this study included how much the child "desired to be the kind of person the parent was" (pp. 94).

2. In 1980 there were 617 mother-child pairs where the mother was continuously married 1962-1980. From 1980 to 1993, 45 mothers were widowed, 18 divorced and

remarried, and 37 divorced and not remarried. Thus, in 1993, 517 mothers were continuously married between 1962 and 1993.

3. We deleted 2 cases from the total sample of N = 770 because of inconsistencies in mothers' reports of marital histories. There were also 29 mothers who were divorced and remarried by 1961 (before the child was born), but we focus on the marital relationship between the child's biological parents after the child was born.

4. We also conducted analyses using the total number of children born to the mother in 1980 instead of birth order. Results were similar to those presented here. For clarity, we have chosen to use birth order for both sets of analyses.

5. The coefficients for the effects of the control variables are similar to those presented in Tables 3 and 4.

6. We acknowledge that given our measure of parental divorce (child's age 0-18), it is likely that these 18-year-old children experienced divorce many years ago. We argue that given the lack of an exact date of divorce, any significant findings of parental disruption on parent-child relations are quite important, and may actually underestimate any immediate or short term consequences.

REFERENCES

Amato, P. (1993). Children's adjustment to divorce: Theories, hypotheses, and empirical support. *Journal of Marriage and the Family, 55,* 23-38.

Amato, P. (1999). Children of divorced parents as young adults. In E.M. Hetherington (Eds), *Coping with Divorce, Single Parenting, and Remarriage* (pp. 147-163), Mahwah, NJ: Erlbaum.

Amato, P.R., & Booth, A. (1991). Consequences of parental divorce and marital unhappiness for adult wellbeing. *Social Forces, 69,* 895-914.

Amato, P.R., & Booth, A. (1996). A prospective study of divorce and parent-child relationships. *Journal of Marriage and the Family, 58,* 356-365.

Amato, P., & Keith, B. (1991). Separation from a parent during childhood and adult socioeconomic attainment. *Social Forces, 70,* 187-206.

Amato, P., Loomis, L.S., & Booth, A. (1995). Parental divorce, marital conflict, and offspring well-being during early adulthood. *Social Forces, 73,* 895-915.

Amato, P.R., Rezac, S.J., & Booth, A. (1995). Helping between parents and young adult offspring: The role of parental marital quality, divorce and remarriage. *Journal of Marriage and the Family, 57,* 363-374.

Aquilino, W.S. (1994a). Impact of childhood family disruption on young adult's relationships with parents. *Journal of Marriage and the Family, 56,* 295-313.

Aquilino, W.S. (1994b). Later life parental divorce and widowhood: Impact on young adults' assessment of parentchild relations. *Journal of Marriage and the Family, 56,* 908-922.

Avenevoli, S., Sessa, F.M., & Steinberg, L. (1999). Family structure, parenting practices, and adolescent adjustment: An ecological examination. In E.M. Hetherington (Eds), *Coping with Divorce, Single Parenting, and Remarriage* (pp. 65-90), Mahwah, NJ: Erlbaum.

Belsky, J., Youngblade, L., Rovine, M., & Volling, B. (1991). Patterns of marital change and parentchild interactions. *Journal of Marriage and the Family, 53,* 487-498.

Bolger, N., DeLongis, A., Kessler, R., & Wethington, E. (1989). The contagion of stress across multiple roles. *Journal of Marriage and the Family, 51*, 175-183.

Booth, A., & Amato, P.R. (1994). Parental marital quality, parental divorce, and relations with parents. *Journal of Marriage and the Family, 56*, 21-34.

Booth, A., & Dunn, J. (1994). *Stepfamilies: Who Benefits? Who Does Not?* Hillsdale, NJ: Erlbaum.

Cherlin, A.J., Furstenburg, F.F., Jr., Chase-Lansdale, P.L., Kierman, K.E., Robins, P.K., Morrison, D.R., & Teitler, J.O. (1991). Longitudinal studies of effects of divorce on children in Great Britain and the United States. *Science, 252*, 1386-1389.

Christensen, A., & Heavey, C.L. (1990). Gender and social structure in the demand/ withdraw pattern of marital conflict. *Journal of Personality and Social Psychology, 59*, 73-81.

Conger, R., Ge, X., Elder, G. Jr., Lorenz, F., & Simons, R. (1994). Economic stress, coercive family process, and developmental problems of adolescents. *Child Development, 65*, 541-561.

Cooney, T.M. (1994). Young adults' relations with parents: The influence of recent parental divorce. *Journal of Marriage and the Family, 56*, 45-56.

Cooney, T.M., Hutchinson, M.K., & Leather, D.M. (1995). Surviving the breakup? Predictors of parent-adult child relations after parental divorce. *Family Relations, 44*, 153-161.

Cowan, C.P., Cowan, P.A. (1992). *When Partners Become Parents*. New York: Basic.

DeGarmo, D.S., & Forgatch, M.S. (1999). Contexts as predictors of structures: A social interactional perspective of risk and resilience. In E.M. Hetherington (Ed.), *Coping with Divorce, Single Parenting, and Remarriage* (pp. 227-257), Mahwah, NJ: Erlbaum.

Easterbrooks, M.A., & Emde, R.N. (1988). Marital and parentchild relationship: The role of affect in the family system. In R.A. Hinde & J.S. Hinde (Eds). *Relationships Within Families: Mutual Influence* (pp. 83-103), New York: Oxford University Press.

Elder, G. Jr., & Caspi, A. (1988). Economic stress in lives: Developmental perspectives. *Journal of Social Issues, 44*, 25-45.

Erel, O., & Burman, B. (1995). Interrelatedness of marital relations and parent-child relations: A Meta-analytic review. *Psychological Bulletin, 118*, 108-132.

Fine, M.A., Coleman, M., & Ganong, L.H. (1999). A social constructionist multi-method approach to understanding the stepparent role. In E.M. Hetherington (Ed.), *Coping with Divorce, Single Parenting, and Remarriage* (pp. 273-294), Mahwah, NJ: Erlbaum.

Furstenberg, F.F., Jr., & Cherlin, A. (1991). *Divided Families: What Happens to Children When Parents Part*. Cambridge, MA: Harvard University Press.

Furstenberg, F.F., Jr., & Teitler, J.O. (1994). Reconsidering the effects of marital disruption. *Journal of Family Issues, 15*, 173-190.

Ganong, L.H., & Coleman, M. (1994). *Remarried Family Relationships*. Thousand Oaks, CA: Sage.

Gronvold, R.L. (1988). Measuring affectual solidarity. In D.J. Mangen, V.L. Bengtson, & P.H. Landry Jr. (Eds.), *Measurement of Intergenerational Relations*. Newbury Park, CA: Sage.

Grych, J.H., Seid, M., & Fincham, F.D. (1992). Assessing marital conflict from the child's perspective: The children's Perception of Interparental Conflict Scale. *Child Development, 63*, 558-572.

Hashima, P., & Amato, P. (1994). Poverty, social support, and parental behavior. *Child Development, 65*, 394-403.

Hetherington, E.M. (1999a). *Coping with Divorce, Single Parenting, and Remarriage,* Mahwah, NJ: Erlbaum.

Hetherington, E.M. (1999b). Should we stay together for the sake of the children? In E.M. Hetherington (Ed.), *Coping with Divorce, Single Parenting, and Remarriage* (pp. 93-116), Mahwah, NJ: Erlbaum.

Hetherington, E.M., & Clingempeel, W.G. (1992). Coping with marital transitions: A family systems perspective. *Monographs of the Society for Research in Child Development, 57,* (2-3, Serial No. 227).

Howes, P., & Markman, H. J. (1989). Marital quality and child functioning: A longitudinal investigation. *Child Development, 60*, 1044-1051.

Hustin, A.C. (1995, August). *Children in Poverty and Public Policy*. Paper presented at the annual meetings of the American Psychological Association, New York City.

Kerig, P.K., Cowan, P.A., & Cowan, C.P. (1993). Marital quality and gender differences in parentchild interaction. *Developmental Psychology, 29*, 931-939.

Kurdek, L., & Fine, M. (1993). The relation between family structure and young adolescents' appraisals of family climate and parenting behavior. *Journal of Family Issues, 14*, 279-290.

Lamb, M.E. & Elster, A.B. (1985). Adolescent mother-infant-father relationships. *Developmental Psychology, 21*, 768-773.

McLanahan, S. (1999). Father absence and the welfare of children. In E.M. Hetherington (Ed.), *Coping with Divorce, Single Parenting, and Remarriage* (pp. 117-145), Mahwah, NJ: Erlbaum.

McLanahan, S., & Sandefur, G. (1994). *Growing Up With a Single Parent: What Hurts, What Helps*. Harvard University Press: Cambridge, MA.

Pearce, L.D., & Axinn, W.G. (1998). The impact of family religious life on the quality of mother-child relations. *American Sociological Review, 63*, 810-828.

Rossi, A., & Rossi, P. (1990). *Of Human Bonding: Parent-Child Relations Across the Lifecourse*. New York: Aldine de Gruyter.

Seltzer, J.A., & Bianchi, S.M. (1988). Children's contact with absent parents. *Journal of Marriage and the Family, 50*, 663-677.

Teachman, J., Paasch, K.M., Day, R, & Carver, K. (1995, February). *Poverty During Adolescence and Subsequent Educational Attainment*. Paper presented at the NICHD conference on Consequences of Growing up Poor, Washington, D.C.

Thornton, A. (1985). Reciprocal influences of family and religion in a changing world. *Journal of Marriage and the Family, 47*, 381-394.

Thornton, A., Orbuch, T., & Axinn, W. (1995). Parentchild relationships during the transition to adulthood. *Journal of Family Issues, 16*, 538-564.

Thornton, A., & Rodgers, W.L. (1987). The influence of individual and historical time on marital dissolution. *Demography, 24*, 1-22.

Umberson, D. (1992). Relationships between adult children and their parents: Psychological consequences for both generations. *Journal of Marriage and the Family, 54*, 664-674.

Webster, P., Orbuch, T., & House, J. (1995). Effects of childhood family background on adult marital quality and perceived stability. *American Journal of Sociology, 101*, 404-432.

Weiss, R.S. (1979). Growing up a little faster: The experiences of growing up in a single-parent household. *Journal of Social Issues, 35*, 97-111.

White, L. K. (1992). The effect of parental divorce and remarriage on parental support of adult children. *Journal of Family Issues, 13*, 234-250.

Zill, N., Morrison, D.R., & Coiro, M.J. (1993). Long-term effects of parental divorce on parent-child relationships, adjustment, and achievement in young adulthood. *Journal of Family Psychology, 7*, 91-103.

Engaging Fathers
in the Post-Divorce Family

Sanford L. Braver
William A. Griffin

SUMMARY. Data we collected in longitudinal and cross-sectional studies of divorcing families provide an empirical basis for understanding the dynamics of divorced fathering. Our findings focus on the difficult circumstances of divorced fathers, rather than on their defective characters. We find that fathers continue visiting and paying at high levels when they perceive that they retain some degree of paternal authority. The loss of this sense of paternal authority appears to occur, in part, because fathers perceive that the legal system and their divorce settlements were unfair to them. We also find that the custodial mother, who sometimes sees little value in the father's involvement, limits the father's role within the post-divorce family. These findings formed the theoretical foundation for an intervention we developed for recently divorced fathers called DADS FOR LIFE. This 8-week program focuses on retraining divorced fathers' attitudes and motivations by

Sanford L. Braver is affiliated with the Department of Psychology, and William A. Griffin is affiliated with the Department of Family Resources and Human Development, Arizona State University.

Address correspondence to: Sanford Braver, Department of Psychology, Arizona State University, Temple AZ 85287-1104 (e-mail: sanford.braver@asu.edu) or William Griffin, Department of Family Resources and Human Development, YHE 2502, Arizona State University, Temple AZ 85287 (e-mail: william.griffin@asu.edu).

Portions of this paper were presented at the 1997 Reintegrating Fathers Conference, sponsored by National Institute of Child Health and Human Development, Bethesda, MD, October 24, 1997. Data presented herein were collected with the support of two grants: NICHD (1R01HD/MR19383), and the NIMH (5P30/MH39246). DADS FOR LIFE is supported by a grant from NIMH (1R01/MH51184).

[Haworth co-indexing entry note]: "Engaging Fathers in the Post-Divorce Family." Braver, Sanford L., and William A. Griffin. Co-published simultaneously in *Marriage & Family Review* (The Haworth Press, Inc.) Vol. 29, No. 4, 2000, pp. 247-267; and: *FATHERHOOD: Research, Interventions and Policies* (ed: H. Elizabeth Peters et al.) The Haworth Press, Inc., 2000, pp. 247-267. Single or multiple copies of this article are available for a fee from The Haworth Document Delivery Service [1-800-342-9678, 9:00 a.m. - 5:00 p.m. (EST). E-mail address: getinfo@haworthpressinc.com].

teaching them skills to manage conflict with the custodial mother, and giving them parenting tools to use during visitation. We are in the process of a randomized trial to evaluate this program. *[Article copies available for a fee from The Haworth Document Delivery Service: 1-800-342-9678. E-mail address: getinfo@haworthpressinc.com <Website: http:// www.haworthpressinc.com>]*

KEYWORDS. Divorced fathers, paternal authority, father involvement, post-divorce conflict, parenting skills

In the late 1960s, the divorce rate rose dramatically, a demographic trend that has tremendous implications for the psychological functioning of our nation's children today. Although a small decline in divorce rates has occurred since the early 1980s, rates remain high enough so that nearly one-half of all couples who are currently married will eventually become divorced (U.S. Bureau of the Census, 1995). The result is that many children are now growing up in single-parent households, stepfamilies, and shared custody arrangements (Faust & McKibben, 1999).

For most children who experience the divorce of their parents, the event will be marked by a considerable loss of contact with their fathers; 90% will become the nonprimary parent (Meyer & Garasky, 1993). For many children, contact will cease altogether, but for most, decreases will occur in the pattern of everyday contact experienced before the dissolution. Although this loss of father involvement commonly results in decrements in the children's well-being (McLanahan & Sandefur, 1994), it can be moderated by the father's maintenance of frequent visits and creation of supportive relationships with children.

A large number of studies have examined the relationship between the child's well-being and the quality contact with the noncustodial parent (e.g., Hess & Camara, 1979; Hetherington, Cox, & Cox, 1978; Kurdek & Berg, 1983; Wallerstein & Kelly, 1980a). For example, a meta-analysis by Amato and Keith (1991) of all the published literature on factors influencing children's adjustment to divorce demonstrates that, in a majority of families, a close relationship with divorced fathers provides unmistakable benefits to children.[1] Moreover, the results obtained from a national sample using multifactor assessments conducted by highly trained evaluators (Guidibaldi, Cleminshaw, Perry, & McLoughlin, 1983) found that the children's good relationships, frequent association, and reliable contact with noncustodial parents were significantly associated with better adjustment in children, but especially for boys.

Despite the clear beneficial effects on children of substantial post-divorce contact with non-custodial parents, several investigators have shown that it is common for this contact to be rather limited in the short term and to drop off substantially as time progresses (Bloom, Hodges, & Caldwell, 1983; Jacobson, 1978; Koch & Lowery, 1984). For example, Hetherington et al. (1978) and Fulton (1979) reported that two years after the divorce about 30% of the fathers rarely saw their children or had ceased to visit altogether.

The most influential and seemingly definitive data on this point were published by Furstenburg and associates (Furstenburg & Nord, 1985; Furstenburg, Nord, Peterson, & Zill, 1983). Using a large, representative national data set, these investigators reported that 49% of the children in their sample had not seen their noncustodial parent in the preceding year and that only one child in six averaged weekly contact or better. Furstenburg and Nord (1985) suggest that this infrequent contact occurs because most of the fathers are only weakly attached to their children. Popenoe (1996) echoes this conclusion by writing that "male biology pulls men away from long-term parental investment" (p. 173) . . . He proposes that "men are only weakly attached to the father role" (p. 184), a circumstance to which Furstenberg (1988) attaches the label "bad dads."

We contend, however, that the interpretation provided above is false or at least open to question. Specifically, we refer to the implication that most divorced fathers are characterologically bad dads who, with volition and a lack of responsibility, abandon their emotional, financial, and physical involvement with their children without sufficient cause (see also Braver & O'Connell, 1998; Hawkins & Dolahite, 1997). Instead, the perspective we investigated assumes that it is the *situation*, rather than their unwholesome personal characteristics, that drives some fathers into undesirable disengagement behavior. Such a perspective is the basis for our empirical exploration of the circumstances faced by divorced fathers.

Substantially different implications follow from these two alternate interpretations. The "bad dad" characterization leads primarily to hand wringing, wholesale condemnations, and often draconian and coercive policies that have led, much too often, to weak remedies for the problem. By comparison, our own perspective is far more hopeful by leading directly to an intervention program that is described later in this paper.

TWO DATA SETS

Analyses presented to support our perspective derive from two data sets we have collected. The first data set (Data Set I) was a longitudinal study that followed over 300 couples within weeks of filing for divorce in 1986. Our first interview preceded the finalization of the divorce decree, the second a year later, and the third occurred two years after the second.

The sample for this study involved (mostly) matched couples from families who divorced in Phoenix, Arizona. In contrast to the highly self-selected samples used by Wallerstein and Kelly (1980b) or Hetherington et al. (1978), however, this sample involved families that were strongly representative of those who divorced in the region.

We obtained the sample in the following manner. Families filing for marital dissolution with at least one child under 15 were randomly selected from court records in Maricopa County (Phoenix), Arizona, within one month of their filing. Subjects were declared ineligible if, once contacted, we found that they (a) were not English speaking, (b) did not currently live in the U.S., (c) were in jail or in a mental hospital, or (d) had reconciled or had plans to reconcile. Eligible participants were interviewed within six weeks of their selection, which was within 2-1/2 months of the time the petition for divorce was filed, and before any of the families was legally divorced. Physical separation of the families was, however, highly variable, and ranged from separated for one week to over seven years. The median time since separation was 4.7 months. Thus, this sample was, as compared to most samples in the divorce literature, quite early in the divorce process.

To ensure as representative a sample as possible, extensive efforts were employed to contact subjects who had relocated; subjects were also paid $20.00 for their participation. We were successful in locating and contacting 74% of the fathers randomly targeted, and only 23% of the eligible parents we contacted refused to participate. Such a response rate was far higher than typically found in the divorce literature (Braver & Bay, 1992).

To assess the representativeness of the total sample, the interviewed sample was compared on 57 variables to subjects who refused to participate and those who were not located (these analyses are reported in detail in Braver & Bay, 1992). These measures included 18 socio-economic variables concerning the Census tract in which participants lived; 8 family composition variables available from the couple's Petition for Dissolution; and 31 variables eventually available from the Divorce Decrees (e.g., amount of child support awarded, custody, and visitation arrangement). Few significant differences were noted between the respondents and the non-respondents, leading to the conclusion that the sample was representative of the targeted population and not subject to selection bias.

Most of the analyses from this first data set presented in the current summary have been previously published. For each such finding reviewed here, we refer the reader to the original publications for more details. The second data set (Data Set II) used a similar sample acquisition methodology. We interviewed both parents in 93 couples, 3-6 months after the finalization of a divorce decree in 1995. Analyses from this second data set have not been published previously in journal articles, so findings from this source are fully documented herein.

One of the primary advantages of these data sets, compared to most in the father involvement or child support literature, is the matched father and mother reports. This feature provides the opportunity to correct for potential reporter biases in past reports. Another important aspect of the data sets is that they contain only divorced parents, and exclude never-marrieds. Many of the national data sets contain both, and the bulk of the published analyses fail to distinguish between these two groups, though virtually everything about them, including their child contact (Seltzer, 1991) and child support records (Peterson & Nord, 1990), are vastly different. A third advantage of the first data set is its longitudinal character, a quality that allows for analyses that examine causal sequences.

FATHER VISITS: WHY NOT MORE?

The initial phase of our analyses explored the various circumstantial reasons for the reported low visitation rates by fathers. Instead of simply concluding that infrequently visiting fathers do so volitionally, because they are only "weakly attached" to their children, we searched for mitigating circumstances. One possibility, though rarely discussed, is that the father's low degrees of contact with the child may be due to factors beyond the fathers' control. Two such factors are immediately evident: (1) relocation by the custodial parent and (2) the divorce decree. With respect to the latter, the divorce decree typically delineates the visitation privileges, or the maximum amount of time that the father can legally visit the child. Although these privileges vary considerably from family to family, the most common provision limits contact to every other weekend. Moreover, additional research is needed that explores, not simply the absolute level of visitation, but also the actual amount that results compared to the amount specified by the decree.

Regardless what the decree states, however, if custodial mothers permit, father-child contact could be virtually limitless. Thus, the real constraining factors are mothers' views about fathers' contacts. If mothers prevent, restrict, interfere with, or otherwise make difficult the contacts of fathers with children, it would be wrong to blame fathers exclusively. This would also make inappropriate the use of such terms as "bad dads" or talk of "fathers' weak and waning ties to their children."[2] Whether fathers who have minimal contact with their children are discouraged or prevented from visiting by custodial parents, or simply choose to visit less, is a distinction with obvious implications for policymakers and other professionals.

To address this issue, we asked parents what proportion of the *scheduled* visits were volitionally missed by the noncustodial parent. We also asked whether the custodial parent had ever denied visitation (see Braver, Wolchik, Sandler, Fogas, & Zvetina, 1991). Non-custodial parents (i.e., fathers) claim they have missed an average of only 3% of all scheduled visits, while custodial parents claim the fathers missed only 12% (the difference is significant; $t[219] = -4.98, p < .001$). These differences suggest that lack of scheduled visits, not "failure to show," determine how often a child sees the father. Moreover, about a third of the noncustodial fathers claim they have been denied visitation privileges at least once, while, surprisingly, a quarter of the custodial parents admit such denials.

Since visitation denial is evidently occurring in a non-trivial proportion of cases, it becomes clearly useful to know why. Why do some mothers prevent or discourage visitation? While many factors are certainly relevant, we choose one to highlight here: If mothers believe they are better parents than the fathers, they may think the children are better off spending residential time with them. We made an attempt to determine whether mothers think they are the better parent in the second data set. We told parents: "The average American parent rates a 5 on a 10-point scale (with 10 being the best) in terms of their parenting impact. This reflects the influence they have on their children so that they grow up healthy, well-adjusted and successful." Then we asked, "How would you rate yourself (and your ex-spouse) on a scale of 1 to 10." We found that mothers gave themselves a mean of 7.53, but gave their ex-husbands a mean of only 5.45, a 2 standard deviation difference ($t[96] = 10.2, p < .001$).

When a mother has custody, she is in a position to act on her perception that the children would be better off with her, and make the father's access to the children difficult. But it is important to note that fathers, who have far less power to act on *their* perceptions, do not agree with mothers' perceptions. Indeed, when fathers answer the same questions, they appear to think almost as strongly that *they* are the better parent (father's perception of own parenting, $M = 7.32$; father's perception of mother's parenting, $M = 6.72$; $t[95] = 3.02, p < .003$). It is also an important observation that both parents seem aware of how the other would do this rating. As shown in Table 1, when we asked, "How do you think your ex will rate you (and him/herself)," mothers thought that fathers would rate fathers ($M = 7.66$) higher than they would rate mothers ($M = 6.88$; $t[96] = 2.82$, $p < .006$), while fathers thought that mothers would rate mothers higher ($M = 8.13$) than they would rate fathers ($M = 6.36$; $t[96] = 6.90, p < .001$).

TABLE 1. How do you think your ex will rate you (and him/herself)?

Respondent	You	Self
Mother	6.88	7.66
Father	6.36	8.13

Clearly, one factor that prevents more father-child contact is the mother's lack of support, and this, presumably, stems in part from the parents' post-divorce relationship. This finding puts the focus, not on inadequacies of fathers, but on the quality of the post-divorce relationship between parents.

VISITATION AND CHILD SUPPORT

One reason that contact and emotional involvement with the children by the noncustodial father is seen as so important, of course, is because it is linked to child support payments and compliance. Although researchers generally agree that a substantial positive relationship exists between visiting and paying, the causal sequence has been unclear (Bay, Braver, Sandler, Wolchik, & Whetstone, in press; Braver, Wolchick, Sandler, Sheets, Fogas, & Bay, 1993; Furstenburg, Nord, Peterson, Zill, 1983; Pearson & Thoennes, 1986; Seltzer, Schaefer, & Charng, 1989), but largely falls in 3 categories. The first explanation proposes that the process of visiting children causes child support compliance. This occurs primarily because visitation induces an urge to shelter and financially enhance the child (Chambers, 1979; Tropf, 1984). An opposite theory proposes that paying child support causes visitation to occur, primarily because a person naturally wants to "look after one's investments" (Weiss & Willis, 1985). A final theory, in turn, proposes that some third variable–such as a "sense of paternal responsibility"–causes both visitation and payment of child support (Seltzer, Schaeffer, & Charng, 1989).

An empirical way of disentangling such questions about the causal sequence is to use a longitudinal design measuring child support payment, visitation, and various candidates for third variables at each wave. Because our data set allowed such analyses, we examined as possible third variables over 30 possible explanations of father dropout. These variables included such possibilities as a sense of paternal responsibility, anger at ex-wife, immorality, lack of strong ties to the child, suspicions that the child support was being abused, and fear of prosecution for non-payment. Essentially, every possible factor that any responsible commentator or social scientist had ever proposed to explain fathers' disengagement–both financial and emotional–was included in our study (see Braver et al., 1993).

DADS PAYING OR VISITING: WHY NOT MORE?

The cross-sectional results were surprisingly unequivocal, with one factor literally rising to the top in terms of its ability to explain lack of father involvement. This factor was the fathers' perceived control over divorce arrangements and childrearing matters, which we refer to as the loss of paternal authority. The cross-sectional correlations of this factor with visitation frequency ranged from .37 (mother's report, Wave 2) to .59 (father's report, Wave 2); the correlations with child support compliance ranged from .29 (father's report, Wave 3) to .37 (father's report, Wave 2).

Additional analyses also were conducted using our longitudinal data. These analyses explored the causal sequence issue, with special attention to the possibility that loss of paternal authority might be the third variable alluded to above. This possibility was investigated in a series of structural equation models, the details of which are in Braver et al. (1993). Briefly, the analyses strongly suggested the following causal sequence: Fathers both pay child support and maintain emotional involvement *because* they perceive themselves as having retained some paternal authority. Compared to our paternal authority hypothesis, therefore, alternative models fit the Wave-to-Wave correlation patterns less effectively. Examples of the tested alternative included the ideas that (a) earlier child support payments led to later visiting; (b) earlier visiting led to later child support; and (c) earlier visiting or paying led to a later sense of paternal authority. Thus, support for the third variable model was found, with the best candidate for the third variable being retention of a sense of paternal authority.

From these statistical findings, it appears that the father's sense of paternal authority is what drives the system of paternal engagement and disengagement. In order to obtain a better qualitative understanding of this construct, we conducted a number of focus groups, which suggested similar impressions. Many of the fathers in our focus groups felt that everything about the divorce, especially anything concerning the way the children were raised, was completely out of their control. These fathers who had lost their sense of paternal authority felt as if the child was in no real sense *theirs* anymore. The child *belonged* now to someone else, someone who, not uncommonly, despised and disparaged them. They had no real right of parenthood anymore, most especially the right to involve themselves in the manner that their children were raised. They were extremely embittered, though, that society was still asking them to assume the responsibilities of parenthood without the benefits. Society, the legal system, and their ex-wives had conspired to rip asunder their connection to their children. In sharp contrast, divorced fathers who thought they shared control with mothers over childrearing issues tended to view paternal obligations (both visitation and financial) as natural accompaniments of divorce and fatherhood.

WHAT PRODUCES THE SENSE OF PATERNAL LOSS OF AUTHORITY?

Although it seems somewhat counterintuitive, paternal loss of authority can be so widespread and pervasive as to explain the degree of non-involvement by fathers. This is especially true given the numerous reports suggesting that the divorce system, administered primarily by male judges, is heavily skewed in favor of fathers (e.g., Mahoney, 1996; Weitzman, 1985), which should add to, not diminish, their sense of paternal authority. Our literature review suggested that, while this view is often voiced, the supporting evidence virtually always involves the writer's own standards about what is fair and unfair, not the standards of the parties themselves (Erlinger, Chambliss & Melli, 1987; Okin, 1989; Seltzer & Garfinkel, 1990; Walters & Abshire, 1995). In our analyses (reported in more detail in Sheets & Braver, 1996), we asked the mothers and fathers themselves.

Measures of satisfaction with various aspects of their divorce settlements were obtained from our sample both at one- and at three-years post-petition.[3] Specifically, subjects were asked how satisfied they were with the custody, visitation, child support, and property/debt division arrangements in their divorce decree. Moreover, a question was asked about their satisfaction with financial issues relating to children other than the child support, such as medical expenses and long-distance visitation. All questions were asked on 7-point scales (1 = extremely dissatisfied, 7 = extremely satisfied). Table 2 presents the average satisfaction ratings of men and women for these divorce provisions.[4] Women reported significantly greater satisfaction than men with four provisions (satisfaction with custody, t [475] = 5.94, $p < .001$; visitation, t [470] = 2.42, $p < .05$; child financial provisions, t [468] = 2.38, $p < .05$; and property settlements, t [467] = 3.16, $p < .01$). The difference in satisfaction with child-support awards, while also showing that women are more satisfied, did not reach conventional levels of significance (t [472] = 1.56, $p < .12$). As Table 2 depicts, mothers were relatively satisfied with their entire divorce settlement, whereas fathers' satisfaction was lower and near the mid-point between satisfied and dissatisfied on each.

What happens as time passes and parents gain more experience with what they have agreed to? Do mothers finally and belatedly realize that they have been "taken to the cleaners" by their ex-spouses, the more experienced, aggressive and adept bargainers? Our Wave 3 interview occurred two years

TABLE 2. Mother's versus father's satisfaction with the provisions of their divorce settlement (Wave 2).

	Custody	Visitation	Child Support	Child Finance	Property Div.
Fathers	4.52	4.91	4.29	4.28	4.38
Mothers	5.60	5.33	4.57	4.68	4.93

after the previous one, with Table 3 showing these long-term ratings. The trends we observed at the earlier period were generally preserved two years later, as parents re-assessed their agreements. The statistical reliability of these trends was examined with a 2×2, Gender (a between subjects factor) $\times$ Time (a two-level repeated measures factor) mixed-factor multivariate analysis of variance (MANOVA). Main effects were noted for Gender [$F (5, 383) = 12.65, p < .001$], and Time [$F (5, 383) = 2.76, p < .05$], and the interaction was also significant [$F (5, 383) = 3.09, p < .01$]. Univariate tests (i.e., 2×2 ANOVAs) were employed to further identify longitudinal patterns in decree satisfaction. Overall satisfaction with custody [$F (1, 413) = 1.66$, ns], visitation [$F (1, 407) = 1.94$, ns], child-support [$F < 1$], and other financial provisions of the decree [$F < 1$], did not change over the two-year post-divorce interval (i.e., no Time main effect). However, satisfaction with the property division increased slightly over this period of time [$F (1, 404) = 6.63, p < .05$]. Further, the absence of significant Gender $\times$ Time interactions confirmed that women's *relative* satisfaction with custody [$F < 1$], visitation [$F (1, 407) = 2.87$, ns], and property settlement provisions [$F < 1$], was also unmodified during this period: Even after two years, women in our sample continued to be more satisfied than men with the custody [$F (1, 413) = 43.41, p < .001$], visitation [$F (1, 407) = 12.79, p < .001$], and the property division, [$F (1, 404) = 10.04, p < .01$], stipulations in their decree. There was still no significant difference in satisfaction with child-support awards at three years post-petition.

In fact, only one substantive change in satisfaction ratings over the two-year interval was apparent: while women initially indicated greater satisfaction than men with the child financial provisions (excepting child-support) of their decree, this pattern was reversed at the later interview. This switch was statistically significant, $F (1, 408) = 12.51, p < .001$ (for the Gender $\times$ Time interaction). Three years after filing for divorce, men were marginally more satisfied with the child financial provisions of their decree than were women, $F (1, 408) = 2.91, p < .10$.

In Sheets and Braver (1996), we also conducted a series of mediation analy-

TABLE 3. Mother' versus father's satisfaction with the provisions of their divorce settlement (Wave 3).

	Custody	Visitation	Child Support	Child Finance	Property Div.
Fathers	4.21	4.61	4.48	4.73	4.54
Mothers	5.52	5.32	4.52	4.43	5.12

ses which attempted to determine *why* mothers were so much more satisfied with the terms of their divorce than were fathers. Since these analyses are quite technical, only the conclusions will be summarized here. The results disclosed that women appear to feel more satisfied with their divorce settlements for two reasons: they are more likely than men to get what they want, and they feel they have greater influence over the settlement process than men. First, women were more satisfied in part because they were simply more likely to get the type of custody they desired than were men. Similarly, mothers' greater satisfaction with their property division was partially explained by being able to obtain in negotiations the custody arrangements they wanted.

The more far-reaching and comprehensive factor, however, turned out to be their feeling that they controlled the legal process. We asked parents how much control they felt they themselves had over (a) the way divorce legal proceedings had gone, (b) the amounts of visitation awarded, (c) the child support awarded, and (d) the final property distribution in the decree. Amount of control in these four decree areas was averaged, with mothers scoring significantly higher than fathers (t [183] = 4.46, $p < .001$; see Bay & Braver, 1990, for additional details). Women (Mean = 3.28) reported feeling more control over the process of divorce settlement than did men (Mean = 2.82). Moreover, in the mediation analyses we conducted, this greater perceived control appeared to be the most effective explanation for females' greater satisfaction with the terms of their divorce.

WHICH GENDER DO THE PARENTS THINK THE DIVORCE SYSTEM FAVORS?

These results directly challenge the contentions of prior writers that highlight women's inferior outcomes in divorce and attribute these results to coercion and intimidation by the ex-husband (Mahoney, 1996; Okin, 1989; Seltzer & Garfinkel, 1990; Weitzman, 1985). Our data suggest that ex-wives do not perceive their awards to be inferior to those of their ex-spouse. And women's greater feelings of control over the settlement contradict the notion that they are pawns in a settlement process controlled by men. On the contrary, mothers feel in control; if anyone perceives themselves as lacking in control, it is the fathers.

Our results also indicate that women do not win custody at the expense of satisfactory outcomes in other respects. If that had been the case, the more satisfied a woman was with the custody arrangements, the less satisfied she should be with the other arrangements. Instead, we found that if she was happy with custody, she tended to be happy with the other provisions as well. That is, we found significant positive correlations with satisfaction with the various terms of the decree, ranging from .28 to .58. If women are indeed "trading-off" desired custody outcomes for less abundant financial outcomes, they nonetheless remain happy with these trade-offs. For fathers, in contrast, the perceived inequity and hopelessness of the divorce process was the highest contributor to men's dissatisfaction. Other investigators have reported similar findings (Arditti & Allen, 1993; Dudley, 1991; Kruk, 1992) in the sense that negativity about the divorce process influenced men's feelings about custody, visitation, and child-support after the divorce.

HOW HAVE RECENT CHANGES IN DIVORCE LAWS AFFECTED THE PARTICIPANTS?

Divorce law changes with social and political shifts. The findings above are derived from Data Set I, collected prior to two general changes in divorce law: less flexible and more generous child support award guidelines and mandatory automatic wage garnishment of child support. Both of these provisions were adopted in 1988 in Arizona as a response to the Child Support Enforcement Amendments passed by Congress in 1984. We wondered if and how the recent changes affected the participant's perceptions of the divorce process.

In our 1995 study (Data Set II), we asked several questions relevant to this issue. First we asked the question, "How satisfied were you with the legal process itself?" Mothers are on average satisfied (Mean = 3.22), while fathers are not [(Mean = 2.82), t (94) = 4.92, p < .001]. Another question was: "How would you describe the slant of the Arizona legal system regarding divorced parents?" The options were "very slanted in favor of mothers," "somewhat slanted in favor of mothers," "slanted toward neither mothers or fathers," "somewhat slanted in favor of fathers," and "very slanted in favor of fathers." The results are presented in Table 4. No father thought that the system favored him, at any level, and 75% thought that it favored mothers. Mothers, albeit to a lesser extent, agreed that the system was slanted in their favor. While 66% thought it was balanced, 3 times as many mothers thought it favored mothers as thought it favored fathers. The difference between fathers' and mothers' views is statistically significant, t (94) = 10.41, p < .001. Even mothers' views alone suggest a statistically significant advantage for mothers; for the test that the mean value differs significantly from the "not slanted" value of 3, t (92) = 2.83, p < .01.

Finally, it has been speculated that "men use superior resources to attain more favorable divorce outcomes" (Arendell, 1995, p. 75), i.e., they are more likely to hire aggressive attorneys who bargain for their advantage (Kurz, 1995). We found otherwise. According to our sample of mothers (Data Set II), in 37% of the cases the mother hired the only attorney or hired her

TABLE 4. How would you describe the slant of the Arizona legal system regarding divorce?

Respondent	Very Slanted to Mothers	Somewhat Slanted to Mothers	Not Slanted	Somewhat Slanted to Dads	Very Slanted to Dads
What Mothers Say	1	24	66	9	0
What Fathers Say	45	29	26	0	0

counsel first. In contrast, significantly fewer fathers (17.5%) were the only party represented by an attorney or had retained an attorney first [t (51) = 2.01, $p < .05$].[5]

A POLICY THAT WILL KEEP FATHERS INVOLVED

These findings go beyond the negative denunciation of fathers' characters and implicate, instead, fathers' post-divorce circumstances. The current findings suggest that paternal non-involvement reflects fathers' sense of powerlessness and inequity, combined with a conflictual post-divorce relationship with the mother, more than it does fathers' unwholesome characters or their weak attachments to children. While wholesale rehabilitation of so many fathers' characters would be difficult, it appears far less daunting to attempt to modify fathers' circumstances. This current interpretation, then, is more hopeful than the "bad dads" perspective. It suggests plausible remedies that ultimately are in the best interests of children. The findings offer hope through policy changes and behavioral intervention programs.

For example, Nord and Zill (1996) have presented findings showing that joint legal custody awards increase child support compliance by 23% and substantially increase father contact as well. Joint legal custody thus appears an effective way to restore a father's sense of paternal authority.

One seemingly plausible account of these findings would be that it is entirely due to self-selection. That is, only couples who get along well and in which the fathers were involved in childrearing prior to dissolution are the ones who chose joint custody. This relative harmony and paternal responsibility play out after divorce in exceptionally high degrees of father involvement. Our results, reported in Braver, Whetstone, and Sheets (1994), support a different interpretation. We found that fathers who "won" joint legal custody (i.e., when the mother was initially opposed) paid and visited at very high rates, even higher than those who obtained joint legal custody with the mother's initial concurrence. We attribute the positive behavior to the interpretation that the "system" was responsive to fathers' needs and wishes and was legally promoting their involvement with their children.

A PROGRAM FOR FATHERS AFTER DIVORCE: DADS FOR LIFE

Besides potential legal or systemic changes, our findings and interpretations also led us to develop an intervention program that assists families in promoting father involvement. With the help of an NIMH grant, we have devised such a program called DADS FOR LIFE. This 8-week program is based on our findings about the causes of father non-involvement.

The primary goal of the program is to increase a child's well-being after a divorce by changing the skills, attitudes, and behaviors of the father. These parental factors, though viewed by some as character features, are seen by us as context sensitive. Our work with focus groups clearly indicated that fathers with a sense of paternal authority were quick to use parenting skills and behavioral self-control, especially around the ex-spouse. A sharp contrast was seen among the fathers who thought that the system had taken away their paternal authority. These dads pointed out that they could not implement parenting plans or tasks requiring coordination with the ex-wife. The common refrain was, "but you don't know my ex." In effect, general despair and hopelessness permeated their perspective of change. Consequently, our intervention efforts to change or implement skills and new behaviors is immersed in an attitude of changing the context, i.e., the assumed ability of the noncustodial father to control his relationship with his child. We assume context, not character, determines the fathering of the child.

In addition we wished to increase child support payments, improve the mental health of mothers and fathers, and decrease court actions. To accomplish these goals, we try to change two proximal outcomes: improve the quality and quantity of the father-child relationship and improve the nature of the father-mother relationship, since conflict between the parents seems to account for the most variance in children's adjustment (Amato & Keith, 1991). Our findings suggested that to impact these relationships favorably, we needed to achieve the following immediate intervention goals: increase the sense of paternal authority among fathers, increase their commitment to the parenting role, improve their parenting skills, and increase their motivation and skill at managing conflict with their ex-spouse.

The DADS FOR LIFE program consists of ten sessions in all, eight group sessions and two individual sessions. All groups are led by a Master's level (either M.S. or M.A. degree) team consisting of a male and a female. Group sessions occur weekly, and individual sessions occur during weeks 3 and 6. Individual sessions allow the fathers to develop individualized strategies for implementing attitudes and skills to their particular family situations. Each session consists of 1.5 hours of didactic teaching, group discussions, and role playing; it is supplemented with approximately 10 minutes of videotape. The videotape segments are drawn from an 83-minute movie entitled, "8 Short Films About Divorced Dads" (Braver & Griffin, 1996). We developed this videotape using information gathered from fathers' focus groups and systematically observing divorced couples' interactions in a behavioral interaction laboratory.

Parenting Skills

The literature is replete with methods and techniques for teaching parenting skills (e.g., active listening, proactive discipline). We adapt each skill or technique to the complexities of parenting in the post-divorce noncustodial environment, where the child may visit only sporadically. We encourage frequent telephone contacts as a means of maintaining consistency.

Because of the newness of the divorce situation and the ill-defined role of noncustodial fathers, many fathers were initially resistant to using discipline techniques. They feared that the child would be angry and unhappy, ruining the short time they had together and decreasing the child's desire to visit. We are able to overcome much of their hesitancy by helping fathers determine the few rules they really want to enforce and by making discipline proactive rather than reactive.

Post-Divorce Conflict Reduction

Our second, and probably larger challenge, is to provide fathers the skills to manage conflict with their ex-spouse. This goal is very important–the evidence we presented above suggested that the relationship with the ex-wife was a formidable barrier to more and better visiting. Considerable evidence suggests the degree of parental conflict is the single strongest independent predictor of children's well-being after divorce (Amato & Keith, 1991). We were keenly aware of several impediments to our success with these fathers. First, there is the legitimate question about whether it is possible to improve a dyadic relationship when working with only one of the parties. Second, is it possible to use psycho-educational techniques to change a relationship that was so bad and hostile that it ended with a divorce? Finally, there were no empirically based intervention programs, therapy models (Griffin & Greene, 1998), or even data, in the literature that might help guide our intervention.

Aside from changing a father's perception that he can control some aspects of his relationship with his children, we also wanted to get fathers to change their behavior toward their ex-wives, at least for the benefit of the child.

We started gathering ideas by running several focus groups, asking fathers to discuss their interactions and experiences with their ex-wives. More importantly, we brought 24 divorced couples into our behavioral observation laboratory and had them engage in a videotaped 15 minute discussion about topics that were relevant to their children. These are the same type of interactions used to investigate interactions in married couples (see e.g., Gottman, 1994). They taught us a lot about divorced couples, especially when compared to what fathers had said they do in these types of interactions. Although the findings are preliminary, several aspects of the interaction stood out. These fathers and mothers interacted similarly to married, distressed couples, showing high levels of negative behavior and escalating cycles. Mothers even had the same pattern of self-report negative affect (Griffin, 1993); they showed a general tendency to report negative affect throughout the interaction, hence a general negative slope for cumulative affect. The results for fathers, on the other hand, were very different and unexpected. On average, they tended to report neutral to slightly positive affect over the course of the interaction. In effect, their self-report affect was not consistent with their behavior. Although preliminary, and awaiting replication, the data nonetheless suggest that fathers are not so angry with their ex-spouses that they cannot be influenced to manage conflict.

Moreover, this is consistent with survey data (including our own findings) that show that divorced fathers are less angry at their ex-spouse than are divorced mothers, and that their anger diminishes faster (Wallerstein & Kelly, 1980b). This consistency across data types convinced us that fathers might be willing and able to institute the changes we promote in the program.

The changes we request from fathers are based on these findings. In short, we ask fathers to refrain from enacting behaviors that would otherwise escalate the conflict. We teach the father to minimize the behaviors his ex-wife may be expecting him to do that escalate animosity. Specifically, we get fathers to show attending behaviors (e.g., looking), reduce contemptuous behaviors (e.g., eye roll), and in general, acknowledge the issue being discussed. Notice that we are not trying to get him to change his ex-wife's behavior, nor do we ask him to do something radically different. Instead we request a few simple attending behaviors, and we ask that he give her views a respectful hearing. Preliminary data indicate, therefore, that these are the behaviors that, if not performed, seem to instigate animosity and negative behavior cycles during interactions. We want fathers to reduce these behaviors that our findings suggest act as triggers to more conflict.

We are currently in the final year of three years of data collection. We are collecting our final of six cohorts, with four waves of data collection each; waves occur at pre, post, 4 months post, and 1 year post. Families are assigned randomly either to receive our intervention or the control condition. The control condition is a compilation of reading material selected from currently popular self-help books. Control condition fathers are instructed to read the material at home at regular intervals. Results should be available in approximately one year.

CONCLUSIONS

These findings suggest that low levels of father involvement in the post-divorce family are more accurately, fruitfully, and optimistically viewed as the reactions of fathers to difficult situations. Specifically, gaining greater understanding about why some fathers disengage will help to alleviate several problems. These remedies are not enforcement oriented, punitive, or draconian, but instead rectify structural problems that contribute to the disengagement. These include joint legal custody and intervention programs such as DADS FOR LIFE, which help fathers focus on the opportunities they have to influence the lives of their children.

NOTES

1. The effects of noncustodial parent contact are unequivocally positive only when any conflict between the parents is well contained. When there is intense, open interparental conflict or domestic abuse, many investigators have found that more father contact may detract from child well-being (e.g., Fitzpatrick, Wolchik, & Braver, 1989; Healy, Malley, & Stewart, 1990; Johnston, Kline, & Tschann, 1989; Maccoby, & Mnookin, 1992).

2. Although no evidence was cited, Furstenburg et al. (1983) consider this possibility, but suggest that such denial is generally in "retaliation" for child support noncompliance. "Lest this observation be taken as a judgement about the motives of the outside parent, we should point out that outside parents are sometimes discouraged or actively barred from seeing their children, especially when custodial mothers are dissatisfied with the level of material support provided by the fathers" (p. 665). However, terms like "bad dad" and "weak ties" appear to present their preferred view that low contact is truly the fault of the father.

3. For this analysis, only subjects whose divorce action was complete by one-year post-petition (when they were first asked about their decree satisfaction) were included. This resulted in a sample of 477 respondents (223 women and 254 men) from 312 different families. Longitudinal analyses are necessarily restricted to those who were reinterviewed at the final wave of data collection (three-years post-petition); this includes 418 respondents (199 women and 219 men) from 282 different families. Note that the actual sample sizes used in analyses may vary with missing data.

4. Although we could match 69% percent of our respondents to their ex-spouses, they were treated as independent samples for the present analyses. Treating the ex-spouses as independent (uncorrelated) samples was justified by the lack of inter-spousal correlations in satisfaction ratings: $rs = -.10, .02, -.08, -.04, .02$, all $ps > .15$, for custody, visitation, child-support, financial, and property division stipulations, respectively, at Time 1. Nonetheless, we also conducted analyses parallel to the ones in the text which utilized the *paired* responses of husbands and wives and resulted in paired t-tests. These analyses revealed substantively identical differences in satisfaction, but they are not presented in detail because of the complexity they introduce.

5. According to the father's report, the figures were 33% and 20.6%, respectively, a difference that did not attain significance.

REFERENCES

Amato, P.R. & Keith, B. (1991). Parental divorce and the well-being of children: A meta-analysis. *Psychological bulletin, 110,* 26-47.

Arditti, J., & Allen, K. (1993). Understanding distressed fathers' perceptions of legal and relational inequities post-divorce. *Family and Conciliation Courts Review, 31,* 461-476.

Arendell, T. (1995). *Fathers and divorce.* Thousand Oaks, CA: Sage.

Bay, R.C., & Braver, S.L. (1990). Perceived control of the divorce settlement process and interparental conflict. *Family Relations, 39,* 382-387.

Bay, R. C., Braver, S.L., Sandler, I. N., Wolchik, S. A., & Whetstone, M.R. (In Press). Child support noncompliance/visitation interference: Reciprocal weapons of engagement in interparental post-divorce conflict. In Depner, C.E., & Bray, J.H.(Eds). *Family Differences: Conflict and its Legacy* (Newbury Park: Sage).

Bloom, B.L., Hodges, W.F., & Caldwell, R.A. (1983). Marital separation: The first eight months. In E.J. Callahan & K.A. McKlusky (Eds.), *Lifespan development psychology: Non-normative events.* (pp. 218-239). New York: Academic Free Press.

Braver, S.L. & Bay, R.C. (1992). Assessing and compensating for self-selection bias (nonrepresentativeness) of the family research sample. *Journal of Marriage and the Family, 54,* 925-939.

Braver, S.L. & Griffin, W. A. (1996). *8 Short Films About Divorced Dads.* [Film]. (Inquires about the film can be sent to either author; see author notes.)

Braver, S.L. & O'Connell, D. (1998). *Divorced dads: Shattering the myths.* NY: Tarcher/Putnam.

Braver, S.L., Whetstone, M.R., & Sheets, V.L. (1994). *Custody preferences versus custody outcomes: Effects of discrepancies on divorcing mothers, fathers, and children.* Presented at Law and Society Association, Phoenix, AZ.

Braver, S. L., Wolchik, S. A., Sandler, I.N., Fogas, B.S., & Zvetina, D. (1991). Frequency of visitation by divorced fathers: Differences in report by fathers and mothers. *American Journal of Orthopsychiatry, 61,* 448-454.

Braver, S.L., Wolchik, S.A., Sandler, I.N., Sheets, V.L., Fogas, B., & Bay, R.C. (1993). A longitudinal study of noncustodial parents: Parents without children. *Journal of Family Psychology, 7,* 9-23.

Chambers, D. L. (1979). *Making Fathers Pay: The Enforcement of Child Support.* Chicago: University of Chicago Press.

Dudley, J. (1991). Increasing our understanding of divorced fathers who have infrequent contact with their children. *Family Relations, 40,* 279-285.

Erlinger, H.S., Chambliss, E., & Melli, M.S. (1987). Participation and flexibility in informal processes: Cautions from the divorce context. *Law & Society Review, 21,* 585-604.

Faust, K.A. & McKibben, J.M. (1999). Marital dissolution: Divorce, separation, annulment, & widowhood. In M. B. Sussman, S.K. Steinmetz, & G.W. Peterson (Eds.), *Handbook of Marriage and the Family, Second edition* (pp. 475-499), New York: Plenum Press.

Fitzpatrick, P., Wolchik, S.A., & Braver, S.L. (1989). *Interparental conflict and children's post-divorce adjustment: Father contact as moderator.* Presented at Western/Rocky Mountain Association Meeting, Reno, NV.

Fulton, J.A. (1979). Parental reports of children's post-divorce adjustment. *Journal of Social Issues, 35,* 126-139.

Furstenberg, F. F. (1988). Good dads-bad dads: Two faces of fatherhood. In A. J. Cherlin (Ed.), *The Changing American Family and Public Policy* (pp. 193-218). Washington, DC: Urban Institute.

Furstenberg, F.F., & Nord, C.W. (1985). Parenting apart: Patterns of child-rearing after divorce. *Journal of Marriage and the Family, 47,* 893-904.

Furstenberg, F.F., Nord, C.W., Peterson, J.L., & Zill, N. (1983). The life course of children of divorce: Marital disruption and parental contact. *American Sociological Review, 48,* 656-668.

Gottman, J. M. (1994). *What Predicts Divorce.* Hillsdale, N.J.: Erblaum.

Griffin, W. A. (1993). Transitions from negative affect during marital interaction: Husband and wife differences. *Journal of Family Psychology, 6,* 3, 230-244.

Griffin, W. A. & Greene, S. M. (1998). *Models of Family Therapy: The Essential Guide.* New York: Brunner/Mazel.

Guidibaldi, J., Cleminshaw, H.K., Perry, J.D., & McLoughlin, C.S. (1983). The impact of parental divorce on children: Report of the nationwide NASP study. *School Psychology Review, 12,* 300-323.

Hawkins, A. J., & Dollahite, D. C. (1997). Beyond the role-inadequacy perspective of fathering. In A. J. Hawkins & D.C. Dollahite (Eds.), *Generative fathering: Beyond deficit perspective,* (pp. 3-16). Thousand Oaks, CA: Sage Publications.

Healy, J.M., Malley, J.E., & Stewart, A.J. (1990). Children and their fathers after parental separation. *American Journal of Orthopsychiatry, 60,* 531-543.

Hess, R., & Camara, K. (1979). Post-divorce family relationships as mediating factors in the consequences of divorce for children. *Journal of Social Issues, 35,* 79-96.

Hetherington, E.M., Cox, M., & Cox, R. (1976). Divorced fathers. *Family Coordinator, 25,* 417-428.

Hetherington, E.M., Cox, M., & Cox, R. (1978). The aftermath of divorce. In J.H. Stevens and M. Mathews (Eds.), *Mother/child, father/child relationships* (pp. 110-155). Washington, D.C.: National Association for the Education of Young Children.

Jacobson, D. (1978). The impact of marital separation/divorce on children: II: Interpersonal hostility and child adjustment. *Journal of Divorce, 2*, 3-20.

Johnston, J.R., Kline, M., & Tschann, J.M. (1989). Ongoing postdivorce conflict: Effects on children of joint custody and frequent access. *American Journal of Orthopsychiatry, 59* (4), 576-592.

Koch, M.A.P., & Lowery, C.R. (1984). Visitation and the non-custodial father. *Journal of Divorce, 8*, 47-65.

Kruk, E. (1992). Psychological and structural factors contributing to the disengagement of noncustodial fathers after divorce. *Family and Conciliation Courts Review, 30*, 81-101.

Kurdek, L.A., & Berg, B. (1983). Correlates of children's adjustment to their parents' divorces. In L.A. Kurdek (Ed.), *Children and divorce* (pp. 47-60). San Francisco: Jossey-Bass.

Kurz, D. (1995). *For richer, for poorer: Mothers confront divorce.* NY: Routledge,

Maccoby, E.E., & Mnookin, R.H. (1992). *Dividing the Child: Social and Legal Dilemmas of Custody.* Cambridge, MA: Harvard University Press.

Mahoney, K. (1996). Gender issues in family law: Leveling the playing field for women. *Family and Conciliation Courts Review, 34*, 198-218.

McLanahan, S., & Sandefur, G. (1994). *Growing up with a single parent: What hurts, what helps.* Cambridge, MA: Harvard University Press.

Meyer, D.R. & Garasky, S. (1993). Custodial fathers: Myths, realities, and child support policy. *Journal of Marriage and the Family, 55*, 73-89.

Nord, C. W. & Zill, N. (1996). Non-custodial parents' participation in their children's lives: Evidence from the SIPP., Vol. I., U.S. Department of Health and Human Services.

Okin, S.M. (1989). *Justice, gender, and the family.* New York: Basic Books.

Pearson, J., & Thoennes, N. (1986). Will this divorced woman receive child support? *Minnesota Family Law Journal, 3*, 65-71.

Peterson, J. L. & Nord, C.W. (1990). The regular receipt of child support: A multistep process. *Journal of Marriage and the Family, 52*, 539-551.

Popenoe, D. (1996). *Life without father.* NY: Free Press.

Seltzer, J.A. (1991). Relationships between fathers and children who live apart. *Journal of Marriage and the Family, 53*, 79-101.

Seltzer, J.A., & Garfinkel, I. (1990). Inequality in divorce settlements: An investigation of property settlements and child support awards. *Social Science Research, 19*, 82-111.

Seltzer, J.A., Schaeffer, N.C., & Charng, H. (1989). Family ties after divorce: The relationship between visiting and paying child support. *Journal of Marriage and the Family, 51*, 1013-1032.

Sheets, V. L. & Braver, S.L. (1996). Gender differences in satisfaction with divorce settlements. *Family Relations, 45*, 336-342.

Tropf, W. D. (1984). An exploratory examination of the effect of remarriage on child support and personal contacts. *Journal of Divorce, 7*, 57-73.

U.S. Bureau of the Census. (1995). *Statistical abstracts of the United States.* Washington, D.C.: U.S. Government Printing Office.

Wallerstein, J.S., & Kelly, J.B. (1980a). Effects of divorce on the visiting father-child relationship. *American Journal of Psychiatry, 137*, 1534-1539.

Wallerstein, J.S., & Kelly, J.B. (1980b). *Surviving the breakup: How children and parents cope with divorce.* NY: Basic Books.

Walters, L.H.,& Abshire, C.R. (1995). Single parenthood and the law. *Journal of Divorce and Remarriage, 20*, 161-188.

Weiss, Y. & Willis, R. J. (1985). Children as collective goods and divorce settlements. *Journal of Labor Economics, 3*, 268-292.

Weitzman, L. (1985). *The Divorce Revolution.* New York: Free Press.

Exploring Fatherhood Diversity: Implications for Conceptualizing Father Involvement

William Marsiglio
Randal D. Day
Michael E. Lamb

SUMMARY. Our analysis, grounded in a social constructionist perspective, explores the theoretical and political complexities facing researchers and policymakers as they attempt to conceptualize, study, and promote fathers' involvement with their children. Taking into account the growing diversity of life course and residency patterns for men and children today, we stress how the definition of fatherhood and conceptualization of paternal involvement are interwoven. As our starting point, we highlight how diverse stakeholders construct differing images and types of fatherhood during an era when men are "doing fatherhood" in a wide range of contexts. Next, we explore issues associated with a broad conceptualization of father involvement, influence, and motivation with an eye toward fatherhood diversity. We then consider how several family processes are implicated in the way men develop, negotiate, and sustain their rights, privileges, and obligations as fathers

William Marsiglio is affiliated with University of Florida (e-mail: marsig@soc.ufl.edu).

Randal D. Day is affiliated with Brigham Young University.

Michael E. Lamb is affiliated with the National Institute of Child Health and Human Development.

An earlier version of this paper was presented at the Theory Construction and Research Methodology Workshop, National Council on Family Relations, Washington, DC, 1997.

[Haworth co-indexing entry note]: "Exploring Fatherhood Diversity: Implications for Conceptualizing Father Involvement." Marsiglio, William, Randal D. Day, and Michael E. Lamb. Co-published simultaneously in *Marriage & Family Review* (The Haworth Press, Inc.) Vol. 29, No. 4, 2000, pp. 269-293; and: *FATHERHOOD: Research, Interventions and Policies* (ed: H. Elizabeth Peters et al.) The Haworth Press, Inc., 2000, pp. 269-293. Single or multiple copies of this article are available for a fee from The Haworth Document Delivery Service [1-800-342-9678, 9:00 a.m. - 5:00 p.m. (EST). E-mail address: getinfo@haworthpressinc.com].

in different types of family structures. We conclude by suggesting how our treatment of these issues can guide future research on fatherhood. *[Article copies available for a fee from The Haworth Document Delivery Service: 1-800-342-9678. E-mail address: getinfo@haworthpressinc.com <Website: http:// www.haworthpressinc.com>]*

KEYWORDS. Fatherhood, father involvement

Scholarly and public policy considerations have combined in the last few years to ignite considerable interest in fatherhood (Federal Interagency Forum on Child and Family Statistics, 1998; Marsiglio, Amato, Day, & Lamb, 2000). In comparison with the social situation that existed a quarter-century ago, contemporary social scientists are struck by the wide range of contexts in which men can lay claim to the label "father." Scholars have recently underscored the extent to which fatherhood is a contested social construction (Lupton & Barclay, 1997) and the notion that diverse types and images of fatherhood are fashioned by the special and heterogeneous circumstances in which men find themselves. We address these concerns by pursuing three primary goals.

First, we identify and discuss the construction of several prominent types of fatherhood in contemporary North American culture with an emphasis on conventional and unconventional approaches to defining the boundaries of fatherhood. Our purpose is to show that various stakeholders (including academics, policymakers, the judiciary, and women's and men's advocacy groups) based their rules for constructing different types and images of fatherhood primarily on biological relatedness. This relatedness usually results from a coital experience, similar residency (prior or current), relationship between mother and father, and legal status involving marriage and paternity.

Next, we explore contemporary conceptualizations of father involvement (the cognitive, affective, and behavioral manifestations of fatherhood) while taking into account fathers' differing circumstances and intrafamilial interpretations of the meaning of fatherhood. Our discussion attends to issues associated with the culture and conduct of fatherhood (LaRossa, 1988), the emergence of a paternal identity, and links between definitions of "father," the social construction of paternal involvement (Lamb, Pleck, Charnov, & Levine, 1987; Marsiglio, 1998; Palkovitz, 1997), and the influence of stakeholders' value-laden and competing interests in defining aspects of fatherhood. Since fathers' experiences and life course patterns have grown increasingly complex and diverse (Marsiglio, 1995a), we have selectively presented examples to show how the varied social and interpersonal processes by which fatherhood is constructed shape: (1) our understanding of the fathering process, (2) the dimensions of paternal influence connected to the various fatherhood categories, and (3) the motivations associated with paternity and fathering.

Our final goal is to show how key family processes are connected to different types of paternal involvement and within various fatherhood types. We emphasize how family processes, in connection with different types of fatherhood, provide opportunities for individuals to define, negotiate, and redefine fathers' privileges, rights, and obligations.

Given the limited scope of our efforts, we will comment only briefly on the specific social processes and interest group politics surrounding the fatherhood terrain (see Marsiglio & Cohan, this volume). Instead, we will focus on the basic distinction between perceptions of fatherhood types and the actual ways fathers participate in their children's lives. In practice, the former come into play most clearly when individuals (men, women, and children) develop ideas about who should be able to lay claim to the status of father. The most fundamental accomplishment in this regard is for men to perceive themselves as fathers with "legitimate" rights and responsibilities. While this designation may be straightforward for many men, it represents an awkward, negotiated, and incremental accomplishment for others, especially when biological paternity or coresidency are absent. Identifying the circumstances under which men are perceived to have specific paternal rights and responsibilities is thus crucial. Both social and personal perceptions are consequential in this regard because they influence the context within which men do "fatherhood" as well as the ways in which they actually think, feel, and act. Discussion of these three principles will be organized by examining: (1) alternative boundaries used to delineate fatherhood in the United States, (2) the diverse and complex conceptualizations of paternal involvement that result from differing definitions or categorizations of fatherhood, (3) motivational issues that influence men's desire to have children and become involved in their lives, (4) how fathers perceive and negotiate their roles in conjunction with ongoing family processes, and (5) how our treatment of these issues can inform future research.

The principal contribution of our analysis, then, rests not with trying to present a comprehensive review of the relevant literature, but rather with our effort to clarify how the issues we explore are interwoven aspects of an interdisciplinary approach to studying fatherhood from a social constructionist perspective.

THEMATIC FRAMEWORK

A number of fundamental themes run through our analysis of contemporary fatherhood. Most importantly, we emphasize how social demographic patterns establish the foundation for contemporary discourses about fatherhood and paternal involvement. The growing diversity of life course and residency patterns for men and children has fostered a new awareness about fathers' roles (Gerson, 1993; Griswold, 1993; Marsiglio, 1995a) as well as the realization that a decreasing proportion of all children today live with their biological fathers (Bianchi, 1995; Mintz, 1998). Moreover, many children have stepfather figures living with them on a regular or irregular basis, and growing numbers of men are becoming custodial single fathers (Marsiglio, 1995b; Brown, this volume; Eggebeen, Snyder, & Manning, 1996). These demographic trends obviously complicate the boundaries of fatherhood and challenge us to consider the diverse manifestations of fathering in numerous settings.

Our analysis also acknowledges gender's significance as a fundamental organizing principle of social life that influences fathers' lives. The gender order continues to reinforce institutional arrangements (e.g., labor markets, corporate culture, and the judicial system) and ideological assumptions regarding men's rights and responsibilities as fathers. In addition, when gender is viewed as an activity that is constructed in specific social contexts (Thompson, 1993; West & Zimmerman, 1987), it provides individuals with opportunities to display and interpret symbolic representations of gender that are closely tied to value-laden meanings associated with the economic provider and caretaker roles. Many men and women experience tremendous anxiety and conflict in sharing parental responsibilities because of their gendered expectations and competing perceptions of family life and parental involvement (Coltrane, 1996; Fox & Bruce, 1996; Hawkins, Christiansen, Sargent, & Hill, 1995). Gender issues therefore affect how men are viewed and treated as fathers, how they think about the prospects of paternity and fatherhood, how they view themselves as fathers, how they perceive their children, and how they are involved in and affect their children's lives (Marsiglio, 1998).

Gender's relevance to father involvement is mediated by the larger ecological context that is shaped by culturally based and economic factors (Burton & Synder, 1998; Doherty, Kouneski, & Erikson, 1998; Furstenberg, 1995; Lupton & Barclay, 1997). The limited scope of our analysis precludes us from exploring systematically how the intersections between race, class, and gender affect definitions of fatherhood, perceptions of paternal involvement, and men's experiences as fathers (see Marsiglio & Cohan, this volume, for a discussion of these connections).

Finally, to fully appreciate fathers' experiences, and family life more generally, it is important to explore the overlapping developmental and life course trajectories of various family members from multiple perspectives over time (Klein & White, 1997). Unfortunately, applying this type of perspective is exceedingly complex when fathers and stepfathers experience transitional periods due to union formation and dissolution with romantic partners.

FATHERHOOD: DEFINITIONS AND TYPES

If we are to advance our conceptualization of fatherhood and paternal involvement while improving our understanding of its implications for children and families, we must update our perception of the diverse forms of fatherhood and the complex ways in which the conceptualization of paternal involvement is affected. Thus, it is useful to identify the multiple forms of fatherhood while considering how these types of fatherhood are linked to paternal rights, responsibilities, and types of involvement. We comment briefly here on the following major permutations of fatherhood: (1) biological fathers married to and living with the children's mothers; (2) biological fathers divorced from (or never married to) their children's mothers but living with their children; (3) unmarried biological fathers living neither with their children nor with the children's mothers; and (4) adoptive or informal stepfathers, both living with and living apart from these children.

Who are fathers? This seemingly simple and somewhat rhetorical question is fraught with conceptual ambiguity because a range of biological, social, and legal considerations come into play when the question is considered from alternative perspectives. Individuals and formal stakeholders (e.g., lawyers, policymakers, child support compliance officials) vary in the way they attempt to clarify the boundaries of fatherhood as well as the attendant rights and obligations of individual fathers. It appears though that a growing array of men are being perceived to have father-like roles in children's lives, in part, because increasing numbers of biological fathers are disengaging from their children or were never actively involved.

The conceptualization of paternal involvement is intimately tied to respective stakeholders' vested interests and the criteria they focus on when they define men as fathers. Consequently, efforts to develop wider conceptualizations of paternal involvement have been fueled by diverse political and scholarly considerations. For example, during recent decades, many feminists have asked men to assume greater responsibility for the everyday care of their children (Hochschild, 1989), thereby reinforcing conceptions that are not limited to breadwinning. Likewise, fathers' rights movements have rejected administrative and legislative attempts to equate responsible nonresident fathering with child support compliance and have instead emphasized that nonresident fathers can be involved with their children in numerous ways when given the opportunity to do so. In both cases, the argument has been made that fathers are capable of assuming roles and responsibilities commonly associated with mothers (Lamb, 1997;1999; Lamb & Goldberg, 1982;

Lamb, Pleck, Charnov, & Levine, 1987; Parke, 1996). However, this has led some to worry about the suitability of using a "mother template" when assessing paternal involvement (Federal Interagency Forum on Child and Family Statistics, 1998), thereby ignoring or devaluing traditionally masculine expressions of paternal involvement such as breadwinning and developing social capital.

Generally speaking, definitions of fatherhood are shaped in part by broader debates about the definition and meaning of family life in industrialized societies (Bahr & Bahr, 1996; Berscheid, 1996; Griswold, 1993; Marks, 1996; Scanzoni & Marsiglio, 1993). These debates evolve largely around competing views about the meaning and relative significance of formal commitments associated with either blood, marriage, or legal ties as opposed to commitments based on less formal interpersonal ties.

Conventional approaches to fatherhood typically accentuate the married, co-resident heterosexual biological father whose child is conceived naturally. Meanwhile, scholars who propose more flexible images of family are less likely to focus exclusively on either the genetic or marital connection when conceptualizing fatherhood; instead they emphasize the significance of social fatherhood. These *nonconventional* approaches are more likely to take into account how men, and others including mothers and children, view men's relationships with children independent of formal criteria. Consequently, adherents of these latter views are less likely to clearly differentiate the borders separating fathering from male mentoring. Although the distinction between conventional and unconventional approaches provides one practical way of delineating the diverse ways in which fatherhood is treated in the relevant literatures and perceived in everyday culture, this scheme is limited because it clearly oversimplifies the complex, multidimensional, and in some instances value laden fatherhood terrain.

Those who accentuate the natural path to paternity (i.e., not asexual sperm donation or stepparenting/adoption strategies) when defining fatherhood sometimes propose that biologically unrelated father figures can never make the same contributions to "their" children and that their childrearing efforts are inherently precarious (Blankenhorn, 1995; Popenoe, 1993). While the legal system may accord certain paternal rights to men if they formally adopt a child, these nonbiological father figures are sometimes perceived as being secondary to or uniquely different from biological fathers. This pattern can be witnessed in judicial efforts to honor paternity claims of biological fathers for their children who have lived with social fathers from birth. Proponents of the natural paternity approach to defining fatherhood are unlikely to seek to provide social or legal status for sperm donors when the donation is formally mediated via a sperm bank or fertility clinic. However, some may feel comfortable with the reality that men who donate sperm informally place themselves at risk of being designated fathers with a legal responsibility to provide child support (*Straub v. B.M.T.,* 1994). Although fatherhood status is seldom achieved by sperm donation, studying this practice is instructive because it clarifies the parameters of fatherhood while illustrating its social construction.

In practice, the *seemingly* clear boundaries of the conventional perspectives are sometimes problematic. This is plainly illustrated when considering the marital presumption of paternity (i.e., children born to a married woman are assumed to be her husband's children). This legal principle is consistent with conventional approaches to the extent that it favors marriage as the legitimate context for procreation (Marsiglio, 1998; Uniform Parentage Act, 1973). However, acknowledging the marital presumption of paternity sometimes means that biological relatedness, another key criterion typically associated with conventional perspectives, must be ignored. In short, the basic assumptions underlying conventional perspectives are not as straightforward as some may think. Some men may be genetically related to children but have no social or legal ties to them, while others may be genetically unrelated but be perceived as fathers by others (and perhaps by the legal system).

The distinction between sexually based, biological paternity and social fatherhood has become more important recently because of the high rates of both out-of-wedlock childbearing and divorce. These factors have led some men to assume paternal roles in relation to children who are not their biological offspring (Da Vanzo & Rahman, 1993), while other men have voluntarily or reluctantly disengaged themselves from their biological, nonresident children's lives (Furstenberg, 1988, 1995). Similarly, the advent of asexual reproductive and DNA fingerprinting technologies have muddled conventional notions of paternity and fatherhood, while increasing the number of images and terms applied to fathers and mothers (Marsiglio, 1998). Although community norms are likely to emphasize sexually based, biological paternity, some communities, as well as legal scholars (Anderson, 1992), may be more willing than others to support attempts by nonbiological fathers to be social (and legal) fathers.

Unique definitional issues are apparent when considering step- and adoptive fathers. Most importantly, individuals and communities often have different perceptions or standards about when father-like rights and responsibilities should be extended to men who are not biologically related to particular children. Social expectations of stepfathers, and their resultant behavior, often depend on the type of relationships they have with the children's mothers, their coresidence status, and the nature of the relationships between biological fathers and the children.

For our purposes here, we do not define fatherhood exclusively using biological lines nor do we emphasize the marital presumption of paternity.

Instead, we focus on social fatherhood, while recognizing that sexually based, biological paternity represents a satisfactory way to conceptualize fatherhood for many scholarly and policymaking purposes, provided that this does not thwart attempts to study and support forms of parenting by men who are not genetically related to "their" children. A more inclusive approach may allow researchers and policymakers to understand a broader range of issues centered on the negotiation and expression of fathering roles (Fox & Bruce, 1996). It also encourages scholars to explore the symbolic and practical significance of the distinctions between the biological, legal, and social bases for paternity.

CONCEPTUALIZING FATHER INVOLVEMENT AND MOTIVATION

Having briefly noted the complexities associated with the definition of fatherhood, we now turn to the equally important, difficult, and in some ways interrelated task of conceptualizing father involvement. Anthropologists, economists, family scientists, legal scholars, developmental psychologists, and sociologists specializing in family and gender studies tend to approach father involvement in unique ways, emphasizing certain features while downplaying or ignoring others. These stakeholders have each contributed to the contemporary conceptualization of father involvement by emphasizing competing though not contradictory criteria (e.g., financial support, emotional sensitivity, hands-on caregiving, social capital) and providing implicit standards by which "good" and "bad" fathering can be evaluated (e.g., direct comparisons with mothers' input, assessment based on mothers' perceptions of equity, threshold level defined by prevailing gendered expectations about stereotypical fathers' contributions).

We conceptualize father involvement by emphasizing men's positive, wide-ranging, and active participation in their children's lives. Developing a theoretically meaningful and tidy categorization scheme for the varied forms of father involvement is clearly difficult. Our modest aim is to underscore the multidimensional and broad parameters of this key concept while showing how it is related to different categories of fatherhood.

Types of Involvement

Obviously, fathers can be involved with their children in many ways and have been assigned different primary responsibilities during different historical periods (Lamb, this volume; Pleck & Pleck, 1980; 1997). Scholars in recent years have become more attentive to the breadth of contemporary fathers' experiences. For instance, Lamb et al. (1987) distinguished among the paternal responsibilities for economic support, emotional support of mothers, and direct interaction with children. They applied the term paternal involvement to those activities that most directly involved joint father-child involvement, distinguishing among three forms of involvement, engagement, accessibility, and responsibility, that had been confused in previous attempts to assess the extent of paternal involvement using time-use methodologies. By definition, engagement involves direct interactions with children (e.g., feeding, helping with homework, playing catch). Accessibility refers to activities involving supervision and the potential for interaction (e.g., cooking in the kitchen while the child plays in the next room or at the parent's feet). Responsibility is defined as the extent to which the parent takes ultimate responsibility for the child's welfare and care (e.g., making childcare arrangements, taking the child to buy clothes). Quantifying the time involved in such activities is particularly difficult because the anxiety, worry, and contingency planning that comprise parental responsibility often occur when the parent is ostensibly doing something else. The importance of responsibility stands in stark contrast to the limited attention researchers have paid to cognitive manifestations of involvement and identification (Hawkins & Palkovitz, 1999; Palkovitz, 1997; Walzer, 1998).

Palkovitz (1997) recently accentuated the need for further conceptual development in this area by explicitly identifying fifteen general forms of paternal involvement (e.g., doing errands, planning, providing, shared activities, teaching, thought processes directly pertaining to children), while emphasizing the need to consider cognitive manifestations of such involvement. Likewise, researchers are more vocal about the various other ways in which father involvement can be demonstrated, whether by providing human capital (e.g., skills, knowledge, and traits that foster achievement), financial capital (e.g., money, goods, and experiences purchased with income), or social capital (e.g., family and community relations that benefit children's cognitive and social development) (Amato, 1998; Coleman, 1988; 1990; Furstenberg, 1998; Hagan, MacMillan, & Wheaton, 1996; Seltzer, 1998).

As we consider an expanded view of paternal involvement, we must also examine the continuity of men's related experiences beginning with procreative decisions, pregnancy, establishing paternity, and culminating in their relationships with their children (Marsiglio, 1998). Even though prospective fathers' feelings and behaviors may affect both child outcomes and individual commitments to particular paternal roles, few researchers have explored this area (Cowan & Cowan, 1992). The relevant social psychological and familial processes surely differ depending on such factors as the prospective father's residency status, type of partner relationship, and the presence or absence of biological connections between the father and child.

General Features of Paternal Influence

A diverse array of sometimes overlapping avenues are associated with how fathers can either be involved with their children or make contributions to their well-being. The relative importance and effort attached to different aspects of fatherhood varies individually, as well as across subcultural groups and fatherhood categories. Although seldom addressed by researchers, it is important to know what fatherhood means when determining how important it is to individuals. As a result, motivational bases of fatherhood remain poorly understood; researchers' conception of paternal involvement may differ from those of the respondents. In addition, not only are different metrics needed to assess the fulfillment of each aspect of fatherhood, but performance is easier to measure in some areas (e.g., economic provisioning) than others (e.g., moral guidance). We highlight four main avenues of paternal influence below.

Nurturance and provision of care. Nurturance and provision of care to young children, including forms of play and recreation, have typically been assessed using time-use data on fathers' activities and are often referred to in the psychological and developmental literatures as "paternal involvement" (Lamb et al., 1987; Pleck, 1997). Although most observers view nurturance as a desirable aspect of fathering, there continues to be widespread disagreement about the importance of this aspect relative to other expressions of fathering, and its importance may still vary depending on the age and gender of the children concerned. Even though (or perhaps because) this aspect approximates "mothering" in many respects, it is almost universally viewed as secondary–less important than mothering done by mothers, and less important than the other dimensions of fatherhood. However, children's own perceptions of their relationships with their fathers suggest that displays of mutuality and recreation are highly valued and more relevant to children's assessment of fathers than mothers (Milkie, Simon, & Powell, 1997).

For many nonresident fathers, this dimension is particularly problematic because they are restricted in their opportunities to nurture and care for their children. To the extent that public policy and many stakeholders emphasize the nonresident fathers' breadwinning role at the expense of their other roles, these obstacles are likely to be exacerbated because the ability to nurture is dependent on opportunities to spend time with their children in diverse social and functional settings (Lamb, Sternberg, & Thompson, 1997).

Moral and ethical guidance. Moral and ethical guidance is viewed as a core feature of fatherhood within most religious traditions even though, in reality, most such guidance or socialization within families is performed by mothers (Lamb, this volume). Furthermore, when fathers are involved in moral socialization, their impact may be indirectly mediated by children's identification with and imitation of their fathers, regardless of any efforts on the fathers' part. Nevertheless, most biological resident fathers are able to provide moral guidance to their children, if they so desire, whereas nonresident fathers and stepfathers have much more limited opportunities. This is particularly true when the quality and depth of the emotional connections with their children preclude them from exerting a strong positive presence as moral guides.

Emotional, practical, and psychosocial support of female partners. Another aspect of paternal influence includes the emotional, practical, and psychosocial support of female partners (biological mothers or stepmothers). These aspects, shaped by social expectations, are likely to influence marital quality and other family process variables that are indirectly tied to fathers' interactions with their children (Cummings & O'Reilly, 1997). For example, some unmarried men may provide similar or even better social support to their partners than husbands do, however, the social expectations are typically lower for cohabiting men than for married men and higher for biological fathers than for stepfathers.

Economic provisioning. Economic provisioning, or breadwinning, is the avenue of paternal influence that is viewed by many stakeholders and most policymakers as one of the most central aspects to fatherhood and paternal involvement. Its importance is highlighted by the fact that legal and community expectations associated with economic provisioning transcend residency status. In some instances, informal recognition of paternity may be sufficient to evoke calls for fathers to contribute to their children financially. By contrast, stepfathers, who have no legal financial obligations to children they have not formally adopted, may have informally negotiated obligations that are often contingent on the continuation of a romantic involvement with the mothers. Men who agree to become nongenetic fathers, through reliance on asexual reproductive technologies and sperm donation, assume financial responsibilities that persist regardless of their romantic relationships, because their situation is viewed as akin to adoption.

Involvement Continua

Our final angle for exploring the nature and complexity of father involvement builds upon Palkovitz's (1997) set of continua (e.g., time invested, degree of involvement, observability, salience, and directness). The most obvious continuum includes the amount of time that fathers invest in different forms of paternal involvement. This level may be affected by people's perceptions about the amount of time different categories of fathers should spend or can realistically spend with their children. How much time fathers devote to their children, however, does not always reflect the depth of fathers' involvement or motivation. Some fathers may spend little time playing with their children, but they may be highly involved in making decisions about how their children's playtime is structured. Other fathers may spend a great deal of time doing things with or for their children but invest little of their heart and soul in these activities. The relationship between time investment and depth of involvement may vary depending upon distinctive features of the various types of fatherhood we defined earlier.

Some modes of father involvement are not observable, thus may go unnoticed, leading others to assume that these fathers are relatively uninvolved, even though fathers' anticipatory planning and worrying about their children may significantly affect interactions with them. This behind-the-scenes involvement may not only influence children's psychological and emotional adjustment and development, it may affect their financial futures as well. Nonobservable activities may often reflect "responsibility" as defined by Lamb et al. (1987), as well as time spent reflecting on the emotional and financial support of their partners. Thus, observability is a continuum with broader relevance to the conceptualization and study of paternal involvement, though it is not clear if the amounts of observable and unobservable involvement need to be correlated, either positively or negatively.

Fathers' and children's perceptions of nonobservable father involvement may differ depending upon both the amount of time fathers spend with their children and their coresident status. Some fathers may be more aware of their nonobservable expressions of fatherhood when they are unable to spend time with their children, whereas mothers' perceptions and evaluations of this involvement are likely to be much weaker when the mothers and fathers do not live together.

Another continuum identified by Palkovitz (1997) involves the salience of particular activities. Tasks may be highly relevant or salient to fathers because they are aversive or attractive. Those tasks toward which fathers are completely indifferent lack salience, and the relative salience of diverse tasks or activities no doubt varies depending on the type of fatherhood represented. Generally speaking, biological fathers are more likely than stepfathers to feel that the provision of financial support is salient, especially when biological fathers are making financial contributions to their children. Likewise, caregiving will be significantly more salient for single coresident fathers than for many resident fathers whose partners are also present.

Since paternal involvement influences children in diverse ways, it is important to recognize that these processes can be direct (e.g., when coaching by father helps the child achieve a desired goal) or indirect (e.g., where the father's overtime work permits the mother to stay home more and coach the child). Given the long-standing importance of the traditional male breadwinner role, much of what fathers have done for their children has had indirect effects on children's socialization and development.

Although it is beyond the scope of this paper to describe or analyze these continua in more detail, scholars would clearly benefit from paying close attention to them as they seek a multifaceted understanding of father involvement. Fathers march to the beat of many different drummers, and the nature and quality of their marching must be viewed in the context of the band by which they are expected, or seek, to be guided.

Motivation

A variety of motivational issues are relevant to the conceptualization of fatherhood and father involvement. These issues have interrelated motives or perceptions associated with various categories of fatherhood (including biological paternity), aspects of social fatherhood, and specific ways of being involved with children. Although different motives are likely to be associated with the various facets of fatherhood, men's desires to procreate are often intimately related to perceptions of specific social roles (e.g., economic provider, moral guide, nurturer), and their commitment to being "responsible" fathers (Marsiglio, 1998; Tanfer & Mott, 1997). Our treatment of motivational issues reflects our decision to incorporate men's prenatal roles into our conceptualization of social fatherhood and to expand the image of father involvement.

The desire to become social fathers and to enhance children's well being through positive involvement with them is shaped by a variety of factors, although research in this area is limited (Marsiglio, 1998). Men may be motivated in varying degrees to become social fathers because they want: (a) the experience of caring for and raising children, (b) an opportunity to strengthen their bonds to romantic partners, (c) to ensure that they are not lonely or financially vulnerable in their later years, or (d) to feel more connected to their extended family and/or friends. Likewise, the motivation to be responsible fathers who are positively involved with their children may stem from some of the above factors as well as: (a) genuine love for the children; (b) societal, religious, and familial incentives/pressures to act like masculine adult males (the "shame" factor in the extreme); (c) early family experiences, particularly their own parents' behavior; and (d) their perceptions of how much their children need their involvement or financial resources.

While these factors may indeed prompt men to be responsible fathers, the task of identifying the principal motives for responsible fathering is made more difficult because of the multiple ways in which paternal involvement can be expressed. Moreover, stakeholders' diverse views about what constitutes "good fathering" by men in different fatherhood situations adds to this complexity. Under the circumstances, it seems most useful to enumerate the most important motivational or explanatory categories that have been hypothesized–usually with respect to first-time biological paternity. In doing so, we recognize that not only is there limited empirical research in this area, but little attention has been given to exploring these motivational forces in light of different categories of fatherhood or types of specific fathering experiences associated with non-firstborn children. For instance, while few men intentionally seek out opportunities to become stepfathers, many men, some of who are biological fathers, are receptive to stepfathering situations. As we explore motives, we can speculate that this latter strategy may be appealing, because it affords some men the chance to satisfy their generative needs while avoiding the opportunity costs associated with the labor intensive infancy period or the formal financial obligations associated with biological paternity.

Turning our attention back to questions of biological paternity, sociobiologists (e.g., Emlen, 1995) emphasize that both men and women strive to maximize the representation of their genes in future generations. Several implications flow from their observation that males (unlike females) can be biologically involved in many pregnancies simultaneously and do not need to make major physiological contributions to the physical survival of their offspring after insemination. The "down side," according to these same theorists, is that men can never really be sure of paternity, and thus always face the risk of investing resources in someone else's children. Numerous predictions flow from these simple (if controversial) observations, including the notion that men invest less in individual offspring because the consequences of not investing are so much lower and the risks of misinvestment are so much higher than they are for women.

Another hypothesis is that the more men invest in partners and their children, the more they want to be sure of paternity. Thus the extent to which they provide economic and socio-emotional support may affect the extent to which their partners' later children have the same fathers. The clarity of these and related predictions is offset by the fact that the motivations are unconscious and must therefore be studied, not by probing attitudes and values in interviews, but by studying the effects, often at the level of population groups rather than individuals. This approach is also limited because its exclusive focus on biological paternity provides no insight into why and how men act as fathers toward non-biologically related children.

Fortunately, the desire to be a father is not driven solely by the desire to propagate one's genes, and sociobiological explanations in terms of ultimate causes involve a different level of analysis than psychological and sociological explanations. Theorists who stress developmental issues and the generativity theme contend that some fathers are motivated to procreate and be involved with their children because such involvement is related to healthy adult development (Hawkins & Dollahite, 1997; Palkovitz, 1997; Snarey, 1993). Indeed, many individuals find fulfillment in shaping the growth and development of another person, and this type of experience represents a motivating force for some fathers. While qualitative research confirms that men highly value the prospects of being able to have a biological connection with their child (Marsiglio, Hutchinson, & Cohan, 1999), some men look forward to raising children whether or not they are biologically related to them. It appears though that compared to women, men are less willing to become a "father" to biologically or nonbiologically related children without the involvement of a romantic partner. Thus, researchers should explore the link between men's motivations for a romantic relationship and their incentives for being involved with their children in particular ways.

The type and extent of fathers' involvement may also be affected by recollections of the fathering that these men experienced as children as well as their interpretation of other men's fathering behaviors in specific social situations. Some men (particularly those who embrace higher levels of hands-on involvement and avoid being defined solely by breadwinning) are motivated to emulate the behavior of their fathers, while others who behave in this way are apparently driven by a desire to be better fathers than their own fathers (Fox & Bruce, 1996). Meanwhile, Daly's (1995) qualitative work suggests that fathers may be less likely to emulate specific individuals and more likely to pick and choose behaviors, values, and standards that are displayed by various parents they encounter in their everyday lives.

Theorists who focus on life course, identity, and gender issues shed light on some men's motivations by suggesting that being a father denotes maturity and confers status in many societies and subcultures. Fathers can reap the benefits of social status when their partners and children are well-provisioned and successful (as denoted by school performance, sports achievement, college admissions, and career attainment).

Identity theory has been extended to address issues associated with men's paternal identity and involvement (Bruce & Fox, 1999; Futris & Pasley, 1997; Ihinger-Tallman, Pasley, & Buehler, 1995; Marsiglio, 1995b; 1995c). This model emphasizes fathers' commitment to role identities that are negotiated within the context of structured role relationships. As such, it implicitly deals with motivational issues in that fathers' commitment to being particular types of men, partners, and fathers may affect their desire to be involved with their children in specific ways. This perspective is valuable because it draws attention to the interpersonal and social context within which men develop their individual dispositions to think, feel, and act toward their children, dispositions that are related to individuals' perceptions of what is expected from men who occupy various types of father or father-like positions. Moreover, it provides a theoretically meaningful link between fathers' perceptions of themselves and their actual paternal involvement. By emphasizing identity within a complex relational context, this theory also underscores how co-parental and co-partner issues may condition men's involvement with their resident and nonresident children within the context of different types of fatherhood (see Dienhart, 1998; Fox & Bruce, 1996).

FAMILY PROCESSES AND FATHERHOOD CLAIMS

In recent years, the growing complexity as well as fluidity of family structures has accentuated the dynamic processes that afford family members opportunities to develop their own working definitions of fatherhood and negotiate paternal privileges, rights, and responsibilities. As a result, efforts to negotiate the meaning of fatherhood, especially during familial transition periods, are increasingly tied to and played out through ongoing family processes–the patterns of interaction or sentiment occurring between family members that can be measured and have a measurable impact on a variety of familial and individual outcomes (Day, Gavazzi, & Acock, 1997). These processes are, in turn, influenced by more general cultural norms concerning familial roles that affect and are affected by the legal and sociopolitical approaches to fatherhood. Much can therefore be gained by studying the social and family processes that define the rights and responsibilities accorded to fathers in diverse situations. We focus here on how three prominent family processes (distance regulation, parental support, and flexibility) affect paternal involvement and the negotiated meanings of fatherhood.

Distance Regulation

Distance regulation contains two primary dimensions: (a) The parent's tolerance for individuality, or the relative tolerance that the system displays for each member to experience a sense of separateness from the family, and (b) the parent's tolerance for intimacy, or the relative tolerance that the system displays for members to be connected emotionally and psychologically to the family (Gavazzi, 1993). Researchers suggest that distance regulation patterns that tolerate both individuality from the family and intimacy within the family create a well-differentiated family system. If the distance regulation patterns display high tolerance for only one dimension of family differentiation–individuality or intimacy–the family is thought to have a moderate level of differentiation. Families that retain a sense of intimacy but do not tolerate individuality well have been labeled "enmeshed," whereas those that tolerate individuality among their members without retaining a sense of intimate belonging have been labeled "disengaged" (Minuchin, 1974). Finally, distance regulation patterns that do not tolerate individuality claims and do not tolerate intimacy within the family are thought to be poorly differentiated (Gavazzi, 1994).

Fathers administer distance regulation within the wide and complex assortment of family structures or categories of fatherhood. These configurations contribute to the father's physical and emotional proximal orientation to his children. When he is estranged from the executive sub-system responsibilities of daily routines and rituals, he may have only limited (if any) opportunity to develop and maintain effective intimacy levels with his children. Fathers who do not maintain a stable physical presence in the household, may have virtually no say in shaping the family climate that establishes implicit and explicit rules regarding child autonomy or individuality. Consequently, fathers who occupy peripheral positions will have to overcome practical and perceptual barriers in order to develop and sustain their intimacy claims as a legitimate father figure.

On the other hand, in many situations where a father is both physically and emotionally present and committed to the family enterprise, that configuration at least allows for the possibility that he may have a voice in distance regulation issues as they pertain to children. Other familial configurations, e.g., a stepfather entering a new marriage with children already present, may create some confusion about a father's ability to promote familial distance regulation. As the new father enters the pre-existing family (often accompanied or followed by a coresidential arrangement) and negotiates for a place within the decision-making, executive sub-system of the "new" family, he may find it difficult to establish the necessary boundaries and relationship ties with his new spouse that exclude children (Pasley & Ihinger-Tallman, 1987). Therefore, his ability or effectiveness to create appropriate intimacy with his new children may be severely limited. In many cases, the previous coalition among the mother and her children may hamper his attempts to influence or have much voice in making rules (formal or informal) or shaping family rituals that would define levels of family distance regulation. He may create a place for himself within the interpersonal household system, but it is unlikely to be as a father figure that has acknowledged claims in distance regulation.

Parental Support

Parental support is another key family process and is conceptualized as physical affection, acceptance, general support, or companionship. Support in these terms has the potential to communicate warmth, affection, rapport, and feelings of being valued (Peterson & Hann, 1999; Stafford & Bayer, 1993). In the case of the parent-child subsystem, nurturant or emotionally supportive relationships encourage the young to identify with parents and incorporate their attitudes, values, and expectations. This process also usually reinforces the legitimacy of biological fathers' legal and informal claims as fathers when they begin to live with and care for their children at birth (or shortly thereafter). Likewise, the claims for "parental" legitimacy that stepfathers negotiate with their partners can be strengthened when stepfathers provide "parental" support to their stepchildren.

However, when fathers are absent from the immediate family residence, it is more difficult to keep the child's well-being as a priority and provide unconditional love. Arendell (1995) found that non-residential biological fathers had to engage in innovative support strategies to maintain the necessary closeness. She also noted that for some men the change in familial configuration (in this case one that takes them out of the daily routine) is something of a wake-up call which resulted in fathers exerting more energy to develop caring strategies than they had before the divorce. This type of paternal involvement may solidify fathers' claims in their children's and former partners' eyes. At the same time it may shape, and in some cases restrict potential stepfathers' opportunities to assert their own legitimate claims.

Flexibility

Flexibility assesses the degree to which members are able to change the power structure, relationship rules, and roles in relation to developmental or situational stressors (Anderson & Sabatelli, 1992). Families that are able to demonstrate greater flexibility in the face of demands for change are thought to respond in healthier ways, thereby meeting the needs of their individual members. The literature in this area contains a number of constructs related to flexibility among family members such as adaptability (Olson, Sprenkle, & Russell, 1983), family problem-solving ability (Reiss & Oliveri, 1980), and family coping styles (McCubbin, Thompson, & McCubbin, 1996; McKenry & Price, 1994).

Regardless of the definition used, fathers who are involved in the family should have some impact on the level of flexibility within that system. As families change in configuration (e.g., from first marriage with children to divorced), the father's ability to contribute to the adaptability level within his family dramatically changes. Changes in the power structure, rules, and daily routines that define a level of flexibility require daily maintenance. If a father is not present (either physically or emotionally), the expressed level of flexibility will reflect the interaction of those who do have a vested interest and are present, for example, the stepfather. In contrast, flexibility issues will be particularly salient for single co-resident fathers. Many of these fathers must demonstrate a great deal of flexibility as they attempt to reorganize family routines and sometimes persuade their children and others to extend more extensive rights and responsibilities to them as fathers/parents than was previously the case.

Until recently, most fathering research focused on the dichotomous notion of fathers' absence or presence as a marker of fathers' impact within a family system. Future research on fathers' involvement needs to examine not only how fathers are involved, but how family processes, which are influenced by dynamic features of family structure, add to our understanding of that involvement. Part of this understanding will therefore come from analyses of how various family processes are tied to family members' efforts to figure out, negotiate, and sustain what men should be doing with or for their children as children experience fathers under new circumstances. These processes, and the associated perceptions individuals have of them, will be closely linked to the more fundamental question we raised earlier: Who are fathers?

ADVANCING A BROADER CONCEPTUALIZATION

As discussed above, the terrain of fatherhood and father involvement is replete with complex and interrelated conceptual issues that are meaningful to a broad audience. These issues, often driven by individuals' and interest groups' value-laden perceptions, speak to how fathers do "fatherhood," how researchers can study fathers, and how policymakers devise public policy. We have provided a snapshot of the theoretical and political complexities facing researchers and policymakers as they attempt to conceptualize, study, and promote fathers' involvement with their children. To conclude, we suggest several foci for future scholarship that draws upon a broader conceptualization of father involvement while contributing to our appreciation of fatherhood as a social construction.

The varied and often negotiated definitions of father as a social status may affect the way men involve themselves in their children's lives in a practical sense. Thus, it is important to empirically determine how the meanings of fatherhood, both as a status and role-making process, are institutionally and interpersonally constructed and negotiated. A concerted effort should be made to develop concepts and measurement strategies that capture these diverse definitions and meanings. This effort should explore how individuals distinguish between fathers' investments or perceptions of their status as father, as opposed to their views and involvement in the process of fathering.

As part of this effort, researchers should examine how individuals, subcultural groups, interest groups, the legal system, media, academics, parenting experts, and diverse professionals construct the images commonly associated with paternity and fatherhood. These images should reference the periods prior to conception, during pregnancy, and across the child's lifespan. More specifically, researchers and policymakers should attempt to understand individuals' perceptions of the varied meanings associated with biological and social fatherhood and the consequences of these perceptions. Under what circumstances does biological paternity entitle men to certain rights or elicit certain obligations? What, according to the various stakeholders, should those rights and obligations be? When do purely social fathers assume the same standing as biological fathers and change their fathering behavior accordingly?

Researchers should also strive to develop a more systematic portrait of how men, women, and children from different family structure, class, and race/ethnic backgrounds view aspects of fatherhood. How is "good" fathering defined and how are these definitions conditioned by individual, interpersonal, and more macro or cultural level factors? Indeed, little is known about such obvious aspects of the parenting role as protecting, breadwinning, and the ethical role model, or about how these interpretations affect paternal involvement. How are these meanings affected by children's developmental stage, personality, and gender, or by community standards and interpersonal ties with the mothers (and grandparents) of the children? Similarly, attention should be given to the relationship between specific family context and family-related processes that either facilitate or impede specific expressions of fathering and shape children's well-being and development. In other words, scholars should devote more effort to understanding how family processes such as distance regulation, parental support, and flexibility (in addition to others) are affected by the varied circumstances and transitional periods associated with the different types of fatherhood. Researchers need to consider how individuals' efforts to define and negotiate fathers' privileges, rights, and obligations are embedded within more generic family processes. In general, researchers must continue to show how conceptual and theoretical concerns, measurement and data questions, and policymaking agendas overlap and mutually inform each other. These efforts are essential if we are to develop better research strategies and, eventually, a more complete understanding of why, how, and with what effect, fathers are involved with their children.

REFERENCES

Amato, P. (1998). More than money?: Men's contributions to their children's lives. In A. Booth & N. Crouter (Eds.), *Men in families: When do they get involved? What difference does it make?* (pp. 241-278). Mahwah, NJ: Lawrence Erlbaum Associates.

Anderson, J. H. (1992). The functioning father: A unified approach to paternity determinations. *Journal of Family Law, 30,* 847-873.

Anderson, S.A. & Sabatelli, R.M. (1992). The differentiation in the family system scale (DIFS). *The American Journal of Family Therapy, 20,* 77-88.

Arendell, T. (1995). *Fathers & divorce.* Thousand Oaks, CA: Sage.

Bahr, H. M. & Bahr, K. S. (1996). A paradigm of family transcendence. *Journal of Marriage and the Family, 58,* 541-555.

Berscheid, E. (1996). The "paradigm of family transcendence": Not a paradigm, questionably transcendent, but valuable, nonetheless. *Journal of Marriage and the Family, 58*, 556 564.

Bianchi, S. M. (1995). The changing demographic and socioeconomic characteristics of single parent families. In Hanson, S. M. H., Heims, M. L., Julian, D. J., & Sussman, M. B. (Eds.), *Single parent families: Diversity, myths, and realities* (pp. 71-97). New York: The Haworth Press, Inc.

Blankenhorn, D. (1995). *Fatherless America: Confronting our most urgent social problem.* New York: Basic Books.

Brown, B. V. (1999). The single father family: Demographic, economic, and public transfer use characteristics. *Marriage & Family Review, 29*, 2-3.

Bruce, C., & Fox, G. L. (1999). Accounting for patterns of father involvement: Age of child, father-child coresidence, and father role salience. *Sociological Inquiry, 69*, 3, 458-476.

Burton, L. M., & Snyder, T. R. (1998). The invisible man revisited: Historical perspectives on men's roles in African American Families. In A. Booth & N. Crouter (Eds.) *Men in families: When do they get involved? What difference does it make?* (pp. 31-39). Mahwah, NJ: Lawrence Erlbaum Associates.

Coleman, J. (1988). Social capital in the creation of human capital. *American Journal of Sociology, 94*, 95-120.

Coleman, J. (1990). *Foundations of social theory.* Cambridge, MA: Harvard University.

Coltrane, S. (1996). *Family man: Fatherhood, housework, and gender equity.* New York: Oxford University Press.

Cowan, C. P., & Cowan, P. A. (1992). *When partners become parents: The big life change for couples.* New York: Basic Books.

Cummings, E. M., & O'Reilly, A. W. (1997). Fathers in family context: Effects of marital quality on child adjustment. In M. E. Lamb (Ed.), *The role of the father in child development* (pp. 49-65). New York: John Wiley & Sons, Inc.

Da Vanzo, J., & Rahman, M. O. (1993). American families: Trends and correlates. *Population Index, 59*, 350-386.

Daly, K. J. (1995). Reshaping fatherhood: Finding the models. In W. Marsiglio (Ed.), *Fatherhood: Contemporary theory, research, and social policy.* Thousand Oaks, CA: Sage.

Day, R. D., Gavazzi, S., & Acock, A. (1997, November). Identifying and measuring compelling family processes. Paper presented at the Theory Construction and Research Methods Pre-conference Workshop. National Council on Family Relations. Washington, D.C.

Dienhart, A., (1998). *Reshaping fatherhood: The social construction of shared parenting.* Thousand Oaks, CA: Sage.

Doherty, W. J., Kouneski, E. F., & Erikson, M. F. (1998). Responsible fathering: An overview and conceptual framework. *Journal of Marriage and the Family, 60*, 277-292.

Eggebeen, D. J., Snyder, A. R., & Manning, W. D. (1996). Children in single-father families in demographic perspective. *Journal of Family Issues, 17*, 441-465.

Emlen, S. T. (1995). An evolutionary theory of the family. *Proceedings of the National Academy of Science, 92*, 8092-8099.

Federal Interagency Forum on Child and Family Statistics. (1998). *Nurturing fatherhood: Improving data and research on male fertility, family formation, and fatherhood.* Washington, D.C.

Fox, G. L., & Bruce, C. (1996, November). Development and validation of measures of parenting for low-income, high-risk men. Paper presented at the Theory and Methodology Workshop, National Council on Family Relations.

Furstenberg, F. F., Jr. (1995). Fathering in the inner city: Paternal participation and public policy. In Marsiglio, W. (1995). *Fatherhood: Contemporary theory, research, and social policy.* Thousand Oaks, CA: Sage.

Furstenberg, F. F., Jr. (1988). Good dads-bad dads: Two faces of fatherhood. In A. J. Cherlin (Ed.), *The changing American family and public policy* (pp. 193-218). Washington, DC: Urban Institute.

Furstenberg, F. F., Jr. (1998). Social capital and the role of fathers in the family. In A. Booth & N. Crouter (Eds.), *Men in families: When do they get involved? What difference does it make?* (pp. 295-301). Mahwah, NJ: Lawrence Erlbaum Associates.

Futris, T. G. & Pasley, K. (1997, November). The father role identity: Conceptualizing and assessing within-role variability. Paper presented at the Theory Construction and Research Methodology Workshop, National Council on Family Relations, Washington, D.C.

Gavazzi, S.M. (1993).The relation between family differentiation levels in families with adolescents and the severity of presenting problems. *Family Relations, 42*, 463-468.

Gavazzi, S.M. (1994). Advances in assessing the relationship between family differentiation and problematic functioning in adolescents. *Family Therapy, 21*, 249-259.

Gerson, K. (1993). *No man's land: Men's changing commitments to family and work.* New York: Basic Books.

Griswold, R. L. (1993). *Fatherhood in America: A history.* New York: Basic Books.

Hagan, J., MacMillan, R., & Wheaton, B. (1996). New kid in town: Social capital and the life course effects of family migration on children. *American Sociological Review, 61*, 368385.

Hawkins, A. J., Christiansen, S. L., Sargent, P. K., & Hill, E. J. (1995). Rethinking fathers' involvement in child care: A developmental perspective. In W. Marsiglio (Ed.), *Fatherhood: Contemporary theory, research, and social policy* (pp. 41-56). Thousand Oaks, CA: Sage.

Hawkins, A. J., & Dollahite, D. C. (1997). *Generative fathering: Beyond deficit perspectives.* Thousand Oaks, CA: Sage.

Hawkins, A. J., & Palkovitz, R. (1999). Beyond ticks and clicks: The need for more diverse and broader conceptualizations and measures of father involvement. *Journal of Men's Studies.*

Hochschild, A. (with A. Machung.) (1989). *The second shift.* New York: Avon.

Ihinger-Tallman, M., Pasley, K., & Buehler, C. L. (1995). Developing a middle-range theory of father involvement post-divorce. In W. Marsiglio (Ed.), *Fatherhood:*

Contemporary theory, research, and social policy (pp. 57-77). Thousand Oaks, CA: Sage.

Klein, D. M. and White, James, M. (1997). *Family Theories: An Introduction*. Thousand Oaks, CA: Sage.

Lamb, M. E. (1997). The development of father-infant relationships. In M. E. Lamb (Ed.), *The role of the father in child development* (pp. 104-120). New York: John Wiley & Sons.

Lamb, M. E. (1999). The history of research on father involvement: An overview. *Marriage & Family Review, 29*, 2-3.

Lamb, M. E..& Goldberg, W. A. (1982). The father child relationship: A synthesis of biological, evolutionary and social perspectives. In L. W. Hoffman, R. Gandelman, & H. R. Schiffman (Eds.), *Parenting: Its causes and consequences* (pp. 55-73) Hillsdale, NJ: Lawrence Erlbaum Associates.

Lamb, M. E., Pleck, J. H., Charnov, E. L. & Levine, J. A. (1987). A biosocial perspective on paternal behavior and involvement. In J. B. Lancaster, J. Altmann, A. S. Rossi, & L. R. Sherrod (Eds.), *Parenting across the lifespan: Biosocial dimensions* (pp. 111-142). New York: Aldine de Gruyter.

Lamb, M. E., Sternberg, K. J., & Thompson, K. A. (1997). The effects of divorce and custody arrangements on childrens behavior, development, and adjustment. *Family and Conciliation Courts Review, 35*, 393-404.

LaRossa, R. (1988). Fatherhood and social change. *Family Relations, 37*, 451-458.

Lupton, D., & Barclay, L. (1997). *Constructing fatherhood: Discourses and experiences*. Thousand Oaks, CA: Sage.

Marks, S. R. (1996). The problem and politics of wholeness in family studies. *Journal of Marriage and the Family, 58*, 565-571.

Marsiglio, W. (1995a). Fathers' diverse life course patterns and roles: Theory and social interventions. In W. Marsiglio (Ed.), *Fatherhood: Contemporary theory, research, and social policy* (78-101). Thousand Oaks, CA: Sage.

Marsiglio, W. (1995b). Stepfathers with minor children living at home: Parenting perceptions and relationship quality. In W. Marsiglio (Ed.), *Fatherhood: Contemporary theory, research, and social policy* (pp. 211-229). Thousand Oaks, CA: Sage.

Marsiglio, W. (1995c). Young nonresident biological fathers. *Marriage & Family Review, 20*, 325-348.

Marsiglio, W. (1998). *Procreative Man*. New York: New York University Press.

Marsiglio, W., Amato, P., Day, R., & Lamb, M. E. (2000). Scholarship on fatherhood in the 1990s and beyond: Past impressions, future prospects. *Journal of Marriage and the Family, 62*.

Marsiglio, W., & Cohan, M. (1999). Contextualizing father involvement and paternal influence: Sociological and qualitative themes. *Marriage & Family Review, 29*, 2-3.

Marsiglio, W., Hutchinson, & S., Cohan, M. (1999). *Young men's procreative self: Becoming aware, being aware, being responsible*. Unpublished paper, University of Florida, Department of Sociology.

McCubbin, H. I., Thompson, A. I., & McCubbin, M.A. (1996). *Family assessment: Resiliency, coping, adaptation*. Madison, WI: University of Wisconsin Publishers.

McKenry P., & Price, S. (1994). *Families and change: Coping with stressful events.* Thousand Oaks, CA: Sage.

Milkie, M. A., Simon, R. W., & Powell, B. (1997). Through the eyes of children: Youths' perceptions and evaluations of maternal and paternal roles. *Social Psychology Quarterly, 60,* 218-237.

Mintz, S. (1998). From patriarchy to androgyny and other myths: Placing men's family roles in historical perspective. In A. Booth & N. Crouter (Eds.), *Men in families: When do they get involved? What difference does it make?* (pp. 3-30). Mahwah, NJ: Lawrence Erlbaum Associates.

Minuchin, S. (1974). *Families and family therapy.* Cambridge, MA: Harvard University Press.

Olson, D.H., Sprenkle, D.H., & Russell, C.S. (1983). Circumplex model of marital and family systems. VI: Theoretical update. *Family Process, 22,* 69-83.

Palkovitz, R. (1997). Reconstructing "involvement": Expanding conceptualizations of men's caring in contemporary families. In A. J. Hawkins & D. C. Dollahite (Eds.), *Generative fathering: Beyond deficit perspectives.* (pp. 200-216). Thousand Oaks, CA: Sage.

Parke, R.D. (1996). *Fatherhood.* Cambridge, MA: Harvard University Press.

Pasley, K. & Ihinger-Tallman, M. (1987). *Remarriage and Stepparenting: Current Research and Theory.* New York: Guilford.

Peterson, G.W., & Hann, D. (1999). Socializing children and parents in families. In M. B. Sussman, S. K. Steinmetz, & G. W. Peterson (Eds.), *Handbook of Marriage and the Family.* New York: Plenum Publishers.

Pleck, J.H. (1997). Paternal involvement: Levels, sources, and consequences. In M. E. Lamb (Ed.), *The role of the father in child development* (pp. 66-103). New York: John Wiley & Sons.

Pleck, E. H., & Pleck, J. H. (1980). *The American man.* Englewood Cliffs, NJ: Prentice-Hall.

Pleck, E. H., & Pleck, J. H. (1997). Fatherhood ideals in the United States: Historical dimensions. In M. E. Lamb (Ed.), *The role of the father in child development.* New York: John Wiley & Sons, Inc.

Popenoe, D. (1993, October). The evolution of marriage and the problem of stepfamilies. Paper presented at the National Symposium on Stepfamilies, Pennsylvania State University.

Reiss, D., & Oliveri, M. (1980). Family paradigm and family coping: A proposal for linking the family's intrinsic adaptive capacities to its response to stress. *Family Relations, 29,* 431-444.

Scanzoni, J., & Marsiglio, W. (1993). New action theory and contemporary families. *Journal of Family Issues, 14,* 105-132.

Seltzer, J. (1998). Men's contributions to children and social policy. In A. Booth & N. Crouter (Eds.), *Men in families: When do they get involved? What difference does it make?* (pp. 303-314). Mahwah, NJ: Lawrence Erlbaum Associates.

Snarey, J. (1993). *How fathers care for the next generation.* Cambridge, MA: Harvard University Press.

Stafford, L., & Bayer, C.L. (1993). *Interaction between parents and children.* Newbury Park, CA: Sage.

Straub v. B.M.T. 1994. No. 10A04-9302-JV-53. Court of Appeals of Indiana, Fourth District.

Tanfer, K., & Mott, F. L. (1997, January). The meaning of fatherhood for men. Background paper prepared for the Working Group on Male Fertility and Family Formation. NICHD, Washington, D.C.

Thompson, L. (1993). Conceptualizing gender in marriage: The case of marital care. *Journal of Marriage and the Family, 55,* 557-569.

Uniform Parentage Act, 9B U.L.A. (1973).

Walzer, S. (1998). *Thinking about the baby: Gender and transitions into parenthood.* Philadelphia: Temple University Press.

West, C. & Zimmerman, D. H. (1987). Doing gender. *Gender and Society, 1,* 125-151.

Public Policies and Father Involvement

Natasha Cabrera
H. Elizabeth Peters

SUMMARY. The last two decades have been marked by a series of social and policy developments that are changing both how men see themselves as fathers and how policies conceptualize and encourage their involvement in the lives of children and families. This paper focuses on several areas of intersection between research on fathers and policy. The paper first summarizes the research that led to the current political and social interest in fathers. The paper then describes the Fatherhood Initiative, a set of activities that stemmed from a 1995 memorandum from President Clinton. This Initiative led to coordinated efforts by U.S. Federal Statistical agencies to collect better data about fathers. The paper concludes with a discussion of what we know about the effects on father involvement of policies such as welfare reform, child support, work place policies, responsible fatherhood programs, and other fatherhood interventions. Examples of new programs and initiatives on father involvement are also given. *[Article copies available for a fee from The Haworth Document Delivery Service: 1-800-342-9678. E-mail address: getinfo@haworthpressinc.com <Website: http://www.haworthpressinc.com>]*

KEYWORDS. Fatherhood, family policy

The last two decades have been marked by a series of social and policy developments that are changing both how men see themselves as fathers and

Natasha Cabrera is affiliated with the National Institute of Child Health and Human Development, Demographic and Behavioral Research Branch.

H. Elizabeth Peters is affiliated with the Department of Policy Analysis and Management, Cornell University.

[Haworth co-indexing entry note]: "Public Policies and Father Involvement." Cabrera, Natasha, and H. Elizabeth Peters. Co-published simultaneously in *Marriage & Family Review* (The Haworth Press, Inc.) Vol. 29, No. 4, 2000, pp. 295-314; and: *FATHERHOOD: Research, Interventions and Policies* (ed: H. Elizabeth Peters et al.) The Haworth Press, Inc., 2000, pp. 295-314. Single or multiple copies of this article are available for a fee from The Haworth Document Delivery Service [1-800-342-9678, 9:00 a.m. - 5:00 p.m. (EST). E-mail address: getinfo@haworthpressinc.com].

295

how policies conceptualize and encourage their involvement in the lives of children and families. This shift in how men's and women's roles are conceptualized is preceded by a large literature that has increased our understanding of father-child relationships, paternal influences on child development, and the impact of father involvement on children and families (see Lamb, 1997, for an in-depth review). This body of research speaks to the importance of father involvement for children's educational and economic attainment, delinquent behavior, and psychological well-being (Harris, Furstenberg, & Marmer, 1998; Lamb, 1997). As evidence accumulates on the important relationship between father involvement and child outcomes, we are learning that specific types of father involvement affect specific outcomes, and that some child outcomes are linked not to specific types of father involvement, but rather to father-child relationships.

However, the research base on fathering has limitations. In their review of studies on father involvement, Coplin and Houts (1991) note that there remains a dearth of longitudinal investigations on changes to father-child interactions over time, the multiplicity of factors that affect those changes, and the consequences for such changes on children's development. There are no prospective studies on father involvement that begin in the prenatal or early infancy periods. We know little about issues surrounding father involvement and fertility, the motivators to fatherhood, relations between intendedness and fathers' long-term investments in children, and whether and how the father-infant relationship affects father involvement and child development over longer time frames. Without prospective studies, it is difficult to ascertain which factors predict healthy father-child relationships versus those that lead to decreased father involvement over time. Another problem with the fathering research is that information about fathers is often based on data obtained from mothers.

In addition to these limitations, and perhaps more relevant to policy design, the bulk of the past and current research on fathers is characterized by small samples of convenience with high levels of exclusion, making the generalization of findings difficult (Greene, Halle, Le Menestrel, & Moore, 1998). The existing studies provide little knowledge about how different cultural, social, and economic circumstances impact fathering styles; how low income fathers relate to their children; why they do (or do not) invest in their children; and how their own investments contribute to the healthy development of their children (Tamis-Lemonda & Cabrera, in press). The studies that have been conducted on minority fathers or economically disadvantaged groups have focused on negative aspects of behavior such as father absence and the nonpayment of child support (see Lamb, 1997).

The limitations outlined above mean that social policies such as child support legislation, that are meant to strengthen the role of fathers in the lives of their children, have often been designed with information gathered from populations other than the ones they were intended to affect. To compound the problem, there is little research that directly evaluates the effectiveness or the potentially harmful consequences of existing social policies and programs targeted to increase father involvement.

Despite its limitations, the body of research on fathers has resulted in a shift in the way federal agencies conceptualize fathers, collect data on fathers, and re-design policies that promote positive involvement of fathers in the lives of their children. Policies are moving beyond an exclusive emphasis on fathers' provider role. Policy makers, researchers, and educators no longer view fathers through the mother lens, they now look at them as men who become fathers, as men who have a different parental trajectory from mothers, and as men who can contribute economic and emotional support for the development of their children.

In this paper, we focus on four areas of intersection between research on fathers and policy: (a) researchers' contributions to the current political and social interest in fathers, (b) the Fatherhood Initiative and its focus on the intersection between research and policy, (c) effects of public policies on father involvement and the role of fatherhood programs and education efforts; and (d) examples of programs and new initiatives on father involvement.

WHY THE CURRENT POLITICAL AND SOCIAL INTEREST IN FATHERS?

In 1996, 20% of American children lived in families with cash income below the poverty line. Today, the largest group of poor people in our population is children, with nearly a quarter of those children being under 6 years of age. Poverty affects the health, cognitive development, social behavior, and psychological well-being in children. One of the most consistent correlates of childhood poverty is the absence of a resident father. The poverty rate for fatherless families is five times higher than in two parent families, and the rate of fatherless families has doubled in the past 15 years. The proportion of children who live with only one parent at some time during their childhood is expected to continue to exceed 50% (Hernandez, 1993).

The alarming notion that fatherless families are becoming the norm in our country for certain groups motivated much of the earlier work and previous focus on the role of the father in child and family well-being. This literature on "absent" fathers has mainly focused on the physically absent (i.e., nonresident father), rather than on the psychologically absent father. Even when controlling for family income, children growing up without their father face more difficulties. Studies have shown that children who grow up without a father are at risk for low school achievement, low involvement in the labor force, early childbearing, and delinquency (Federal Interagency Forum on Child and Family Statistics, 1998). Holding race, income, parent's education, and urban residence constant, Harper and McLanahan (1998) found that boys with nonresident fathers had double the odds of being incarcerated; those boys who grew up with a stepfather in the home were at even higher risk of incarceration, roughly three times that of children who remained with both their natural parents.

Boys growing up without fathers seem especially prone to exhibit problems in the areas of sex-role and gender-identity development, school performance, psychosocial adjustment, and in the control of aggression (Hetherington & Stanley-Hagan, 1986). Girls are affected by father-absence too, although the effects on girls may be less enduring, dramatic, and consistent than the effects on boys.

While this apocalyptic picture of the consequences of father's absence has the power to sustain public attention, it characterizes the father's role as unidimensional–either physically present or not. When we account for the distinction between physical versus psychological absence, both the patterns of involvement and the consequences of physical absence are less straightforward. For example, it is not clear how "absent" men have been from their families. Lerman and Sorensen (this volume) report that two-thirds of fathers of children born out of wedlock have a substantial amount of contact with at least one nonmarital child. There is also little understanding of the non-financial ways that some fathers–especially nonresidential fathers–contribute to their families. Green and Moore (this volume) report that nonresident low income fathers often provide financial support informally, rather than through the formal child support enforcement system. Fathers may prefer these less formal systems, because they feel they have more control over how money for the child is spent.

In contrast to the trends in father-absent families, father involvement in intact families appears to be increasing (Casper; 1997; Pleck, 1997; Yeung, Sandberg, Davis-Kean, & Hofferth, 1999). Fathers' motivations for these changes are difficult to ascertain. They may reflect changing conceptions of fatherhood or changes in macro and micro economic conditions. For example, Averett, Gennetian, and Peters (this volume) found that when working mothers had non-traditional gender role attitudes, fathers were more likely to provide child care. Other research has shown that increased rates of maternal employment, periods of economic decline, joint work schedules, flexible work hours, irregular work schedules, part-time employment, job sharing, and home-based work are all associated with increases in paternal responsibility for child care (Averett et al., this volume; Brayfield, 1995; Casper & O'Connell, 1998; Presser, 1995). The U.S. Bureau of Labor Statistics (1997) projects that the largest job growth through 2006 will be in low-wage jobs which involve night and weekend shifts; thus the trend today for fathers to assume greater responsibility for the care of their young children is likely to continue into the 21st century.

Thus, for a variety of reasons paternal involvement, responsibility, and care has increased over the past three decades (Pleck, 1997; Yeung et al., 1999). Whereas fathers in intact two-parent families formerly spent about 30% to 45% as much time with their children as mothers did, they now spend 67% as much time as mothers on weekdays and 87% as much on weekends (Yeung et al., 1999). In addition, the number of single fathers living with their children has increased by 25% in the past three years, reflecting an increased acceptance by courts and society of paternal custody, an increased tendency on the part of men to seek custody, and a greater willingness on the part of mothers and judges to agree to paternal custody (U.S. Bureau of the Census, 1999).

Specific changes in the participation of fathers have paralleled, and perhaps prompted, a major shift in how men and women define their parental roles. National campaigns, the popular media, researchers, policy makers, practitioners, educators, and leaders of social and religious organizations are popularizing a new image of emotionally-involved nurturant fatherhood (Wilkie, 1993). As a result, fathers have moved from relative obscurity into a central position in efforts to understand and promote child well-being (Tamis-Lemonda & Cabrera, in press). New types of fathers–in stepparent, recombined, and cohabiting families–are being acknowledged and studied. Many men express the desire to be the father they wish they had (Pruett, 1987), and one-third of the men surveyed defined the ideal father as unlike, rather than like their own fathers (Hofferth, 1999).

THE FATHERHOOD INITIATIVE

While research has been almost unanimous in their findings that fathers are important for the healthy development of their children, it has been largely confined to academic publications and thus absent from a parallel public debate going on about how and when fathers' involvement matters. This situation changed dramatically in 1994 when the Interagency Forum on Child and Family Statistics (Forum), a collection of Federal statistical agencies, was created to coordinate data collection efforts across major statistical agencies.[1] On June 16, 1995, President Clinton issued a one-page memorandum requesting that Federal agencies review their programs and policies with the purposes of strengthening the role of fathers in families and highlighting the contributions that fathers can make to their children's well-being. One goal of this request was to improve current data collection efforts to increase the information available on fathers.

To accomplish this goal the Forum co-sponsored a series of workshops on Male Fertility, Family Formation, and Fathering that were held between 1996-1997. These activities came to be known as "The Fatherhood Initiative." This Initiative provided a forum where academics, researchers, policy makers, educators, and practitioners came together to present different views on how research and policy can jointly strengthen the roles of fathers in all families. The Fatherhood Initiative echoed several of the themes discussed earlier. Specifically, the Initiative highlighted the importance of understanding the multiple contributions of fathers in a variety of family situations and structures and across diverse socioeconomic, racial, and ethnic groups. The Initiative also pointed out that responsible fatherhood may be important to the personal development of men in motivating them to engage in economically productive and pro-social behaviors.

In its report, the Fatherhood Initiative put forth several recommendations about improving data on the nature and outcomes of father involvement. They urged researchers and policy makers to attend to both marital and non-marital relationships from the perspectives of women and men; conduct longitudinal studies that follow the process of fertility and family formation across the life course; improve data on the motivations, attitudes, and intentions underlying childbearing among men and women in all types of relationships; and to further investigate the meaning of fatherhood, the motivational bases of fatherhood, and the impact that father involvement has on child development across cultural and ethnic groups (Federal Interagency Forum on Child and Family Statistics, 1998b).

The impact of the Fatherhood activities and these emerging social trends have already led to important developments in the way federal agencies conceptualize and collect data on fathers; the initiative has stimulated new national data collection efforts, new national studies, and shifts in social policies and research directions that are linked to policy. Consequently, there exists a current national momentum and agenda for reconceptualizing fatherhood and the ways fathers are incorporated into policies, improving federal data on fathers, and designing policies that recognize the emotional, psychological, and economic contributions that fathers can make to the development of their children.

Despite substantial gains made in recognizing the importance of fathers for child development and policy design and implementation, there are still barriers to overcome. Some have suggested that socio-cultural blocks continue to exist in how men see themselves. Women largely see themselves as advocates for children's well-being, but men are less likely to define themselves in such an activist or nurturing role. While there is a cultural shift in the image of fatherhood, empirical evidence shows that women continue to be children's primary caregivers (LaRossa, 1997). Legal processes, which traditionally have favored women over men in custodial decisions, feed into the larger image of women as caregivers. Moreover, the responsibilities of men as detailed in such decisions largely focus on the single dimension of father involvement, namely financial or material supports.

EFFECTS OF PUBLIC POLICIES ON FATHER INVOLVEMENT

Historically, public policies have tended to constrain the positive development of fathering behaviors, especially in non-traditional families, because they were constructed through the lens of the traditional nuclear family. These policies have focused primarily on fathers' provision of child support as the most important and regulatable form of father involvement and responsibilities. Programs designed to increase positive paternal involvement in non-economic ways, however, are few.

Successful child support collection is a key area of the 1996 Federal welfare reform legislation. The law requires custodial parents who apply for public assistance to cooperate in establishing paternity (for nonmarital children) and pursuing child support. Individual states have developed their own strategies for collecting child support. For example, in 1997 Virginia launched the Virginia's Kids First Campaign, which has netted $25 million from noncustodial parents who owed back support (Sisk, 1998). Methods of collection included letters to delinquent fathers, arrests, use of boots to disable their cars, and notices to suspend drivers, hunting and fishing licenses.

Paternity establishment policies traditionally operated under the assumption that nonmarital fathers would try to avoid their responsibilities; thus coercive measures such as genetic testing and default proceedings (e.g., failure to show up at a paternity hearing is presumptive grounds for paternity in many states) were assumed to be necessary. More recently, however, there has been an emphasis on voluntary acknowledgment of paternity (Lundy, Peters, & Venohr, 1999). Sonenstein, Holcomb, and Seefeldt (1994) found that states and counties that encouraged voluntary acknowledgments had a paternity establishment rate of 65%, 43 percentage points more than the paternity establishment rate of states and counties that had no or limited opportunities for consent.

Research also shows that unmarried mothers frequently continue their relationship with the father during pregnancy and through the first few years after the child's birth (Price & Williams, 1990). This suggests that efforts to establish paternity voluntarily should be made early in the child's life, when the father is more likely to be involved with the child. The 1996 welfare reform legislation required all states to have voluntary paternity acknowledgment programs in birthing hospitals. The policies are based on the hope that these kind of programs will increase paternity establishments, child support payments, and fathers' involvement with their children. However, there is no research to date that examines the relationship between legal paternity establishment and father involvement. We do not know whether the act of paternity establishment, itself, leads to greater father involvement or whether fathers are more likely to develop long-term positive relationships with their children when policies encourage and facilitate voluntary acknowledgment.

Evaluations of child support policies suggest that they may have unintended consequences and might discourage family formation and paternity establishment, and impede father involvement. Welfare policies also tend to reduce the incentive to pay child support through the formal child support system, because welfare payments are reduced by one dollar for each dollar of child support that is collected.[2] Men and women often decide not to declare paternity, so that any payments the father makes go directly to the child and mother (Achatz & MacAllum, 1994; Anderson, 1993; Doherty, Kouneski, & Erickson, 1998; Wattenberg, 1993).

Studies of the impact of child support payments on children's outcomes is mixed. While many studies have found that income from child support is more beneficial to children than other sources of income (e.g., Knox & Bane, 1994; McLanahan, Seltzer, Hanson, & Thomas, 1994), there are other studies that have found select or limited effects of child support. For example, Peters and Mullis (1997) found positive effects of child-support income on cognitive test scores measured during adolescence, but not on later outcome measures such as educational attainment, earning, and labor market experience. Knox (1996) found significant child-support effects for achievement test scores, but not for measures of the home environment. Argys and Peters (1996) argued that the differential effects of child support dollars on children's outcomes may depend on the relationship between the mother and father. Parents who get along are more likely to be able agree about how the money should be spent and to make expenditures on children in a cooperative and efficient way.

A cumulative body of evidence is showing that child support, itself, may influence parent-child and mother-father relationships, which, in turn, affect children's well-being. For example, payment of child support is an indicator of a fathers' success in the "economic provider role"; this success may then enable nonresidential fathers to become involved with their children in other beneficial ways. Similarly, mothers who are "gatekeepers" may only allow the father access to the children if child support is paid. On the other hand, the positive relationship between child support and father involvement may simply reflect selection: fathers who care more about their children and want to maintain involvement are also more likely to want to pay child support.

McLanahan et al. (1994) argue that child support payments influence the degree of conflict between the two parents either positively or negatively. Conflict is likely to decrease when fathers fulfill their financial obligation. However, if child support increases the involvement of the father in the child's life, this may also increase opportunities for conflict between the parents. Argys, Peters, Brooks-Gunn, and Smith (1998) report findings that make the important distinction between cooperative and noncooperative awards. They found that the effects of child support on cognitive development persist even after accounting for unobserved characteristics of fathers and families. They also showed that voluntary child support, rather than no support or court-ordered support, affects cognitive outcomes, perhaps because it does not negatively affect family processes. The most relevant finding from a policy perspective is the impact of policies on family processes which have important consequences for child well-being.

Intimately tied to child support is the issue of custody. Braver and O'Connell (1998) argue that custody laws, which often choose the mother as the custodial parent, keep men from maintaining involvement with their children. As custody laws begin to be gender neutral, there is an increasing prevalence of shared custody, which has implications for child support and father involvement. Cancian and Meyer (1998) find that although mother-sole custody is the dominant arrangement in divorce cases, there is a small but significant increase in fathers and mothers sharing custody in recent years. Seltzer (1998) found that joint legal custody also helped increased father involvement. Braver and O'Connell argue that joint legal custody is beneficial for children and parents. They propose some type of mediation between mothers and fathers, as well as giving absent fathers more rights. For example, visitation rights could be tied to child support payment, which is currently not the case. Making visitation and custody rights more explicit and enforcing them might also help keep fathers involved. Another argument for joint custody laws is the argument that nonresident fathers do not always support their children because they lack control over the allocation of resources within the resident parent's household (Weiss & Willis, 1985). Awarding joint custody would then lead to increased financial support for children and higher paternal involvement.

Welfare policies may also have an impact on father involvement. In place of Aid to Families with Dependent Children (AFDC), the 1996 Federal welfare legislation created a block grant called Temporary Assistance for Needy Families (TANF) that provides funds to allow states to run welfare programs of their own design, within broad federal guidelines. The new welfare law obliges mothers to enter the workforce by imposing work requirements on those who receive cash assistance for more than two years, and by placing a five-year lifetime limit in eligibility for assistance. The 1996

Welfare Reform establishes four interrelated goals: (a) to enable children to stay with their families, (b) to encourage work and marriage, (c) to prevent and reduce out-of-wedlock pregnancies, and (d) to encourage the formation and maintenance of two-parent families.

The Act includes bonuses for "high performing" states in meeting the Act's overall objectives. The emphasis on promoting marriage expressed in the welfare reform bill is intended to increase the incidence of two-parent families, which has been shown to have beneficial effects on child well-being even after controlling for family income (McLanahan & Sandefur, 1994). One path by which positive benefits may occur in two-parent families is that this kind of family structure can facilitate the ability of fathers to interact with their children.

Evidence about the effect of AFDC benefits on family structure is mixed (see Moffitt, 1992, for a review). The consequences of TANF for men, women, and children are yet to be known. However, again researchers anticipate mixed effects. For some women, the work requirement will open opportunities for employment that will benefit their children (Joint Center for Poverty Research, 1998). For other single mothers, it means more hardship and fewer resources to support their children emotionally and financially. Yet for men, the potential hardship, added to mothers already in distress, might represent an opportunity to play an important role in the well-being of their families. Men have come to represent an untapped resource for welfare families moving into the workforce.

While changes in social norms and policies are giving some men the opportunity to become more involved in their children's lives, there are still barriers. Furstenberg (1998) argues that the "gender distrust" between men and women is widening. The focus of welfare reform on finding employment for single mothers may leave men unemployed and hence "undesirable" as marriage partners. Policy makers are now considering ways to improve the lot of these men. Thousands of programs have sprung up across the country that target men specifically and provide job training and parenting advice (e.g., National Center on Families and Fathers [NCOFF], Association of Practitioners, and the Baltimore Men's Start). Activism at the community level and a desire to bring men back into their families have motivated policy makers to include men in social policies. In the U.S. Congress, Representative E. Clay Shaw, Jr. (who was a key author of the 1996 welfare law) introduced a "Fathers Count" Bill. This Bill would fund community groups, including religious organizations, to give poor fathers job training and parenting advice and encourage them to marry.

Even when fathers live with their children, there are structural barriers that might hinder their ability to fulfill their parental obligations. In 1993 President Clinton signed the Family and Medical Leave Act (FMLA) that allowed parents to take up to six weeks of unpaid leave to care for a newborn or adopted child or another family member who is sick. The Federal law restricted these benefits to those working in establishments with 50 or more employees, employed for a full year, and working at least 1250 hours during the year prior to taking the leave. Before the passage of FMLA, 11 states had similar family leave policies (Klerman & Liebowitz, 1997). Paid parental leave in the U.S. is fairly rare. In 1993, only 3% of medium and large establishments and 1% of small establishments offered parental leave (Blau, Ferber, & Winkler, 1998).

Even when benefits are available, fathers are much less likely to take parental leave, or they take leave for much shorter durations than do mothers. In the U.S. it has been estimated that fathers take about 5 days of leave when their child is born. The good news is that 91% of fathers took at least some leave (Hyde, Essex, & Horton, 1993). It is interesting to note that when fathers took time off from work, they were much more likely to use paid vacation or sick leave than parental leave, which is most often unpaid. This observation leads to an interesting hypothesis. Because of the importance of the breadwinner role, fathers are less likely to take a leave if it is unpaid.

The availability of parental leave in the U.S.–both paid and unpaid–is a recent phenomenon. To get an idea of how fathers' behaviors might change over time, it is useful to look at studies of patental leave in Sweden. Haas (1991) reports that in 1974, the first year that paid paternal leave was available, only 3% of fathers took a leave; by 1989 44% of fathers in Sweden took parental leave (Pleck, 1993). Even in Sweden, however, Haas (1991) notes that fathers take much less leave than do mothers (53 versus 225 days, on average).

There are strong grounds for hope that public policy in the U.S. is ready to confront the barriers to father involvement for both residential and nonresidential fathers and to enhance effective services and outreach to low-income fathers. The Department of Health and Human Services' policies on fathers are now shaped by five principles: (a) All fathers can be important contributors to the well-being of their children; (b) Parents are partners in raising their children, even when they do not live in the same household; (c) The roles fathers play in families are diverse and related to cultural and community norms; (d) Men should receive the education and support necessary to prepare them for the responsibility of parenthood; and (e) Government can encourage and promote father involvement through its programs and through its workforce policies.

In addition to these national goals, the states have also set forward a set of efforts that have increased public awareness of the importance of fathers' involvement in the lives of their children by convening statewide summits and conferences and sponsoring statewide media campaigns to promote positive father involvement. These efforts have focused on all fathers, including fathers in two-parent families, teen fathers, noncustodial fathers (both divorced and never married), and single fathers. The National Governors Association has published a list of the best programs to promote responsible fathering across states. The initiatives profiled by the states fall into six categories: services for low-income, noncustodial fathers; parenting skills training; public awareness campaigns; state fatherhood commissions; comprehensive funding streams; and premature fatherhood prevention (Knitzer, Brenner, & Gadsden, 1997).

Most states have recently undertaken strategic initiatives to address this issue and promote responsible fatherhood. Welfare reform has provided the impetus for many of these state level initiatives. There is no question that the problem of fatherless families is finally beginning to receive public attention. However, there is no consensus about the values that provide the foundation for strategies; nor is there research-based evidence about what approaches work best for which groups of fathers. Moreover, there is concern that program evaluations rarely accompany initiatives. Nevertheless, there is enormous opportunity for innovation and leadership by the states in promoting responsible fatherhood. Government and philanthropic support have created a network of programs across the country that seek to raise the income of low income men and strengthen their ties to their children. Nearly all states given substantial Federal welfare-to-work grants this year have pledged to include fathers in their programs

PUBLIC EDUCATION AND INTERVENTION PROGRAMS

Public policies focus on behaviors that can be manipulated or affected by policy mechanisms. Sometimes the behaviors targeted for change also have indirect impacts on outcomes of interest. For example, men who have greater income, education, healthy self-esteem, greater parenting knowledge, and more modern sex-role attitudes tend to be more involved with their children. Public education efforts that promote sexual responsibility and responsible fatherhood have focused on teen fathering. These programs are believed to have beneficial effects on children, because they focus on training and parenting skills, and involve fathers in programs such as Early Head Start, and school activities

However, most national programs that serve low-income families and young children have worked exclusively with mothers. In the case of teen pregnancy, knowledge and service have been hampered by an exclusive focus on adolescent mothers. In almost every case, teen mothers are studied without regard for their partners (Elster & Lamb, 1986). During the past decade, society has come to tolerate, and even actively support, adolescent mothers. No such support exists for teen fathers. They are blamed for the pregnancy, and society's reaction is punitive and harsh. Kiselica (1995) surveyed 149 agencies in Ohio serving teenage parents. He found 28 of 39 offered significantly fewer, if any, services to teen fathers compared to teen mothers.

However, the recent cultural shift on how men are reconceptualized into their families has tremendous implications for program design and implementation. Thousands of programs have arisen across the United States at the state and county levels that seek to help fathers, oftentimes unmarried and adolescent males, become better fathers (e.g., Responsive Fathers Program at the Philadelphia Children's Network, as discussed by Louv, 1994). Generally, these programs focus on employment, training, and parental involvement.

There are little evaluative data on the effect of these programs. But researchers have argued that programs can be effective if they take away the built-in disincentive to provide support (e.g., substituting child support dollars for welfare dollars), allow fathers to be involved with their children, and identify fathers through paternity establishment. A recent evaluation of a program called "Parents Fair Share" revealed no gains in employment or earnings, and the program had only modest success in enhancing child support payments. An important finding, however, identified the distinction between those fathers who could and those who could not pay support. Payments were 19% higher from men who could pay (Doolittle & Lynn, 1998).

EXAMPLES OF PROGRAMS AND NEW INITIATIVES ON FATHER INVOLVEMENT

Public attention and academic research on fathers has led to a number of programs across the country. We briefly discuss four initiatives, which are either ongoing or will be in the field by the year 2000–Early Head Start (EHS), Fragile Families, and Early Child Longitudinal Survey-Birth Cohort (ECLS-B), and Welfare studies. These initiatives are important because they improve past research on at least five fronts: (a) They collect nationally representative and longitudinal data on men in the context of families and communities; (b) They collect information from the fathers themselves; (c) They collect data from men of diverse ethnic and economic background; and (d) They represent partnerships between public and private organizations. These studies will also provide empirical evidence to answer questions such as (a) How do father-infant relationships develop in the context of these families? (b) What sustains the relationships? and (c) How can public policies go beyond child support to foster responsible fathering?

The study of Fathers in the Early Head Start Evaluation is one of two national studies that will have data on fathering from fathers themselves rather than from mothers. This study of fathers is looking at father-child interactions in the context of an early intervention program. It includes three waves of data collection (when the children are 14, 24 and 36 months old) and a wave of qualitative data collection in which men are asked about their own conceptualizations of fatherhood and child development. The study will examine the roles of both biological and social fathers in the lives of children from birth to 3 years. For a subsample of fathers this study will also collect data on father-infant interactions that are comparable to the mother-infant interaction data being collected as part of the EHS national evaluation.

The study will address questions about the timing, frequency, and nature of father involvement; how paternal involvement is sustained over time; and what the barriers and facilitators are to parental involvement. It will provide valuable data about how men interact with their children, how they view themselves in their roles of fathers, and the type of social and emotional investments they make on behalf of their children. In order to capture important processes and interactions that begin at birth, a study of newborns and their fathers and mothers has been added to the EHS evaluation. For low income populations we know very little about how early in life infants develop attachments to their fathers, how fathers become involved with their infants, and how that involvement at birth is sustained over time and affects different developmental trajectories.

The other national study that will collect data from fathers is the ECLS-B. This study begins in the year 2000 and is designed to track a large, nationally representative sample of infants at six-month intervals from birth to two years and yearly thereafter until the children reach grade one. The principal purposes of the study are to assess children's health status and their growth and development in domains that are critical for later school readiness and academic achievement. The study will address children's transitions to non-paternal care and early education programs, kindergarten, and first grade. It will provide nationally representative data on the relationships between children's early care and education experiences and their growth and development in key developmental domains. An important component of assessing the child's environment is parenting. This study will collect important information on mother and father involvement as well as on other variables related to father involvement that are believed to be related to positive child outcomes.

The Fragile Families and Child Well-Being Study addresses three areas of great interest to policy makers and researchers–non-marital childbearing, welfare reform, and the role of fathers–and brings these three areas together in an innovative, integrated framework. Specifically, the study will follow a new cohort of unwed parents and their children and will provide previously unavailable information on the conditions and capabilities of new unwed fathers, the nature of the relationship between unwed mothers and fathers, the factors that push new unwed parents together or apart, how public policies affect parents' behavior and living arrangements, and the consequences for parents, children, and society of new welfare regulations.

Three major studies–Children, Families, and Welfare Reform; the Los Angeles Study of Families and Communities; and New Hope–collectively known as the Welfare Studies, are currently underway. These studies will provide longitudinal, ethnographic, and qualitative data on how welfare reform affects poor children and their families. An important goal of these longitudinal studies is to assess how families, fathers, mothers, and children, negotiate the new policies, and how this context influences the way they relate to one another.

Collectively, the knowledge we gain from these studies will give us a better understanding of what it means to be a father under economically impoverished conditions. This information will be critical in the development and implementation of policies that promote positive father involvement in the lives of children in low-income populations.

In addition to these research initiatives, the "male undercount" problem has led to a major data collection effort at the national level to improve the representation of men in national surveys. Together with others interested in charting the well-being of children, Federal statistical agencies are also looking at how to improve the information base on fathers. The planned data collection ranges from basic demographic information (e.g., about male fertility) to family process information on how men become involved with their children and families and what sustains or deters their involvement. For example, the National Longitudinal Survey of Youth, 1997 Cohort (1998) plans to field a special module on fathers, mothers, and parenting. The Panel Study of Income Dynamics (Hill, 1992) is asking the same questions of fathers as they do of mothers and has plans to expand data on nonresident fathers' involvement. The Census Bureau and the National Center for Health Statistics are working on a methodology project to incorporate men. The National Study of Family Growth (1998) has support to add men in the next round. It will survey approximately 7,200 men by the year 2000. The National Survey of Family Household (1998) also has father-related questions.

CONCLUSION

More than ever, there is growing appreciation for the diversity of fathers, their roles, and their influences on children across familial, sub-cultural, and cultural contexts. There is no single definition of a successful father, or of an optimal "father's role." Rather, fathers' expectations about what they should do, what they actually do, and their effects on children must be viewed in the broader familial context. This is not an easy task. Research to date has shed light into how positive father involvement can have beneficial effects on children and families. But it has also highlighted some limitations that have led, in turn, to some important policy initiatives.

These policies face the challenge of addressing two opposing trends: the increase of father involvement in intact families and the absence of nonresident fathers from their children's lives. While some children are experiencing more nurturant and involved fathers, unfortunately, many others are growing up with little if any contact with their fathers. Will the gap between involved and uninvolved fathers continue to widen? Or, will society respond to this crisis by implementing policies that better empower fathers to become active participants in their children's lives? In either case, it is clear that the boys (and girls) of today are being reared with different expectations about their future roles–expectations that are continually being reinforced by direct experiences, media images, and changing institutional structures.

However, in order for policymakers to build programs and design policies that are beneficial for families, regardless of how these families are structured, they must have access to relevant and useful data. The Fatherhood Initiative and other partnerships between private and public organizations are creating an integrated knowledge base that is beginning to address policy concerns. This is paving the way for better policies and programs that will, in turn, stimulate further research. Although research on fathers has been underway since the 1960s, the latest surge of interest in fathers and their role in the well-being of their children has created an urgent impetus to revise social and cultural conceptions of fatherhood. This cultural shift will have important consequences for policies and research that examine how parents–both mothers and fathers–can best contribute to the development of their children. We leave the 20th century with fathers out of obscurity, and will begin the 21st century with important insights about how policies and programs can best integrate both parents to maximize benefits for children.

NOTES

1. The Forum also puts out an annual report of indicators of child well-being (Federal Interagency Forum on Child and Family Statistics, 1998a).

2. Before 1996, mothers were allowed to keep the first $50 per month in child support before welfare benefits were reduced. The 1996 welfare legislation allowed states to increase or decrease the amount of this child support disregard.

REFERENCES

Achatz, M., & MacAllum, C. A. (1994). *The young unwed fathers demonstration project: A status report.* Philadelphia: Public/Private Ventures.

Anderson, E. (1993). Sex codes and family life among poor inner-city youths. In R. I. Lerman & T. J. Ooms (Eds.), *Young unwed fathers: Changing roles and emerging policies* (pp.74-98). Philadelphia: Temple University Press.

Argys, L. M., & Peters, H. E. (1996). *Can adequate child support be legislated? A theoretical model of responses to child support guidelines and enforcement efforts.* Mimeographed document, Department of Policy Analysis and Management, Cornell University.

Argys, L. M., Peters, H. E., Brooks-Gunn, J., & Smith, J. R. (1998). The impact of child support dollars on cognitive outcomes. *Demography, 35,* 2, 159-173.

Averett, S. L., Gennetian, L. A., & Peters, H. E. (1999). Patterns and determinants of paternal child care during a child's first three years of life. *Marriage & Family Review, 29,* 2-3.

Blau, F., Ferber, M., & Winkler, A. (1998). *The economics of women, men, and work.* Upper Saddle River, NJ: Prentice Hall.

Braver, S. L., & O'Connell, D. (1998). *Divorced dads.* New York: Putnam.

Brayfield, A. (1995). Juggling jobs and kids: The impact of employment schedules on fathers' caring for children. *Journal of Marriage and the Family, 57,* 321-332.

Cancian, M., & Meyer, D. (1998). Who gets custody? *Demography, 35*(2), 147-157.

Casper, L. M. (1997). My daddy takes care of me! Fathers as care providers. *Current Population Reports,* 70-59. Washington, DC: U.S. Bureau of the Census.

Casper, L. M., & O'Connell, M (1998). Work, income, the economy, and married fathers as child care providers. *Demography, 35*(2), 243-250.

Coplin. J. W. & Houts, A. C. (1991). Father involvement in parent training for oppositional child behavior: Progress or stagnation? *Child and Family Behavior Therapy, 13* (2).

Doherty, W. J., Kouneski, E. F., & Erickson, M. F. (1998). Responsible fathering: An overview and conceptual framework. *Journal of Marriage and the Family, 60,* 277-292.

Doolittle, F. & Lynn, S. (1998). *Working with low-income cases: Lessons for the child support enforcement system from Parents' Fair Share.* Report of the Manpower Demonstration, Research Corporation.

Elster, A. B., & Lamb, M. E. (Eds.), (1986). *Adolescent fatherhood.* Hillsdale, NJ: Earlbaum.

Federal Interagency Forum on Child and Family Statistics. (1998a). *America's children: Key national indicators of well-being.* Washington, D.C.: U.S. Government Printing Office.

Federal Interagency Forum on Child and Family Statistics. (1998b). *Nurturing fatherhood: Improving data and research on male fertility, family formation, and fatherhood.* Washington, D.C.: U.S. Government Printing Office.

Furstenberg. F. F. Jr. (1998, May). *The effects of welfare reform on the family: The good, the bad, and the ugly.* Paper presented at the Family Process and Child Development in Low Income Families Conference organized by the Joint Center for Poverty Research, Chicago, IL.

Greene, A. D., & Moore, K. A. (1999). Nonresident father involvement and child well-being among young children in families on welfare. *Marriage & Family Review, 29,* 2-3.

Greene, A. D., Halle, T. G., Le Menestrel, S., & Moore, K. A. (1998). Father involvement in young children's lives: Recommendations for a fatherhood module for the ECLS-B. Paper prepared for the National Center for Education Statistics by Child Trends, Inc., Washington, D.C.

Haas, L. (1991). Equal parenthood and social policy: Lessons from a study of parental leave in Sweden. In J.S. Hyde & M.J. Essex (Eds.), *Parental leave and child care: Setting a research and policy agenda* (pp. 375-405). Philadelphia: Temple University Press.

Harper, C. C. & McLanahan, S. S. (1998 August). *Father absence and youth incarceration.* Paper presented at the 1998 annual meetings of the American Sociological Association, San Fransico, CA.

Harris, K., Furstenberg, F. F. Jr., & Marmer, J. K. (1998). Paternal involvement with adolescents in intact families: The influence of fathers over the life course. *Demography, 35*(2), 201-216.

Hernandez, Donald J. 1993. *America's Children: Resources from Family, Government and the Economy.* New York: Russell Sage.

Hetherington, E. M., & Stanley-Hagan, M. (1986). Divorced fathers: Stress, coping, and adjustment. In M. E. Lamb (Ed.), *The father's role: Applied perspectives* (pp. 103-134). New York: Wiley.

Hill, M. S. (1992). *The Panel Study of Income Dynamics: A user's guide.* London: Sage Publications.

Hofferth, S. (1999). *Race/ethnic differences in father involvement with young children: A conceptual framework and empirical test in two-parent families.* Paper presented at the Urban Seminar on Fatherhood, April 23-24, Harvard University, Cambridge, MA.

Hyde, J. S., Essex, M. J., & Horton, F. (1993). Fathers and parental leave: Attitudes and experiences. *Journal of Family Issues, 14*, 4, 616-641.

Joint Center for Poverty Research (1998 May). Family process and child development in low income families. Chicago, IL. Additional material at: http://jcpr.org/sept1999.html.

Kiselica, M. S. (1995). *Multicultural counseling with teenage fathers: A practical guide.* Thousand Oaks, CA: Sage.

Klerman, J. A. & Leibowitz, A. (1997). Labor Supply Effects of State Maternity Leave Legislation. In F. D. Blau & R. G. Ehrenberg (Eds.), *Gender and family issues in the workplace* (pp. 65-85). New York: Russell Sage Foundation.

Knitzer, J., Brenner, E., & Gadsden, V. (1998). *Map and Track: States initiatives to encourage responsible fatherhood.* National Center for Children in Poverty, New York.

Knox, V. W. (1996). The effects of child support payments on developmental outcomes for elementary school-age children. *The Journal of Human Resources, 31*, 816-840.

Knox, V. W., & Bane, M. J. (1994). Child support and schooling. In I. Garfinkel, S. S. McLanahan, & P. K. Robbins (Eds.), *Child support and child well-being* (pp. 285-310). Washington, DC: The Urban Institute Press.

Lamb, M. (Ed.), (1997). *The role of the father in child development.* New York: Wiley.

LaRossa, R. (1997). *The modernization of fatherhood: A social and political history.* Chicago: University of Chicago Press.

Lerman, R.I., & E. Sorensen. (1999) Father involvement with their nonmarital children: Patterns, determinants, and effects on their earnings. *Marriage & Family Review*, 29(2/3).

Louv, R. (1994). *Reinventing fatherhood.* Occasional Papers Series, No. 14. New York: United Nations.

Lundy, B., Peters, H. E., Venohr, J. (1999, June). *Telephone Survey of State Paternity Establishment Policies and Practices.* Unpublished document. Cornell University.

McLanahan, S.S., Seltzer, J. A., Hanson, T. L., & Thomas, E. (1994). Child support enforcement and child well-being: Greater security or greater conflicts. In I. Garfinkel, S. S. McLanahan, & P. K. Robins (Eds.), *Child support and child well-being* (pp. 239-254). Washington, DC: The Urban Institute Press.

McLanahan, S. S., & Sandefeur, G. (1994). *Growing up with a single parent: What hurts, what helps.* Cambridge: Harvard University Press.

Moffitt, R. (1992). Incentive effects of the U.S. welfare system: A review. *Journal of Economic Literature, 30,* 1-61.

National Survey of Family Growth (1998). http://www.cdc.gov/nchswww/products/catalogues/subject/nsfg/nsfg.htm

National Survey of Families and Households (1998). http://www.ssc.wisc.edu/nsfh/home.htm.

National Longitudinal Survey of Youth, 1997 Cohort. (1998). http://www.bls.gov/nlsy97.htm.

Peters, H. E. & Mullis, N. (1997). The role of family income and sources of income in adolescent achievement. In G. J. Duncan & J. Brooks-Gunn (Eds.), *Consequences of growing up poor* (pp. 340-382). New York: Russell Sage Foundation.

Pleck, E. H. (1997). Paternal involvement: Levels, sources, and consequences. In M. E. Lamb (Ed.), *The role of the father in child development.* (3rd ed., pp. 66-103). New York: Wiley.

Pleck, J. H. (1993). Are "family-supportive" employer policies relevant to men? In J. C. Hood (Ed.), *Men, work, & family* (pp. 217-237). Newbury Park, CA: Sage.

Price, D. A., & Williams, V. S. (1990). *Nebraska Paternity Project, Final Report.* Denver, CO: Policy Studies, Inc.

Presser, H. (1995). Job, family, and gender: Determinants of non-standard work schedules among employed Americans in 1991. *Demography, 32,* 577-598.

Pruett, K. (1987). *The nurturing father.* New York: Warner Books.

Seltzer, J. A. (1998). Father by law: Effects of joint legal custody on nonresident fathers' involvement with children. *Demography, 35,* 2, 135-146.

Sisk, P. J. (1998, July). Virginia Kids First campaign: First year nets $25 million. *Child Support Report, XX*(7), 1-2.

Sonenstein, F. L.; Holcomb, P. A., & Seefeldt, K. S. (1994). Promising Approaches to Improving Paternity Establishment Rates at the Local Level. In I. Garfinkel, S. S. McLanahan, & P. K. Robins (Eds.), *Child Support and Child Well-being* (pp. 31-59). Washington, DC: The Urban Institute.

Tamis-LeMonda, C. & Cabrera, N. (In press). *Perspectives on father involvement: Research and Policy.* Social Policy Report. Society for Research in Child Development.

U.S. Bureau of the Census. (1999). *Current Population Reports: Growth in single fathers outpaces growth in single mothers.* (Series P-20 No. 1344). Washington, DC: U.S. Government Printing Office.

U.S. Bureau of Labor Statistics (1997). Marital and family characteristics of the labor force from March 1997. *Current Population Survey.* Unpublished statistics. Washington, DC: U.S. Department of Labor.

Wattenberg, E. (1993). Paternity actions and young fathers. In R. I. Lerman & T. J. Ooms (Eds.), *Young unwed fathers: Changing roles and emerging policies* (pp. 213-234). Philadelphia: Temple University Press.

Weiss, Y., & Willis, R. J. (1985). Children as collective goods in divorce settlements. *Journal of Labor Economics, 3*, 268-292.

Wilkie, J. R. (1993). Changes in U.S. men's attitudes toward the family provider role, 1972-1989. *Gender and Society, 7*, 261-79.

Working Group on Conceptualizing Male Parenting (1997). *Social fatherhood and paternal involvement: Conceptual, data, and policymaking issues.* Presented at the NICHD Conference on Fathering and Male Fertility: Improving Data and Research, Bethesda, MD.

Yeung, W. Jean; Sandberg, John F.; Davis-Kean, Pamela; Hofferth, Sandra L. (1999, April). *Children's time with fathers in intact families.* Paper presented at the Annual Meeting of the Population Association of America, New York, NY.

V. GENERAL EDITORS' EPILOGUE

The Diversity of Fatherhood: Change, Constancy, and Contradiction

Gary W. Peterson
Suzanne K. Steinmetz

The articles in this volume seek to examine the many faces of fatherhood. As we edited this very informative collection, the message conveyed very clearly is that fatherhood is no simple phenomenon, but a complex tapestry of many things. Contemporary fatherhood is both diverse in its manifestations and subject to contradictory qualities, forces, and trends. Acquiring an accurate view of contemporary fatherhood is not possible without images of constant change, lingering traditionality, and, above all, a complex set of roles that vary from having very clear expectations to being highly ambiguous. This collection of original articles conveys the reality that fatherhood is not a static phenomenon, but more like a moving target, only some of which has constant meaning. Like so many things in social life, we also need to accommodate constant changes in what each generation expects of paternity.

Gary W. Peterson is Professor and Chair, Department of Sociology, Arizona State University, Tempe, AZ 85287-2101.

Suzanne K. Steinmetz is Professor, Department of Sociology, Indiana University-Purdue University at Indianapolis, IN 46236.

[Haworth co-indexing entry note]: "The Diversity of Fatherhood: Change, Constancy, and Contradiction." Peterson, Gary W., and Suzanne K. Steinmetz. Co-published simultaneously in *Marriage & Family Review* (The Haworth Press, Inc.) Vol. 29, No. 4, 2000, pp. 315-322; and: *FATHERHOOD: Research, Interventions and Policies* (ed: H. Elizabeth Peters et al.) The Haworth Press, Inc., 2000, pp. 315-322. Single or multiple copies of this article are available for a fee from The Haworth Document Delivery Service [1-800-342-9678, 9:00 a.m. - 5:00 p.m. (EST). E-mail address: getinfo@haworthpressinc.com].

315

In so many ways, the complexities of contemporary fatherhood reflect the great diversity of America's family life at the brink of the 21st century and a new millennium. In 1999, for example, 48.2 million children live with both of their parents, a figure that is not statistically different from the number of such families in 1980 (U.S. Bureau of the Census, 1999). Despite considerable population growth, therefore, this constancy in the absolute number of traditional families also reflects the dramatic growth of families that experience divorce, single-parenthood (never married), stepfamily circumstances, declines in marriage rates, and the growing numbers of individuals who remain single for longer periods of time. Although traditional nuclear families with breadwinner dads and stay-at-home moms certainly have die-hard advocates (Popenoe, 1993), this family structure has become increasingly questionable as a realistic goal for many in our society. Replacing this time-bound conception of western families are several "alternative" family forms, which, taken as a whole, compel us to recognize the current demographic reality that *diversity has become the norm* that defines our domestic relations. Thus, acknowledging family diversity as the norm is not a value judgement about how things "ought to be," but a simple recognition that things have changed and will most likely do so again in the future.

The fact that no particular family form currently dominates numerically does not suggest that the family is close to extinction as a central aspect of our social lives (Popenoe, 1993). Instead, what is suggested is that families are changing and adapting to meet the current and emerging demands of a dynamic society (Coontz, 1997). Despite great debates about the costs or benefits of these changes, many of the same generalizations can be applied to the nature of fatherhood, a central component of our current pattern of family diversity.

A contemporary way of understanding fatherhood is to compare and contrast it with contemporary maternal roles. That is, motherhood today is characterized by diversity, contradictory images, a complicated array of role involvements, and engendered role expectations (Barnard & Martell, 1995). Women become mothers by choice, failing to plan, natural child birth, technological innovations, and adoption. Mothers are married, single, partnered, employed, non-employed, young, old, rich, and poor. Fatherhood can also be achieved by a similar range of options, but only relatively recently have social scientists begun to investigate the meaning of fatherhood and the variety of ways in which men fulfill this role (Peterson, Bodman, Bush, & Madden-Derdich, in press). Consequently, this information deficit is rapidly being erased as research on paternity grows and journals devote publication space to research on men who occupy a variety of roles, including those of fatherhood. These volumes, with chapters by some of the leading experts who study fatherhood, have joined this growing number of resources that devoted space to the examination of paternal roles.

The complexity of contemporary fatherhood is evident throughout this collection of articles and the existing research on this topic. Fatherhood in our society consists of a variety of roles that illustrate how engendered social expectations differentiate what fathers are expected to do in some ways from what mothers are expected to do. Such roles may include breadwinner, companion, care provider, moral guide, protector, disciplinarian, playmate, and co-parent (Lamb, 1997a; Pleck, 1997). Compared to mothers, for example, paternal roles are often described as being less culturally scripted and as being difficult for boys to learn in the absence of clearly defined role models (Marsiglio, 1995). For a variety of reasons, many fathers remain in secondary parenting roles (i.e., "helpers") and are more difficult for children to develop clear images of and to use as role models (Lewis, 1997).

In two-parent families in which mothers are not employed, fathers spend only 20 to 25 percent as much time as mothers in direct interaction with children and only about a third as much time being accessible to them (Lamb, 1997b; Lamb, Pleck, Charnov, & Levine, 1987; Pleck, 1997). Fathers are especially unlikely to have overall responsibility for managing children's environments or for structuring their schedules and setting limits (Lamb, 1997a; Parke, 1995). Fathers' direct interaction and accessibility increases only modestly when mothers work outside the home, whereas changes in fathers' overall responsibility for managing children's lives are virtually negligible within these circumstances (Lamb, 1997b; Pleck, 1997). According to one study, for example, parenthood appears to crystallize rather than moderate a gender division of labor by reshaping the wives' routines Sanchez and Thomas (1997). Moreover, mothers tended to view their household duties as obligatory, while fathers viewed them as voluntary (Perkins & DeMeiss, 1996). Even the serious tasks of providing care to disabled children did not significantly increase the contributions of fathers to domestic responsibilities (Cuskelly, Pullman, & Hayes, 1998). Such patterns suggest that, both historically and currently, fathers face fewer social expectations to identify with (or become committed to) parental roles, and spend substantially less time performing parental roles than mothers (Marsiglio, 1993, 1995).

Comparisons between mothers and fathers, at least in part, seem to indicate that many fathers still behave consistently with Parsonian conceptions of the instrumental role as the primary linkages to the larger society and the secondary or "back-up" parent (Parsons & Bales, 1955). Beginning in infancy, for example, fathers are characterized as novel playmates (i.e., frequently rough-and-tumble play), whereas mothers are caretakers (Lamb, 1997b; Parke, 1995). Such patterns of interaction appear consistent with those of middle-childhood, during which fathers are more involved in physical/outdoor play interactions, whereas mothers report more frequent interactions involving caregiving and household tasks (Russell & Russell, 1987). Moreover, fathers compared to mothers engage in less punitive episodes, conflictual interactions, negative emotional expressions, and positive emotional communications with elementary school children (Russell & Russell, 1987; Straus, 1994). However, much of this comparatively different pattern of paternal interaction reflects the fact that fathers spend less time with children at all ages than mothers (Parke, 1995).

During adolescence, in turn, fathers engage in more leisure time activities with the young, whereas mothers are again primarily responsible for taking care of youth. Relationships are characteristically less close between fathers and adolescents than between mothers and teenagers, with fathers being primarily involved in giving practical advice to sons (Collins & Russell, 1991). Both sons and daughters are likely to view their fathers as authoritarian and less authoritative than mothers (Klein, O'Bryant & Hopkins, 1996; see also Steinmetz, 1999). Teenage daughters are especially inclined to view their fathers as distant authority figures with whom little interaction occurs, a result that some observers have labeled "nonrelations" (Starrels, 1994; Youniss & Smollar, 1985).

Although such gender differences in parenting certainly hearken back to the Parsonian view of traditional (and perhaps lasting) gender-of-parent differences, sufficient evidence also exists to indicate that fatherhood roles are subject to historical change, substantial variability, and social construction within specific parental relationships. Partly in response to feminist thought, and the greater numbers of women entering the labor force, the attitudes of men and the general society have changed toward the acceptance of coequal responsibility for parenting roles by fathers (Lamb, 1997a; Pleck & Pleck, 1997). Despite arguments that such changes in fatherhood are largely cultural myths, the prevailing view is that slow but moderate change has occurred in fathers' identification with and actual performance of coequal parenting roles (see Peterson & Hann, 1999; Peterson, Bodman, Bush & Madden-Derdich, in press, for a discussion of these studies). This does not mean, unfortunately, that we have now achieved real co-equal responsibility by fathers and mothers to actually provide care and to socialize children. Much additional change is required before trends in social attitudes become realities in terms of actual behavior that is coequal.

Beyond assessing change or stability in fatherhood is the recognition that substantial variation already exists in paternal role performance, especially in reference to more contemporary expectations of fathers as *caregivers*. Variations in fathers' involvement in care-giving is predicted by (or varies depending upon) men's attitudes (or motivations) to do so, perceived parental competence, self-confidence in parental roles, supportiveness of the spouse, degree of mother's involvement in work roles, as well as formal supports from the workplace (e.g., parental leave) and other institutions (Lamb, 1997b; Haas, 1992; Parke, 1995, Pleck & Pleck, 1997). Such variability implies that couples negotiate or socially construct aspects of their parental roles as their family circumstances vary.

Although Pleck and Pleck (1997) suggest that recent trends toward co-equal parenting tend to be localized within samples of highly educated, primarily European-American fathers, other studies (e.g., Deutsch, Lussier, & Servis, 1993; Houssain, Field, Pickens, Malphurs, & Del Valle, 1997) have provided a different view. For example, in a study of low income Hispanic and African-American families, the fathers were found to spend about half as much time as mothers in caregiving (a percentage that is considerably more time than is typical of middle class, white fathers). Moreover, these findings did not vary as a function of ethnic group, employment status (full-time versus part-time), or a range of sociodemographic variables (Houssain, Field, Pickens, Malphurs, & Del Valle, 1997; Hossain & Roopnarine, 1994). Some evidence suggests, in fact, that fathers with less education, lower incomes, and more traditional attitudes toward child care, as well as those working a different shift, may be more likely to care for children (Tuttle, 1994). Supporting this view is a study by Deutsch (1999) who found that, contrary to stereotypes about working class men being unwilling to change dirty diapers, the evidence actually pointed to considerable involvement by these blue-collar fathers in childcare. This increased participation, however, does not mean that fathers' involvement in care-taking has increased in equal proportion to mothers' greater identification with and performance of breadwinner roles (Haas, 1992, in press). Consequently, current conceptions of fatherhood remain at least moderately consistent with functionalist views (see Parsons & Bales, 1955) that fathers are (or should be) disproportionately linked to roles outside families and, compared to mothers, are only secondarily involved in parenting.

Although certain aspects of fatherhood retain traditional roots, other trends suggest that fathers' behavior is changing in directions that parallel those avenues previously taken by mothers. According to the Census Bureau, for example, the fastest growing family structure is the single father-headed family (U.S. Bureau of the Census, 1999). Recent data indicate that 2.8 million children, nearly triple the number in 1980, are living with single fathers. The number of single fathers grew an additional 25% between 1995 and 1998, from 1.7 million to 2.1 million, while the number of single mothers remained constant at about 9.8 million (U.S. Bureau of the Census, 1999). Consequently, men comprised 1 in 6 of the nation's 11.9 million single parents in 1998, an amount that was up from the figures of 1 in 7 in 1995 and 1 in 10 in 1980. About 63% of these fathers cared for only one child under 18 years of age, whereas three or more children were cared for by 11% of these fathers (U.S. Bureau of the Census, 1999).

Although we are aware of the wide range of ways in which mothers can become single parents, fathers present a similar picture. In 1998, 44% of the single-parent fathers were single as a result of divorce, 35% had never married; 12% were separated, 5% widowed and 5% were separated due to circumstances other than marital discord (e.g., in prison, the military, long-term care, or mental health facility). Data from the same year revealed that 83% of the single fathers were white (an increase from 76% in 1997), whereas 13% were African Americans (down from 19% in 1977); the percentage of Hispanics, 13%, remained the same (U.S. Bureau of the Census, 1998, 1999).

The median family income in 1997 for single fathers was $29,313 with 20% being categorized as poor, whereas median income for intact families was $52,553, with 9% being poor. A substantial percentage (77%) of single dads had high school diplomas, with about 11% having a bachelor's degree or higher. About half of these families lived in rental housing and about 55% had other adults in the household besides the father (U.S. Bureau of the Census, 1999).

As we enter the 21st century, we need to direct our focus toward new issues in the growing literature on fatherhood. For example, what is the role of genetics and hormones in facilitating emotional connections and the bonding of fathers to the young? As fathers become increasingly more involved in parenthood, especially as they take on primary caregiving roles, what is the impact of fathers' work on their parenting roles? What is the effect on children when househusbands return to work? What contributions do fathers make to the development of children besides those contributions that result from direct interaction? And finally, as an increasing number of fathers obtain joint and sole custody, what impact will this have on separation and divorce rates?

It has now become clear that many of our simplistic images about what fathers are or should be must be laid to rest similar to the manner that older images of the dinosaurs (i.e., as maladaptive, stupid, slow-moving creatures) have been revolutionized. Fatherhood is not something simply dominated by static patterns of the past, but, despite many social concerns, is a dynamic aspect of our social lives that is changing along with families and the forces at play in the larger society.

REFERENCES

Barnard, K. R., & Martell, L. K. (1995). Mothering. In M. H. Bornstein (Ed.), *Handbook of Parenting: Vol. 3. Status and social conditions of parenting* (pp. 3-26). New Jersey: Erlbaum.

Collins, W. A., & Russell, G. (1991). Mother-child and father-child relationships in middle childhood and adolescence: A developmental analysis. *Developmental Review, 11*, 99-136.

Coontz, S. (1997). *The way we really are.* New York: Basic Books.

Cuskelly, M., Pullman, L., & Hayes, A. (1998). Parenting and employment decisions of parents with a preschool child with a disability. *Journal of Intellectual and Developmental Disability, 23*, 4, 319-332.

Deutsch, F. M. (1999). *Halving it all: How equally shared parenting works.* Cambridge, MA: Harvard University Press.

Deutsch, F. M., Lussier, J. B., & Servis, L. J. (1993). Instrumental and expressive family roles among African American fathers. Husbands at home: Predictors of paternal participation in childcare and housework. *Journal of Personality and Social Psychology, 65*, 6, 1154-1166.

Field, L. F., Mussetter, B. W., & Powers, G. T. (1997). Children denied two parents: An analysis of access denial. *Journal of Divorce & Remarriage, 28*, 1-2, 49-62.

Haas, L. (1992). *Equal parenthood and social policy.* Albany: State University of New York Press.

Haas, L. (1999). Families and work. In M. Sussman, S. Steinmetz, and G. Peterson, (Eds.), *Handbook of marriage and the family (Second ed.).* (pp. 571-612) New York: Plenum.

Hossain, Z., Field, T., Pickens, J., Malphurs, J. Del Valle, C. (1997). Fathers' caregiving in low-income African-American and Hispanic-American families. *Early Development and Parenting, 6*, 2, 73-82.

Hossain, Z. & Roopnarine, J. L. (1994). African-American fathers' involvement with infants: Relationship to their functioning style, support, education, and income. *Infant Behavior and Development, 17*, 2, 175-184.

Hyde, J. S. (1995). Women and maternity leave: Empirical data and public policy. *Psychology of Women Quarterly, 191*, 3, 299-313)

Hyde, J. S., Essex, M.J., & Horton, F. (1993). Fathers and parental leave: Attitudes and experiences. *Journal of Family Issues, 14*, 4, 616-638).

Klein, H. A., O'Bryant, K., & Hopkins, H. R. (1996). Recalled parental authority style and self perception in college men and women. *Journal of Genetic Psychology, 157* (1), 517.

Lamb, M.E. (1997a). Fathers and child development: An introductory overview and guide. In M. E. Lamb (Ed.), *The role of the father in child development* (pp. 1-18). New York: Wiley.

Lamb. M. E. (1997b). The development of father-infant relationships. In M. E. Lamb (Ed.), *The role of the father in child development* (pp. 104-120). New York: Wiley.

Lamb, M. E., Pleck, J. H., Charnov, E. L., Levine, J. A. (1987). A biosocial perspective on paternal behavior and involvement. In J. B. Lancaster, J. Altmann, A. S. Rossi, & L. R. Sherrod (Eds.), *Parenting across the lifespan: Biosocial dimensions* (pp. 111-142). New York: A. De Gruyter.

Lewis, C. (1997). Fathers and preschoolers. In M. E. Lamb (Ed.), *The role of the father in child development* (pp. 121-142). New York: Wiley.

Marsiglio, W. (1993). Contemporary scholarship on fatherhood: Culture, identity, and conduct. *Journal of Family Issues, 14*, 484-509.

Marsiglio, W. (1995). Fathers' diverse life course patterns and roles: theory and social interventions. In W. Marsiglio (Ed.), *Fatherhood: Contemporary theory, research, and social policy* (pp. 78-101). Thousand Oaks: Sage.

Parke, R. D. (1995). Fathers and families. In M. H. Bornstein (Ed.), *Handbook of parenting: Vol 3. Status and social conditions of parenting*, (pp. 27-63). Hillsdale, NJ: Erlbaum.

Parsons, T. & Bales, R. (1955). *Family socialization and interaction process.* New York: Free Press.

Perkins, H. W. & DeMeis, D. K. (1996). Gender and family effects on the "second-shift" domestic activity of college-educated young adults *Gender and Society, 10*, 1, 78-93.

Peterson, G. W., Bodman, D. A., Bush, K. R., & Madden-Derdich, D. (in press). Gender and Parent-Child Relationships. In D. H. Demo, K. R. Allen, & M. A. Fine (Eds.) *The handbook of family diversity.* New York: Oxford University Press.

Peterson, G. W. & Hann, D. (1999). Socializing children and parents in families. In M. B. Sussman, S. K. Steinmetz, & G. W. Peterson (Eds.) *Handbook of marriage and the family, Second edition* (pp. 327-370). New York: Plenum Publishers.

Pleck, J.H. (1997). Paternal involvement: Levels, sources, and consequences. In M. E. Lamb (Ed.), *The role of the father in child development* (pp. 66-103). New York: Wiley.

Pleck, E. H., & Pleck, J. H. (1997). Fatherhood ideals in the United States: Historical dimensions. In M. E. Lamb (Ed.), *The role of the father in child development* (pp. 33-48). New York: Wiley.

Popenoe, D. (1993). American family in decline, 1960-1990. A review and appraisal. *Journal of Marriage and the Family*, 49, 527-555.

Russell, G., & Russell, A. (1987). Mother-child and father-child relationships in middle childhood. *Child Development, 58*, 1573-1585.

Sanchez, L. & Thomson, E. (1997). Becoming mothers and fathers: Parenthood, gender, and the division of labor. *Gender and Society, 11*, 6, 747-772.

Starrels, M.E. (1994). Gender differences in parent-child relations. *Journal of Family Issues, 15*, 148-165.

Steinmetz, S. K. (1999). Adolescence in Contemporary Society. In M. B. Sussman, S. K. Steinmetz, & G. W. Peterson (Eds.) *Handbook of marriage and the family, Second edition* (pp. 371-424). New York: Plenum Publishers.

Straus, M. A. (1994). *Beating the devil out of them: Corporal punishment in American families.* New York: Lexington Books.

Tuttle, R. C. (1994) Determinants of father's participation in child care. *International Journal of Sociology of the Family, 24*, 1, 113-125.

U. S. Bureau of the Census (1998, June 15th) Census Bureau Facts for Fathers's Day 1998: June 21. Census Bureau Fact Sheets for Media, Facts for Features. (http:www.census.gov/Press-Release/www/ cb98-ff.07.html).

U. S. Bureau of the Census (1999, June 10th) Census Bureau Facts for Fathers's Day 1998: June 20. Census Bureau Fact Sheets for Media, Facts for Features. (http:www.census.gov/Press-Release/www/1999/cb99ff08.html).

Youniss, J. & Smollar, J. (1985). *Adolescent relations with mothers, fathers, and friends.* Chicago: University of Chicago Press.

Index